939/EPN

(59226)

POLITICS IN
AN ARABIAN OASIS

POLITICS IN
AN ARABIAN OASIS
The Rashidi Tribal Dynasty

MADAWI AL RASHEED

I.B.Tauris & Co Ltd
Publishers
London · New York

Published in 1991 by
I.B.Tauris & Co Ltd
110 Gloucester Avenue
London NW1 8JA

175 Fifth Avenue
New York
NY 10010

In the United States of America
and Canada distributed by
St Martin's Press
175 Fifth Avenue
New York
NY 10010

A CIP record for this book is available from the British Library
Library of Congress catalog card number: 91–65139
A full CIP record is available from the Library of Congress
ISBN 1–85043–320–8

To my parents

CONTENTS

LIST OF MAPS, TABLES
AND DIAGRAMS

ACKNOWLEDGEMENT

This book is based on a Ph.D. thesis presented to the Department of Social Anthropology at Cambridge University in 1988. I would like to take this opportunity to express my gratitude to Professor Ernest Gellner for all his patient, diligent, and generous supervision throughout my three years in Cambridge. I am also greatly indebted to Dr Robin Bidwell for introducing me to the archives of London and for reading an early draft of the thesis. I also wish to thank Dr Bruce Ingham, Dr Ugo Fabietti, Dr Tim Wright and Dr François Pouillon for reading chapters of this book and for their constructive criticisms. I would like to thank my internal examiner Dr Paul Sant-Cassia for his comments and suggestions. Finally, I owe a lasting debt of gratitude to Professor Michael Gilsenan whose stimulating criticism and genuine support have been most valuable.

I would like to thank my colleagues in the Department of Social Anthropology of Cambridge University for their constant encouragement, comments and criticisms.

My greatest debt is to my parents whose selfless support, encouragement, and understanding made this research possible. I would also like to express my gratitude to my Rashidi informants who responded to my inquisitive questions with patience and tolerance as they were asked to repeat stories of the past which reactivated painful memories. I am grateful for their help, without which this research would have been impossible. However, I am wholly responsible for all opinions, errors and omissions.

M. Al Rasheed
London 1990

INTRODUCTION

This book deals with the Rashidi dynasty which emerged in the nineteenth century among the Shammar camel-herders of central Arabia. Throughout the century, the Shammar and their amirs were engaged in a process of dynastic expansion intended to unify central Arabia into one polity under Rashidi hegemony.

The present study is an attempt to bridge the gap between two disciplines, history and anthropology. I was trained as an anthropologist who became interested in those political processes that can only be studied over time. I realized that the formation of tribal dynasties and the transformation of political leadership are diachronic phenomena best understood by combining anthropological knowledge with an historical perspective. I chose to explore the history of the Rashidi dynasty which enabled me to reconcile my academic concerns with my own personal interest.

This book is a case study of a process whereby a tribe established its hegemony over an oasis which became the capital of a tribal dynasty. Two controversial notions in anthropology are invoked, namely tribe and dynasty. The Shammar regarded themselves and were regarded by others (including other tribes in the region, other dynastic rulers, and the Ottoman officials) as a *gabila* which is translated as a tribe, a large association of people who claim common ancestry. The unresolved anthropological debate over the notion of tribe has made anthropologists hesitate to mention the word without qualifications, definitions, and further elaborations, a symptom of the lack of consensus among them as to what this notion means and whether it is a useful sociological–analytical tool. This problem will be discussed in Chapter 1.

Once we know that the majority of the Shammar were nomadic camel-herders with some sedentarized tribal lineages, the two

1

notions, tribe and dynasty – which mainly describe cultural and political processes – become entangled with the economy of the group and further complicate the issues involved. The economy within which the Shammar tribe and dynasty operated consisted of a combination of pastoralism, trade, and to a lesser extent agriculture.

A second complication arises from the fact that the Shammar were Muslim tribesmen who operated within the general cultural framework of Islam. Since the eighteenth century, central Arabia had witnessed the emergence of Wahhabism, a religious movement which was opposed to the ethos of the tribes, mainly their tribal loyalty, but became dependent on them for the spread of the call. The Shammar opposed, not the doctrines of Wahhabism, but its political implications. When they defended their territory against Saudi–Wahhabi expansion towards the end of the eighteenth century, their actions were in defence of their tribal autonomy. In other words, their military encounters were directed against political rather than religious domination.

The Shammar inhabited an area which was within the claimed jurisdiction of the Ottoman Empire. This places the discussion of the Shammar tribe and dynasty within a wider context, showing how local formations (both tribe and dynasty) are not isolated and self-contained systems. The Shammar combined their nomadism with their control over an oasis where some lineages, such as the Rashidis, settled. This lineage began to centralize its powers, a process which led to the development of dynastic rule. This is not unusual, as some tribal groups in what is now called the Middle East have gone through similar developments (L. Beck 1986, G. Garthwaite 1983, Van Bruinessen 1978, R. Tapper 1983).

The majority of these tribes had some sort of tribal leadership although they were believed to have retained a degree of political decentralization fostered by the conditions of nomadism and lack of surplus. To take a few examples, the Rwala bedouins of the Syrian desert, the Al Fadl and Al Hassanna of the Beqaa Valley, and the Al Murrah of the Empty Quarter called their leaders sheikhs and amirs (W. Lancaster 1981, D. Chatty 1877 & 1986, and D. Cole 1975). Iranian nomadic tribes had khans and ilkhanis who were tribal chiefs (L. Beck 1986, G. Garthwaite 1983). However, the degree of power exercised by these tribal leaders varied. Differences in political centralization among the various nomadic tribes of the Middle East were dependent on a number of factors such as the diversity of the economy in terms of combining pastoralism with agriculture and trade, the capability of the system to generate surplus, the degree of geographical isolation of the group involved, its encapsulation by centralized states or empires, and the level of internal differentiation within the group.

Anthropologists who adopt an evolutionary approach tend to regard the formation of centralized political organization among nomads as a stage in a linear evolutionary framework (M. Sahlins 1968, E. Service 1975, M. Fried 1967). Societies are believed to evolve from simple political organizations, i.e. bands, tribes, and chiefdoms, to more complex political systems which are found in state societies. However, this approach with its rigid stages of development fails to explain how political decentralization does sometimes take place after a society goes through a period of centralization. It is not always the case that societies follow a linear evolutionary political development leading in one direction to the establishment of complex forms of political organization. Some north African tribes, for example, have oscillated between two systems, moving from dispersion and political decentralization to more centralized dynasty-like political systems (Ibn Khaldun 1987, R. Montagne 1930, E. Gellner 1981). Also dynasties collapsed and tribes reverted to decentralized political systems. In other words, their political evolution has been cyclical rather than linear. Instead of considering political centralization as an evolutionary stage in a linear model, I investigate the factors which stimulate such processes.

One of the factors responsible for political centralization among nomads is their contact with the outside world, in particular their relations with sedentary societies and interaction with more centralized states and empires (A. Khazanov 1984, R. Tapper 1983). On the assumption that nomads maintain social, political and economic relations with the wider society, these are held responsible for altering the nomads' political and economic structures – as a result of which they become prone to political centralization. When nomads' interaction with the outside world is examined over a historical period, oine can assess the relevance of this approach to the study of political centralization among them. This is particularly relevant to understanding the rise of the Rashidi dynasty among the Shammar tribe. In this book, the notions of tribe and dynasty are not regarded as describing two evolutionary stages whereby the first, i.e. tribe, was followed by the second. In the case of the Shammar, tribe and dynasty coexisted and were initially a single polity.

METHODOLOGICAL REMARKS

As a member of the Rashidi family, my interest in Rashidi history started when I was a child. At an early age, I became familiar with stories and anecdotes that members of my family told about their past. As some of them were born in Hail and lived there for some time, they had vivid descriptions of that episode of their history. They also were members of the first generation forced to leave Hail and settle in Riyadh, the Saudi capital after Ibn Saud captured the oasis and put an end to Rashidi rule in 1921. Other members of the family such as my father were born in Riyadh and were never allowed to return to Hail not even for a short visit. Such people lived through the experience of exile in Riyadh. I listened to their stories out of politeness, but never took them seriously. I thought that Rashidi history belonged to a distant past which did not impinge on our daily lives.

Born in Paris of a Rashidi father and a Lebanese mother, and brought up as a child in Riyadh, I knew only one home until the age of twelve. I lived there together with my close relatives and family. I was aware of my family's history which I was told not to discuss with school friends and teachers. I was warned that we did not need new problems. I never understood what was meant by these warnings until 1975 when King Faisal of Saudi Arabia was killed by his nephew Prince Faisal Ibn Musaid whose mother was my paternal aunt, my father's sister. History became alive again. There were rumours that the Rashidis were involved. These rumours became suspicions as the Saudi secret police entered our house and that of my uncle, searched our belongings, took my father for interrogation and put my uncle in prison. As my father was not imprisoned, he remained in the country for a period of three months at the end of which he decided to voluntarily leave Saudi Arabia. My uncle stayed in prison for almost a year although Saudi enquiries established that the king's murderer was acting on his own and did not collaborate with anybody else. After his release, my uncle left Saudi Arabia and renounced his Saudi citizenship. He now lives in Iraq.

As a twelve-year-old child, I was struck by these events and turned to members of the family in an attempt to find out why we were harassed and indirectly forced to leave home. Because of our history, I was told, we now had to go through this new experience of exile. My interest in Rashidi history and politics in general began to crystallize. I read the accessible literature of the European travellers who had visited Hail and met my ancestors. I also became more interested in Rashidi oral poetry which some members of my family memorized and recorded.

After Riyadh, I lived in Lebanon where I was sent to school. I became detached from Rashidi history as the turmoils of the Lebanon during its civil war and the Israeli invasion of 1982 impinged on my daily life and diverted me from my early concerns. After graduating from school, I came to England for higher education. I studied anthropology and sociology. Anthropology was the academic discipline in which I found serious attempts at answering the number of questions I had accumulated. I chose to continue my exploration of the discipline whose founders spoke a language I could relate to and understand.

As I was searching for a research topic to present to the Anthropology Department at Cambridge University, I could not overcome the temptation to write a Ph.D thesis on the Rashidi amirs of Hail. However, I was not sure of the department's reaction to me being the subject and object of my own research, a dichotomy which anthropologists have been keen to maintain. My uncertainties about the prospects of such a research proposal were aggravated because I knew I would not be able to do fieldwork in Hail. In 1986, I was not in a position to do so for various political reasons. To my surprise, my proposal was accepted.

This account of the circumstances which resulted in writing this book and my close personal interest and background are essential for evaluating and interpreting my work. As my research started to progress, I began to realize the positive advantage I had as an insider and the shortcomings resulting from being the subject and object of research. Anthropologists concerned with methodology issues have dealt with this problem (P. Rabinow 1977, D. Messerschmidt 1981, S. Altorki and C. El Solh 1988), and I shall only say that my close personal connection with the Rashidi family has opened many doors which would most probably have remained closed for outsiders. However, having grown up after the age of twelve outside Saudi Arabia, I have always been regarded by my own relatives as distant from my own history and past. They often commented on my naïvity as I asked questions which revealed my limited knowledge of tribal affairs, tribal custom, and the past in general. They were, nevertheless, tolerant of my ignorance which they wished to eliminate in the context of the interviews that I designed and carried out. In their eyes, these interviews became the means to socialize me and enrich my knowledge of my own history.

Being an insider by birth, I also began to realize the disadvantages which this entails. The first was related to my inability to carry out fieldwork in Hail, thus limiting my access to a wider group of informants whose opinions could have enriched this study. Secondly, throughout this research I always felt the pressure of trying to avoid bias, which might not have been strongly felt by an outsider. I recognized that I could be accused of being an apologist for the Rashidis and was aware of my strong personal feelings about my own history, affiliations, and allegiances. Researching one's own society or family involves unavoidable personal struggles which the researcher has to learn to live with and resolve. Recognizing one's allegiances can only be the first step towards resolving this struggle.

The ethnographic data on which my research is based does not describe in detail the present situation among the Shammar which has been recently studied by two anthropologists (U. Fabietti 1984 and R. Fernea 1987). Instead, I focus on Shammar and Rashidi nineteenth-century history which is most relevant to our understanding of the present situation. In the course of this research, I used data gathered through interviewing members of the Rashidi family outside Saudi Arabia, archival material, and the literature of European travellers.

In December 1986 and between June and September 1987, I collected folktales, oral poetry, narratives and life histories related to the subject matter of this study. Some of my informants were close relatives still living in Saudi Arabia, whom I interviewed when they travelled outside the country. Others were in exile and these I interviewed in London and Paris. My oldest informant was in his early fifties, belonging to the first generation of the family born after the capture of Hail in 1921.

The archival material which I used is found in London and Paris. I consulted the archives of the India Office Library and Records (London) where I looked at the correspondence of the British consuls, political agents, political residents and high commissioners with the Government of India and the Foreign Office. As there was no British representative or political agent in central Arabia in the nineteenth century, I relied on the correspondence of the British representatives in the Persian Gulf, mainly in Bushire, Bahrein, and Kuweit. I also worked in the archives of the Foreign Office in Paris (Archive du Ministère des Affaires Etrangères) where I consulted the series of Correspondance Politique et Commerciale, Correspondance Consulaire et Commerciale, and Mémoires et Documents. The numbers and references of the files consulted are given in the bibliography section. In addition, I used published archival data from the National Archives of Cairo (Cairo, Abdeen) which document the Egyptian invasion of central Arabia by the troops of Mohammad Ali. These were originally in Ottoman Turkish and were later translated by the Egyptian government into Arabic. Unfortunately I was not able to use the Ottoman Archives in Istanbul. In 1987, I applied to the Turkish Embassy in London for a research permit which would enable me to carry out archival research in Turkey. This would have allowed me to explore Ottoman policy and relations with the amirs of Hail towards the end of the nineteenth century. As my application was rejected, I had to rely on British sources covering the same period. I hope that in the future the Turkish authorities will realize the value of Ottoman documents for research and loosen their restrictions.

The literature of the European travellers has also been consulted in the course of this research. From the mid-nineteenth century, Hail attracted the attention of travellers such as G. Wallin, W. Palgrave, C. Doughty, A. Blunt, C. Guarmani, C. Huber, E. Nolde, and J. Euting who visited the oasis and described how it became a central nub of Arabian politics at that time (see bibliography for references). Common to this literature was an underlying puzzle: how could an oasis situated in the midst of the desert become the capital of a prosperous dynasty where law and order were enforced? Travellers at that time had an image of Arabia as an area dominated by wandering bedouin tribes who lived in a Hobbesian state of nature and knew only raids, chaos, and plunder. In Hail, they saw something which they did not expect and were not able to explain. This literature has recently been reconsidered and critically reevaluated (K. Tidrick 1981, R. Bidwell 1976, R. Brent 1977). Tidrick argued that the European travellers of the nineteenth century failed to make the distinction between the value system of the community as expressed in what its members say about it and the value system which can be deduced from the behaviour of its members (K. Tidrick 1981: 29). Unfortunately, this fundamental distinction which seems simple and obvious to any social scientist trained in the last fifty years or so was not so obvious to most of the European travellers. In spite of any shortcomings, their writing has always been and is still an important source of information on the history of the Arabian Peninsula in general. Both historians (R. Winder 1965) and anthropologists (H. Rosenfeld 1965, L. Sweet 1965, M. Meeker 1979) have relied on it for their research.

Rosenfeld drew heavily on this literature for his anthropological construction of the Rashidi dynasty. The travellers' fascination with tribal military organization, raids and warfare seems to have influenced Rosenfeld's understanding of the mechanisms which led to the emergence of what he calls the state-type dynasty of the Rashidis. In fact, he begins his analysis with the hypothesis that the key to understanding the level of development of a society is the social composition of its military. His complete reliance on travellers' literature prevented him from exploring other relevant areas of social life and relating local political processes to a wider historical context. Unlike Rosenfeld, I used the travellers' studies in conjunction with other sources to avoid the trap of a reductionist approach resulting from dependence on this literature alone.

1

THE COUNTRY AND
THE PEOPLE

The Shammar homeland was in the central north of what is now
Saudi Arabia. It consisted of the south-east of the Great Nafud
Desert and Jabal Shammar. Before the rise of Islam, the latter was
known as Jabal Tayy, the homeland of the ancient Arab tribe
called Tayy (R. Montagne 1932: 63). Perhaps the mountain came
to be known as Jabal Shammar after the Shammar moved to the
area.

Neither historical sources nor Shammar oral tradition provides
accurate documentation concerning the Shammar move to Jabal
Shammar. In their oral narratives, the Shammar state that they
moved to this region from the Yemen four centuries earlier. The
reasons for migration remain unclear. However, most of the tribal
migration in the region used to occur as a result of drought, tribal
competition over natural resources, or military pressures from
other groups. As the Shammer located their origins in the Yemen,
they established their status among the Arabian tribes. They were
Yemenites of an exclusive status as they claimed to be descendants
of Qahtani origin. In their legends, the Shammar claim they were
the descendants of an apical ancestor, Shimmer Ibn al Amluq, one
of the kings of the Yemen in ancient times.[1]

The Shammar claim that one of their tribal sections, the Abde,
assumed leadership in Jabal Shammar soon after their arrival and
pushed away the local leader, a man called Bahij.[2] Shammar
narratives tend to elaborate on the migration and settlement in
Jabal Shammar. However, the narratives become thinner with
regard to the period after their settlement in Jabal Shammar. In
other words, there are no detailed accounts of the events of the
sixteenth and seventeenth centuries. Consequently, it is difficult, if
not impossible, to reconstruct Shammar history during these two
hundred years from their oral tradition. However, one gets a

9

clearer picture of the later period of the eighteenth and an even
better one of the nineteenth century as Shammar accounts become
richer and full of detailed descriptions of their position in their
territory.

This is not surprising. Most tribal histories constructed from
people's oral tradition show similar patterns. Tribes tend to have a
rich reservoir of memories with regard to their origins and
migration. However, memories fade away and a sort of historical
amnesia follows when individuals are asked about succeeding
events. Narratives and memories of the last hundred years,
however, become alive and tend to be detailed. The Shammar are
not unique in this respect. Scholars of tribal history have observed
the richness of the myths which relate to the group's tribal origin,
the gaps in the narratives with regard to subsequent events, and
their detailed knowledge of recent history.[3] The collective memoirs
of the tribe, however, cannot be considered as historical truths as
understood by historians. They are sociological truths, consequently, they are relevant to our understanding of people's
perceptions of themselves and their claims and justifications of
their presence in a given territory. The geographical features of this
territory are discussed in the following section.

THE COUNTRY

The Great Nafud Desert

The Great Nafud Desert covers about 2,500 sq. miles of sand dunes
at an elevation of about 3,000 ft. It extends about 140 miles from
north to south, and about 180 miles from east to west.
Longitudinal dunes, scores of miles in length, as much as 300 ft.
high and separated by valleys as much as 10 miles wide, are the
main features of this desert. Iron oxide gives the sand a reddish
tint, particularly when the sun is low. Within the desert there are
several watering places, and winter rain brings up short-lived but
succulent grasses which permit nomadic herding during later
winter and spring. The major wells in this desert are Al Shaqiq,
Atwa, Hafar, Hayaniya, and Artayan. Contrary to traditional
beliefs, the Great Nafud is not barren. It is considered to be better
wooded and richer in pasture than any part of the deserts to the
north or south (A. Blunt 1968: 157 vol I).

The Shammar regarded the south-east section of the Nafud

Desert as part of their traditional tribal territory. They had communal ownership of its pasture and wells, and encamped there in winter and spring when pasture and water became abundant. Their camps were usually situated around the wells which had their tribal *wasm* (brand). During the hot and dry season, the Shammar either remained near their wells or moved closer to the villages and oases of Jabal Shammar. They were forced by the hot summer climate to spend at least five months near wells or oases. They claimed control of these wells, and exclusive rights over both the water and pasture of the area. The Rumal section had access to the only oasis in the area, Jubba, which was an isolated location with eighty houses. The chiefly lineage of the Rumal settled in the village and were considered the sheikhs of the settlement (U. Fabietti 1984).

Jabal Shammar

To the south of the Great Nafud Desert, Jabal Shammar consists of two ranges of mountains, Jabal Aja and Jabal Salma, both granite ridges of considerable height. Jabal Aja averages 1,000 ft. above sea level. The range covers an area of about 100 miles, over 420 miles south-west of Baghdad and more than 480 miles south-east of Damascus. Jabal Salma is not much lower in altitude, but is considerably less in area. The region can be divided into two zones: the western and north-western sandstone plain, dotted with sandstone crags, shelving finally into the Nafud sand bed; and the southern and eastern basaltic plains out of which rise the granite ridges, cropped with basalt. Jabal Aja rises abruptly out of the plain, and is dominated by imposing crags. The barrenness of its flanks is intensified by a considerable amount of vegetation in its gullies. Brushwood, acacias, and palms show that these hills attract a certain quantity of moisture. There was also a considerable amount of animal life: ibex, gazelle, fox, wolf, jackal and partridges (Admiralty 1920: 375).

Jabal Shammar attracts sufficient rainfall to ensure a certain supply of grazing. The first rains start in November and if abundant ensure good pasture. The water below the surface is so near and so easily tapped that there is an unusually large cluster of oases – situated between Jabal Aja and Jabal Salma – which can be described as areas of vegetation surrounded by desert. In the nineteenth century, Hail became the 'capital' of Jabal Shammar.

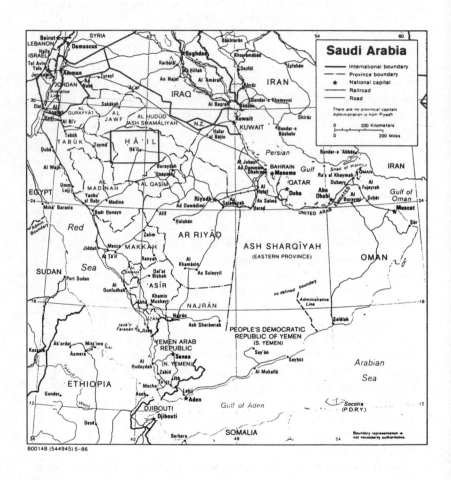

MAP 1: *Area of Jabal Shammar*

In addition to Hail, there were a number of small oases and villages in Jabal Shammar. Feid was 45 miles south-east of Hail. Its palm groves extended for two or three miles, and there was considerable cultivation of cereals. Its inhabitants, who were partly Shammar and partly Bani Tamim, numbered about 1,000. Gofar, the second oasis, was almost equal to Hail in the number of its population. The oasis was extensive and its palm groves were even more numerous than those of Hail. It was inhabited by the Bani Tamim. Agdah consisted of a group of scattered villages situated in a large area of palm groves, which filled an enclosed valley in Jabal Shammar. It was entirely shut in by steep granite crags, and was regarded by the Rashidi family as their ancestral stronghold (Admiralty, 1920: 386). It had a total population of 1,500. Mouwaqaq, Saban, Mustajjiddah, Ghazalah, and Raudhah were other smaller oases in Jabal Shammar. They were inhabited by a mixture of the Shammar and Bani Tamim tribes.

The population of Jabal Shammar was estimated to be 20,000 in 1877 (C. Doughty 1979: 20 vol II). The *Handbook of Arabia* gave an estimate of 18,000 in 1920.[4]

Hail

Hail, situated at an altitude of 979 metres, had a population of 3,000 inhabitants in 1877 (C. Doughty 1979: 20 vol II). Estimates of the population of Hail are unreliable in the nineteenth and early twentieth centuries. The *Handbook of Arabia* suggests a figure of 5,000 in 1946 (Admiralty, 1946: 566). Wallin mentions that 'Hail is probably one of the latest founded villages in the land, owing its origin principally to its being the birthplace of the present and preceding sheikh family. There is no mention made in the work of Arab geographers of Hail as a village, but only as a place in the Aga chain.' (G. Wallin 1854: 200)

The quarters of Hail were listed as, in roughly west–east order, Samah, Barzan, Subhan, Abid, Lubdah, Mughithah, Atiq, Jubarah, Jarad, Qoraishi, Rakhis, Faraikh, Dhubaan, Ziqidi, and Wasitah (J. Lorimer 1908: 600–1 vol IIA). Hail was surrounded by a 15–20 ft. wall of mud brick; the wall was 3–4 miles in circumference. It had round towers and five gates; the Madina Gate on the south-east, the Mubbah Gate on the east, the Najaf Gate on the north, the Jubbah Gate to the west and another small gate to the south-west.

Land inside the wall was planted with figs, wheat and other crops, while cultivation outside the wall was mainly of date palms, sweet lemon, pomegranate, apricot, apples, and oranges. Lorimer describes the main square in Hail, called Al Mishab, as being 250 yards long and 25 yards wide. The main *suq* (market) was called Al Mabi and had 140 shops (J. Lorimer 1908: 601 vol IIA).

The houses had an upper storey and were built of sun-dried brick, date palms, or tamarisk wood. The main building material was unfired mud-brick, and the completed walls were made smooth by the application of mud-plaster. These walls were very thick and provided insulation against the extremities of the local climate. The roofing consisted of wooden beams, with palm mattings or twigs spread above, usually covered with a layer of mud. Stone was only used for the foundation of the houses and in fortifications. The houses were often built around a central courtyard with only a few openings on the street. The entrances to the houses were closed by large rectangular elaborately shaped mud finials which stood at the corners.

In 1836, Abdullah Ibn Rashid succeeded in establishing his power base in Hail which started to assume a predominant political and economic role not only in Jabal Shammar, but in central Arabia as a whole. He completed the construction of the palace in Hail, which is described in detail in Chapter 3. Before 1836, Hail was simply a village with date groves and a small market. During the second half of the century, this village was transformed into an important oasis. It began to have some urban characteristics such as high population density. It witnessed the growth and concentration of its population (3,000 inhabitants) in a circle of 3–4 miles in circumference, which can be contrasted with the other sparsely populated oases of Jabal Shammar. In addition, Hail had major urban sites such as the mosque, market, and ruler's castle.

Furthermore, the population of Hail was becoming more and more heterogeneous as it attracted merchants from Syria, Mesopotamia, and the Qasim. Both Christian and Jewish merchants settled there, drawn by the prosperity and safety under the leadership of the Rashidi amirs. Doughty couned thirty-five Shiite trading families and merchants from Mashad Ali in Iraq who had already settled (C. Doughty 1979: 656 vol I).

The establishment of Hail as a caravan station for merchants and pilgrims coming from Persia and Mesopotamia to visit Mecca and Madina led to the enlargement of Hail's role. This fostered both cultural and economic contacts between the local population and people of more established sedentary civilization such as the inhabitants of Baghdad, Basra, and Persia.

In Hail, status groups began to form along demarcated lines.[5] The Rashidi ruling group and the Shammar chiefly families who settled in the oasis occupied the highest position in the hierarchy. The merchants of Hail were the second prosperous group whose wealth was derived from involvement in the trading caravans. They became influential as they were allied to the ruling group whose commercial interests coincided with those of the merchants. The third group consisted of the sedentary Bani Tamim agriculturalists who owned their own land in the oasis and cultivated mainly dates. The fourth category included the artisans who occupied a low status as a result of their occupation and lack of tribal origin. The last category in the system of stratification in Hail consisted of the slaves who were domestic servants and agricultural labourers.

The heterogeneity of the Hail population was reflected in the arrangement of space. The various quarters were grouped into three main neighbours; Lubdah the quarter of the artisans and merchants, Barzan the quarter of the slaves and strangers in the town, and Magidah the quarter of the ruling group (R. Montagne 1947: 77). Hail was not, however, unique in this respect.[6] Describing the oases of north Arabia, Musil claims that: 'Each oasis or settlement is divided into districts inhabited by members of the same kin or clan. Each district has its chief, and the most powerful of the chiefs is regarded as the head chief of the whole settlement.' (A. Musil 1928a: 302) The various groups of the population remained to a great extent physically isolated from each other. The *hayy* (quarter) population represented a close network rather than the population of the oasis as a whole. Residence in the *hayy* depended on the family's origin and profession.

In spite of its urban features, life in Hail remained an extension of desert life. This stemmed from the fact that Hail was situated in Jabal Shammar, an area where there were almost equal numbers of sedentary and nomadic population – in contrast to southern Najd, which was mainly occupied by settled communities in clusters of oases. In the absence of precise statistics, one has to rely on the available estimates. Wahba estimated that in Jabal Shammar there were 20,000 nomads and 22,000 sedentary people in the 1900s (H.

Wahba 1935: 73). Consequently, as a desert town, Hail became part of two worlds which were not necessarily different from each other. The wall of Hail did not demarcate solid frontiers between the desert and the oasis, rather there was a continuum between the two which blurred the divisions between the sedentary and nomadic population.

In the nineteenth century, it was not an unusual sight to see nomads with their tents a short distance from the oasis. In the hot and dry season, Hail used to attract a considerable number of the Shammar who were forced by the climate to retreat to areas where water was abundant. Doughty observed the presence of 'resident nomads' who were encamping around the wall of Hail when he visited the region: 'They are Shammar, whose few cattle are with their tribesfolk in the wilderness: in spring months they also remove thither, and refresh themselves in the short season of milk ... I counted their tents, thirty, nearer the Gofar gate were other fifteen booths of half resident Shammar, pitched without clay building.' (C. Doughty 1979: 671–2 vol I)

Perhaps these comments allow us to reconsider the dichotomy between the nomads and the sedentary at least in the context of Jabal Shammar. When the term 'nomad' is used to describe the Shammar, it refers to a group of people who practised animal herding, followed a pattern of migration, settled in the oases for some time especially during the dry season, perhaps owned houses and date plantations in the oases, and were involved in trade relations with the sedentary people. In other words, nomadism was only one aspect of their life. On the other hand, the term 'sedentary' refers to those oasis dwellers who permanently resided in houses, were farmers, artisans, or merchants, and perhaps had animal herds in the desert.

The division between the nomad and the sedentary population was further blurred as a result of the symbiotic relations which existed between the two categories. The regional economy of Jabal Shammar was characterized by the juxtaposition of three economic activities, pastoralism (i.e. animal herding), agriculture (mainly dates) and trade. These did not constitute three separate and specialized zones, rather they were part of a single economy. It was not unusual to find Shammar families practising animal herding on a regular basis and being involved in trade at the same time. Some families participated in the caravan trade with Mesopotamia. They transported the merchandise, and some of them were traders themselves. Also, it was common among Shammar families to own agricultural land and date plantations in the oases, and some chiefly families had permanent houses there.

Similarly, some oasis dwellers had herds in the desert. Sedentarized Shammar families in Hail continued to own camels which they kept with members of their families or shepherds in the desert. The oasis dwellers relied on those who owned animals for their supply of meat, clarified butter, wool, and animal products in general. Some oasis dwellers were traders who represented a link between the nomads and the sedentary population. Traders had commercial links with Mesopotamia where they imported various products including grain, dates, rice, coffee, sugar, clothes, shoes, and weapons.

The regional economy was, therefore, characterized by relations of symbiosis between the 'nomads' and the 'sedentary' population. The economic interdependence between the desert and the sown fostered the existence of cultural continuity rather than dichotomy between the two sections of the population.

THE PEOPLE

The Shammar who inhabited the Great Nafud Desert and Jabal Shammar regarded themselves and were regarded by others[7] as belonging to a *gabila*, an indigenous term used by many groups in the Middle East and often translated as tribe. However, this term represents perhaps one of the most controversial notions in anthropological literature, stemming from the claim that it describes a variety of groups who may or may not have common features with regard to economic and political organization. In Arabia, for example, there were sedentary people such as Bani Tamim who called themselves a *gabila*. There were also camel-herding people such as the Shammar, the Al Murrah of the Empty Quarter, the Anizah, and the Rwala of the Syrian Desert, who were known as *gabail* (singular *gabila*). Furthermore, there were sheep- and goat-herding *gabail* such as the Hawazim and the Shararat. Outside the Arabian Peninsula and across north Africa, the term *gabila* is used by many groups. In Egypt, for example, Awlad Ali were reported to use the term (L. Abu-Lughod 1986).

Among the Bani Saada of Cyrenaica (E. Evans-Pritchard 1949 and
E. Peters 1967) and the Bni Bataw of Morocco (D. Eickelman
1976), the word *gabila* occurs again and again.

The list is very long and these examples are not meant to be
exhaustive. The point which I emphasize here relates to the variety
of so-called tribal people in terms of their economic activity (they
can be pastoralists, agriculturalists or merchants in the case of the
Koreish tribe of the sixth century), ethnic origin (in the case of the
Middle East, tribes can be Arab, Berber, Kurdish, Turkic, Persian
and so on), socio-political organization (they can be acephalous
with no headship or centralized with powerful chiefs, sheiks, and
amirs), and degree of political autonomy (they can be encapsulated
by states or independent of central authority).

The variety of societies that regard themselves as tribes
encouraged some anthropologists to argue that the notion is void
and has no sociological value (M. Godelier 1977, M. Fried 1975).
Others considered tribes as creations of colonial powers for
administrative purposes. In cases such as Morocco and the Sudan,
the colonial powers formerly promoted 'tribal' identities and
developed tribal administration to a fine art in an attempt to retard
nationalistic movements (D. Eickelman 1981: 89). A third group of
anthropologists accepted the term *gabila* because it represented an
indigenous notion referring to identity, unity, and cohesion among
individuals who claim to have common blood relations.

Once the notion has been accepted, the problem of definition
becomes acute. Many articles and books have been published on
the notion of 'tribe'.[8] Almost all anthropologists using the word
'tribe' feel the need to define what they mean by it, which indicates
the lack of consensus on the meaning of the word. Sometimes, these
definitions are given in general and broad terms in order to
encompass the variety of societies which call themselves 'tribes'.

Defining the term 'tribe', anthropologists have emphasized three
dimensions. First, common descent and kinship ties are often
invoked by people when they claim they belong to a tribe. People
say 'we are related genealogically, therefore we are one tribe', or
'we are one tribe, therefore, we must be related genealogically'. For
example, Tapper stresses that kinship is the dominant idiom of
organization among tribes (R. Tapper 1983: 9). Second, the
political functions of the tribe have also been emphasized. What
makes a tribe is the fact that it is a local mutual aid association,
whose members jointly help maintain order internally and defend

the unit externally (E. Gellner 1983: 438). Third, sometimes definitions are given in terms of how tribes orginate. Beck argues, for example, that the tribe is a polity emerging out of the contact between local resource sharing, non-state organized people and larger more complex polities, states in particular (L. Beck 1986: 14–15). Fourth, instead of giving one definition, some anthropologists distinguish between four usages: the local native ideology of tribal identity, the administrative notion, the implicit practical notion held by the people, and finally the analytical–anthropological notion of tribe (D. Eickelman 1981: 88). According to this approach, every time the word 'tribe' is mentioned, one has to make clear whether one is referring to the ideology, the practical notions, the administrative definition, or the sociological definition of the scholars.

In this study, however, the definition of the tribe will not be given in general terms, but will be derived from the features of the notion among the Shammar. Consequently, it may or may not apply to tribes in general.

The Shammar

In the seventeenth century, the Shammar split into two groups: the Shammar of Mesopotamia (or northern Shammar) and the Shammar of Jabal Shammar (or southern Shammar). The northern group inhabit, with other groups, the area between the Tigris and Euphrates. They moved from Jabal Shammar to the north in search of better pasture grounds and water. However, towards the end of the eighteenth century, a new migration took place as a result of confrontation with the expanding Saudi–Wahhabi dynasty.[9] The major sections of the northern Shammar are the Jarba, Toqah, and Zakarit. Some of these groups continued to practise animal herding whereas others became sedentarized agriculturalists. Toqah and Zakarit, for example, became semi-nomadic in the sense that they went out into the *Jazirah* (Syrian Desert) west of the Euphrates in the spring and returned to their villages in the summer. They adopted Shiism in Mesopotamia under the influence of the Shiite communities in the area whereas the southern Shammar remained Sunnis of the Hanafi sect.[10] The southern Shammar are the major concern of this book and will be referred to as the Shammar for simplification.

Before embarking on any definition of the *gabila* among the

Shammar, it is important to identify the size of the unit. In the absence of accurate statistics, one has to rely on the available estimates of the Shammar in the nineteenth century. According to the *Handbook of Arabia*, the Shammar were estimated to have had 4,000 tents (Admiralty 1920: 77). Montagne, on the other hand, claims that 'Les Semmar forment une confédération dont on peut, en l'absence de tout dénombrement, éstimer l'importance à 150 ou 200 000 âmes' (R. Montagne 1932: 63). Montagne's estimates included the sedentarized Shammar of the oases which numbered approximately 20,000.

Those 150,000–200,000 people constituted the Shammar *gabila* which consisted of an amalgamation of smaller units. According to Shammar genealogies, they were divided into four tribal sections called *ashair* (singular *ashira*): Aslam (1,200 tents), Sinjara (1,000 tents), Abde (1,500 tents) and Tuman (300 tents) (estimates in the *Handbook of Arabia* 1929). Those sections claimed descent from one apical ancestor and shared a defined territory whose resources, pasture, water and oases, were divided among them. The Abde Shammar used land between Jabal Aja and Jabal Salma whereas the Aslam camped to the east of the Abde. Sinjara inhabited the central part of the Great Nafud Desert (Map 2).

The *gabila* was, therefore, a large association of people who claimed common ancestry, which endowed it with a fragile unity. The fact that the *gabila* consisted of a large group dispersed over the Great Nafud Desert and Jabal Shammar acted against the development of a strong sense of unity.[11] Furthermore, until 1836, the Shammar *gabila* had no single chief or head. It was only after the rise of the Rashidi amirs to power in Hail that the Shammer became identified with a common leadership. In contrast with the *gabila*, the *ashira* had political and military unity, reflected in the role of the tribal sheikhs. The head of the *ashira* represented a nob around which its members gathered.

Each *ashira* consisted of a number of maximal lineages (*fukhud*). The Shammar use the metaphor of the human thigh (*fakhd*) which by definition proliferates from a body, in this case the *ashira*. The maximal lineages (*Fukhud* = 100–150 tents) were the basic herding and camping units which moved and camped together with their animals. The maximal lineage claimed ownership of wells and pasture in their territory. The wells had the maximal lineage's *wasm* (brand) which indicated the exclusive right of the smaller lineages to use the wells. The maximal lineage consisted of a

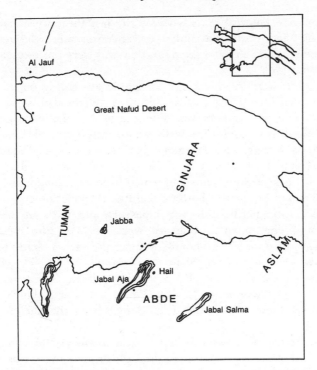

MAP 2: *Distribution of the Shammar*

number of smaller lineages (*hamula*). The *hamula* was a patrilineal corporate group which consisted of grandfather and grandmother(s), ego, his wife(ves), his sons, his brothers, their wives and their sons. In other words, the lineage consisted of a group of actual *ibn amm* (patrilateral parallel cousins). Members of the *hamula* usually encamped in close proximity to each other, and herded their animals as one unit.

The *hamula* was further divided into smaller households, called *beit*. The *beit* was the residential unit. It consisted of ego, his wife(ves) and children and tended to be formed upon marriage. The marriage of a son enabled him to move out of his father's tent and set up his own. The son was also given his share of the herd which would enable him to remain self sufficient with respect to his household consumption of milk and meat.

The tribe (*gabila*), the tribal section (*ashira*), the maximal lineage (*fakhd*), the lineages (*hamula*) and the household (*beit*) were units which had different size and political importance. The first two groups were political units whereas the last three were economic, camping and residential units. These terms were derived from Shammar terminology of segmentation and were not unique to the Shammar.[12]

The *beits* were in most cases incapable of existing on their own due to their small size and inability to defend themselves solely with their limited manpower. The size of its herd was sometimes insufficient to maintain the well-being of the *beit*, which remained tied to its lineage. The lineage pooled its resources and herded the animals together, although it did not own pasture and water. Several lineages were joined together to form a maximal lineage, which was the major herding camp. It had control over its resources and herds and owned pasture and wells in the tribal territory. The maximal lineages were parts of the *ashira* and whereas they were economic units, the *ashira* had political importance. Each of the Shammar *ashair* had a sheikh who was usually a member of one of the prominent lineages. Leadership of the Sinjara was provided by Ibn Thunayan. The Aslam had Ibn Twala as their sheikh and Ibn Timyat was the sheikh of the Tuman.

The Abde Shammar was the largest *ashira* (1,500 tents). The Rashidi dynasty in Hail represented the hegemony of this section as the Rashidi amirs were descendants of the Abde. The Abde were divided into two maximal lineages: Yahia and Rabia. The Yahia were further divided into two lineages: the Fadl with Ibn Jibrin as their sheikh and the Mufadal whose sheikh was Ibn Ajil. The Rabia consisted also of two lineages; Ibn Ali was the sheikh of the Jaafar whereas Ibn Jadi was the sheikh of the Weibar. The Jaafar was comprised of seven households: al-Jashm, al-Himiar, al-Atu, al-Ali, al-Khalil, al-Shirhan, and al-Rasin (Diagram 1). The ruler of Hail before 1836, Ibn Ali, was a descendant of the al-Khalil and so were the Rashidi amirs.

In spite of the presence of various levels of segmentation, the Shammar adhered to a practical ideology in which they stressed their unity at the level of *gabila*. By practical ideology, to use Eickelman's definition, I mean the 'sets of beliefs constituted by largely implicit shared assumptions concerning such basic aspects of the social order as notions of tribe, kinship, family, and person . . . etc' (D. Eickelman 1981: 86). The Shammar held shared assumptions with direct relevance to their everyday life. These covered the political, military, and economic spheres and had a

DIAGRAM 1: *The Segmentation of the Abde Shammar*

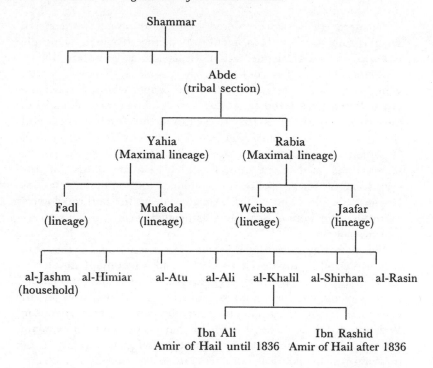

common emphasis on enforcing the group's unity and cohesion. Political assumptions stressed the peaceful settlement of inter-tribal disputes and mutual support. The *gabila* represented also the arena for potential political alliances. At the military level, the Shammar held strong obligations regarding the avoidance of military confrontation with each other and military co-operation in the face of external threat. These obligations were expressed as cultural norms. They were occasionally put into practice, but most of the time they remained as ideal beliefs describing the 'appropriate action'. Evidence from Shammar history supports this formulation.[13] It is difficult to imagine that the Shammar, a group of 150,000–200,000 people co-operated at the military level to defend each other when one section or maximal lineage was attacked. It would be impossible to mobilize such a large group for defence or offence. At the economic level, the Shammar also had a set of assumptions regarding the obligation to share the economic resources of their territory, and to help each other during times of drought and scarcity.

The term *gabila* is considered here as an important concept sociologically because it is a cultural notion invented by people under conditions of fragmentation, dispersion, and constant threats of attack. This notion confers on the people a sense of identity which is not static or rigid. When the people who inhabited the Great Nafud Desert and Jabal Shammar claimed they belonged to one tribe, they made assertions regarding their exclusiveness and the presence of communal bonds which by definition involved co-operation and peaceful coexistence. Therefore, the *gabila* can be regarded as a dynamic notion which sets standards for the regulation of social, political, economic, and military relations between people who claim kinship ties. In anthropological literature, the notion has been associated with the segmentary lineage model.

This model appeared for the first time as a systematic theory in the writings of Evans-Pritchard (1940) and was initially developed to account for the political organization of the Nuer, the cattle-herders of the southern Sudan. Later the model was used in the context of north Africa and in particular among the Cyrenaican Bedouins of Libya (1949). Evans-Pritchard endeavoured to explain the existence and functions of elaborate tribal genealogies and the mechanisms of political alliances in tribal societies with no centralized authority. He argued that the principal function of the tribal genealogy is to provide a paradigm for political action such as, for example, the settlement of disputes between the various groups represented in the genealogy. For the segmentary lineage theory to be applicable, the following should be present. First, groups should hold a strong ideology of unilineal descent. Secondly, groups should be balanced by other groups of equal strength at each level of segmentation. And thirdly, groups and individuals should hold a strong ideology of equality based on equal birth. As Evans-Pritchard tried to explain order and peace in acephalous societies, he claimed that in the absence of centralized leadership, peace is maintained as a result of the balanced opposition between segmentary groups. A situation of ordered anarchy exists rather than complete disorder and perpetual conflicts (1940: 6). The segmentary political system results from the unsettled political conditions among peoples without developed political institutions.

The segmentary lineage theory has been used by many anthropologists working with tribal material drawn from Africa and the Middle East (M. Fortes 1953, J. Middleton & D. Tait 1958, I.M. Lewis 1961, and E. Gellner 1969). Recently, this theory has been criticized by many anthropologists (M.G. Smith 1956, E. Peters 1967, A. Hamoudi 1980, H. Geertz 1971, C. Geertz, H. Geertz & L. Rosen 1979, M. Meeker 1979, J.P. Digard 1978, and D. Eickelman 1976 & 1981). The debate between the supporters of the theory and its critics has been reproduced elsewhere (E. Gellner and C. Micaud 1973, E. Gellner 1981, M. Sahlins 1961, and D. Eickelman 1981) and there is no need to repeat it. However, what concerns us here is Peters' contribution to our understanding of the theory. In his study of the Cyrenaican bedouins, he argues that the segmentary lineage model is not a sociological one, but a frame of reference used by a particular people to give them a common-sense kind of understanding of their social relationships (1967: 261). Peters claims that as the segmentary model is a kind of ideology which enables the bedouins to understand their social relations, it would be an error to mistake such a folk model for sociological analysis. He lists four objections to the model. First, the corner-stone in the theory of lineage systems is that they consist of parts which are in balanced opposition to each other all the time, yet this is not true of segmentary groups. Secondly, according to this theory, groups come together to constitute larger segments in opposition to like segments, yet when groups combine in Cyrenaica, they do not do so according to the rules of segmentary lineage theory. Thirdly, according to the model, all groups must have equal resources and equal size. However, in reality groups vary in size and economic wealth. Fourthly, lineage theory does not take into account the role of women and the ties created through them. Peters' criticisms of the segmentary lineage theory are based on emphasizing the discrepancy between what the bedouins say and what they actually do. Because of this discrepancy he concludes that the segmentary model is useless as an analytical and sociological framework.

Other anthropologists, such as Meeker, criticized the segmentary lineage theory on formal grounds. Meeker argues that 'while it implies that the nomads are practical men who think in terms of self-interest, it fails to explain the highly formal way by which they conceive of their self-interest' (M. Meeker 1979: 13). When the model is applied to the north Arabian bedouin, Meeker argues that it does not work. Their pattern of political segmentation fails to conform to the 'classical notion of a segmentary political system' as developed by Evans-Pritchard. Meeker argues that among the north Arabian bedouins, political relationships were not represented in terms of a politically segmenting genealogy. Instead, one level of political grouping, the tribe, stood out as a clear-cut political community with clear-cut political authority. In addition, he claims that there was certainly no great genealogical tradition among these people, which analysed the structure of their tribal confederation at its upper levels, and analysed the patrilineal descent of each individual male tribesman at its lower levels. Inter-tribal genealogical relationships were not normally represented in genealogical terms. The north Arabian tribes were not structured communities and their political relations were not structured either. Meeker concludes that it is not possible to describe the political relationships of the north Arabian bedouins as a fixed pattern of segmentary political alliances. Within the tribe, there was no systematic representation of the tribe as a politically segmenting structure. Beyond the tribe, inter-tribal relations were represented in a segmentary form, but these representations did not take the shape of a politically segmenting ideology since the inter-tribal alliances were not quite stable enough to be conceived in a genealogical idiom (ibid: 192). It is worth noting that Meeker arrived at this conclusion through analysing Rwala political literature.

Both Meeker and Peters give examples of situations where tribal organization, the settlement of feuds, and political alliances did not follow the segmentary model. Such examples allowed them and other critics to claim that it is useless as a sociological framework for analysing political organization among tribal people. To arrive at an evaluation of the model, Dresch makes the distinction between lineage theory and segmentation. The first deals with sequences of events at the level of observation (and in particular with the appearance of groups), while the second deals with formal relations that characterize the types of events possible (P. Dresch 1986: 309). In other words, segmentation relates to the structure of groups whereas segmentary lineage theory provides one of the matrixes of organization between the segments. Dresch accepts the notion of 'segmentation' as it provides an essential aid to the prospect of delineating 'the implicit assumptions which people themselves make' (ibid: 319), but discards the segmentary lineage model which does not allow room for individual actions and diversions. He adds that segmentation is not by any means the only principle at work in tribal society as groups may form or combine in a great many patterns other than those suggested by tribal classifications. He introduces the notion of honour as an option informed by the notion of segmentation: 'A tribesman cannot have honor by himself (in the Yemeni case he needs someone to defend it from), nor can a tribe or section, and sections and tribes have little substance apart from this honor that their members share.' (ibid: 311)

Dresch's distinction between segmentation and segmentary lineage theory is useful. Segmentation can be regarded as a framework for political action and organization which cannot be explained solely by reference to a segmentary lineage model. The Shammar adhered to a general notion of segmentation which was known to all Shammar tribesmen. Although ordinary tribesmen were unable to give detailed accounts of their genealogical relations with other distant groups, they were more or less aware of their genealogical connection with these groups. People of high authority, especially those belonging to chiefly lineages, were more genealogically conscious as they were able to give elaborate genealogical accounts of how people were related and connected. They perceived their inter-tribal relations and political alliances as a function of segmentation which explained in the form of the genealogy the existence of various tribal sections, maximal lineages, lineages and households. The notion embodied an emphasis on common genealogical unity as descendants of one apical ancestor (in the case of the tribal sections), or a common *jid* (grandfather) in the case of the lineages. It provided a set of rules for social and political co-operation and action at each level of segmentation.

Arguments about tribal unity were put forward by Shammar tribesmen and in particular their sheikhs to account for inter-tribal relations. In most cases, these arguments were formulated in response to questions asked by outsiders. Tribesmen responded by referring to present alliances or by creating hypothetical situations of alliances and demonstrating how the group would react. These arguments explained how relations should be rather than how they actually were. Looking at Shammar inter-tribal relations and alliances with an historical perspective, one cannot fail to observe that these relations did not follow the segmentary lineage model invoked by the people themselves.

Knowledge of segmentation was one thing and political action was another. Shammar segmentation was the general structural framework for organization, but it was not the determining factor for political action. Historical observation of Shammar tribal organization, political alliances, conflict, and opposition reveal that these did not always follow the principles of the segmentary lineage model. The various Shammar sections, for examples, made peace with other groups on the basis of self interest, political expediency, and economic necessity.[14] Furthermore, the historical context of political action was far more important sociologically than the rules of the segmentary lineage model. In the following chapter, this context will be described.

2
CENTRAL ARABIA IN TURMOIL
(1744–1841)

From the sixteenth century, central Arabia was officially part of the Ottoman Empire although the poor resources of the region, coupled with its geographical isolation prevented its full incorporation in the empire. This situation was maintained until the rise of the Wahhabi movement in the middle of the eighteenth century. The Saudi adoption of the movement and the expansion of Saudi–Wahhabi forces threatened the integrity of the empire in the Arabian Peninsula in general and above all in the Hijaz. This expansion and the Ottoman reaction to it put Central Arabia into turmoil for almost one hundred years. The internal wars which the Saudis started to spread their message devastated the country. This was aggravated by the Ottoman intervention orchestrated by Mohammad Ali, the *wali* of Egypt, on behalf of the Ottoman Sultan.

THE WAHHABI MOVEMENT

The term 'Wahhabism' is used here to refer to the eighteenth century religious revivalist movement of Sheikh Mohammad Ibn Abdul Wahhab, whose followers preferred to call themselves *ahl al tawhid* or *muwahidun* (the unitarians) rather than Wahhabis.[1] The origins of the movement were found among the oasis and settled communities of southern Najd, the central region of what is now Saudi Arabia. The founder of the movement himself was a sedentary agriculturalist who cultivated date palms and raised some cattle in Uyayna, a small village in central Arabia (Abu Hakima 1967: 26).

Ibn Abdul Wahhab, a student of the Hanbali school of Islamic

29

jurisprudence and a follower of the fourteenth century revivalist, Ibn Taymiyya,[2] called for a return to the simple and pure beliefs, austere living and strict application of the law of early Islam. He developed the first principle of the movement, the call for the doctrine of the oneness of God, in his book, *Kitab al Tawhid*. The objective of his call was to return to the fundamentals of seventh century Islam and to purify the faith from *bida* (innovations), which he observed among the sedentary and nomadic population of central Arabia, the Hijaz, Syria, and Mesopotamia. They consisted of saint worship, animistic rituals and indulgence in luxuries. Visiting holy trees for *baraka* (grace), the use of saints for *shafaa* (absolution), building shrines on holy men's tombs (including the prophet's tomb, that of his cousin and the four caliphs) were practices condemned by Wahhabi doctrine. The second principle of Wahhabism was concerned with *ijtihad* (independent judgement by religious personnel). Ibn Abdul Wahhab restricted *ijtihad* to three sources, the Koran, the *sunna* (the prophet's sayings and deeds) and *sirat al salaf* (sayings and deeds of the early caliphs). The third principle of Wahhabism was concerned with *jihad* (holy war). He considered this as an important duty to be respected by the *muwahidun* (the unitarians). Ibn Abdul Wahhab stressed that the true Muslims had a responsibility to fight *ahl al bida* (the innovators), a category which included all those who did not share the Wahhabi beliefs. This principle proved to be essential for the expansion of the movement.

Ibn Abdul Wahhab first started to preach openly and spread his teachings in his village, Uyayna, whose ruler Othman Ibn Muamar promised to adopt the sheikh's message (Ibn Bishr 1930: 18–19). Encouraged by the ruler's willingness to support him, Ibn Abdul Wahhab began to put his teachings into practice. He tried to enforce the *sharia* law in all aspects of life. For example, Ibn Ghanam mentions that an adulterous woman was stoned in Uyayna in compliance with Islamic law. The severity of the punishment and the uncompromising teachings of the Wahhabis invoked reactions from the religious sheikhs of the Hasa region who rejected the *dawa* (call) and threatened to suppress it in Uyayna. Ibn Abdul Wahhab was asked to leave Uyayna because its ruler feared adverse repercussions by the religious authorities who opposed the Wahhabi movement (Ibn Ghanam 1971: 97 vol II). He then moved to Deraiya in an attempt to win the sympathy of its ruler, Mohammad Ibn Saud.

DIAGRAM 2: *Saudi Rulers (1744–1818)*

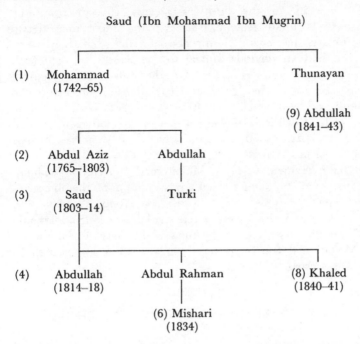

THE SAUDIS ADOPT THE MOVEMENT

Shortly after the arrival of Ibn Abdul Wahhab in Deraiya in 1744, a meeting was arranged between him and Mohammad Ibn Saud – at which the foundation was laid for an alliance between the two men. It was concluded by a *mithaq*, a covenant which formed the basis of the first Saudi–Wahhabi dynasty.

Mohammad Ibn Saud's influence was restricted at that time to his town and the alliance was a vital opportunity to enable his expansion beyond its limited confines. He offered to put Ibn Abdul Wahhab under his wing subject to two conditions: firstly, he was not to abandon him after the success of his *dawa* and should not offer his allegiance to any other ruler in the area. Secondly, he should not interfere or try to stop Mohammad Ibn Saud from extracting the tribute which was collected by the Saudi rulers from their subjects (ibid: 81 & Ibn Bishr 1930: 12). Ibn Abdul Wahhab accepted these conditions and assured Mohammad Ibn Saud that he should not worry about the tribute for 'God promises more material benefits in the form of *ghanima* (booty) from the unbelievers'. Wahhabi teachings stressed the importance of two Islamic pillars, the *zakat* (Islamic tax) and the *jihad* (holy war). These two had an obvious appeal to the Saudis as they both promised considerable revenues for the ruler. Ibn Ghanam described Deraiya in the age of *shirk* (polytheism), i.e. before the spread of Wahhabi teachings, as a poor town with no basic supplies of food, while in the age of *tawhid* (monotheism), it had excessive amounts of food, gold and silver money, horses, camels and clothes (Ibn Ghanam 1971: 23).

After the agreement of 1744, Mohammad Ibn Abdul Wahhab and Mohammad Ibn Saud started a mission of *jihad*, the objectives of which were religious and political. Ibn Abdul Wahhab was motivated by his desire to see a reformed Islam and an Islamic *umma* (community) guided by the rules of the *sharia*. On the other hand, Mohammad Ibn Saud was interested in seeing himself as leader of this *umma*.

SAUDI–WAHHABI EXPANSION IN ARABIA 1744–1818

From Deraiya, Mohammad Ibn Saud tried to incorporate all of central Arabia under his control. This proved to be difficult but not necessarily impossible, given the strong military orientation, the uncompromising fanaticism and the unshakable determination of Ibn Abdul Wahhab's followers. The fulfilment of this religious mission was bound to bring them into confrontation with the various power centres in the region which regarded the Saudi–Wahhabi expansion as a threat to their political autonomy.[3] The local rulers of the towns of Riyadh, Kharj, and Qasim resisted and this delayed the unification of Najd but did not succeed in preventing it. By 1792, all the mentioned towns came under the control of the Saudi–Wahhabi forces. Representatives and *gadis* (judges) were appointed in the conquered areas which became administrative units in the first Saudi–Wahhabi dynasty.

Four factors facilitated the expansion of the Saudis and the spread of Wahhabism in Najd (Abdul Rahim 1976: 73). Firstly, the disunity of the Najdi rulers meant that the Saudis could defeat them one-by-one. Secondly, the internal familial disputes among members of the ruling groups weakened their resistance and enabled the invaders to use dissidents for their purposes. Thirdly, the migration of certain Najdi tribes to Iraq because of the mounting Saudi–Wahhabi pressure and the effects of a drought further aided the conquest. And fourthly, the peaceful adoption of Wahhabism by a number of groups provided grass-root support for the expansion even before its occurrence (ibid).

After the completion of the campaigns in central Arabia, Saudi forces tried to expand to the east, in particular to the Hasa region. A substantial population there consisted of Shiites representing in the eyes of the Wahhabis, an extreme case of *ahl al bida*. The subjugation of the Qatif in the Hasa region in 1780 opened the road to the coast of the Persian Gulf and Oman. Bahrein acknowledged the suzerainty of the Wahhabis by paying the *zakat*. The growing influence of Wahhabism in the Persian Gulf was regarded as a threat to foreign interests, particularly those of Britain and France, but neither country had the resources to directly influence the course of events.

The expansion of the Saudi forces to the west and in particular in the Hijaz brought them into conflict with the Sherif of Mecca. In spite of the strong resistance of the Hijazis, the Saudis established their hegemony over Taif in 1802 after massacring its inhabitants and Mecca in 1803. Sherif Ghalib of Mecca became a mere representative of the Saudis (ibid).[4] He was asked by the Wahhabi *ulama* (scholars) to destroy the domed tombs of the prophet and the caliphs in accordance with Wahhabi doctrine.

Saudi success in the Hijaz encouraged the southward expansion to Asir, where the leaders adopted the Wahhabi cause and joined their forces to march on the Yemen. The strong resistance of the Shiite Zaidis, coupled with the unfamiliar geographical features of the region, prevented the incorporation of the Yemeni highlands.

To the north Saudi expansion reached the fertile regions of Mesopotamia, thus threatening the security of the more vital areas of the Ottoman Empire. In 1801 the Shiite holy city, Karbala, was raided by 10,000 men on 6,000 camels and resulted in the destruction and plundering of Husein's tomb, the holiest site in the Shiite tradition (J. Glubb 1961: 44). In 1808, 1810 and 1812 even Baghdad came under threat as a result of Wahhabi raids. However, severe ideological and theological differences between Shiism and Wahhabism, and the distance between Mesopotamia and the base of Saudi–Wahhabi power in central Arabia, prevented the Saudis from maintaining a continuous .presence there. Wahhabi preoccupation at that time revolved around gaining booty from these rich provinces of the Ottoman Empire without having the intention of establishing a permanent presence.

A similar pattern may be observed in Syria. The Saudis continued to raid cities and towns without establishing a permanent base there. They also raided pilgrim caravans, especially those going from Syria to the Hijaz. In 1810 the villages south of Damascus were raided and the Saudis were also able to extract taxes from the tribes in the vicinity of Aleppo. At certain times they refused to allow pilgrims from Syria to enter Mecca and Madina.

SAUDI–WAHHABI EXPANSION IN JABAL SHAMMAR 1792

This deserves to be discussed in detail as it constituted the historical context for the rise of the Rashidi amirs to power in Hail. In the 1770s, Saudi–Wahhabi expansion reached the Shammar territory.

The first encounter took place when the Shammar allied themselves with the ruler of the province of Hasa, Sadoun Ibn Urayir from the Bani Khalid tribe, who organized a raid on the town of Boreidah in the Qasim district which had already been put under Saudi control. The alliance with Bani Khalid was not successful as the Saudi representative in Boreidah was able to retaliate. He organized an expedition against Jabal Shammar which fell under Saudi domination in 1779 (Ibn Bishr 1930: 94 vol I & Ibn Ghanam 1971: 130 vol II). Only the oases of the Jabal, including Hail, Gofar, and Mustajjidah, became part of the Saudi realm – the Shammar nomadic population retreated to the Great Nafud Desert and escaped control. Those who managed to escape maintained their independence and autonomy while waiting for the appropriate moment to attack the Saudi forces.

The Shammar allied themselves with the Sherif of Mecca during the defence of his territory against the Saudi–Wahhabi invasion in 1790 (Ibn Bishr 1930: 108–9 vol I). The leader of the Shammar, Muslat Ibn Mutlaq, was killed in the battle between the two groups and the Shammar lost 6,000 camels and 10,000 sheep (ibid: 109–10 & Ibn Ghanam 1971: 150–2 vol II). Some sections of the Shammar migrated under the leadership of Sheikh Mutlaq Al Jarba to Mesopotamia. Those who left the Jabal remained hostile to the Wahhabis. They were followed by the Saudi forces which attacked them in a place near Samawah in 1795. Again their leader Mutlaq was killed in the battle (ibid: 150 & 157). Those Shammar sections who stayed in Iraq belonged to the Jarba section. They still live in the country and are referred to as northern Shammar.

The history of those who stayed in central Arabia, the southern Shammar, followed a different course. Their oral tradition stresses that although the majority were nomadic, they had a power base in Hail, the central oasis in Jabal Shammar. The ruler of this oasis belonged to *beit* Ibn Ali of the Abde section. Members of this *beit* provided leadership throughout the eighteenth century (Ibn Bishr 1930). However, it is difficult to find evidence concerning when and how its members reached the position of leadership. At the beginning of the nineteenth century, nevertheless, one finds reference to the ruler of Hail at that time, Mohammad Ibn Abdul Mohsin Ibn Ali. This is confirmed by the oral narratives of the Shammar which mention that Mohammad was settled in Hail. He also had agricultural fields, mainly date groves, which were cultivated by slave labour whereas his camel herd was looked after by the nomadic section of his lineage around Hail and the Great Nafud Desert.

As the area of Jabal Shammar fell under the control of the Saudi–Wahhabi forces, the role Ibn Ali played was ambiguous. We do not know to what extent his authority was undermined by the fact that Jabal Shammar had already become one of the Saudi provinces. The local Najdi historians, Ibn Bishr and Ibn Ghanam, refer to the fact that Ibn Ali occasionally collected the *zakat* from the Hail population and handed it to the Saudis. We definitely know that at the beginning of the nineteenth century, Mohammad Ibn Ali became an ally of the Saudis and maintained friendly relations with them. Ibn Bishr mentions that he provided military support to the Saudis on many occasions. His relations with the Saudis were the opposite of the Jarba nomadic section of the Shammar in Iraq. Mohammad Ibn Ali gave military support to the Saudi–Wahhabi forces in 1805 during their attempt to prevent the Syrian pilgrims, under the leadership of Abdullah Pasha Al Adhm, from visiting Mecca and Madina. Later in 1810, Mohammad Ibn Ali attacked the Syrian desert on behalf of the Saudi–Wahhabi forces. Furthermore, in 1814 the ruler of Hail provided military support to the Saudis in the province of the Qasim at the beginning of the Egyptian invasion which started in

1811 under the leadership of Tosun Pasha (ibid: 188–9, 215, 223, 249, and 291).

OTTOMAN REACTION: THE FIRST EGYPTIAN INVASION
(1811–18)

The Saudi–Wahhabi expansion in all directions resulted in the disruption of the *hajj* caravans which came under the threat of raids, not only on their way to the Hijaz, but also in the holy cities themselves. These events encouraged the Ottoman Sultan, who was officially responsible for the security of the pilgrims and the holy cities to take serious measures aimed at curbing the rising influence of Wahhabism. This influence had been carefully watched by Sultan Mohammad II who was waiting for the right moment to organize an expedition to put an end to Saudi power in Arabia.

The Sultan arrived at the conclusion that the *wali* of Baghdad and that of Damascus were not strong enough to carry out the plan to destroy this new threat which so far had succeeded in both embarrassing the Ottomans in the Muslim world and undermining their authority. They had been unsuccessful in confronting Saudi–Wahhabi expansion on the borders of these two major cities of the Ottoman Empire. The Sultan looked for an alternative *wali* to carry out the mission. This was provided by the energetic leadership of Mohammad Ali, the *wali* of Egypt. By choosing Mohammad Ali for this mission, the Sultan was seeking to achieve two objectives. The first was the collapse of the Saudi–Wahhabi dynasty and the second was the exhaustion of Mohammad Ali's forces during a fierce struggle in central Arabia. The Sultan recognized the dangers that Mohammad Ali represented, and subsequent history fully justified his fears.[5] The decision was taken to keep Mohammad Ali busy for some time in the southern regions of the Ottoman Empire and away from the vital northern areas of Mesopotamia. Mohammad Ali received the first orders from the Sultan to organize an expedition against the Saudi–Wahhabi forces in 1807 (Abdul Rahim 1976: 298).

Mohammad Ali sent letters to the sultan in which he expressed his inability to embark on such a major expedition without the necessary weapons, ammunition, and food supplies for his soldiers during their transport to the fields of battle (Cairo Archives,

Mihfadhat Abdeen 1808, Daftar I, P. 6, 9, 12 and 13). It was only after the sultan promised to supply Mohammad Ali with the necessary weapons and money that he sent the first troops which landed in Yanbo on the Red Sea in 1811 under the leadership of his son Tosun Pasha. The Egyptian army soon advanced on Madina, destroyed the Saudi forces, and captured the town after a fourteen-day siege. The Saudis lost 1,500 men in the battle of Madina.

The Egyptian troops captured Mecca from the Saudis in 1813 and continued the march on Taif which fell soon after Mecca. Later in 1813, Mohammad Ali himself landed in Jeddah with 2,000 cavalry and 2,000 infantry to give a new impetus to the invasion (N. Safran 1985: 13). With the capture of the holy cities of the Hijaz, Mohammad Ali restored the sultan's authority over these important regions. He then sent his son Tosun to the Qasim in 1815. In addition to the regular troops, the Egyptian army was joined by members of the Mutair and Harb tribes, who had already expressed submission to Saudi–Wahhabi domination, but wished to free themselves from it.

From the Qasim, Tosun Pasha started negotiations with the Saudi ruler, Abdullah, in an attempt to extract Saudi recognition of Tosun's authority in the Hijaz. However, no agreement was reached as Tosun was asked by his father to go back to Cairo. He was replaced in 1816 by another son, Ibrahim Pasha, who continued the march on the Saudi capital with 2,000 cavalry, 5,600 infantry, 12 guns, and a number of tribesmen (ibid). The siege of Deraiya started in 1818 and lasted for five months. The Saudi ruler, Abdullah, was put under pressure to give himself up, and was captured by Ibrahim Pasha who sent him to Cairo and then to Istanbul where he was beheaded. The Egyptian troops completely destroyed the town, burnt its date plantations, and plundered the population. The death of Abdullah and the destruction of Deraiya put an end to the first Saudi–Wahhabi dynasty after almost seventy years of expansion.

The Egyptian troops continued to maintain their presence in central Arabia, aiming to conquer all those territories which had been incorporated in the Saudi realm. Being on friendly terms with the Saudi rulers, the population of the oases of Jabal Shammar was attacked by the Egyptian troops in the 1820s. Ibrahim Pasha invaded the area with 600 Turkish soldiers and 1,000 bedouins and managed to force the population to recognize his authority over

DIAGRAM 3: *Saudi Rulers (1824–1891)* *

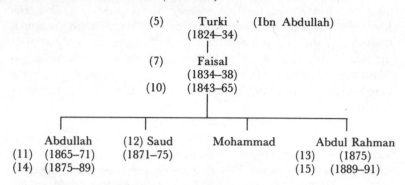

```
                    (5)       Turki      (Ibn Abdullah)
                              (1824–34)
                                │
                    (7)       Faisal
                              (1834–38)
                    (10)      (1843–65)
                                │
  ┌──────────────┬─────────────┴──────────┬──────────────────┐
  Abdullah      (12) Saud      Mohammad         Abdul Rahman
(11)  (1865–71)  (1871–75)                   (13)    (1875)
(14)  (1875–89)                              (15)    (1889–91)
```

*For rulers number 6, 8 and 9 see Diagram 2.

their territory (Al Utheimin 1981: 13). During the expedition on Jabal Shammar, the ruler of Hail, Mohammad Ibn Ali, was killed and his brother Saleh became ruler of the town – continuing his brother's policy of supporting the Saudi leadership.

THE WEAK SAUDI REVIVAL 1824

In 1824, the Saudis succeeded in establishing a new Saudi–Wahhabi power base in Riyadh south of their old capital. Imam Turki Ibn Abdullah, a grandson of the first ruler in the Saudi–Wahhabi realm, can be considered the founder of the second dynasty (see Diagram 3). After settling down in Riyadh, Turki endeavoured to reconquer the Hasa region in 1830 and sought to enforce recognition of Saudi hegemony along the coast of the Persian Gulf by 1833. Although a strict Wahhabi, he was careful not to fan the embers of fanaticism and tried to avoid clashes with the Ottoman–Egyptian forces still in the Hijaz. However, the greatest challenge which faced Turki came from elsewhere.

In 1831, while on an expedition against some tribes, Turki received word that a cousin of his, Mishari whom he had appointed governor of Manfuha, had revolted against him. Turki got back to Riyadh to find out that his cousin had already escaped. Having failed to mobilize additional support from the Sherif of Mecca, Mishari submitted to Turki's authority and returned to Riyadh where he was put under house arrest. In 1834, Mishari successfully plotted the assassination of Turki while the Saudi forces were, under the leadership of Turki's son Faisal, occupied in a war with Qatif and Bahrain. Turki was killed while coming out of the mosque after the Friday prayers.

Within forty days of Turki's assassination, his son, Faisal, returned to Riyadh from Bahrain and defeated Mishari. However, peace for Faisal did not last for long. Mohammad Ali of Egypt, having broken with the Ottoman Sultan, defeated his forces, brought what is now Palestine, Syria and Lebanon under his rule and looked set to incorporate the entire Arabian Peninsula in his empire. In 1836, new Egyptian troops landed in Yanbo to start a second invasion, this time putting forward the claims of Mohammad Ali himself rather than the sultan. The Egyptian troops brought with them a cousin of Faisal called Khalid, whom they aimed to install as puppet ruler of central Arabia. In 1838, Faisal was defeated, captured and sent to Cairo for detention.

The Egyptian troops left Khalid to rule in Najd when they were forced to withdraw from the Arabian Peninsula in 1841. The withdrawal was stimulated by pressures from European powers, mainly Britain.[6] Consequently, the year 1841 witnessed the end of Egyptian intervention in Arabia. Faisal escaped from his jail in Cairo, returned to Najd and was able to recover his position in Riyadh in the absence of foreign troops. He refrained from challenging the sultan's authority in the Hijaz and paid an annual tribute to him in recognition of his submission. Faisal ruled in Riyadh until his death in 1865.

After Faisal's death, his son, Abdullah became ruler in Riyadh. However, Saudi power entered a phase of decline due to the power struggles between Faisal's four sons, which undermined Saudi legitimacy in central Arabia and facilitated the disintegration of their realm. They were, however, able to maintain a fragile power until 1890 when they were expelled from Riyadh by the Rashidi amirs of Hail, thus ending the second Saudi-Wahhabi realm.[7]

JABAL SHAMMAR BETWEEN TWO INVASIONS 1818–41

After the success of the first Egyptian invasion (1811–18) in destroying Deraiya, and the weakening of the second Saudi dynasty by the second invasion (1836–41), Hail and Jabal Shammar began gradually to assume a history separate from that of the Saudis. Although the Saudis recovered from the invasions and succeeded in establishing a new fragile power base in Riyadh in 1824, this second episode in their history did not enable them to influence the course of events in the northern regions of central Arabia.[8]

The continuous presence of the Egyptian forces prevented the expansion of the Saudis. Turki Ibn Abdullah was able to recover only some of the districts lost as a result of the Egyptian invasion and was not able to enforce Saudi rule in Jabal Shammar, although he maintained friendly relations with the rulers of Hail. These two decades saw an escalation of events in the area.

THE RISE OF THE RASHIDIS TO POWER

In 1818 the ruler of Hail, Mohammad Ibn Ali, was being challenged by the rising influence of his two patrilateral cousins Abdullah and Obeid Ibn Rashid. Although Mohammad Ibn Ali died during the Egyptian invasion in the 1820s, the dispute between the Rashidi brothers and Mohammad's successor, Saleh, continued afterwards.

The dispute between *beit* Ibn Ali and the Rashidi brothers lasted until 1836 when *beit* Ibn Ali's leadership over Hail was terminated. Mohammad Ibn Ali was a descendant of *beit* al-Khalil, a Jaafar chiefly family of the Abde section of the Shammar. Both Mohammad Ibn Ali and the Rashidi brothers shared a common great grandfather, Ali al-Kabir. However, this genealogical relation was not very clear even in the minds of their descendants. They referred to their relationship as being *ibn amm* (patrilateral parallel cousins). The degree of this relation remained vague and the term *ibn amm* was used in a classificatory manner to refer to a rather distant genealogical connection.

Neither historical sources nor the Shammar oral narratives give us a clear description of the causes of the dispute and its resolution. A. Musil claims that Abdullah Ibn Rashid and his brother Obeid were ambitious and active in accompanying the trading caravans from Iraq to Hail. The two brothers offered their protection to the caravans against attack and raids by the nomadic tribes. They acquired a reputation for bravery and a considerable number of supporters among the Shammar. They started infringing on the authority of the Hail ruler who arranged for Abdullah to marry his daughter, Salma. However, this did not deter Abdullah from expressing his interest in running the political affairs of Hail. After the death of the ruler of Hail, Mohammad Ibn Ali, during the first Egyptian invasion, his brother Saleh refused to recognize Abdullah Ibn Rashid's claims. Abdullah immediately left Hail as his relations with Saleh started to deteriorate (A. Musil 1928a: 237 & F. Hamza 1933: 341).

W. Palgrave's account differs from that of Musil. He claims that the dispute between Abdullah Ibn Rashid and Saleh Ibn Ali started after the withdrawal of the Egyptian forces from Najd. He argues that Abdullah left Hail because he lost some of his supporters, especially among the people of Gofar, a village near Hail, who decided to back Saleh Ibn Ali (W. Palgrave 1865: 120–1 vol I).

Again historical sources do not agree on Abdullah Ibn Rashid's destination after he left Hail. Huber mentions that the two brothers took refuge in Jabal Aja (C. Huber 1888: 151–2). The ruler of Hail knew about them and sent one of his trusted slaves to bring them back to face punishment. After killing the slave, Abdullah Ibn Rashid managed to escape to Iraq where he stayed for two years. His father was later forced to leave Hail. Abdullah's second destination, according to Huber, was Riyadh, the new capital of the Saudis. Musil offers a different story. He claims that Abdullah Ibn Rashid went first to Jubba, an oasis in the Great Nafud Desert, then to the Fedaan tribe. He later headed for Iraq where he stayed with the Jarba, the sheikhly lineage of the Shammar (A. Musil 1928a: 237).

Palgrave mentions that Abdullah Ibn Rashid initially wanted to go to Al Jauf, an oasis on the northern edge of the Great Nafud Desert, but realized that he might not be able to gather enough supporters there (W. Palgrave 1865: 121–2 vol I). He then changed his destination to Wadi Sirhan where he was attacked by the Anizah tribe. A Syrian merchant helped him to recover from his wounds and he then went to the south and stayed in Riyadh. The mythical tone of Palgrave's story is clear as he offers a detailed account of Abdullah's wounds when he was found in the desert and how he was saved by the Syrian merchant.

This confusion among the European travellers who visited Hail in the nineteenth century concerning the origin of the dispute and the destination of Abdullah Ibn Rashid afer his exile can be partially clarified by reading the accounts of the local historians and checking these with the Shammar narratives. There is an agreement in all these accounts that Saleh Ibn Ali was the ruler of Hail in the 1820s. The dispute between Saleh and his Rashidi cousins was caused by their disobedience of his orders. Apparently, the Anizah tribe raided a group of Shammar nomads near Hail and the Rashidi brothers wanted to help their tribesmen in defending themselves. Saleh, however, feared that this might increase their popularity. To keep order and peace, Saleh Ibn Ali asked them not to participate in the dispute.

Abdullah and his brother Obeid raided the Anizah and defeated them, gaining a reputation for bravery which added to Saleh's fears concerning their rising power. He ordered Abdullah, Obeid and their mother to leave Hail. It seemed that the Anizah affair had been used by Saleh as an excuse to expel his ambitious cousins. Abdullah's destination after exile was with the Jarba Shammar of Iraq, where he stayed until he returned to Najd. In Iraq, he assisted the Shammar Jarba in their battle against the Ottoman governor of Iraq, Daoud Pasha (D. Ibn Rashid 1966: 64). Abdullah's reputation as a skilled military leader was growing and this encouraged the Saudi Imam, Turki Ibn Abdullah Ibn Saud, to offer him a warm welcome when he appeared in the Saudi capital.

In Riyadh, Abdullah Ibn Rashid developed a friendship with Imam Turki's son, Faisal, who wanted Abdullah to accompany him in his raids against the dissident tribes rebelling against Saudi domination. In 1833, Abdullah was with Faisal during the expedition against the Qatif and Bahrain when Faisal's cousin Mishari killed Imam Turki. As mentioned earlier, Faisal immediately returned to Riyadh to punish his cousin and Abdullah Ibn Rashid played an important role in the attack on Mishari. Expecting the arrival of Faisal, Mishari took refuge in the town's castle where he was put under siege. This attack resulted in Mishari's death in 1834. Abdullah Ibn Rashid's participation in the resolution of the conflict in the house of Saud increased his popularity with the new Imam, Faisal Ibn Turki. Later Abdullah married Faisal's daughter Al Jawhara.

This friendship encouraged Imam Faisal to sanction Abdullah Ibn Rashid's activities in Hail and Jabal Shammar and his ambition to overthrow his cousin Ibn Ali. Imam Faisal had only a moral authority over Jabal Shammar which had been politically independent after the first Egyptian invasion. He had neither the resources nor the power to actively participate in upsetting the balance of power between Ibn Ali and Ibn Rashid. Imam Faisal was busy re-establishing his leadership after the Mishari incident and also had to face the Egyptian presence in the area. Once Abdullah realized the limited prospects of his alliance with the Saudi Imam, he left Riyadh and headed towards Jabal Shammar without actually going to Hail.

While Abdullah was in Jabal Shammar, news about a visit by Saleh Ibn Ali to the Saudi Imam reached him. Faisal was to act as a mediator in the dispute. In his *majlis* (council) the two parties explained their position but Imam Faisal was indecisive because so far he had maintained good relations with both disputants. Huber argues that Faisal finally suggested that they should both go to Hail and act together as rulers of the oasis. When they returned, Abdullah was in a stronger position and refused to share power with Ibn Ali, who left Hail and went to Boreidah (C. Huber 1888: 152–4).

Ibn Bishr points out that Abdullah Ibn Rashid accompanied Imam Faisal on his raid against the area of Shaara when Faisal appointed Abdullah Ibn Rashid as ruler of Hail. To confirm his story, Ibn Bishr mentions that a *qadi* (judge) was sent with Abdullah to Hail (Ibn Bishr 1930: 84 vol II). This view was repeated by a recent Saudi historian, Al Utheimin (1981: 43). It would be misleading, however, to conclude that Imam Faisal appointed Abdullah Ibn Rashid as ruler of Hail. The presence of the Egyptian forces in the Arabian Peninsula determined the course of events not only in Jabal Shammar but in the Saudi capital itself and Imam Faisal had no power to enforce any such decision.

After the meeting in Riyadh at the *majlis* of Imam Faisal, Saleh Ibn Ali returned to Hail whereas Abdullah Ibn Rashid remained in the area of Jabal Shammar where he tried to gather some supporters among the Shammar nomads (D. Ibn Rashid 1966: 68–77). There Abdullah heard from a man called Al Uraifi that the Egyptian *wali* of Madina and his officers were enquiring about competent persons to help them in the second invasion of Najd. Abdullah went to Madina and co-operated with the *wali*. His cousin Saleh Ibn Ali wanted to use the rivalry between Mohammad Ali's troops in Arabia and the Ottomans in Iraq to his advantage.[9] He headed for Iraq hoping to raise a military force under Ottoman sponsorship to repel the Egyptian backed invasion, but failed to reach the Ottoman representative in Iraq. Saleh began to doubt whether his journey to Iraq would yield any benefit. Returning to Hail, he stopped in a village called Suleimi where he was killed with two of his sons by Abdullah Ibn Rashid's brother, Obeid. The third son, Issa escaped to Madina and took refuge with the *wali*.

Issa wanted the *wali* to guarantee his safe return to Hail to replace his father. Before reaching Madina, Issa met Ismail Agha, the commander of the Egyptian troops in the Qasim, who was interested in winning his allegiance, believing that Issa would be a better ally than Abdullah Ibn Rashid. The commander supplied Issa with 400 men to accompany him during his return to Hail, and this enabled him to establish himself as ruler of the oasis in 1836 (Ibn Bishr 1930: 62 vol II). However, the support of the Egyptian troops was resented by the population of Hail.

Later most of the Egyptian soldiers withdrew from Jabal Shammar, leaving Issa with only one hundred men to consolidate his power. When Abdullah Ibn Rashid heard of Issa's return, he immediately left the oasis and headed for Gofar, from where he planned to overthrow Issa. Abdullah tried to rely on the support of the Shammar tribe and in particular the lineage of Jaafar. In addition, his immediate kin group, his brother, and his slaves provided the bulk of the force with which he was to conquer Hail. The solidarity of the Jaafar lineage and their support of Abdullah Ibn Rashid were important in distinguishing his leadership from that of Issa Ibn Ali, who was apparently relying heavily on the support of the Egyptian troops. Palgrave described how Abdullah used his marriage connection with the Jaafar to strengthen his position (W. Palgrave 1865: 127 vol I):

> He had at an early period contracted a marriage alliance with a powerful chieftain's family of Djaafar, his near kinsmen by blood. Strong in the support of this restless clan, he subdued with their help the rivalry of town and country nobles, and gratified at once his own ambition and the rapacity of his bedouin allies by the measures that crushed his domestic enemies and ensured his pre-eminence.

Abdullah spent most of the period of his exile with the Jaafar lineage, but even with their support, he knew that it would be impossible to oppose the Egyptian troops. Abdullah therefore sent his brother Obeid with 2,000 camels to Khurshid Pasha, the commander of the Egyptian forces in the Hijaz. Musil claims that as early as 1834, Abdullah Ibn Rashid 'supported the Egyptian governor, Hursid Pasha, in his plundering raids against the Harb and Htejm tribes' (A. Musil 1928a: 239). His aim was to win the support of this pasha and negotiate a peaceful settlement which would guarantee his return to Hail. Khurshid Pasha accepted the offer in return for Abdullah's services which consisted of providing the necessary camels to transport the weapons, soldiers and ammunition to Najd. Khurshid Pasha described Abdullah Ibn Rashid's co-operation in a letter to Mohammad Ali, reporting that Abdullah was now independent from Imam Faisal and could therefore be trusted and be helpful to the Egyptians. Abdullah was asked to provide a constant supply of camels and in return Khurshid Pasha recognized Abdullah Ibn Rashid as the sole ruler of Hail and Jabal Shammar instead of his cousin Issa Ibn Ali (National Archives of Cairo Mihfadhat Abdeen 240). Khurshid Pasha suggested to the Egyptian government the payment of a monthly allowance to Abdullah, claiming that his revenues were not enough to cover his expenses and that his services were indispensable for the success of the Egyptian invasion. In addition, Khurshid Pasha allowed Abdullah to keep one-third of the *zakat* (Islamic tax) of Jabal Shammar for himself (ibid: 264). While Abdullah was busy with the Egyptian forces, his brother Obeid returned to Hail and drove Issa out, Abdullah Ibn Rashid then returned to Hail and announced himself ruler in 1836.

Issa Ibn Ali decided to meet Khurshid Pasha and ask for explanations. He received a warm welcome from the Egyptian commander who was interested in keeping the loyalty of Abdullah Ibn Rashid by threatening to support his rival. In compensation for his lost post as ruler of Hail, Issa was appointed by the Egyptians as an administrator of *beit al mal* (public treasury) of the Hasa district. He died in 1839 leaving Abdullah Ibn Rashid as the undisputed ruler of Hail and Jabal Shammar.

The dispute between Ibn Ali and the Rashidis took place at a crucial episode of central Arabian history, coinciding with the destruction of the first Saudi–Wahhabi dynasty and the decline of Saudi hegemony in the Arabian Peninsula. The area was officially part of the Ottoman Empire which acted through the Egyptian *wali* to curb Saudi expansion. This was a reminder to all those who in the past had been acting independently that their actions were in fact watched and could be restricted depending on the will of the

Ottoman Sultan. The latter lost control of the situation when Mohammad Ali's influence began to grow beyond the expected level. In 1841 Mohammad Ali had to withdraw his troops from the Arabian Peninsula under international pressure, thus leaving the future of central Arabia to be determined by its local power centres.

On the eve of the Egyptian withdrawal from Najd, the Saudis in Riyadh had already been weakened and their forces exhausted by a series of military encounters with the Egyptians. Their power was still not well established in their new capital Riyadh and their influence among the bedouin tribes had started to wither away. On the other hand, in Jabal Shammar and Hail, the Egyptian invasions resulted in the establishment of a new ruling house, that of the Rashidis.

The Rashidis slowly began to act independently as they felt no need to ally themselves with a weakened Saudi dynasty. They were able to do so as a result of the support of the Shammar tribe which gathered around this leadership and regarded it as theirs. Although Abdullah Ibn Rashid was able to win the support of the Egyptian officials, he realized at an early stage that this was not enough to achieve his political ambitions. His brother Obeid and the Jaafar lineage were his close allies from the very beginning. He also won to his side the majority of the population of Hail who thought that their commercial interests would be better served by someone like him as he had already developed an interest in the protection of trading caravans. Historical sources do not refer to any strong resistance on the part of the population of Hail. Only J. Lorimer mentions a revolt against Abdullah Ibn Rashid by the inhabitants of Gofar (J. Lorimer 1908: 1161): 'Abdullah succeeded in gaining to his side a majority of the citizens of Hail, but the people of the neighbouring town of Qafar supported his adversary.' Abdullah Ibn Rashid recognized the importance of the nomadic sections of the Shammar whom he favoured to break the strength of the sedentary population of Gofar. Although Abdullah was brought up in Hail, he spent a considerable time with the nomads during his exile and was popular for his military skills, bravery, courage and eloquence.

The Shammar support of Abdullah Ibn Rashid also arose from their fears at that time. Firstly, they had witnessed the growth of Saudi–Wahhabi domination and had been defeated by them towards the end of the eighteenth century. Secondly, in 1818, they were attacked by the Egyptian troops who regarded their territory as part of the Saudi domain. The Egyptian interest and influence in central Arabia at that time created conditions of uncertainty among the Shammar. Although the aim of the Egyptians was to destroy the Saudi–Wahhabi power base, they were later concerned with incorporating Najd into a sort of Egyptian empire. Consequently, they were eager to encapsulate the autonomous tribal groups in the area. Once the Saudi–Wahhabi hegemony over central Arabia was diminished, there seemed to be a power vacuum in the region. This was a favourable condition for a successful Egyptian domination.

By supporting the Rashidis, the Shammar were seeking a leadership which would guarantee their security and autonomy. The measures taken by the various Shammar tribal sections can be regarded as an adaptive strategy aimed at mitigating encapsulation by outside powers. In backing the Rashidis who were connected genealogically to the Abde section of the Shammar, the Shammar laid the foundation for organizing their defence and offence and strengthening their unity which in the past had been expressed in terms of common origin. The centralization of power in the hands of the Rashidis stemmed from this context of political upheaval, military turmoil, and foreign intervention. Subsequently the Shammar were able to cope with foreign encroachment on their territory and preserve their autonomy not only during the later period of the Egyptian invasion, but also during later Ottoman attempts to incorporate central Arabia in the empire.[10]

Abdullah Ibn Rashid emerged from the political struggle stronger than his predecessor. His powers increased with the support of the Shammar as this gave him a wider political constituency which included the sedentary population of Hail and Jabal Shammar in addition to the Shammar nomads. This was a privilege which Ibn Ali had not enjoyed. Abdullah Ibn Rashid's role was expanding and was beginning to be invested with extra powers which had simply not been available to his cousin. The expansion of Abdullah's sphere of influence and the crystallization of his power were products of Shammar fears and the uncertainty of their political situation at that time. The centralization of power among the Shammar was the first step towards polity (or dynasty) formation.

The crystallization of political and military leadership among the Shammar in the middle of the nineteenth century has parallels among other nomadic groups in the Middle East where these groups were faced with expanding centralized state structures. It has been argued that the development of centralized leadership among segmentary tribal societies is a reaction to an external stimulus manifested by the attempts of states to encapsulate autonomous tribal groups. This has been observed by Garthwaite (G. Garthwaite 1983) in his study of Bakhtiyari tribal history. Political centralization among the Bakhtiyari nomads of Iran and the crystallization of the role of ilkhani, the paramount chief of the tribal confederation, were highly dependent on the external influence and pressures of the Iranian state. He argues that this resulted from political development initiated by the state, but built on the pastoral nomadic base of the tribal community itself (ibid: 4–15). Beck's study of the Qashqai nomads in the south-west of Iran is also an attempt to relate the centralization of power in the hands of a tribal élite to external factors. In the Qashqai case, the growth of western interest, influence and power in the Persian Gulf appeared to be precisely the event that created the economic and political conditions facilitating Qashqai polity formation (L. Beck 1986: 25). Khazanov also arrives at the conclusion that nomadic polities and the centralization of power among tribally organized groups are products of and reactions to interaction with sedentary people and states (A. Khazanov 1984: 303–4). These studies and many others (W. Irons 1971 & 1979, and Van Bruinessen 1978) look at nomadic groups within a wider historical and political context and see nomadic political organization as being constantly changed and transformed by external stimuli. However, although the formation of the Shammar polity was stimulated by the historical context of intervention by foreign powers, this polity was later shaped and maintained by the specificity of Shammar political organization and economic conditions.

3

PATTERNS OF LEADERSHIP
Amir, Sheikh and Imam

THE AMIR'S RESIDENCE

Once Abdullah Ibn Rashid had succeeded in expelling his cousin from Hail, he was eager to create a permanent physical location for his rule.[1] Abdullah chose to complete the construction of the Barzan site which had been started by his predecessor. It was described in the accounts of the European travellers who visited the oasis in the nineteenth and early twentieth centuries (G. Wallin 1854, W. Palgrave 1865, C. Doughty 1979, A. Blunt 1968, C. Huber 1888, J. Euting 1896, G. Bell 1914, A. Musil 1928a). The site occupied, claimed Palgrave, one-tenth of the oasis (W. Palgrave 1865: 103). Abdullah Ibn Rashid died in 1847 and his son completed the construction of the palace (A. Musil 1928a: 239) which became the amir's official residence in Hail. Wallin claims that the size of Barzan distinguished it from other houses: 'The residence of Ibnu Alrashid is distinguished from other houses by nothing but its largeness and extent, which the accommodation of his own ample household, and the numerous guests which the chief entertains throughout the year, make necessary'. (G. Wallin 1854: 200)

Perhaps Euting's map of Barzan was the clearest and most detailed (see Map 3). The palace was near the market and the mosque and was surrounded by a wall with large towers. It consisted of two courtyards, a guest reception room, the amir's private reception room, stables, kitchen, prison and a private quarter. The main entrance overlooked a central square called Al Mishab. The amir's daily *majlis* (council) was held in Al Mishab which was outside the palace, thus reflecting the public nature of these regular meetings and their openness to a wide audience. Opposite this public square, the amir's warehouses (*makhzen*) and

49

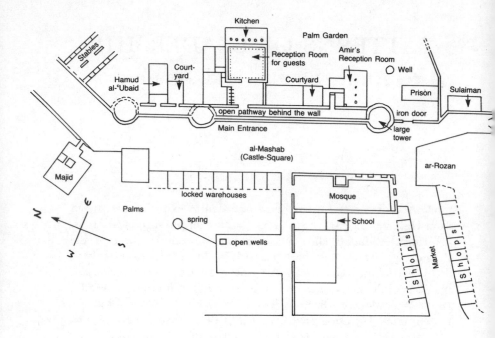

MAP 3: *Barzan Palace*

the guest chambers were found. Small houses were attached to both sides of the building, in which Hamud Ibn Obeid and Suleiman, relatives of the amir, resided. Wells, the major source of water supply, were found nearby. Other maps such as that of Palgrave show the location of a slave market behind the palace (W. Palgrave 1865).

The completion of the Barzan site by Abdullah Ibn Rashid and his son Talal was related to the desire of the Rashidi amirs to establish a permanent, strong and visible base in Hail. The location of the palace, its fortification, and the use of space reflected the political system which was beginning to emerge during the second half of the nineteenth century. First, its location near the great mosque where the Friday prayers were held and the central market of Hail is crucial to our understanding of the nature of the amirs' leadership and their role. As oasis rulers, the Rashidi amirs represented a political leadership which had economic and religious dimensions. Their economic involvement in trade, the centrality of the market which was the outlet for such an involvement, and their military role as protectors of trading caravans were reflected in their decision to reside near the market. On the other hand, the proximity of the residence to the mosque indicated the presence of a sort of relationship. Although the amirs did not lead the Friday prayers themselves, they appointed an imam to carry out the task. Their control and supervision over this important religious institution was guaranteed by this practice. Wallin noted that: 'In the great mosque of Hail the prayers are said by an Imam, whom the prince himself appoints and pays. He is generally a man who has received some literary education in Almedina, Alkahira, or Alriiad.' (G. Wallin 1854: 184)

Secondly, the palace fortification and its protection by high walls marked a need for the physical isolation of the ruler and his entourage – an indication of the existence of both a sort of fear on behalf of the ruler and a danger of assassination, robbery, and so on. The walls represented the emerging tendency towards a greater physical, but not necessarily social or political segregation between the ruler and his subjects. This was maintained by the presence at the main gate of a number of guards, usually of slave origin, who controlled access to the amirs and protected them from unwanted guests and dangerous visitors. This particular feature was an expression of the transformation of the leadership pattern in Hail. The need for protection was not a characteristic of the Shammar sheikhly leadership who lived and encamped with their tribal section. Their tents were the only frontiers existing between them and their group.

Thirdly, the arrangement of space inside the palace reflected the political concerns of the rulers. For example, the kitchen and the reception rooms occupied a substantial part. The first was used for the preparation of daily meals for the amirs' guests. These feasts contributed to the consolidation of the amirs' leadership and the maintenance of their relationship with their followers. Doughty estimated the cost of these meals in 1888 to be £1,200 (C. Doughty 1979: 35 vol II). This was a political strategy aimed at increasing the ruler's popularity and legitimacy.

The amirs' stables were another important spatial arrangement. During the second half of the nineteenth century, the stables of the Rashidi amirs and the reputation of their horses attracted the attention of the imperial powers such as the Ottoman, the Egyptian and the British governments. European travellers also

showed an interest as they visited and described these stables
where the finest breeds of the Arabian horses were kept. Some of
these horses were sent as gifts to other notables, tribal sheikhs, and
Ottoman governors to cement political alliances. Wallin noted:

> These animals are more numerous here than in any other part of
> Arabia which I have visited . . . The Stud of Abd Allah alone, I
> was told, contained nearly 200 horses, quartered upon the
> different villages of his land. A couple of these animals are sent
> yearly to Almedina with the pilgrim-Karawan as a present for
> the Turkish Pasha, another couple to Mekka for the Governor of
> that town, sometimes a third for the Pasha of Baghdad, and
> during the late years Abbas has sent an expedition almost every
> year from Egypt, in order to purchase a number of horses for his
> extensive stud in Alkahira. Others are occasionally presented to
> the princes of the family of Saood, or sold privately to the
> Badawis of the neighbourhood. (G. Wallin 1854: 188).

A small number of these horses found their way to the market of
Kuweit where they were purchased by the representatives of the
British government and sent to Bombay. This was a small-scale
commercial activity as horses were precious animals to be
appreciated and looked after. Their military value was the most
important reason for keeping them. They guaranteed a military
hegemony which exceeded that brought about by camels, which
are slow and unsuited for hit-and-run military strategies although
easier to maintain for long periods without water and food. In
contrast, horses are well-suited for short military encounters near
wells or water sources. The amirs' stables were again a spatial
arrangement reflecting the political and military necessities of the
time. The Hail leadership became stronger as a result of conquest
and military expansion. Consequently, stables and horses were
part of their military reservoir as well as enhancing their social and
political prestige.

The customary law of the bedouin population of Arabia did not
envisage imprisonment. However, with the establishment of the
Rashidi amirs' leadership in Hail, such an institution was enforced
and a hostage system began to emerge. A prison was attached to
the palace and used to punish criminals, political dissidents and
traitors. Also, defeated tribal sheikhs and town rulers were
sometimes kept in this prison after the subjugation of their

territory. The prison was, therefore, a place for punishment and for holding hostages.[2] These two aspects of the prison were not common among the bedouins but developed in the oases and towns. The maintenance of a prison system needed both the presence of a permanent physical location and a permanent police force to watch and guard it. These two became available to the Rashidi leadership which was gradually being transformed.

Abdullah Ibn Rashid's legitimacy sprung from a combination of attributes, both ascribed and achieved. First, he was a descendant of *beit* Rashid, one of the prominent households of the Jaafar lineage. The lineage was a branch of the *ashira* of Abde, one of the four Shammar *ashair*. Abdullah's noble origin as a member of the Jaafar was recognized and valued by the Shammar. The ascribed prestige of nobility granted him undisputed loyalty among the Shammar and a sort of unquestioned legitimacy. Secondly, before his establishment in Hail, Abdullah had already succeeded in maintaining his reputation for courage, eloquence, bravery, generosity, and advanced military skills. These achieved attributes were highly valued among the Shammar. They invoked respect, admiration and loyalty.

Abdullah's leadership (1836–48) was initially an extension of his role as a tribal sheikh who had managed to establish his reputation and legitimacy among the Shammar. During the first decade of his leadership, he was still known as the sheikh, a term which was equally used to refer to the leader or head of the *ashira*. In Hail, the transformation of the role of sheikh was gradual. It was only during the rule of Talal Ibn Rashid (1848–68) and Mohammad Ibn Rashid (1869–97) that this transformation was completed. This meant more political centralization, consolidation of power, increase in military hegemony, and the establishment of dynastic rule. It is important to stress that this qualitative change was accompanied by the appearance of a new title to refer to political leadership. The Rashidis began to be known as amirs rather than sheikhs. The adoption of this title reflected the beginning of a process whereby a tribal 'leader' became an oasis 'ruler'.

THE AMIRS' LEADERSHIP

The Rashidis derived their name from Abdullah's grandfather, Rashid, who had one son called Ali. According to some genealogical accounts, Rashid had a second son called Jabr. Since the descendants of Jabr did not have any political influence, their line of descent will not be investigated further.

Rashid's son, Ali had two sons, Abdullah and Obeid, the founders of Rashidi hegemony in Hail. Two lines of descent can be identified within the Rashidi ruling group; the descendants of Abdullah and those of Obeid (see Diagram 4). Abdullah had three sons, Talal, Mohammad, and Mitab. The descendants of Abdullah had a monopoly over the office of amir for almost ninety years. During this period, ten out of a total of twelve amirs were the sons and grandsons of Abdullah. On the other hand, although Obeid played an important role in the consolidation of his brother's rule in Hail, he did not become ruler after his brother's death. Furthermore, only two of Obeid's grandsons, Sultan and Saud, occupied that position for a short time. The reason why neither Obeid nor his descendants were officially involved in political leadership was perhaps related to the fact that Abdullah Ibn Rashid demanded from his brother an *ahd* (covenant) according to which succession to the office of amir remained in the line of Abdullah.[3] However, despite the fact that Obeid's descendants did not hold public office, they became an important support group for the amir. Table I provides a list of the twelve amirs who ruled in Hail between 1836 and 1921.

There is agreement among European travellers and local historians of central Arabia that the establishment of Rashidi hegemony in the oasis was related to the success of Abdullah Ibn Rashid.[4] During his visit to central Arabia, Wallin observed that Abdullah was '. . . by most people admitted to be the de facto governor of Negd'. Wallin added that Abdullah's efforts led to the establishment of his family's dynastic rule: '. . . they have become the mightiest and most influential sheikh families in all Arabia' (G. Wallin 1854: 182). The importance of Abdullah's noble origin as a member of the Jaafar lineage and his personal qualities were also noted by Wallin:

He owed it far more to his own great personal qualities, his intrepidity and manliness, his strict justice, often inclining to severity, his unflinching adherence to his word and promise, of a breach of which he was never known to have rendered himself guilty, and, above all, to his unsurpassed hospitality and benevolence towards the poor, of whom it was a well-known

DIAGRAM 4: *The Genealogy of the Rashidi Ruling Group*

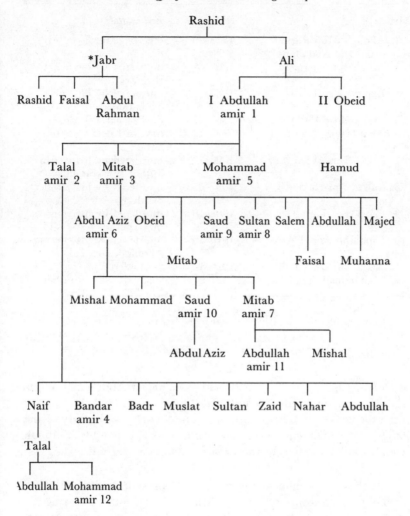

: Abdullah's line of descent.

I: Obeid's line of descent.

': Jabr's connection with Ali is not clear. Some members of the Shammar tribe claim that Jabr was adopted by Ali whereas others claim that it was Rashid who adopted Jabr. A third group claim that Jabr was an orphan from Bani Tamim, the settled tribe in Hail.

TABLE 1: *The Rashidi Amirs (1836–1921)*

Amir	Rule	End of Rule
1. Abdullah. Ibn Rashid	1836–48	died of natural causes
2. Talal Ibn Abdullah	1848–68	died in an accident
3. Mitab Ibn Abdullah	1868–69	murdered by his nephew Bandar
4. Bandar Ibn Talal	1869	murdered by his uncle Mohammad
5. Mohammad Ibn Abdullah	1869–97	died of natural causes
6. Abdul Aziz Ibn Mitab	1897–1906	died in battle with Ibn Saud
7. Mitab Ibn Abdul Aziz	1906–7	murdered by his cousin Sultan Ibn Hamud
8. Sultan Ibn Hamud	1907–8	murdered by his brother Saud
9. Saud Ibn Hamud	1908–10	murdered by his cousin's maternal uncles
10. Saud Ibn Abdul Aziz	1910–20	murdered by his cousin Abdullah Ibn Talal
11. Abdullah Ibn Mitab	1920–1	surrendered to Ibn Saud
12. Mohammad Ibn Talal	1921	surrendered to Ibn Saud

thing, none ever went unhelped from his door. These virtues, the highest a Badawy can be endowed with, Abd Allah was endowed with in a high degree. (ibid)

Perhaps one of the greatest achievements of Abdullah was his success in maintaining law and order not only in Hail, but also in the other oases of Jabal Shammar. The security and safety of the oases and settlements were new conditions created by Abdullah Ibn Rashid according to the inhabitants of the region:

There is a common saying among the present inhabitants, that one may go from one end of their land to another, bearing his gold on his head, without being troubled with any questions. Formerly I was told, the villagers were divided into parties, who lived in open defiance, plundering and rubbing each other, on every opportunity, in the streets and in the very houses of their quarters. (Wallin: 183).

This was confirmed by Musil who claimed that Abdullah 'soon established peace and order in all the settlements about the two ranges of Ega and Salma and endeavored to win the various head chiefs of the Sammar by kindness and generosity' (A. Musil 1928a: 238). Abdullah's desire to guarantee peace and enforce the security of the settlements was an indication of the beginning of a process whereby his role as sheikh was being transformed, complicated and redefined. He began to assume new responsibilities relating to the maintenance of law and order. Abdullah began to 'rule' and behave like a ruler. He had at his disposal a permanent force consisting of his slaves and bodyguards which was capable of enforcing his decisions and punishing criminals and robbers.

In general, the period of Abdullah's leadership laid the basis for the establishment of dynastic rule. After his death in 1848, he was succeeded by his eldest son, Talal. Palgrave claims that Talal was unanimously appointed as amir of Hail after his father's death: 'Telal was already highly popular ... All parties united to proclaim him sole heir to the kingdom and lawful successor to the regal power, and thus the rival pretensions of Obeyd, hated by many and feared by all, were smothered at the outset and put aside without a contest'. (W. Palgrave 1865: 128).

Talal became amir of Hail without any complication relating to succession. His uncle Obeid, the other potential candidate, had already given his brother, Abdullah, his word in which he agreed to leave the post of amir to his brother's descendants. Furthermore, Obeid was known as the wolf, a term which stressed his war-like character, and was prone to devote himself to leading and organizing the military expansion of the Rashidi domain on behalf of his brother and later his nephew. These attributes were soon recognised by Talal who 'managed to secure at once the fidelity and the absence of his dangerous uncle by giving him charge of those military expeditions which best satisfied the restless energy of Obeyd' (ibid: 129).

During Talal's rule (1848–68), trade and commerce flourished in Hail due to his continuous effort to maintain the achievements of his father in the establishment of peace and security. Talal was often described in the literature as someone with an interest in commerce and a taste for luxuries. He encouraged traders from different parts of Najd, merchants from Basra and Mashad Ali in Iraq to establish themselves in Hail. The majority of these were Shiites, towards whom Talal showed a liberal attitude and granted protection. Palgrave commented on this: 'Many of these traders belonged to the Shiyaa sect, hated by all good Sonnites, doubly hated by the Wahhabees. But Telal affected not to perceive their religious discrepancies, and silenced all murmers by marks of special favour towards these very dissenters, and also by the advantages which their presence was not long in procuring for the town.' (ibid: 130)

Talal was also known for his 'urban' interests. Under his supervision, the construction of Barzan palace was completed as well as the palace warehouses and the renovation of the market place to which he added eighty shops. 'Round the palace, and in many other parts of the town, he opened streets, dug wells, and laid out extensive gardens, besides strengthening the old fortifications all round and adding new ones.' (ibid: 128) In addition, Talal endeavoured to rebuild the settlements of Jabal Shammar which had been damaged during the first half of the century as a result of the invasions of the Saudi–Wahhabi forces and the Egyptian troops. He ordered 800 slaves belonging to his family to move to Gofar, an oasis to the south of Hail, where they were required to work as agricultural labourers on his family date gardens. Musil noted that: 'The choked-up wells were cleared, the old palm groves were cleaned and new ones planted and protected from the sand by high walls, fortified houses (ksur, pl. of kasr) were built in the midst of the palm gardens, craftsmen and merchants from Irak and Syria were introduced and a regular trade connection was established with Irak.' (A. Musil 1928a: 239)

This involvement in urban construction and public works marked a further complication of the amir's role and an increasing tendency towards settlement and urban life. According to Musil, the measures taken by Talal increased not only the prosperity of his subjects but also his own influence and power. As Hail entered a phase of sustained growth and prosperity, Talal was able to think about extending his dominions (ibid: 240). To the west, Rashidi rule was first expanded to the oases of Kheibar and Teima, abandoned by the Turko-Egyptian troops who left central Arabia in 1841. Later, the southern district of Qasim, between Jabal Shammar and the Saudi–Wahhabi domain, came under the Rashidi sphere of influence. According to Palgrave, the inhabitants of Qasim began to 'annex' themselves to the amir of Hail:

> The inhabitants of Kaseem, weary of Wahhabee tyranny, turned their eyes towards Telal, who had already given a generous and inviolable asylum to the numerous political exiles

of that district. Secret negotiations took place, and at a favourable moment the entire uplands of that province – after a fashion not indeed peculiar to Arabia – annexed themselves to the kingdom of the Shommer by universal and unanimous suffrage. (W. Palgrave 1865: 129)

To the north, the expansion reached Al Jauf, an oasis on the northern edge of the Great Nafud Desert in 1853. This oasis had already been within the sphere of influence of the Rashidis as its population recognized their authority by paying tribute. As soon as internal disputes among the inhabitants of Al Jauf broke out, the amir of Hail sent out a strong force under the leadership of his uncle Obeid and his brother Mitab to enforce his control over the oasis (A. Musil 1928a: 239).

Talal died in 1868 in a mysterious accident. Doughty recalls the story that Talal became ill after being poisoned in eastern Najd and sent for a Persian *hakim* (doctor) who told him that his disease would lead to mental illness. Talal refused to accept his insanity and died as a result of a shot which escaped from his own gun as he was holding it. Doughty concludes that Talal must have committed suicide (C. Doughty 1979: 28 vol II). Musil, however, claims that Talal suffered for several years from an abscess which embittered his life. He died as a result of a gunshot while he was testing a revolver of an unfamiliar type and his death could have been an accident rather than an intentional attempt at suicide (A. Musil 1928a: 240). He left seven sons, Bandar, Badr, Muslat, Nahar, Abdullah, Zaid, and Naif. After his death, his eldest son, Bandar, did not inherit the post of amir as Talal had done when his father died in 1848. This was perhaps because he was only eighteen or twenty years old at the time and was unable to win the necessary support.

The office of amir was occupied by Talal's brother, Mitab, who was supported by the senior members of the Rashid family and the sheikhs of the Shammar sections. Mitab ruled only for one year and was then shot by Bandar in Barzan Palace. He left a two-year-old son, Abdul Aziz. After the murder of Mitab, the senior members of the family, including his uncle Obeid, Obeid's son, Hamud, and Mitab's brother, Mohammad, left Hail for Riyadh, the Saudi capital. Once established in office, Bandar encouraged his uncles to return to Hail. Obeid died in Riyadh and only Hamud returned; Mohammad preferred to join the trading caravans which travelled between Arabia and Iraq. This was done in an attempt to gather supporters among both the sedentary and the nomadic population. Mohammad was a renowned caravan leader and was known to have supported the commercial interests of the townsmen. He possessed military skills without which he would not have been able to guarantee the security and safe passage of the trading caravans.

On one of his journeys back from Iraq, Mohammad was met by his nephew Bandar, the new ruler of Hail. It is not clear what Bandar's intentions were at that time. Musil claims that Bandar, who could rely only on his young slaves, rode out at the head of his bodyguard to prevent his uncle from uniting with the settled population of Hail (A. Musil 1928a: 242). However, Bandar was immediately shot by his uncle who could forsee danger. Mohammad continued the journey to Hail and announced himself amir. To prevent the possibility of revenge, Mohammad gave orders for the execution of Bandar's brothers, the sons of Talal. Talal's line of descent, however, was not completely terminated since one of his sons, Naif, escaped the massacre.

These violent disturbances were watched by the sedentary population of Hail who regarded the matter as a private issue of the ruling family, and did not interfere. Musil claims that it was all the same to them which member of the ruling house they had to give tribute and military service to (ibid: 241). Nevertheless, Mohammad's commercial interests and involvement in the caravan trade must have guaranteed him at least implicit support among the merchant community of Hail – although they did not have the means to actively participate in the dispute over leadership. Furthermore, the Shammar sheikhs were in favour of Mohammad from the very beginning for he was sensitive to their interests – especially those related to the caravan trade in which the nomads played an active role as escorts, guides, and customers and for which they provided the means of transport.

Mohammad realized that the risks he had taken to reach the position of amir were very high and throughout his life he feared the possibility of revenge. In an attempt to win the greatest number of supporters among the family, Mohammad maintained close contacts with the Obeid branch which seemed to be outnumbering the branch of Abdullah as a result of the massacre of Talal's sons. Hamud, the eldest son of Obeid became a close ally of Mohammad. Doughty described this alliance:

The princely Hamud has bound his soul by oath to his cousin the emir to live and die with him; their fathers were brethren and as none remained of age of the prince's house, Hamud Ibn Rashid is next after Mohammad in authority, is his deputy at home, fights by his side in the field and he bears the style of Emir. Hamud is the ruler's companion in all daily service and council. (C. Doughty 1979: 647 vol I)

Mohammad realized that members of the branch of Obeid constituted a potential danger and the fact that Mohammad was childless aggravated the situation. To restore the demographic balance, Mohammad looked for potential heirs among the remaining descendants of Abdullah. The only possibility was offered by a young child of Mohammad's brother, Mitab, the first murdered member of Abdullah's branch. Mohammad adopted his brother's orphan, a young boy called Abdul Aziz whom he was determined to prepare for leadership.

In spite of the complications and massacres which brought Mohammad to the office of amir, his rule turned out to be the longest in the history of the Rashidi dynasty as he remained amir of Hail and Jabal Shammar until his death in 1897. His leadership was accompanied by a period of stability, expansion and prosperity. By the end of the nineteenth century, his sphere of influence extended to most of Najd including the region of the Qasim and the Saudi capital, Riyadh. In 1891 the Saudi family was expelled from Riyadh by Mohammad Ibn Rashid. The ruler of Riyadh, Abdul Rahman and his son Abdul Aziz (known as Ibn Saud, the founder of the present Saudi Kingdom) took refuge in Kuweit. Ibn Rashid's expansion reached Al Jauf and Palmyra to the north, and Teima and Kheibar to the west. Musil claims that:

Prince Muhammad now consolidated his power in al Gowf and extended it to all the settlements in the depression of Sirhan as far as the mountains of the Hawran and even to Tudmor (Palmyra), which was also forced to pay yearly tribute to him ... the power of Eben Rasid was in full flood, his influence extending from Aleppo and Damascus to al Basra, Oman and al Asir. (A. Musil 1928a: 243)

Mohammad died of natural causes. By that time, his brother's son, Abdul Aziz whom he had brought up, had reached an appropriate age to assume the responsibility of leadership. Abdul Aziz Ibn Mitab became amir without the complications which surrounded the succession of the previous rulers. To maintain the Shammar hegemony established by Mohammad, Abdul Aziz needed a constant supply of arms and ammunition. His predecessor relied on the port of Kuwait which was under the control of the Al Sabah family, and the Turkish port of Aqir in the Hasa district in eastern Arabia. However, the rulers of Kuwait had already allied themselves with the house of Saud. This made access to the port of Kuwait very difficult. Abdul Aziz wanted to expand his realm to include an outlet on the coast but was occupied with defending his territory. The only challenge that Abdul Aziz Ibn Rashid had to face was the rising power of Ibn Saud who succeeded in 1902 in returning from Kuwait and re-establishing his ancestors' position in Riyadh. Abdul Aziz Ibn Rashid was killed in the battle of Rawdat Muhanna which took place between him and Ibn Saud in 1906. Abdul Aziz's eldest son, Mitab, inherited the position of his father and was amir of Hail for only one year.

Mitab was recognized as amir of Hail only by the supporters of his father and not by the family of Hamud Ibn Obeid. As Mitab was not able to win the consensus of the majority of his family, he was not able to influence any political or military development. In 1907 he was killed by a rising member of the Obeid's branch, Sultan Ibn Hamud. Although Hamud Ibn Obeid and his descendants had become close to the powerful amir Mohammad Ibn Rashid, they were unable to make further political claims as a result of the agreement between their grandfather and Abdullah Ibn Rashid. None of Obeid's descendants had occupied the post of amir so far. Sultan Ibn Hamud now announced himself amir of Hail in spite of his father's objections, who expressed in his oral poetry his dissatisfaction with his son's violation of the agreement:

> Sultan, you betrayed the covenant, if you rise
> when the sun disappears, the shadow does too
> Sultan khunt al ahad lau taraqeit
> esh shams iliya zalat yazoul al dhalali

In these verses, Hamud disapproves of his son's actions which according to him represent no victory. He tells his son that he broke the agreement and he will not prosper as a result, adding that when the main branch of the Rashidi family is defeated, this will be accompanied by the decline of the Obeidis. Hamud uses the image of the sun and its shadow: whenever the sun shines, there is shadow and sunset is always accompanied by the disappearance of shadow.

In an attempt to minimize the chances of Mitab's brothers avenging his murder, Sultan in co-operation with his half-brother Saud, executed two sons of Abdul Aziz Ibn Mitab Ibn Abdullah. The fourth son Saud, a young boy of eight years, was taken by his maternal uncles the Sibhan to Madina in an attempt to save his life.

Sultan was ambitious and eager to expand his sphere of influence beyond Hail and central Arabia. A report by G.P. Devey to the British government in 1907 described him: 'Sultan Ibn Hamud has a wider ambition than being Emir of Hail. He is communicating with the Druses of Jebel Hawran through his agent at Jauf, Sheikh Saleh el Muzeini, avowing to them eternal friendship and strong alliance, to say nothing of his promises and expressed devotion to the tribe of Anezah, Muteir, Oteibah and the natives of Qasim.'[5] Nevertheless, Sultan lost several districts especially those in the Qasim. Musil argues that in Hail and the other oases of Jabal Shammar, the different opposed groups fought one another and the land was economically and politically ruined. In addition, the pilgrim caravan no longer passed through Hail, severely damaging the economic prosperity of the townsmen.[6] Musil added: 'Sultan was unable to prevent the plundering of several settlements by the troops of Eben Saud at the end of 1907 and as a result was murdered by his own brothers, Saud and Fejsal, towards the close of January 1908.' (A. Musil 1928a: 247)

After the assassination, Sultan's brother Saud proclaimed himself amir of Hail and his brother Faisal was appointed as governor of Al Jauf. Saud ruled for only two years before his leadership was challenged by the maternal uncles of Saud, the now ten-year-old son of Abdul Aziz Ibn Mitab. They gained support among the Shammar tribe, surrounded Hail and massacred the remaining sons of Hamud Ibn Obeid – except Faisal who was in Al Jauf. The Sibhan maternal uncles, Zamil and Hamud, declared their sister's son, Saud, amir of Hail and Jabal Shammar. He was to rule under the regency of his maternal uncles as he was too young to occupy the position of leadership.

Although Saud Ibn Rashid occupied the position of amir in Hail until 1920, the actual leadership was in the hands of members of the Sibhan family. His uncle Zamil Ibn Sibhan was *wazir* (minister) until he was murdered by one of his kinsmen, Saud Ibn Saleh Ibn Sibhan, in 1914. The latter became the *wazir* of Saud Ibn Rashid and immediately took advantage of the inability of the young amir to exercise any power. According to Musil, Saud Ibn Sibhan felt himself so strong that he desired to set himself up as amir (ibid: 250). Although he managed to win to his side a considerable number of the Shammar, in particular the *ashira* of Aslam, and a few supporters among the Jaafar lineage of the Abde Shammar, neither group was eager to see him officially replacing the young amir. Ibn Sibhan's mother was of slave origin and this perhaps was behind the reluctance of the Shammar sheikhs to support his plans to take over the post of amir. Saud Ibn Sibhan and his followers were finally forced to leave Hail by the same group who had initially supported them. He fled to Iraq where he was murdered in 1919. The office of *wazir* was later occupied by Okab Ibn Ajil, Saud Ibn Rashid's father-in-law.

In 1920, Saud Ibn Rashid was killed by his cousin Abdullah Ibn Talal who was in turn immediately murdered by Saud's slaves. Abdullah Ibn Mitab was then announced the eleventh amir of Hail and immediately imprisoned the murderer's brother, Mohammad Ibn Talal, fearing revengeful assassinations.

Abdullah Ibn Mitab faced the rising power of Ibn Saud who had already been planning to terminate the leadership of the Rashidi family over Hail and Jabal Shammar. Ibn Saud reached an agreement with Ibn Shaalan, the sheikh of the Rwala tribe, to attack Hail from the north while his troops approached the town from the south. In 1921, the camp of Abdullah Ibn Mitab was attacked by Ibn Saud who forced him to surrender. In Hail Mohammad Ibn Talal was released from prison after the surrender of Abdullah, proclaimed amir and required to continue the battle against Ibn Saud. In November 1921, Ibn Saud entered Hail and terminated the leadership of the Rashidi family.[7] Mohammad Ibn Talal, the last amir of Hail, and the rest of his family were taken to Riyadh where they stayed under house arrest. They were not allowed to return to Hail because Ibn Saud feared they might gather supporters among the Shammar who were still willing to defend the Rashidi claims to power. It was a general policy of Ibn Saud that all defeated tribal sheikhs, amirs and town rulers reside in his capital Riyadh. This marked the end of the Rashidi leadership over Hail and Jabal Shammar.

Throughout this period of leadership, members of the Rashidi family who did not become rulers of Hail were none the less regarded as important political figures. They were the brothers, paternal uncles, nephews and paternal cousins of the amir. Although not involved in formal political leadership they often provided auxiliary political and military support to the amir. Some members of the family entertained military careers, consequently, they played an important role in the expansion of the boundaries of their family dynasty. For instance Obeid, Abdullah's brother, was a successful military leader who played an active role in establishing his brother's leadership and in the later military expeditions and expansion of his brother's rule. Consequently, Obeid was known to have valuable military skills, a war-like character and indispensable personal attributes such as courage, bravery, and toughness in battle.

Obeid was also known for his eloquence and poetic talents. His oral poetry, known as *qasaid*, in which he documented the hegemony of his family and the supremacy of the Shammar tribe as a whole, is still remembered and recited. These particular poetic talents predisposed Obeid to play the role of spokesman of his group, an important role in a society where the word was as mighty as the sword and where literacy was still not well-developed. This particular skill guaranteed Obeid respect and admiration and enhanced his reputation.[8]

Another valued attribute of Obeid was his generosity towards those in need. Generosity, however, was not a simple benevolent act but an important political strategy which guaranteed the donors undisputed loyalty. Generosity was a sort of 'bribe'. The leader who gave generously and spent lavishly on his followers accumulated a massive capital of a non-material nature. He had his reputation enhanced. If this was accompanied by poetic skills, as in the case of Obeid, he could spread his fame and prestige, thus increasing his followers and often guaranteeing him material assets.

Obeid continued to be respected as a senior member of the family until his death. His son Hamud followed in the steps of his father and allied himself with Mohammad Ibn Rashid, the ruler of Hail. The alliance between the two men was encouraged by the fact that Mohammad had come to power as a result of massacring his brother's sons, thus alienating himself from his own immediate kinsmen, the descendants of Abdullah's line.

The relationship between the amir and the rest of the Rashidi family was not always amicable. All members were competing for leadership as they had equal claims to power. The one who succeeded in establishing himself as amir always feared the rivalry of the other members who constituted a group of potential amirs. Certain amirs tried to curb the influence of the others either by imprisonment or by physical elimination. For example, Mohammad Ibn Talal (the twelfth amir) was put in gaol by his cousin Abdullah Ibn Mitab as soon as the latter became amir of Hail in 1920. Also Mohammad Ibn Abdullah came to power in 1869 after massacring four young amirs, the sons of his brother. These were assassinated in infancy as they were considered to represent a potential danger for the stability and continuity of Mohammad's rule. Competition between male members of the family over political office was so strong that assassinations became almost the rule.

Members of the Rashidi family represented both a threat and a potential reservoir for political alliances. The amir was often caught in a difficult dilemma. If he ignored the claims of his brothers, cousins, and uncles to have more political participation, he would risk their alignment against him. However, if he chose to share power with them and increase their popularity and participation in the political and military affairs, he would risk being replaced by one of them. The repetitive assassinations of young members of the family give an indication of the tension and difficulty of achieving the necessary balance.

SUCCESSION TO THE OFFICE OF AMIR

With regard to succession to the office of amir, a general hereditary principle was respected and followed for almost ninety years. The office was occupied by people who claimed descent from Rashid and constituted the Rashidi family. The legitimacy of the office was granted to the *beit* including all its members, rather than to a particular individual and his line of descent. This practice guaranteed the continuity of leadership. The Shammar granted their loyalty to *beit* Rashid, thus perpetuating the hegemony of the Rashidis and their political leadership. The Rashidi family provided the amirs of Hail and no recruitment was possible from outside this family. The strict adherence to this rule was demonstrated in the case of the Sibhan family whose power was strengthened during the leadership of Saud Ibn Rashid. As the power of the young amir's Sibhan maternal uncles was gradually increasing and they tried to substitute their leadership for that of the Rashidis, they lost the legitimacy and tolerance of the Shammar sections who had initially supported them.

Although the general hereditary principle was established, its internal dynamics were not explicitly spelled out and regulated. It was a well-established fact among the Shammar that the office of amir was to remain in *beit* Rashid. Yet, how was it regulated to pass smoothly from one amir to the other? Was the amir's son more eligible to succeed his father or was the amir's brother the legitimate heir to the office? Was there a rule of primogeniture? In other words, was succession horizontal or vertical among the Rashidi ruling group?

The account given earlier concerning the succession of the twelve amirs of Hail reveals the oscillation between horizontalism and verticalism. After the death of the amir, it was not clear who would succeed him; both sons and brothers had an equal chance. All these were in theory equal as potential claimants and heirs to the office. As a result, succession followed an indeterminate pattern. Also, the amir did not appoint his successor before his death and this was reflected in the absence of the institutionalized post of 'crown prince'. However, at an informal level, certain amirs had preferences for particular members of the family to succeed them. Mohammad Ibn Rashid (1868–97) was childless and adopted his nephew, Abdul Aziz, whom he favoured to replace him after his death. As expected, Abdul Aziz became amir without any complication or resistance from other members of the family. However, the uncle/nephew relationship was not always a relationship of alliance, support and co-operation. The fiercest competition and internal rivalries took place along this kinship line. As there was no explicit rule dictating that leadership pass vertically from father to son, nor horizontally from the ruler to his brother, the relationship between uncle and nephew was ambiguous, competitive and conflict laden. The indeterminacy of the system of succession generated a zig-zag pattern of conflict, although this does not necessarily mean that had there been explicit rules, these internal conflicts would have been avoided. Even in cases whereby the rules are clear, succession struggles seem to be endemic.

Goody argues that succession to office, like the inheritance of property, involves the allocation of scarce resources. Consequently, close succession, as for example, in a next of kin rule, means that the tension of the struggle for office falls on the nuclear domestic relationship. The indeterminacy of such a system, coupled with its very openness, tends to increase the possibility of strained relations between the potential heirs. Furthermore, the existence of two structures, the lineage and the state, produces interpersonal conflict and institutionalized instability that are reflected most clearly in the position of the ruler. If he is both head of state hierarchy and a member of the royal clan and lineage, his unique position at the head of the state is in conflict with his membership in the royal company of equals. However, it is not the existence of a lineage system in itself, Goody argues, that gives rise to strain. The conflict derives from the presence of a plurality of royals who regard the crown as common property even though it has to be held *de facto* by one member (J. Goody 1966: 23–5).

Such factors were present in an exaggerated form among the Rashidi amirs. Conflict and competition over the office of amir were highly intensified since both uncles and nephews regarded the office as theirs. The first incident of the uncle/nephew conflict took place after Talal's death in 1868. Talal's brother, Mitab, immediately became ruler due to his seniority, but the young sons of Talal, Bandar and Badr, co-operated to kill their uncle as they regarded themselves more eligible to inherit the post of their father. They were in turn killed by a second paternal uncle, Mohammad Ibn Abdullah. These events started a sequence of murders, revenge and counter-revenge among closely related members of the family.

In situations where murder occurs between members of two tribes, tribal sections or even lineages, the matter is more likely to be terminated as soon as blood money (*diya*) is received by the victim's family. However, when homicide occurs within the same family or extended family, there seems to be no way of terminating hostilities. Peters argues that among the Cyrenaican bedouins, in such cases, homicide brings about an impasse in relationships. Neither the payment of blood money nor vengeance appears to be appropriate since the first means that those who pay would be the same as those who receive the payment, whereas the second strategy would only aggravate the problem and double the original loss (E. Peters 1967: 263). Peters witnessed cases where the murderer voluntarily exiled himself and returned to the camp after the lapse of a number of years. Among the Rashidis, when an amir was killed by a close relative the murderer was aiming to install himself in the victim's office. Therefore, expulsion was not a feasible strategy since this would render the act of killing meaningless and unnecessary. In all but one of the homicide cases among the Rashidis, the murderer succeeded in establishing himself as amir at least for a short time before he was killed by another member of the family.

The post of amir represented a position of multiple powers as it included being the oasis ruler, the head of the Shammar tribe, and the head of the ruling group. The post placed its holder in a higher political position *vis-à-vis* the other members of the ruling group. There was no justification for this since the equality of birth of all members of the family was still adhered to and respected. The genealogical equality, in other words, was contradicted by the political conditions emerging from the occupation of the post of amir by one single person. These contradictions which were inherent in the system remained unresolved and proved to be detrimental to the stability of leadership in the Rashidi dynasty.

Struggle between paternal parallel cousins was also endemic in this system. The first such incident occurred when Sultan Ibn Hamud killed his paternal cousin, Mitab Ibn Abdul Aziz in 1907. This was a revolt by a descendant of the Obeid line against the hegemony of the descendants of the Abdullah line. The second incident took place when Abdullah Ibn Talal murdered his cousin, Saud Ibn Abdul Aziz in 1920. This was a murder between cousins of the same line of descent, i.e. that of Abdullah. Political struggle at this level can be regarded as a continuation of the struggle which took place at the first uncle/nephew level. The two conflicts were structurally similar and they were generated by the same principle of antagonism between the descendants of one ruler and his sons on one hand, and his brother and his descendants on the other hand. At a third level, conflict was also expressed between brothers, as when Sultan Ibn Hamud was murdered by his brothers, Saud and Faisal in 1908.

Despite the indeterminacy of the system of succession, there was a strong implicit principle according to which some guidance regarding the transfer of leadership was provided. This principle was related to seniority. The ruler was usually succeeded by his brothers until the generation was exhausted, when the succession moved down to the most senior son of the first ruler. Violation of the seniority rule undermined to a certain extent the legitimacy of the amir. Succession conflicts reflected the opposition between young and old members of the ruling group. The legitimacy of the ruler was partly derived from his wisdom, good mediation, military skills and so on, all attributes associated with old age. Youth was synonymous with ignorance, lack of experience, rebellion, and undeveloped leadership skills. On the other hand, youth was desired and valued for its association with military supremacy, bravery and courage.

Early marriages for males and females and the practice of polygamy contributed to blurring the lines between generations. For example, it was very common to find a generation of siblings in which there was more than thirty years difference between the eldest and the youngest sons. Also, it was common to have uncles younger than their nephews, and cousins of the same generation with huge age differences. As a result, horizontal and vertical successions were not fixed patterns because they sometimes did not coincide with the seniority principle. Conflict between equal claimants then became inevitable.

The intensification of succession struggles between members of the Rashidi family was related to the fact that competition took place for a scarce and indivisible post. The political system lacked the presence of institutionalized means by which political power could be shared. The only way for the young amirs to prove their leadership skills was in the military domain. The amir frequently sought the military expertise of one close member of the family, usually a younger brother or a cousin, to assist in leading military expeditions. As a result, successful war leaders became popular and represented a threat to the authority of the ruler, for military leadership was often a prelude to permanent political leadership.

The frequency of internal power rivalries and succession struggles among the Rashidi ruling group is not a phenomenon peculiar to them. In his search for the principles that generally govern succession, Burling admits that such struggles are inherent and almost inevitable features of the transfer of office (R. Burling 1974: 254). Goody also points out that succession struggles are characteristics of corporate dynasties where the pattern of succession tends to be indeterminate, i.e. lacks explicit or fixed rules (J. Goody 1966: 25). Middle Eastern early and later history is full of examples of succession struggles stimulated by the indeterminacy of the pattern of succession.

Within the Islamic context, and in particular the Sunni tradition, there are no definite or explicit rules for succession. The Prophet himself died without designating a successor. This contributed to various power struggles which threatened to split Muslims for centuries, thus undermining the stability of the Muslim community. During the Ummayad and Abbassid periods, the principle of seniority was the underlying rule but whether the seniority applied to brothers, cousins, or uncles remained unsolved. However, strong caliphs had a tendency to appoint or show preference for their sons, thus setting a pattern for vertical succession. By definition, this meant the exclusion of the caliph's brothers who from time to time revolted and installed themselves in his place. As a result, succession to the office of caliph followed both the vertical and horizontal lines.

During the early days of the Ottoman Empire and until the eighteenth century, the rule of primogeniture was followed. Later, the principle of seniority was respected, although accompanied by fierce succession struggles, fraternal rivalries, and assassination.[9]

Equally, in the Arabian Peninsula, there was no fixed pattern of succession among the various dynasties. For example, the Hashemite Sherifian family of the Hijaz passed the title of Sherif of Mecca from father to son (W. Ochsenwald 1984). In other tribal dynasties in the area such as that in Yemen and Oman, succession had been by primogeniture (F. Halliday 1974: 61, 94–6, 280, 299–300). In some Gulf sheikhdoms, a ruler was succeeded by his brothers until a member of the next generation who was older than the next youngest of the original brothers came of age and then became next in line. This *de facto* system – there is no evidence that it is seen as *de jure* – is implemented peacefully at times, and at times through military revolt (A. Bligh 1984: 10). Succession by assassination accompanied this system. For example, in Abu Dhabi, the local Sheikh, Tahnun was assassinated by his brother in 1833 (P. Lienhardt 1975: 61). In Kuwait, fratricide among the Al Sabah ruling family was very common (Z. Freeth and H. Winstone 1972: 66). Sheikh Mubarak (1896–1915) became ruler of Kuwait after assassinating his two brothers (A. Bush 1987: 101). Furthermore, the history of the Rwala tribe of the Syrian Desert in the twentieth century reveals the occurrence of fratricide. In 1901, Sattam Ibn Shaalan, the amir of the Rwala died. He was succeeded by his brother's son, Fahad Ibn Haza who tried to increase the taxes collected from his tribesmen. As a result, he lost popularity and was killed in 1904 by his brother, Nuri, who became amir *de jure* as well as *de facto* (W. Lancaster 1981: 126).

In the nineteenth century, Saudi succession largely followed the seniority system but started to depart from this pattern when Imam Faisal (1834–65) nominated his son Abdullah to succeed him before his death in 1865. Imam Faisal had three other sons who rebelled against their appointed brother together with their uncle, Abdullah Ibn Turki. The second half of the century was characterized by fierce internal power struggles among the Saudi brothers and other branches of the family. These struggles weakened them and paved the way for the decline of their hegemony in central Arabia and the loss of their territories to the Rashidi family. In the twentieth century, the Saudi kingdom adopted the principle of horizontal succession only after the exclusion of Abdul Aziz Ibn Saud's brothers. Ibn Saud designated his son Saud as heir in 1933, thus excluding his brother Mohammad. Since then, subsequent successions have been between brothers, the sons of Abdul Aziz Ibn Saud (A. Bligh 1984).

Some general conclusions can be drawn from this brief account of the patterns of succession in the Arabian Peninsula. It is clear that succession followed an indeterminate pattern, oscillating between horizontal and vertical succession. When the system was leaning more towards vertical succession, assassination tended to bring it back to the horizontal line for some time and vice versa. Struggles for power were fought within a very narrow circle of kinsmen which either included the immediate family, in the case of fratricide, or the lineage, in the case of conflicts between uncles, nephews and cousins.

Succession struggles generated a demographic imbalance among the ruling group as young members of the family were assassinated in infancy. This narrowed the demographic base from which future amirs were to be drawn. In some cases, due to the unavailability of a suitable heir, a young and inexperienced amir was installed in office under the regency of the amir's maternal uncles. This was the case during the rule of Saud Ibn Rashid (1910–20).

With frequent assassination and internal rivalries, the loyalty and support of the immediate paternal kinsmen could no longer be taken for granted. Two solutions were sought by the amirs. First, the maternal link was strengthened to counterbalance the uncertainty and usually competitive relationship with the paternal relatives. The maternal uncles represented a kinship refuge for political alliances to be used by the amirs. Sometimes, the maternal kin acted as guardians of young amirs who were unable to press their claims to power because of their age.[10]

Second, loyalty and support were sought outside the kinship system altogether. The amirs had a group of trusted bodyguards, generally of slave origin, who had the advantage of being foreigners with limited local kinship ties. As their livelihood was completely in his hands, they devoted themselves wholeheartedly to their amir, his security and well-being. Their low status and complete dependence on their masters prevented them from assuming more powers in the dynasty. However, at a later period, some slaves interfered in the succession struggles which took place between members of the ruling group. In 1920, when Saud Ibn Rashid was killed by his cousin, Abdullah Ibn Talal, the latter was immediately assassinated by Saud's slaves who had witnessed the murder of their master.

The indeterminacy of the succession pattern operated as a control mechanism on leadership. As there was no fixed rule for the transfer of office, the political claims of all members of the ruling group were considered to be legitimate. Consequently, the success of one of them and the stability of his leadership was to a certain extent dependent on maintaining a balance between these claims and an implicit recognition of their validity. This was a check on the possibility of abusing power. The amir who coerced his brothers or cousins, by using violence against them or by putting them in gaol, would certainly risk being overthrown or assassinated by other members of the group. In short, indeterminate succession acted as a check on the amir's powers *vis-à-vis* his group.

The Rashidi ruling group represented a microcosm of the Shammar tribal structure in which power was diffused within the various sections of the tribe. In this structure, power was distributed rather than concentrated in the hands of individuals. Among the Shammar, the alternative to succession by assassination was fission and the subsequent formation of new small groups within the general framework of the tribe. The fission and fusion of groups was the mechanism which prevented the formation of permanent authority structures and power enclaves. In the Rashidi case, power resided within the ruling group as a whole. However, the attempts of the amirs to centralize their authority to the exclusion of the others resulted in violence. The internal struggles of the Rashidis were resolved, not by splitting from the group with the intention of forming other power centres, but by violence and physical elimination.

In his discussion of the Middle Eastern tribal quasi-state, Gellner argues that succession depends on the balance of power and prestige, rather than on the simple application of a rule: 'Hence the succession may be determined either by an informal vote – it may go to the man whose leadership potential is demonstrated by the support he receives from other segments – or by conflict, in which case the leadership potential is demonstrated by what one might call bloody praxis.' (E. Gellner 1991)

This suggests that informal vote and bloody praxis are means by which succession struggles are resolved. To succeed, one has to either gather supporters, or develop supremacy in competition, even if that involves the elimination of the rival. Both are legitimate strategies in succession struggles. However, under what conditions is the first option, the informal vote, usually adopted? And what conditions induce the claimants to resort to the second option, i.e. bloody praxis, to use Gellner's terminology? One might argue that if the claimant had failed to gather enough supporters among the segments, he might adopt the second option. Equally, it is possible to claim that only when someone had gathered a huge number of supporters, would he not fear the consequences of physically eliminating his rival. These answers do not resolve the problem. Among the Rashidis, the question of why succession by assassination took precedence over 'informal vote' cannot be answered in this manner. All claimants had supporters and the only way to upset the balance was by the assassination of the rivals. Among the twelve rulers of Hail, only four became amirs as a result of 'informal vote', while the remaining eight had assassinated the previous amir. Succession by assassination was directly proportional to the level of political centralization brought about by the settlement of the amir in Hail. These new conditions made informal vote or quasi-election, give way to succession by assassination.

AMIR AND SHEIKH

The rise of the Rashidi amirs to power marked the beginning of a new era in Shammar political history which did not necessarily represent a complete break from their traditional tribal pattern. Until 1836, the shammar had no leadership beyond the *ashira* which had its own sheikh. The four Shammar *ashair* remained politically and economically autonomous, but claimed common descent and territory. They interacted with each other at the economic, political and social levels. As heads of the sections, the tribal sheikhs were involved in communicating and negotiating with other heads and discussing issues relevant to the tribe as a whole. Nevertheless, the Shammar did not have a tribal assembly in which all the *ashair* were represented. The sheikhs met irregularly with their counterparts at no fixed meeting place and the meetings were *ad hoc* and informal. Sheikhs visited each other occasionally in their respective camps to discuss issues relating to defence, to mediate disputes, and to organize the distribution of pasture land.

The maximal lineages comprising the *ashira* had their heads who were drawn from one of the prominent *biut* in the lineage. The head of the lineage was the grandfather or a senior son who was responsible for the management of the internal affairs of his lineage. Within the *ashira*, some lineages were more prominent than others and they provided sheikhs for the whole *ashira*. A lineage became prominent due to a combination of factors which did not necessarily stem from economic prosperity – since all lineages tended to be more or less equal in wealth and size of herd. Although some sheikhs owned date groves in the oases within their tribal territory, they were under the obligation to share the produce with the rest of their group. The redistribution of the agricultural produce prevented the accumulation of wealth in the hands of the sheikhs. A lineage became dominant as a result of the association of its members with defending the camping unit during times of external threat and raids. The reputation of the lineage members for eloquence, wisdom, and knowledge of tribal history and genealogy, justice and good judgement in internal dispute, and good mediation with outsiders, all increased the lineage's popularity among the rest of the *ashira*. In other words, the head of the lineage who had a non-material capital consisting of a set of valued attributes was likely to be placed in a higher position than the rest of his group. He would have better prospects than other heads of becoming the head of the *ashira* as a whole and his sphere of influence would then be extended beyond the limited confines of his own lineage. A headman who became a sheikh would be a representative or a spokesman of all the lineages but would have no authority over the other *ashair* who in turn had their own sheikhs.

After the death of a sheikh, his son, brother, or even a distant male relative would have an equal chance of becoming sheikh. Sometimes a successor was chosen from another lineage altogether. The system of succession did not provide clear guiding principles. Tribesmen were intolerant of sheikhs or heads of lineages who were more likely to lead their groups for an indefinite time. At the same time, the sheikh did not have the means to ensure that succession remained within his own lineage. If a sheikh was known to have expressed preferences towards maintaining leadership within his immediate relatives or descendants, he would lose respect among his group or even be abandoned by dissatisfied lineages of the *ashira*. These would probably attach themselves to other sections of the tribe. The fluidity of the system stemmed from the fact that the sheikh had no coercive force under his command to strengthen his position and consolidate his powers. Furthermore, the limitations of the pastoral economy prevented the accumulation of wealth or surplus which could be used either to attract followers or bribe them to accept the sheikhs' authority. In addition, the danger that lineages might split up as a result of dissatisfaction concerning the authority of domineering sheikhs acted as checks on the possibility of coercing tribesmen. The splitting up of lineages threatened the unity of the *ashira* as this process led to smaller lineages being swallowed up by bigger ones. The fragmentation of the *ashira* increased the vulnerability of the groups during external threats. Fear of loss of autonomy resulting from fragmentation brought the lineages together around the sheikh and prevented him from indulging in authoritarian government.

At the economic level, the sheikh dealt with matters related to the seasonal migration of the camping units. Since a considerable number of the Shammar remained nomadic, their livelihood was highly dependent on migration to areas where water and pasture were abundant. The sheikhs served as a focal point in an information network concerning the availability of these important resources. It is worth noting that some Shammar sheikhs settled down in the oases in their tribal territory during the dry season. They also owned land in the oases which was often cultivated by slave labour. The produce consisted mainly of dates which were distributed by the sheikh among the rest of his group. This supplemented the pastoral economy and lessened its vulnerability, especially during the frequent periods of drought. However, in the nineteenth century, only a few of the Shammar sheikhs settled permanently in the oases.

Politically, the sheikh was the head of the *ashira* who represented his group and negotiated alliances. He was a representative of an autonomous unit and was, consequently, not compelled to participate in any Shammar raids or join any alliance with them which did not serve his *ashira*'s interests.

Sheikhs were war leaders if they were able, or they appointed young and energetic members of the group to lead military campaigns. Generally the sheikh was responsible for the distribution of booty among the raiders. All male members of the *ashira* carried weapons and constituted a body of potential warriors. They were not segregated from the rest of their group and after raids and military encounters with other groups all participants resumed their normal life.

The sheikh also had judicial functions as he was the mediator in disputes between members of his group. He resolved feuds with outsiders or with other sections of the Shammar and dealt with cases of blood revenge, theft and robbery. However, the Shammar sheikh was a *primus inter pares* and lacked the means to enforce his decisions. He had no command over his followers other than his eloquence, wisdom, and power of persuasion (G. Wallin 1854: 180). The sheikh relied on his authority among his group and his status as a knowledgeable person and this authority guaranteed that disputants obey his recommendations.

The establishment of the Rashidi amirs in Hail did not undermine the role of the Shammar sheikhs. An oasis-based leadership emerged, i.e. that of the amirs, whose powers were more centralized than those of the sheikhs. The amirs also had greater economic resources and more military hegemony than the sheikhs. However, the amirs coexisted with the sheikhs, each having separate political spheres in which they exercised their authority.

The terms amir (ruler, commander or prince) and sheikh (head of tribal section) refer to two types of leadership. The desert-based Shammar section sheikhs never used the title of amir. In contrast, the Rashidi amirs were often referred to as sheikhs by the Shammar. In other words, the amir was a sheikh, but the reverse was not true. This indicates that the role of the sheikh was more or less well defined and there was no confusion relating to his position as a tribal leader. As the Shammar sheikhs considered the Rashidis to be sheikhs too, they were making a political statement. They emphasized their equality with the Hail leadership. The Shammar and their sheikhs did not perceive the amir's leadership as a distinct type chracterized by the exercise of power over them, although it was clear that the amir played a larger role than their sheikhs. This was related to the fact that at the beginning of the Rashidi rule, the terms amir and sheikh were only terminological distinctions which described two manifestations of the same leadership. Common to both manifestations was a single underlying legitimating ideology. In the 1830–40s, both the amirs and the Shammar sheikhs derived their legitimacy from two sources: patrilineal descent from a noble lineage and achieved attributes.

Although the amir's basis of legitimacy was to a great extent similar to the sheikh's, the settlement of the former in Hail led to the departure of this leadership from the traditional tribal pattern and the beginning of dynastic rule. The founder of the Rashidi dynasty was initially regarded as a bedouin sheikh, a leader who spent a long time among his Jaafar lineage. When he settled in Hail, he became an oasis ruler.[11] This was an important step which marked the emergence of differences between the amir and the sheikh. These differences were manifested at the level of their sphere of influence, economic, political and military power, and relations with outside government.

With regard to their sphere of influence, while the leadership of the Shammar sheikh was limited to his tribal section, the amir had a wider constituency which included the tribe, the settled population of the oases in Jabal Shammar, and the conquered nomadic groups. The Shammar recognized the amir's leadership which coexisted with that of their own tribal sheikhs. Montagne noted how the Shammar accepted the amirs as their leaders: 'nous ne connaissons d'autre chefs que les Al Rashid' (R. Montagne 1932: 65). This statement did not undermine the role of their own sheikhs through whom the Shammar expressed this recognition. The sheikhs represented their groups to the amir and had access to his *majlis* (council). During their regular visits to Hail, the sheikhs were the guests of the amir. They visited to renew their allegiance and loyalty and to enquire about matters relating to future military and political plans. For example, the sheikhs were often told about future military expeditions while the amir investigated whether they were willing to take part. The Shammar sections and their sheikhs were in theory free to join the amir's expedition or abstain from participation. In most cases they preferred to take part as this guaranteed a share of any booty. In addition, as the Shammar could not rely entirely on their animals, they supplemented their pastoral economy by the purchase of agricultural produce. These economic transactions were initially conducted in the markets of Iraq. Later, with the growth of Rashidi power, caravan trade brought all sorts of products to the market of Hail which was more convenient to them. The commercial transactions of the Shammar were dependent on their access to the market which was under the control of the amirs. In return for access, the Shammar were required to put their military skills and human resources at the disposal of the amir. This was important in ensuring the flow of trade, the protection of the caravans, and the maintenance of peace and order in the market-place. The amir had little control over the economic base of pastoral production, but maintained strong control over trade and commerce by virtue of his political and military supremacy.

The economic basis underlying the amir's leadership started to differ from that of the ordinary Shammar sheikh whose revenues were derived from a combination of pastoralism, limited agriculture, and trade. This mixed economy was not prone to the generation of wealth and surplus accumulation. As a result social differentiation was not a characteristic of the sheikh who remained economically indistinguishable from the rest of his section. The revenues of the Hail amir, however, were not entirely dependent on this mixed economy; they were derived from a variety of sources such as landownership in the oases, subsidies from the Ottoman government, tax on trading and pilgrims' caravans, and tribute extracted from the conquered sedentary and nomadic population. The amir's revenues contributed to the growing social differentiation between him and his subjects; he became a member of a distinct socio-economic group with dynastic and aristocratic features. Even when the amir encamped in the desert, a tradition which was maintained throughout the history of the dynasty, his tent was marked separately from the others as it had nine poles. Montagne commented on this: 'Les sheikh de la famille des Al Rashid, qui commandaient à tout les Semmar du Negd, avaient, lorsqu'ils comptaient au milieu de leurs tribus, une tente de neufs piquets ... le nombre est d'ailleurs approximativement proportionnel à leur fortune.' (R. Montagne 1932: 65)

The amir's political power was qualitatively different from that

of the Shammar sheikh, who can be described as a leader with no
actual power to influence people's decisions or impose his own,
while the amir's political power was entangled with his military
supremacy. G. Wallin commented on these differences when he
visited Hail: 'The latter [Shammar sheikhs] have no other
influence over the meanest of the tribe, nor any means of enforcing
obedience to decisions, than their own eloquence and power of
persuasion, and the authority and credit their own personal
qualities and merits have procured them among their people.'
(G.A. Wallin 1854: 180) By contrast, the amir had at his command
a body of armed men, slaves and supporters who were ready to
enforce his rule: 'Through his body of servants, constituting, so to
say, his life guard, and through his own personal influence, Abd
Allah had the power to execute his will and to enforce obedience to
the sentences he passed, and, in case of disobedience and
obstinacy, to punish the refractory.' (ibid)

It was this power to enforce orders and inflict punishment that
distinguished the amir's leadership from the sheikh's. While all
male members of the tribal section carried weapons, they were not
the personal bodyguard of the sheikh. They neither served his own
personal interests nor enforced his own commands. This tribal
force was not paid by the sheikh to fulfil particular tasks. Their
voluntary participation in raids and in the defence of their section
was a moral duty and an obligation respected by all. Abstention
from participation for reasons other than old age or illness brought
about shame, ridicule, and even social ostracism. It meant the loss
of economic, political, social and jural rights, i.e. the suspension of
membership rights in the group. However, while participating in
military expeditions, tribesmen were fulfilling their duties towards
the group rather than towards the sheikh. In contrast, the amir's
armed men formed a distinct body which constituted a professional
force employed on a permanent basis. It consisted of slaves and
volunteers from villages and oases, in addition to the conscripts
who joined the amir's military force as a result of the imposition of
military service. These were paid in cash or kind in return for their
service. As a result, the amir's power rested on the possession of
actual means of coercion which the tribal sheikh lacked, and this
facilitated the process by which the centralization of the oasis-
based leadership was enforced.

The leadership of the amirs started to surpass the local level as
they began to take part in international politics. They maintained

external political relations with the Ottoman government which claimed a nominal suzerainty over the Arabian peninsula. The amirs sent their messengers to negotiate alliances with Ottoman officials in Basra, Baghdad, Damascus, and Madina. These relations guaranteed a flow of external subsidies in return for their loyalty and that of the population under their influence. Towards the beginning of the twentieth century, these relations were intensified under the pressures which preceded the First World War. In a desperate attempt to win the loyalty and co-operation of local power centres in the region, the Ottoman government almost doubled the subsidies to the Hail amirs. In contrast, section sheikhs had limited contacts with external agents and did not directly receive subsidies from outside. The Rashidi amirs acted as mediators between the Shammar and the Ottoman government, which expected the amirs to act like 'state rulers'. The Ottomans thought that these expectations would be translated into reality by a continuous flow of arms and weapons which would guarantee the control of the amirs over the Shammar and the loyalty of the latter. Their leadership thus became endowed with actual military powers which gave them control rather than mere influence. This control was not mainly directed towards the Shammar; it was successful in the process of the amirs' dynastic expansion whereby their realm began to include non-Shammar groups.

The existence among the Shammar of two types of leadership which were different at the level of constituency and powers, contributed to the emergence of underlying political tensions. These emerged from the coexistence of a centralizing agent (the amir) and a decentralized political structure ideology which was unfavourable to the crystallization of power in the hands of a single amir.

The growing tendency towards greater centralization and the creation of more stable forms of government were constantly being checked by the inherently decentralizing tendencies of the Shammar tribal system. This system was not favourable to the maintenance of permanent political relations and alliances. It was based on the principle of local group autonomy at the political, military and economic levels. The central political authority of the amir had to coexist with tribal autonomy which meant that sovereignty was diffused in the tribe and among its various sections. The tension between the two tendencies was dispersed, encompassed and partially overcome through the system of subsidies to tribal sheikhs. The amirs maintained a tradition of subsidizing these sheikhs through the continuous distribution of cash and gifts of rice, coffee, sugar, camels, and weapons. These gifts operated as a bribe to maintain the allegiance of the sheikhs, who remained to a great extent autonomous. The subsidies cemented, enforced and strengthened what would otherwise have been a loose, fragile, and weak political relationship between the Hail leadership and the Shammar. The system remained operative as long as the amirs were able to provide these subsidies and as long as their interests coincided with those of the Shammar.

In general, the relationship remained fairly strong in terms of political loyalty until the amirs were threatened by external rival power centres, i.e. that of the Saudis at the beginning of the twentieth century. Both the amirs and the sheikhs recognized each other's sphere of influence and neither tried to trespass on the other's political field.

Anthropologists working among nomadic Middle Eastern tribes have often underestimated the distinctions at the level of leadership by stressing the existence of an 'inherent egalitarian tradition' among these nomads.[12] In his study of the Rwala of north Arabia, Lancaster does not see the two leaderships as distinct. He argues that both the amir and the sheikh are mediators on behalf of the tribe with other tribes or with national governments. Lancaster stresses that: 'No individual has political power, no group has political power and no family has political power; power is restricted to the workings of public opinion.' (W. Lancaster 1981: 81)

Among the Rwala, the term 'sheikh' is used as a courtesy title for the most influential members of the Shaalan family, the prominent ruling group, while the title 'amir' was given to Nuri Ibn Shaalan by the Ottoman government, and later confirmed by the French mandatory authorities. Lancaster recognizes only terminological differences between the two types of leadership although others were recognized by Lawrence and Glubb, two of the sources he used for his study. Lawrence described Nuri as someone who had gained his headship by sheer force and all feared and obeyed him whereas Glubb added that Nuri's authority was probably unique among the bedouins (ibid: 84). Lancaster dismisses these comments and does not recognize the fact that Ibn Shaalan was no longer a traditional tribal sheikh. The basis of his authority changed as he was drawn closer to international politics and central states interested in subjugating and encapsulating his tribe.

His power now rested on his slaves, the taxes which he collected on behalf of the central government, and his contacts with a wider political élite. Consequently, his leadership departed from that of a bedouin sheikh.[13]

In her study of the Al Hassana and Al Fadl semi-nomadic tribes of Syria and the Beqaa valley, Chatty recognizes two distinct types of leadership which emerged during the colonial period and lasted until the 1960s and 1970s. The Al Hassana sheikhs represent an authority different from that of the Al Fadl amirs. Chatty argues that the amir's basis of authority rests not so much on the pre-eminence of his *beit* within the tribe, but more so on the pre-eminence of his *beit* throughout the system of bedouin tribes. In addition, the amir maintained 'semi-feudal' relations with the rest of his tribe as he became the owner of the land which was registered under his name by the colonial authorities, and demanded rent from those who used it. He was an absentee landlord who lived in the city and became removed from his group; and his family became a wealthy and sophisticated part of the national élite. By contrast, the sheikh's pre-eminence rested only within his tribal section (D. Chatty 1977: 393). The sheikh never requested land rental payments from his tribesmen who made annual presentations to him – voluntary donations which were occasionally converted into feasts.

However, Chatty does not refer to the military basis of power in the case of the amir and sheikh. The question whether the amir enjoyed more military powers, or possessed a separate force than that consisting of his tribesmen is not answered. Moreover, no mention is made of tension or resentment arising from the increasing exercise of economic power by the amir over his followers. As mentioned before, the strong decentralized political tradition shared by a considerable number of nomadic tribes in the region acted as a check on the centralizing tendencies represented by the leadership of the amirs.

In Jabal Shammar, the crystallization of the Rashidi amir's role set in motion a process of dynastic rule. This does not seem to have been the case among the nomadic tribes of the north. This is perhaps related to the fact that the northern tribes such as those studied by Chatty in Syria were in close proximity to well-established urban government centres which were able at an earlier phase to encapsulate and restrict the development of more advanced tribal government.[14] The restraints on the amir's leadership in central Arabia, however, came from within the system, i.e. from the decentralized political tradition in which the local autonomy of the tribal sections was dominant. A second challenge came from another type of leadership which, in addition to being a political leadership, had an important religious dimension. This leadership was provided by the Saudi imams of the nineteenth century.

AMIR AND IMAM

In 1824 a second Saudi–Wahhabi dynasty was established in Riyadh, with Turki Ibn Abdullah as the founder.[15] As seen in Chapter 2, he was murdered and succeeded by his son, Faisal. Faisal was known as the imam, a term which, in the Saudi–Wahhabi context, meant both leader of prayer and political leader of the Muslim community, i.e. the term stood for political and religious leadership as there was no distinction between the two.

After a number of clashes with the Egyptian forces, Faisal was defeated and replaced by his cousin Khalid, who had been raised in Cairo by the Egyptians. After the withdrawal of the Egyptian troops in 1841 Abdullah Ibn Thunayan, another member of the Saudi family, captured Riyadh from its Egyptian appointed ruler who fled to the Hijaz. Ibn Thunayan's leadership did not last for long as Imam Faisal had escaped from gaol in Cairo and succeeded in establishing himself for the second time in Riyadh.

Because of his policy of avoiding clashes with the Ottomans, Imam Faisal tried to expand to the south-east especially along the coast of the Persian Gulf where confrontations with Ottoman troops and officials were less likely. His reign turned out to be one of stability as Wahhabism ceased to be a strong driving force for an uncontrolled external war. In the conquered areas, acceptance of Wahhabism came to signify mere willingness to receive Wahhabi judges and religious teachers who were appointed by Imam Faisal and sent to the oases and towns of the region (N. Safran 1985: 16). The bedouin tribes who accepted Faisal's authority were even exempted from that requirement. Imam Faisal realized the importance of establishing political alliances with these tribes in an attempt to win approval for his policies and curb dissension among them. To cement these alliances, he encouraged his sons to marry the daughters of powerful tribal sheikhs. He and his son Saud married into the powerful Ajman tribe whereas his son Abdullah married the daughter of Abdullah Ibn Rashid, the founder of the Rashidi dynasty.

Before his death in 1865, Imam Faisal nominated his son Abdullah to succeed him after ensuring the approval of the *ulama* (religious scholars) of Riyadh. This, however, did not guarantee the peaceful succession of his son, who was challenged by his brother, Saud. Abdullah sought to centralize his powers and exercise more control over both the provinces under Saudi domination and the bedouin tribes which had already accepted his father's rule. As a result, Abdullah antagonized these groups who refused to compromise their autonomy. His brother, Saud, who coveted the succession for himself, and had his own sources of support, particularly within the powerful Ajman tribe, took advantage of his brother's mistakes and challenged and defeated him. He was able to capture Riyadh in 1871 (ibid: 17). Abdullah left Riyadh in an attempt to gather supporters and took refuge in Jabal Shammar whose amir was Mohammad Ibn Rashid. Being married to Mohammad's sister, Abdullah hoped to find some support and sympathy for his cause in Hail. However, Mohammad Ibn Rashid was not willing to restore the Saudi imam to his position, rather, his plans included the subjugation of the southern Saudi–Wahhabi dynasty and the incorporation of its territory in his realm.

Saud's leadership lasted until his death in 1875. Soon after this, his brother, Abdul Rahman, became imam in Riyadh but was challenged by the sons of Saud who thought they were more eligible to inherit the post of their deceased father. Abdul Rahman was driven out of Riyadh by his nephews.

In spite of his disappointment in Hail, Abdullah managed to return to Riyadh with the support of some nomadic tribes. He installed himself as imam after reaching an agreement with Saud's sons. Peace for Abdullah did not last for long, however, as he was captured by Saud's sons and put in gaol. Mohammad Ibn Rashid took advantage of these events by advancing to Riyadh and liberating Abdullah – who was taken to Hail as a 'permanent guest' to prevent his return to power. Mohammad Ibn Rashid appointed a governor to Riyadh which became part of Ibn Rashid's sphere of influence (R. Winder 1965: 264–5). Because of his old age and illness, Abdullah Ibn Faisal was allowed to return to Riyadh while retaining his title as imam until his death in 1889.

After Abdullah's death, his brother Abdul Rahman became imam. Abdul Rahman tried to free himself from the Rashidi domination over his capital. He organized a revolt against Ibn Rashid in 1890 with the support of the people of central Najd and in particular the Qasimis, who occupied the territory between Hail and Riyadh. The ruler of the major towns in the Qasim responded to Abdul Rahman's call to join him in the revolt, but Ibn Rashid defeated this joint alliance in the battle of Muleida in 1891. After the defeat of his allies, Imam Abdul Rahman immediately left Riyadh with all members of his family and took refuge first with the Al Murrah tribe of the Empty Quarter. Later he went to Kuweit where he was adopted by its ruler, Ibn Sabah. The escape of the last Saudi imam to Kuwait brought about the collapse of the second Saudi–Wahhabi dynasty. This was carried out by a local power centre, that of the Rashidis, rather than by an external agent.

Many aspects of leadership in the second Saudi–Wahhabi dynasty were a continuation of what existed in the eighteenth century. This leadership continued to derive its guiding lines from the application of the laws of the *sharia* and the Islamic principles as explained by Mohammad Ibn Abdul Wahhab, the founder of the Wahhabi movement. The religious basis of this leadership was reflected in the adoption of the title of imam. Throughout Arabia, the Saudi rulers were known as imams and maintained a system of primogeniture with respect to succession. This was a clear departure from the principles of succession to tribal leadership in which the sheikh was usually chosen from amongst the lineage of the preceding ruler, but without any fixed rule. In the Saudi case, the role of imam was passed from father to son, although this pattern was occasionally disrupted during the fraternal strife of the second half of the nineteenth century.

As the Saudi imams expanded their realm over other provinces in Arabia, they appointed representatives whose major role was to keep order and peace and to see the application of the laws of the *sharia*. The representatives also collected the *zakat* (Islamic tax) which was regulated as follows: 10 per cent of the agricultural produce from non-irrigated areas and 5 per cent of the produce from irrigated fields, 2.5 per cent tax on capital stored in silver and gold, 2.5 per cent tax on capital used for trade, and finally the *zakat* of cattle, camels and sheep. These taxes constituted a considerable revenue which was sent to *beit al mal* (public treasury). Other revenues included the booty which was collected from the conquered areas and distributed among the fighters according to the Islamic law of the *ghanima* (booty). One fifth of the booty was sent to *beit al mal* whereas the remainder was distributed among the soldiers and commanders. The Saudi imams also appointed *qadis* (judges) in the conquered provinces. The *qadis* settled disputes over inheritance, marriage and divorce, thefts, murder and so on, according to the rules of the *sharia*, and were paid annually from the public treasury (Abu Hakima 1967: 50).

The leadership of the Saudi imams provided an alternative to tribal leadership as it derived its ideological foundation from Islam. The imams aimed to establish an Islamic rather than a tribal government. In this context, it is worth comparing the two leaderships, i.e. the tribal leadership as represented by the Rashidi amirs of Hail and the Islamic leadership as represented by the Saudi imams of the nineteenth century. The amir's role differed in many aspects from that of the Saudi imam. Hogarth commented on these differences:

> Society in Hail differs from that of the other oasis lands of central Arabia. This resides in the fact that its main constituent, now settled and in part of fellah life, has not lost the spirit of the custom of the bedouin population from which it sprang. To take the ruling family for example, the chiefs of the house of Rashid are not as the chiefs of the house of Saud in Riad, rulers of settled communities with which they are at one, and surrounding tribes of bedouins, distinct from themselves, but they are chiefs, in the first instance, of a great dominant bedouin tribe, and in the second of the settlements which serve that tribe for markets and rallying points. (D.G. Hogarth 1905: 166)

Hogarth's comments stressed the unity and cohesion between the Hail amirs and their Shammar tribe. Although the amirs were physically separated from their fellow Shammar, there was a strong genealogical bond between them. The Saudi leadership, however, lacked the tribal depth of the Rashidis, for they had been established in a sedentary environment long enough to have lost their tribal ties – for example, they were settled in Deraiya as early as the fifteenth century. Since then they had been oasis rulers. Also, Wahhabism, the ideological umbrella for Saudi leadership, did not originate among the bedouins, though some of them enthusiastically adopted it. It had its roots in the oasis-culture of southern Najd. Saudi expansion in the eighteenth and nineteenth centuries represented the political and ideological domination of the sedentary world as it existed in southern Najd at that time over the hinterland, i.e. the domain of the nomadic tribes. These facts led the Saudi leadership to adopt and invoke sources of legitimacy different from those behind the Rashidi leadership.

The legitimation of authority, domination or leadership, Weber argued, is a prerequisite for the development of a harmonious relationship between ruler and ruled. Acceptance of domination, in the case of the exercise of power where an actor obeys a specific command issued by another, may rest on automatic habituation or appeal to self-interest. Continuity in leadership requires the presence of legitimacy, of which Weber distinguishes three ideal types: traditional, charismatic and legal (M. Weber 1947: 226 vol I). However, only the first is relevant here. Lineage elders, patriarchalism, and patrimonialism are variations of leadership based on traditional legitimation. The Hail amirs can be considered as one of the variants of traditional authority. Their leadership was legitimized by reference to traditional values of nobility and patrilineal descent from a prominent lineage.

However, these were combined with 'personal' sources of legitimacy. Strong attributes such as military skills, wisdom, courage, bravery, hospitality, and generosity were themselves sources for legitimation. It is true that the personality of the ruler constitutes a source of legitimation in both traditional and non-traditional leadership (D. Easton 1965: 302–3). The leader must demonstrate his personal competence if he is to earn the traditional oath of allegiance. His personal attributes determine to a great extent his pre-eminence. This was a factor of considerable relevance to the establishment of Abdullah Ibn Rashid's leadership in Hail. In contrast, as the Saudi leadership lacked the tribal connection it derived its legitimacy from an ideology of Islam, and in particular the Wahhabi version of it. With Saudi adoption of the movement, Wahhabism became a 'political religion' to use Easton's terminology. The sacred was employed to develop a system of political legitimacy and to aid in mobilizing the community for secular ends. In this case, the ends were political.

The founder of the Rashidi dynasty, Abdullah Ibn Rashid did not question the religious leadership of imam Faisal of Riyadh. The former's leadership was not based on religious legitimation. With respect to the Shammar, the Rashidi amirs were above all their tribal sheikhs. In contrast, the authority of the Saudi imams rested on their adherence to an Islamic ideology with a mission to establish an Islamic state where Islamic law ruled supreme. The Saudi imams were not initially sheikhs of a strong tribe within the Arabian Peninsula, neither were they of Sherifian descent like the Hashemite rulers of the Hijaz. They had been the rulers of the settled population of Deraiya since 1446 (A. Abdul Rahim 1976: 73). As in most sedentary parts of southern Najd, the population of Deraiya consisted of farmers (mainly of date palms), craftsmen, traders, religious personnel (*qadis* and imams) and slaves. Before the rise of Wahhabism and its adoption by the Saudis in 1744, the power of the Saudi rulers rested on their ability to collect the tax from the settled population in return for protection. Wahhabism provided the ideological mechanism by which Saudi domination was extended beyond Deraiya as the Saudis imposed their religious and political leadership over most of the Arabian Peninsula.

Both the Rashidi amirs and the Saudi imams enjoyed a high status in the eyes of their followers. The Hail amirs derived their status from their privileged descent which guaranteed them respect not only among the Shammar, but also within the bedouin society of Arabia in general. In contrast, the Saudi imams derived their status from their role as the guardians of Islamic law. Their knowledge of the *sharia*, their willingness to enforce it, and their piety enhanced their position.

The amirs and imams played military and political roles. They took part in military expeditions and were involved in the expansion of their realm. The amirs imposed their own hegemony and that of the Shammar tribe on the conquered towns and oases whereas the imams regarded their expansion as a holy war to spread the 'true beliefs of Islam'. The amirs used tribal manpower, slaves, mercenaries and conscripts for their military expeditions whereas the imams relied heavily on the converts who were willing to spread the teachings of Wahhabism. The Rashidi amirs justified warfare by reference to an ideology of tribal supremacy; the Saudi imams highlighted the concept of *jihad* (holy war).

With respect to their judiciary functions, the Rashidi amirs were mediators in disputes whereas the imams were judges who had at their disposal the divine law of the *sharia*. The Rashidi amirs made use of Islamic law and sought the judgement of the Hail *qadis* on various occasions, yet they did not rule out customary law

TABLE 2: *Tribal and Islamic Leadership*

Characteristics	Tribal Leadership	Islamic Leadership
Title:	Amir	Imam
Legitimation:	tradition and personality	political religion
Status:	high derived from descent, personal qualities and military skills	high derived from piety and knowledge of Islam
Roles:	political and military roles and mediator in disputes	political and military roles and judge in disputes
Military power:	tribal force recruited according to custom, slaves, conscripts	Muslims ready to fight for the spread of Islam, slaves
Objective of war:	expansion and defence of Shammar supremacy	expansion and spread of Islamic government
Revenues:	tribute, booty, and tax collected according to custom	*zakat* and booty collected according to Islamic law
Succession:	indeterminate	*shura* in theory, but primogeniture in practice

according to which many disputes especially those relating to murder were settled.

Both rulers relied on revenues from raids and taxes which were imposed on the conquered territories. The amirs collected a protection tax (*khuwa*) according to tribal custom whereas the imams amassed the *zakat* tax (Islamic tax). The Rashidi amirs followed tribal *urf* (custom) when distributing the booty whereas the imams used Islamic law (see Table 2).

With respect to succession to the office of amir, it was mentioned earlier that this passed to brothers, sons, and even patrilateral cousins. In contrast, succession to the office of imam was in theory based on the Islamic concept of *shura* (negotiation and consultation) which was dominant at least within the Sunni tradition. However, in practice, the Saudi imams tried to win the approval of the Wahhabi *ulama* for a particular heir before the death of the imam, for example when Imam Faisal appointed his son Abdullah to succeed him. In general, the Saudis adhered to the system of primogeniture which was not a common practice for tribal leadership at least among the tribes of central and northern Arabia. It was a characteristic of succession in the Yemen and Oman in the nineteenth century (A. Bligh 1984: 9–10). Among the Saudis, this system did not operate without fratricide, internal rivalries and succession struggles.

Although the Rashidi amirs did not invoke a religious legitimating ideology, it would be misleading to conclude that their leadership was completely 'secular' and that religion did not have any significance. At the beginning of their rule in Hail, the Rashidi amirs together with the Shammar tribe, were influenced by Wahhabism which had already been present in Arabia for almost a century. Travellers visiting Hail in the nineteenth century commented on the religiosity of the sedentary population, a feature common in almost all towns and oases of central Arabia at that time. Wallin wrote:

> The two principal tenets of the Wahhaby doctrine, to which the Shammar still unalterably adhere, are the rejection of all saints, even the Prophet himself, as mediator between God and man; and 2ndly, the necessity of saying the prayers publicly in a mosque, in common with a congregation, and not alone at home . . . The Wahhaby princes keep a strict eye upon assembling the people to the Friday prayer, and there were in Hail many instances of Abd Allah's having severely punished several men for default of attending to that service. (G. Wallin 1854: 185)

In addition, Abdullah Ibn Rashid's brother, Obeid, was often described as a 'fanatic Wahhabi'. Doughty described him as the 'conductor of the military power of J. Shammar, in Abdullah his brother and in his nephew Telal's days. He was a martial man, and a Wahhaby . . .' (C. Doughty 1979: 27 vol II).

The Friday prayers were attended by the amirs who appointed the imam of the mosque. The imam was usually someone who received religious education in Madina, Cairo or Riyadh (ibid). In Hail there were also a number of *khatibs* (preachers) who taught people the basic tenets of Wahhabism. The amir appointed a *qadi* who had an education in Islamic jurisprudence. Some historical records refer to the presence of a Wahhabi *qadi* in Hail at the beginning of the rule of Abdullah Ibn Rashid. The *qadi* was often sent from Riyadh to Hail to settle disputes and collect *sadaqa* (Islamic charity) and *zakat* (Islamic tax) from those who paid it voluntarily. This was usually done during spring-time when the farmers were ready to collect their agricultural produce, mainly dates. After fulfilling these tasks, the *qadi* returned to Riyadh. During Abdullah Ibn Rashid's rule, four *qadis* were sent to Hail – Abdullah Ibn Suleiman Ibn Obeid, and his brother Ahmed, Abdul Aziz Ibn Abdul Jabar, and Mohammad Ibn Saif (A. Alhindi 1380 AH: 80). Hail also had its own *qadis* who were appointed by the amirs and were there on a permanent basis. It seems that the amir had the final say over the decisions of the *qadis*. These decisions were arrived at by consulting rather than obeying the religious authority. Palgrave described the *qadi* of Hail as someone who was more tolerant than the *qadis* in the Saudi capital: 'Besides being a tolerable representative of what here may be called the moderate party, neither participating in the fanaticism of the Wahhabee, nor yet, like the most of the indigenous chiefs, hostile to Mohometanism, he takes his cue from the court direction and is popular with all factions because belonging properly to none.' (W. Palgrave 1865: 158 vol I)

Palgrave's account stresses that the amir and the tribal sheikhs were hostile to the application of Islamic law.[16] Nevertheless, the presence of a *qadi* whose main function was to settle disputes according to the *sharia* was an indication that he at least occasionally did so. It seems that in Hail, the settlement of disputes followed both the Islamic and the Shammar customary law. The *qadi* dealt with disputes relating to commerce, marriage, divorce and inheritance. Other cases, especially those related to the bedouin population such as murder, theft, disputes arising from the allocation of economic resources such as wells and pasture, and robbery were perhaps dealt with according to customary law. Lady Blunt who visited Hail towards the last quarter of the nineteenth century when Wahhabi influence in Arabia in general was already declining, claimed that in Hail most disputes were settled according to customary law rather than the *Sharia*:

> Where, however, quarrels are not to be settled by the intervention of friends, the disputants bring their cases to the Emir, who settles them in open court, the mejlis, and whose word is final. The law of the Koran, though often referred to, is not, I fancy, the main rule of the Emir's decision, but rather Arabian custom, an authority far older than the Musluman code. I doubt if it is often necessary for the soldiers to support such decisions by force. (A. Blunt 1968: 266 vol I)

The settlement of disputes took place in the amir's *majlis* (council) which was held daily in the public square and was open for the public. Among those who attended the meetings were the amirs of the Rashidi family, the Shammar sheikhs who happened to be present in Hail, other non-Shammar sheikhs, and the oasis notables. The amir was the head of the *majlis* and this was reflected in the seating arrangement. The amir with his cousins, brothers, and uncles sat on a slightly raised bench the central part of which was occupied by himself. Access to the *majlis* was not regulated by any rule; anyone who had a case, a request, or an enquiry to make attended the meetings. The amir played the role of mediator between disputants. Euting attended the *majlis* during his visit to Hail; thus he was able to describe these meetings:

> Someone steps forward and announces that a couple of sheep have been stolen from him by such and such a person. The amir promises him that he will see to it that they are given back or replaced, and has the sheikh of the tribe to which the thief belongs informed of this with the observation that he must clear the matter up. This simple announcement implies the tacit threat that in case of delay, the sheikh in question, together with his tribe, may, at the next year's distribution of grazing grounds, be allotted a region inferior to their previous one. (J. Euting in P. Ward 1983: 467)

It is clear that the amir used to seek the co-operation of the tribal sheikhs of the disputants. The sheikhs usually had closer contacts with their followers and a grass-root knowledge of their behaviour. The tribal sheikhs, in the amir's *majlis*, were held responsible for returning stolen property and arranging for blood money (*diya*) to be paid in cases of murder. The failure of the sheikh to do so resulted in punishment and violence against the whole group. The amir's threat to allocate a less favourable grazing land to the group was one of the means employed to encourage groups to abide by the resolutions arrived at in the *majlis*.

During the first decades of their rule (1840–60s), the amirs did not question the religious role of the Saudi imams. Their rather moderate religious fervour during the second half of the nineteenth century was tolerated and accepted as a spiritual leadership. The moderation of the imams followed the first and second Egyptian invasions which had succeeded in destroying their first power-base in Deraiya. The imams were unable to recover their initial might, unlimited zeal, and the support of the population of central Arabia who had suffered for almost a century from Wahhabi fanaticism followed by the Egyptian devastation of the country. This population was reluctant to carry the Saudi–Wahhabi flag again in a process of holy war launched at the unbelievers. Now the consequences were almost predictable because of historical precedence and the presence of the Egyptian troops in the Hijaz. This background explains the relationship between the Hail amirs and the Saudi imams. There was a considerable degree of tolerance in Hail for Wahhabi teachings and knowledge of religious matters. Saudi leadership was respected as long as it did not constitute a political threat. In other words, the imams' leadership was respected and tolerated, but their political hegemony was resented and rejected. Throughout the second half of the nineteenth century, the Rashidi amirs maintained their local autonomy and independence. Their tolerance of the religious leadership of the imams was translated into actual hostilities in the 1880s and 1890s, culminating in the battle of Muleida and the expulsion of the last Saudi imam, Abdul Rahman, together with his family to Kuwait.

4

THE CARAVAN ECONOMY
Trade, Pilgrims and Tribute

TRADE

The hegemony of the Rashidi amirs rested on their control of the caravan commercial network which existed between Iraq and Persia in the east, and the Hijaz in the west. Hail became a major caravan transit station attracting foreign merchants and pilgrims; and also began to have its own commercial caravans which brought to the region a variety of goods. These were vital to both the local oasis dwellers and the Shammar.

Pastoralism in Jabal Shammar was vulnerable due to the unpredictability of rainfall and the length of the summer season when the nomads had to stay near their desert wells or the permanent wells in the oases. The Shammar, however, had control over the basic means of their pastoral production; i.e. pasture land and wells in their tribal territory. The Shammar had collective ownership rights over these resources whereas the various tribal sections had rights to use them. The Hail amirs had neither the authority nor the means to alter this traditional arrangement. The distribution of pastoral resources was left to the sections and their sheikhs who co-operated to organize the seasonal migration of their groups and the regular use of wells and pasture land.

The vulnerability of the pastoral economy induced the Shammar to diversify their resources. Both agricultural products and manufactured goods were essential. Also, they needed access to permanent water springs which did not dry up during the dry season. These were often found in the villages and oases of Jabal Shammar which produced a variety of fruits, vegetables, wheat and barley, and above all dates, which were the most important part of the nomads' diet. Those Shammar who did not own their own date plantations in the oases were obliged to exchange their pastoral products such as wool, butter, and animals for dates. Some Shammar families, however, owned their own date fields which were usually situated near a permanent well (G. Wallin 1854: 189).

The agricultural labour force consisted of sedentary farmers and slaves. The Shammar sheikhs who owned a considerable number of slaves were able to benefit from their labour whereas others had arrangements with local sedentary families to look after their date plantations. The farmers were allowed to keep one-fifth of the agricultural produce whereas the landowner took four-fifths, an arrangement common in most of the oases of central Arabia. Other Shammar families left a few members of their group to settle near the plantation to look after it while the rest of the group kept the family herd in the desert. This was common in one of the plantations of Agde, a small desert village in the Aja mountain near Hail (ibid). The owners visited the plantation at least twice or three times every year to collect the ripened dates and, if the plantation failed to produce enough dates as a result of shortage of water, they looked for other sources to supplement the mixed economy. The Shammar had rights over the produce of date plantations belonging to their kinsmen in other villages. If these failed too, they tried to purchase quantities of dates from the markets in the region.

The dependence of the Shammar on oasis agricultural production was not a one-way process. Oasis dwellers also required products which they were not able to produce themselves – camels to deliver water from their wells and to plough the fields, meat (camel, sheep and goat), wool, butter, and other dairy products. The oases also relied on the import of a variety of agricultural products (dates, grain, wheat, barley, rice, coffee, sugar) and manufactured goods (clothes, shoes, weapons, perfumes and saddles). These were imported to Jabal Shammar from the more fertile regions of Iraq and the port of Basra and Kuwait on the Persian Gulf. The symbiotic relation between the nomads and the sedentary people was reinforced by their dependence on caravan trade.

Both groups participated in this trade and had a stake in its continuity. The Shammar provided the means of transport for the commercial caravans, acted as guides and escorts and were also consumers of the products – as were the oasis dwellers. During the second half of the nineteenth century, Hail was transformed from a small oasis where only local desert–oasis exchanges had taken place into a major trading station almost equal in importance to the ancient commercial centres of the Hijaz such as Mecca and Madina.

Trade routes from Iraq and Persia to the Hijaz had always been important not only for commerce, but also for the pilgrims who made the *hajj* (pilgrimage) journey every year. As there were no marked roads in the vast desert area between Iraq and the Hijaz, it was absolutely essential for travellers, merchants, and pilgrims to follow routes which would eventually lead to desert wells or to villages and oases where permanent water sources would be found. Jabal Shammar had the advantage of being situated along the route which started from Karbala in Iraq and stretched in a southwesterly direction to reach Hail in the central north of Arabia. From Hail, the route continued to its final destination in the Hijaz region. This route was called Darb Zobeida (the route of Zobeida, the wife of the Abassid Caliph, Haroun Al Rashid). During the rule of her husband, Zobeida gave orders to rebuild the chains of wells along the route and construct caravan stations where travellers and pilgrims could stay and recover from the fatigue of the journey. The proximity of the wells to each other and the convenient relays found along this route facilitated the journey and made it possible to cover the distance in nine to eleven days (S. Al Rasheed 1981: 63, and G. Wallin 1854: 336). Towards the end of the eighteenth century, travellers from Persia and Iraq still used Darb Zobeida which started in Baghdad then turned off to the east where the village of Linah was, to avoid crossing the Great Nafud Desert. From Linah, the road went across the desert to Hail, then continued to Madina. (Manzil al Hajj itinerary, from Iraq to Mecca, MS, British Museum, Add 16. 741)

In the nineteenth century, Hail continued to play an important role as a caravan station along this route in spite of the emergence of other stations and routes. Some trading caravans started their journey from Kuwait, the Hasa region, Zubeir and Najaf in Iraq, and Syria to Hail, Boreidah, and the Hijaz (see Map 4). The following table shows the diverse trade and pilgrim routes. The starting stations of the caravans were prosperous urban centres in the Arabian Peninsula and outside it. Some were coastal towns with a well-established trade network with Europe and India. For example, the port of Kuwait had commercial relations with the Persian coastal towns and Bombay. The Hasa region on the Arab side of the Persian Gulf also maintained trade relations with India.

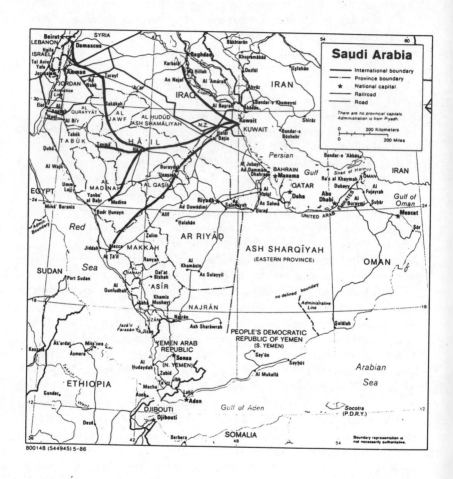

MAP 4: *Trade Routes*

TABLE 3: *Long-distance Trade*

First Station	Towns en Route	Final Destination
Kuwait	Boreidah (Qasim)	Mecca
The Hasa	Riyadh	Mecca
Najaf (Iraq)	Zubeir-Kuwait	Hail
Zubeir (Iraq)		Boreidah (Qasim)
Syria	Al Jauf	Hail

TABLE 4: *Distance between Hail and Major Towns*

From	To	Distance in Miles
Hail	Teima	235
	Al Jauf	270
	Kheibar	230
	Madina	275
	Boreidah	160

Source: *Western Arabia and the Red Sea*, Naval Intelligence Division, Geographical Handbook Series, 1949: 567.

Indian and European products reached the towns of Iraq from India and Persia. These products found their way to central Arabia and Jabal Shammar as they were carried along the ancient *hajj* route.

Wallin was among the first European travellers to notice the advantages of the geographical position of Jabal Shammar: 'Situated in the middle of Northern and Central Arabia, on the very limits of them both, at nearly an equal distance from Damascus, Baghdad and Mekka, midway between the Red Sea and the Persian Gulf, it is the most fit place from which to exercise power and command over the neighbouring countries.' (G. Wallin 1854: 198) However, for Hail to dominate caravan trade and channel commercial traffic to its advantage, it needed a strong political and military leadership without which the protection of trading caravans would have been difficult if not impossible. In the second half of the nineteenth century, this leadership was provided by the Rashidi amirs, who were able to establish peace and order in the oases under their control and along the trade routes leading to Hail.

The amirs created a police force whose main role was to enforce

order and protect property in the market of Hail. The security of
the Rashidi territory, coupled with the advantages of its geographical position, predisposed Hail to compete with other towns
in central Arabia, such as Unaizah, Boreidah and Riyadh, over the
control of the caravan trade. Most of these towns were not self-
sufficient; consequently, their population and that of the surrounding deserts depended for their livelihood on the caravan
trade. With the rise of Saudi–Wahhabi domination in the
eighteenth century, Deraiya started to play the role of a caravan
transit station. Saudi–Wahhabi expansion and military hegemony
enabled them to force pilgrims and trading caravans to cross their
territory and pay tribute to them. However, the rise of Deraiya was
linked to the military and political hegemony of its leadership. In
the nineteenth century, the weakened imams were unable to
exercise any further control over the caravan trade coming from
Mesopotamia. Their new capital, Riyadh, was not established as
an important commercial centre and their decline was followed by
the withdrawal of the Turko-Egyptian troops from central Arabia
to the Hijaz, leaving a power vacuum in central Arabia. When the
major towns and oases of the region entered into competition with
each other for the caravan traffic, Hail was able to win as its amirs
extended their domination over territories outside Jabal Shammar
and sent their own trading caravans from Hail to Mesopotamia.
Revenues from trade enabled them to maintain their political
leadership as it accrued to them substantial revenues derived from
the tribute which they collected from the merchants and those who
were involved in trade. This tribute was partially invested in the
amelioration of their military force which in turn further enforced
their control over the commercial traffic.

The existence of a relatively 'liberal' attitude towards trade and
foreign merchants among the Rashidi amirs has been referred to in
Chapter 3. The European travellers who visited Hail in the
nineteenth century described the oasis as a place where the security
of the foreigner and the non-Muslim was established. Palgrave
described Hail under the leadership of Talal Ibn Rashid, asserting
that Talal 'exerted his ability to persuade Jews and Christians from
the north to take up their abode in his capital, where he promised
them entire security and free exercise of religion.' (W. Palgrave
1865: 130). Doughty also claimed that he stayed in a small house
in Hail which had already been occupied by a Jew from Baghdad
who had converted to Islam and was married to a woman in the

town (C. Doughty 1979: 596). Consequently, 'the Emir licensed him to live at Hayil, where buying and selling . . . he was now a thriving tradesmen.' (ibid 602)

The amirs also expressed tolerance for the religious beliefs of Shiite merchants who needed the protection and the assurance that their lives and property were safe. While in Hail, Doughty reported that he met a rich foreign merchant, Seyyid Mahmud, 'the chief of the Meshahada [the Shiite tradesmen from Mashad Ali], some thirty five families, who are established in Hayil; the Bazaar merchandise [wares of Mesopotamia] is mostly in their hands.' (ibid) Palgrave also confirms that 'merchants from Basra, from Meshid Alee and Wasit, shopkeepers from Medinah and even from Yemen, were invited by liberal offers to come and establish themselves in the new market of Hayel.' (W. Palgrave 1865: 130)

The amirs also allowed local merchants – especially those of the Qasim region – to migrate to Hail to set up their shops and businesses. The Qasimi merchants were renowned in central Arabia for their trading and entrepreneurial skills (S. Altorki and D. Cole 1989). For years they had resented Wahhabi fanaticism in their territory, which condemned the sale and consumption of a number of luxury items such as coffee, tobacco and silk. In southern Najd, the Saudi–Wahhabi imams imposed on themselves and the communities which fell under their domination a strict moral code and were hostile to those local merchants and foreign traders who brought such goods from Mesopotamia and Persia, the majority of whom were Shiites. Wallin noticed this hostility:

In the first days of the Wahhabees, tobacco for instance, was prohibited without any reserve . . . the use of silk was interdicted . . . music, poetry and the other amusements were condemned; restrain was put upon rice, as a food not in use among the Arabs at the time of the prophet . . . friendly intercourse with every other sect of Muslims was regarded as illicit, and war preached against them as a holy duty. (G. Wallin 1854: 183)

Wahhabism regarded Shiism as an innovation worse than *kufr* (blasphemy). As both Shiite pilgrims and traders were physically harassed in Saudi–Wahhabi territory, they avoided it. In contrast, the Hail amirs tolerated religious differences and encouraged trade in luxury goods – some indeed, were themselves consumers of these goods. For example, Palgrave mentions that Talal Ibn Rashid was 'rumoured to indulge in the heretical pleasures of tobacco, to wear silk' (W. Palgrave 1865: 131). Wallin also confirms that the Hail population was more tolerant of certain ways of dress: 'for instance, a man may perform his devotion in a dress which is mixed with one-half silk; at other times he may dress wholly in silk . . . Tobacco is tolerated, and seems to become more common again.' (G. Wallin 1854: 183) Euting described smoking in the streets of Hail without invoking hostility: 'I began to smoke in the streets and it seems that this was accepted so smoothly that the people from the Bazaar, the shops and the houses brought me out a light whenever I needed one.' (J. Euting in P. Ward 1983: 625)

Thus, Hail became an important transit station on the trade routes which linked the markets of Iraq, Persia and the Persian Gulf to central Arabia and the Hijaz. The major commodities of this long-distance commercial network were weapons, carpets, jewellery, shoes, rice, corn, tobacco, coffee, spices, and perfumes. These products were produced or manufactured in Iraq, Persia, India or Europe. Although Hail was not the major producer or consumer of these products, its leadership succeeded in both attracting the caravan trade and forcing it to pass through their territory – as well as having an active involvement in this trade. The Hail caravans left the oasis four times every year; they proceeded with their animals, mainly camels and horses, wool, and clarified butter to Iraq. These products were basically produced by the Shammar.

It was common for the Hail caravans to be accompanied by a leader and a group of armed men who were responsible for security. Once the caravans left Shammar territory, they became vulnerable to attacks as they entered the customary territory of other tribes. It was the responsibility of the caravan leader and the armed men under his command to guarantee the safe passage of the caravan and the merchants who placed themselves under their protection. In most cases, the caravan leader was appointed by the amir who expected him to levy a toll from the caravan after keeping a sum for himself. The toll was paid by the merchants who had their commodities carried by the caravan. Musil described this arrangement:

> The leader counts the camels before they enter Irak and levies a toll for the prince of a quarter Megidijje (23 cents) on each camel from the bedouins, a half Megidijje per camel from the

merchants and also an indeterminate sum for himself. As the
caravans often number more than a thousand camels and a toll
is demanded on the return journey, also the leader earns a
considerable sum. (A. Musil 1928a: 241)

Some members of the Rashidi family were themselves caravan
leaders. Talal Ibn Rashid, for example, provided an escort of 600
men, commanded by his brother Mitab, for the Mesopotamia
caravan which went every year from Baghdad to Mecca (C.
Guarmani 1938: 92). Also, Mohammad Ibn Rashid was an active
supporter of the long-distance trade as he was a renowned caravan
leader before he became amir of Hail in 1869. The amir put the
Hail caravans under his protection in exchange for the toll paid by
those participating in trade.

The commercial links between Hail and Mesopotamia encouraged the prosperity of the oasis market which became the
trading centre for the Shammar and the sedentary population of
the adjacent oases. Hail became the seat for oasis–desert exchanges
as it was at the heart of Shammar tribal territory and its safety
encouraged the Shammar to carry out their exchanges there
instead of making the long journey to Iraq. Both the Shammar and
the sedentary population of the oases were attracted to the Hail
market which provided a number of services for commercial
transactions. For example, a *maslakha* (slaughter house) was
available in the market and this encouraged the organization of the
sale of animals.

In addition, Hail had a small community of manufacturers and
artisans. Lorimer claims that:

artisans are not many; they belong to the smiths' caste and their
implements are few and clumsy; nevertheless, copperware,
spearheads, and horse shoes are manufactured, wooden bowls
are turned, and camel saddles are built . . . Women embroiderers
in silk and metal thread do a small business. The largest trading
capital in Hail probably does not exceed £300. (J. Lorimer 1908:
601 vol IIA).

This limited industry, coupled with the flourishing caravan trade
provided a variety of essential and luxury goods. The market was
no longer a small open space where nomads and oasis-dwellers
carried out local exchanges which were almost an extension of their

subsistence economy. The market was distinguished from those of other small oases by the fact that its trade was a specialized activity carried out by a merchant community which resided in Hail and owned permanent shops in the oasis.

The market-place called Al Mabi consisted of almost 140 shops in which the various goods were displayed on a permanent basis. These shops were constructed by the amir in the 1860s and rented to the merchants of the oasis (ibid: 601 vol. IIA). There was also an enclosure set apart for female stall-keepers who sold a variety of products such as ornaments, perfumes, female attire, dates and vegetables. Lorimer claims that even cooked food was displayed for sale in the open market and there were many cook-shops mostly kept by Persians in Hail (ibid). Perhaps these catered for the travellers and pilgrims who arrived in Hail during the *hajj* season and stayed in the oasis for some time.

In addition to oasis–desert trade, Hail also served local oasis trade between the inhabitants of the oasis itself. These included the merchants, farmers, craftsmen, and slaves. The farmers sold their produce – which consisted mainly of dates and, to a lesser extent, wheat, vegetables, fruits, and corn – to the consumers either directly or through a broker who acted as a link between the two groups. Both immediate and postponed modes of payment were practised. Postponed payment required the buyer to pay a sum of money to the producer at the beginning of the agricultural season. When the produce was ready, usually at the end of the summer season in the case of dates, the farmer had to provide an amount of dates in return for the cash received earlier in the year. Postponed payment operated as a credit system which helped the farmers at the beginning of the agricultural cycle when they often had nothing to sell and lacked the cash to buy what they needed.

The currencies used in these commercial transactions varied. In Hail and most parts of the Arabian Peninsula the Ottoman lira and magidi were frequently used. In addition, local currencies such as the ahmar, tawila, qirsh, and bara were common (see Table 5). Doughty reported that the commercial transactions in Hail were carried out in foreign money: 'All their dealings are in foreign money; reals of Spain, Maria Theresa dollars, Turkish mejidy crowns; gold money is known more than seen among them. They call doubloon the piece of 5 Turkish pounds, English sovereigns ginniyat or bintu, and the 20 fr. piece lira fransawy.' (C. Doughty 1979: 9) Paper money was not used in the Rashidi dynasty. Euting

TABLE 5: *Currencies in Central Arabia*

Currency	Equivalent in Foreign Currency	Make
Ahmar	½ Ottoman Lira	Gold
Mohamadia		
Qirsh	⅓ French Riyal	5 g silver
Tawila		Silver or copper
Bara	Turkish money	
Magidie	Turkish money	

described the Hail amir enquiring about the existence of such notes in Europe. He explained that this was true and showed the amir a note of 100 marks. (J. Euting in P. Ward 1983: 559–60). It is worth noting that the Hail amirs did not attempt to issue any currencies or coins for use within their territory. This would inevitably have been regarded by the Ottoman government which still claimed sovereignty over the region, as an infringement on its jurisdiction and hegemony.

In summary, the Hail market prospered as a result of three types of interrelated trade: long-distance caravan trade, oasis–desert trade, and local oasis trade. Without the caravan trade and the commerical link with Mesopotamia and the Persian Gulf, a whole range of goods would not have been made available in the market. The caravan trade was also entangled with the availability of substantial means of transport, the camels of the Shammar provided such means. Oasis–desert trade brought these animals to the market where they were hired or purchased by the merchants to use in long-distance caravan trade. Limited local production and the inability of the population to maintain self-sufficiency made trade links with more productive and fertile regions essential.

Trading relations had, in addition to their economic benefits, a non-financial advantage. Caravan trade and oasis–desert trade contributed to the creation of information networks between various groups. These networks covered a variety of issues ranging from the conditions of grazing land, to the availability of water in distant regions. This information was essential for the nomadic population which was dependent for migration on such news. Foreign traders travelling between regions outside the reach of the nomads were able to bring news concerning the climatic conditions existing in distant areas. Trading caravans were also useful for the sedentary population in Hail and all those unable to travel outside the oasis. The caravans diminished the social isolation of the oasis dwellers as they became aware of the social and political conditions in Iraq, Syria, the Hijaz, and the Persian Gulf. The variety of imported spices, consumption of rice, coffee, and tobacco changed the life-styles and food habits of the Hail population.

The Hail amirs also benefited from the trading caravans in a non-financial way. Their messengers to the Ottoman officials and governors in Syria and Iraq travelled along the same routes as the merchants and negotiated with the Ottoman officials on their behalf. On their return to Hail they brought various kinds of subsidies in cash and kind such as gifts of rice, grain, ammunition and weapons. The amirs also sent spies to seek out information regarding the military strength of their adversaries, news about the alliances which were being formed between the various tribes in the neighbouring territories, and the preparation for raids by hostile groups. Such information was either delivered by their own messengers or brought to their attention by travellers and merchants.

An important characteristic of the Hail market was that it became an intra-tribal market. The Shammar and the oasis-dwellers, the majority of whom belonged to Bani Tamim, were not the only participants in trade. Other non-Shammar groups under the protection of the Rashidi amirs were encouraged to visit Hail as they were guaranteed safety and protection from attack. The amirs' expansion brought under their control a tribally heterogeneous population which either resided in the adjacent oases or remained nomadic in the surrounding deserts. For example, the inhabitants of Jubba, a very isolated oasis in the Great Nafud Desert, were a mixture of Shammar and non-Shammar tribesmen. Its Shammar inhabitants belonged to the Rumal section whereas others claimed descent from the Rwala, the Bushir, and the Tukara sections of the Anizah tribe. Moreover, others were members of the Shararat and Hawazim who had already allied themselves with the Shammar. The isolation of the oasis in the middle of the desert made it less attractive for merchants to visit or lead their caravans near its borders. Consequently, its tribally mixed population got their clothes and the small supplies of rice which they wanted from Hail (G. Wallin 1854: 163).

Hail became a place where a tribally mixed population could meet and intermingle peacefully. This interaction in the market was achieved in a manner different from that observed by anthropologists working on north African or Yemeni tribal markets (E. Gellner 1969, F. Benet 1970, D. Eickelman 1976, H. Geertz, C. Geertz and Rosen 1979, R. Dunn 1977, P. Dresch 1989). To take one example, Dunn argues that everywhere in Morocco, two basic rules governed the operation of the markets to ensure peace and a free flow of trade. First, the market-place had to be a neutral territory, sheltered from the violent eruptions which characterized inter-tribal relations. Secondly, an authority acceptable to all groups who used the market had to enforce peace by imposing sanctions of one kind or another (R. Dunn 1977: 121). The most common and most effective solution was to award jurisdiction to a reputable saint and locate the market near his tomb. The *baraka* (grace) of the saint would cast a protective mantle over the market-place, restraining any potential market-breaker 'with the threat of divine wrath' (ibid: 122).

Similarly, in pre-Islamic Arabia, this pattern was described by Wolf in his study of Mecca. The ancient Arab sanctuary, the Kaaba, was surrounded by a sacred area, the Haram, where no blood could be shed. The famous Meccan tribe, Koreish, consciously sought to extend the sacred precinct as a means of increasing the stability of social relations in their trading territory (E. Wolf 1951). The sacredness of the territory made Mecca a safe place for trade, consequently, its market attracted a tribally heterogeneous population. Kister also argued that Mecca, a small centre for the distribution of goods for the bedouin tribes in the vicinity of the city, rose to the position of an important centre of transit trade. It was the merchants of Mecca who carried the wares to Syria, Abyssinia, Iraq, and Yemen:

> The trade based on the pacts of ilaf was a joint enterprise of the clans of Quraysh headed by the family of Abd Manaf. The pacts concluded with tribes were based on a hitherto unknown principle of trade interest . . . The ilaf agreements were set up on a base of share of profit for the heads of the tribes and apparently employment of the men of the tribes as escort of the caravan . . . This accrued to the tribes a stable profit . . . They were welcomed in Mecca and could enter without fear. (M. Kister 1965: 120–1)

According to Kister, one may assume that the *ilaf* agreement referred to the observation of the sacred months, namely keeping of peace during these months and respecting the sanctity (or the inviolability) of Mecca. Apparently, the *ilaf* system was invented by the Koreish merchants of Mecca as a further guarantee for the safety of the caravans, as there were in the vicinity of the city some nomadic tribes who did not respect the sanctity of the Haram. They consequently created this economic bond to further the ties with the nomads who became entangled with the caravan traffic.

Peace in the Hail market which enabled non-Shammar tribesmen to carry out their exchanges without the threat of an uncontrolled outbreak of violence was established without invoking an authority of a religious or sacred nature. It must be remembered that in the eighteenth and nineteenth centuries, Wahhabism condemned saint worship and endeavoured to destroy the tombs of saints including that of the Prophet Mohammad and the early caliphs. This was done in an attempt to eliminate mediation between man and God as these sites were the physical representation of such practices. However, although actual Wahhabi power was on the decline in the nineteenth century, its influence and teachings were still respected and felt in central Arabia including Jabal Shammar. The basic tenet of Wahhabism which the Shammar adhered to was 'the rejection of all Saints, even the Prophet himself as mediator between God and man' (G. Wallin 1854: 184). Rejection of saint worship rendered impossible the north African alternative relating to the sacredness of saints' territory and tombs which contributed to the maintenance of peace. Consequently, peace in the market-place was established as a result of two mechanisms: first, the amirs created a permanent armed force whose duty was to enforce peace and order, protect property and punish criminals, thieves and robbers.[1] This was combined with an important traditional arrangement, the *khuwa* system (brotherly tax or a tribute collected in return for protection).[2] The maintenance of peace and order were essential conditions for the promotion of caravan trade, and were also important in attracting the pilgrim caravans.

THE PILGRIMS

Hail was also established as a major pilgrimage station in central Arabia in the nineteenth century. As mentioned before, pilgrimage routes from Iraq and Persia to the Hijaz coincided with the routes of the trading caravans. The hegemony of the Rashidi amirs and the security of their territories enabled them to maintain the safe passage of the annual *hajj* caravans through their capital and on the routes leading to the capital.

The majority of pilgrims from Mesopotamia and Persia were Shiites. At the end of the eighteenth century, Saudi–Wahhabi military activities in southern Iraq led to the plundering of the Persian pilgrims who were travelling between Hilah and Meshad Ali (S. Al Rasheed 1981: 64). Consequently, these pilgrims felt unsafe while travelling in Saudi territories and in later years tried to avoid the route which led to Deraiya. The pilgrims preferred the ancient route, Darb Zobeida, which passed through Hail and Jabal Shammar. The rulers of the first Saudi–Wahhabi dynasty tried constantly to divert the pilgrim caravans from Hail to Deraiya and other parts of their territories. Burckhardt reported that the pilgrims' caravan from Iraq and Persia had perforce to travel through the territory of the Wahhabis in 1815 (Burckhardt 1831: 251). During the second Saudi–Wahhabi dynasty, the Saudi imams also wanted to establish their new capital Riyadh as a major *hajj* station and an alternative to Hail. However, the fanaticism and hostility of the eighteenth-century followers of Wahhabism continued to deter the Shiite pilgrims.[3] Palgrave described how they were still badly treated in southern Najd in the second half of the nineteenth century:

Feyzul, after extracting the exorbitant sum which Wahhabi orthodoxy claims from Shiite heretics as the price of permission to visit the sacred city and the tomb of the Prophet, had assigned them for a guide and a leader one Abdulaziz abu Botein, who was to conduct and plunder them in the name of God and the true faith all the rest of the way to Mecca and back again ... 40 gold Tumans were fixed as the claim of the Wahhabee treasury on every Persian pilgrim for his passage through Riad and 40 more for a safe conduct through the rest of the Empire. (G. Palgrave 1865: 160 vol I)

Such treatment of the Persian pilgrims acted in favour of the promotion of the route passing through Hail. The fairly liberal attitude in Hail encouraged the pilgrims to use the oasis and the

Rashidi amirs took the responsibility of protecting the Persian pilgrims in their territory. Palgrave states that Talal Ibn Rashid conducted negotiations with the Shah of Persia to obtain the passage of the annual *hajj* caravans through his territory. Palgrave also claims that the Persian pilgrims expressed their gratitude for the good treatment of Ibn Rashid and his brother Mitab who was in charge of the *hajj* affairs at that time (W. Palgrave 1865: 196–7 vol I). Guarmani confirms that Talal Ibn Rashid provided 600 armed men to escort the Persian pilgrims under the command of his brother Mitab (C. Guarmani 1938: 43). However, negotiations were not the only means which allowed the pilgrims to travel via Hail on their way to the Hijaz. Musil says of Mohammad Ibn Rashid that 'by means of presents and threats, he induced all the caravan leaders to conduct their caravans by way of his capital Hajel. Thus the pilgrim caravan travelled no longer by al Hasa and ar-Rijad but by Abu-Rar, Tkajjec and Hajel.' (A. Musil 1928a: 239)

The pilgrimage season benefited the Shammar who offered their camels to be rented by the pilgrims as means of transport. Their knowledge of the desert routes and location of wells meant that they were sought by the foreign pilgrims as escorts and guides. The Shammar travelled with the *hajj* caravans back to Iraq to purchase rice and wheat. Blunt commented that 'They are going on afterwards with the Haj as far as Meshad Ali, or perhaps to Samawa on the Euphrates to buy rice (tummin), and wheat. It is only twice a year that the tribes of Jebel Shammar can communicate with the outside world; on the occasion of the two Haj journeys.' (A. Blunt 1968: 40 vol II) The involvement of the Shammar in the *hajj* caravans supplemented their pastoral economy and contributed to the diversification of their economic resources.

Equally, the sedentary population of Hail and particularly the merchants benefited from the diversion of the *Hajj* caravans to Hail. The pilgrims brought with them various goods which they were prepared to sell or exchange for services needed for their journey to the Hijaz. As they encamped for a few days in the vicinity of Hail, they visited the market and carried out their economic exchanges, hired camels and bought food. The Rashidi amirs used to delay the departure of the caravans so that the pilgrims would spend more time selling and buying various products. As the pilgrims were not allowed to travel without the amir's permission which guaranteed their safety and protection, they had no choice but to wait in Hail.

The amirs supervised the *hajj* caravans by appointing a leader for each. Their flag (*bairag*) was carried with the caravan, a gesture indicating that the caravan was under their protection. The amirs also assigned a police force mounted on camels to protect the pilgrims and interfere in case of an outbreak of violence. The main task of this force was to protect the pilgrims against attacks by the tribes encamped along the pilgrimage route. Raids on the caravans and the plundering of their possessions constituted an important source of income for groups such as the Harb tribe whose territory was between Hail and Madina. In return for protection, the amirs collected a toll from the pilgrims. Musil claims that:

> Everyone of the pilgrims, who sometimes numbered ten thousand, had to pay for water and for his camels thirty megidijjat ($25) on the outward and fifteen megidijjat on the return journey. Furthermore a portion of all goods imported or transported by the pilgrims was exacted as toll. In this manner Mohammad increased the prosperity not merely of the ruling house but of the settlers who acted as merchants and of the bedouins who were accustomed to hire out their camels to the caravans. (A. Musil 1928a: 239)

The tax imposed on the caravans varied from year to year according to the security of the routes, the amir's needs and the number of travelling pilgrims. Leachman mentions that during his visit to Ibn Rashid's camp in 1909, Ibn Rashid had only taken 2½ liras (45 shillings) from each pilgrim and 17 reals (51 shillings) for the hiring of each camel (G.E. Leachman 1910: 265–74 vol 37). This toll from the pilgrims, coupled with the tax levied from trade, accrued to the amirs a substantial income. They were able to further increase their revenues through the *khuwa* system.

TRIBUTE: THE *KHUWA* SYSTEM

The term *khuwa* is derived from the Arabic root *akh* meaning brother. In this context, it is translated as tribute to denote occasional or regular requisitions from conquered tribes. Tribute is defined as a tax levied not upon the collector's own community, but rather upon a conquered alien community which remains more or less autonomous (A. Pershits 1979: 149–56 and 1966). Traditionally strong camel-herding tribes of the Arabian Peninsula such as the Shammar and the Rwala imposed on the weaker groups, usually the sheep- and goat-herders and the weakened camel-herders, a tribute paid in cash or kind such as sheep, dairy products, and clarified butter. This tribute was an economic arrangement with a social and political significance. The payment of the *khuwa* symbolized an arrangement between two unequal parties joined together in a brotherly relationship. In return for payment, the givers were guaranteed a number of rights. First, when the givers were sheep- or goat-herders, they were entitled to encamp in the tribal territory of the receivers. They gained rights to share the use of pasture land and wells of the *khuwa* receivers, hence the economic function of the system.

Secondly, the economic transaction which was established upon payment, was extended to cover the obligation to protect and defend the weaker party in the relationship. The receivers were expected to act as patrons who were under an obligation to guard the interest of the *khuwa* givers. Thus, the system fostered the development of obligations and rights which were usually created as a result of kinship and tribal descent. Consequently, the *khuwa* established social and political relations which were otherwise created out of traditional social organization.

In addition, the *khuwa* was a form of partnership which joined together the nomadic and the sedentary population of the oases and towns. In Jabal Shammar, the oases were encircled by the desert area inhabited by the nomads who, because of their mobility and military supremacy, could control all routes leading to the oases and villages. The sedentary population paid the *khuwa* to the camel-herders in return for the protection of their markets, property and agricultural fields. This also ensured that trade and caravan routes leading to the oases remained safe, open, and immune from attack by the surrounding nomads. Oasis dwellers gave the nomads a share of their agricultural produce, mainly dates, in return for protection against attacks often by the receivers themselves or by other nomadic groups. Consequently, this guaranteed that the nomads and the oasis dwellers were bound in an organic exchange system at the economic, social, and political levels. The nomads needed the agricultural produce of the oases and the goods in their markets. Equally, the oasis dwellers relied on the nomads for their supply of meat, wool, and other animal products. Above all, the oasis dwellers had to maintain good relations with the nomads who were capable of disrupting all lines of supplies and trade routes leading to the oases, plundering the oases, cutting their date plantations and ruining the sources of their livelihood. The *khuwa* was, therefore, an insurance token paid to cement the peaceful coexistence of the nomads and the sedentary populations.[4]

When the Rashidi amirs took control of Hail in 1836, this system remained operative. Their expansion beyond Hail and Jabal Shammar in the nineteenth century brought under their control a nomadic and sedentary population of non-Shammar tribal origin. Whether they placed themselves willingly under the protection of the amirs or were forced to come under their domination, these groups became tributary to the amirs as they paid the *khuwa*. The majority of the nomadic tributary community consisted of sheep- or goat-herders and weakened camel-herders who were forced out of the best productive areas for camel breedings into less suitable or marginal areas (H. Rosenfield 1965: 76 and Glubb 1935: 14). Those who paid *khuwa* were given permission to utilize the grazing land of the Shammar. In the nineteenth century, the nomadic tributary community consisted of Bani Wahhab, the Fejir, Bishr, and Awlad Ali in addition to sections of the Hetym and Shararat tribes (C. Doughty 1979: 35 vol II). These were protected against raids by other powerful tribes in the area. The amirs were under the obligation to restore their stolen property and camels if they came under attack.

In addition to the nomadic tribes, the population of the oases – merchants, artisans and farmers – also became tributary to the Hail amirs. The payment of tribute guaranteed the security of the market, trade routes and agricultural land. In return for tribute, the amirs played a policing role as they inhibited theft and robbery. The amirs' protection was extended to the oases of Al Jauf, Kheibar, and Teima. During the rule of Mohammad Ibn Rashid even Palmyra in the Syrian desert became tributary.

Payment of tribute was regulated in cash, agricultural produce, or in animals. The amirs were eager to fix the amount of tribute as follows: ¼ Maria Theresa dollars on each camel under ten camels being exempt, ¼ Ottoman lira on each 40 sheep under forty sheep

being exempt. With respect to the agricultural tributary community, tribute amounted to 5 per cent of the agricultural produce
including dates (IOR, R/15/5/25).[5] The tribute collected from the
oases exceeded that collected from the nomadic population.
Doughty claims that 'the burden of the Emir's public contribution
is levied in the settlements upon the fruits of corn and dates . . .
nearly £1 sterling from every head; and among the nomads . . .
about £1 sterling for eight or ten persons.' (C. Doughty 1979: 34–5
vol II)

The amir's revenue from tribute was estimated to be £40,000 in
1876 and £60,000 in 1888 (ibid and A. Blunt 1968: 267). It is
noteworthy that the tributary groups were not constant over time.
Various nomadic tribes and oases dwellers were forced to enter
into *khuwa* relations with Hail whereas others were lost to
neighbouring rival power centres. The collection of tribute was
dependent on the amirs' military ability. With the decline of their
hegemony in the twentieth century, they lost their domination over
the oasis of Al Jauf which switched allegiance to the Shaalans, the
amirs of the Rwala tribe (on the Shaalan, see A. Musil 1928, W.
Lancaster 1981 and IOR R/15/5/25). Rosenfeld describes this
interconnectedness between the *khuwa* system and military hegemony: 'Greater power means increased tribute payments, tributary
groups and honour, reduced power means less ability to receive
tribute, less recognition and, as the group itself becomes tributary,
gradual reduction on the status scale of honour.' (H. Rosenfeld
1965: 79)

Rosenfeld argues that the Rashidi dynasty was a trade state at
its core, a tribute state in relation to its periphery. He claims that
the tribute payers were left with their social structures intact –
structures which were often no different from that of their overlord
(ibid 183–4). In other words, while the ruling group maintained its
commercial interests, their subjects remained either nomadic or
oasis agriculturalists. No attempt at economic integration was
made.

Three criticisms and elaborations of Rosenfeld's arguments can
be made. The first is related to his proposition that increase in
tribute payment was proportional to increase in power. This was
very true in Hail, but most importantly increase in power led to
change in the meaning of *khuwa*. With the consolidation of Rashidi
power, *khuwa* relations gradually lost their 'brotherly' connotation.
The expansion of the Rashidi realm prevented the maintenance of

face-to-face interaction between the *khuwa* givers and receivers, in particular the relationship between the *akh* who put the former under his wing and defended his interests.[6] The *akh* played the role of advocate for the weak party among his tribal group. He was under the obligation to restore to the *khuwa* givers any property which his fellow tribesmen had stolen from them (A. Musil 1928a: 60). With the rise of Rashidi hegemony, the *khuwa* began to stand for an economic transaction symbolizing relations of political domination rather than relations of a brotherly nature. The amirs did not wait for weaker groups to voluntarily place themselves under their protection, rather they imposed the *khuwa* on other groups, including the nomads and the sedentary population.

Secondly, Rosenfeld's claims that there was no social and economic integration between the amirs and their nomadic and sedentary subjects need to be qualified. Social integration, as will be shown in Chapter 7, was maintained through the marriage practices of the amirs. As the latter married into the nomadic Shammar sheikhly families, they created kinship, social, and political ties with the hinterland. With respect to economic integration, as discussed earlier both the sedentary and nomadic groups had a stake in the maintenance of the Hail power structure for they were both involved in the caravan economy.

Thirdly, part of the tribute collected by the amirs was redistributed among their subjects in the form of subsidies to tribal sheikhs, gifts and daily feasts for their guests. An obligation to share the *khuwa* revenues was strongly held by both the amirs and their subjects. The importance of the ruler's reputation for generosity and benevolence acted as a check against the accumulation of wealth. In order to maintain their position as legitimate rulers, the amirs had to spend lavishly on their followers, entertain them in Hail and bestow on them various favours. The redistribution of wealth took place through the institutionalization of generosity. The amirs kept the tradition of offering daily meals for those who attended their *majlis* (council) and expressed their loyalty (A. Blunt 1968: 268 vol I and C. Doughty 1979: 35 vol II). This increased their popularity in the eyes of their subjects. This policy was in line with Shammar expectations which were reflected in their saying '*al amir saif wa mansaf*'. Literally this means that the amir is someone who owns a sword and gives food. In other words, the true amir is one who is militarily strong and is capable of giving generously.

Subsidies from the amirs to Shammar and non-Shammar tribal

sections were another means through which wealth was re-distributed. The subsidies consisted of cash handouts to individual tribesmen and their sheikhs as well as dates, rice, grain, weapons and so on. The sheikhs visited Hail with the intention of asking for help, often during periods of drought, natural disasters, and raids which considerably diminished the number of nomadic herds. To maintain their subsistence, the Shammar relied on handouts from the amirs. The amirs realized that failure to provide these subsidies would jeopardize their legitimacy. The subsidies guaranteed the loyalty of the Shammar and of other non-Shammar groups who were not ready to offer their allegiance for nothing.

The subsidy system functioned as a mechanism for the circulation of wealth which promised the loyalty of the subjects. The revenues from the trade economy, consequently, benefited not only the amirs, but also their nomadic subjects and it is, therefore, inappropriate to talk about lack of economic integration between the two groups.

However, as the nomads remained militarily strong, they challenged from time to time the authority of the amirs. For example the tributary Harb tribe whose territory was between Hail and Madina, continued to raid the trading and pilgrims' caravans which had already placed themselves under the protection of the amirs. Despite the economic and social integration between the Hail centre and its nomadic periphery, there was no real military integration. The amirs did not have monopoly over the means of coercion as it was difficult to break the military strength of the tribal nomadic sections.[7] The military hegemony of the tribes was occasionally neutralized through subsidies and the frequent raids which the amirs launched against disobedient and disloyal tribes.

To sum up, the rise of the Rashidi amirs to power and their expansion contributed to their control over trade and pilgrims' caravans, and allowed them to have control over a wider base which consisted of tributary sedentary and nomadic population. This accrued to them substantial revenues which they invested in subsidizing tribal groups and in increasing their means of coercion. The inter-connection between military power and economic power was a cyclical process. The two factors, power and tribute, were interdependent; the alteration of one factor automatically affected the other. The more power the amirs had, the more they were able to collect tribute. Equally, more tribute meant more powers. The reverse of the cycle was also possible. Less military power meant

no effective control over trade, pilgrims, and subjects, consequently, less tribute. Any decrease in tribute meant less subsidies,
less loyalty, and a diminished ability to invest in the means of
coercion. As a result, the amirs' power would inevitably be affected
and would tend to decrease.

The caravan economy was a significant factor in the consolidation of the amirs' leadership and the further centralization of their
powers. The Rashidi case is not unique in this respect. Lacoste, in
his commentary on Ibn Khaldun's work, noticed the relevance of
trade routes and in particular, *tarik al dhahab* (the gold route), in
the establishment of centralized authority in the Maghreb (Lacoste
1966). Furthermore, the region between Damascus and Riyadh
witnessed the emergence of the three powerful dynasties in Arabia,
the Rwala (A. Musil 1927 and W. Lancaster 1981), the Rashidi
and the Saudi (R. Winder 1965) power centres. Trade provided the
surplus which guaranteed the manipulation of tribal raids and a
substitute for these raids. Consequently, stable political leadership
emerged along the Damascus–Riyadh axis and provided the means
to ensure the safety of trade routes by exercising direct control over
the tribes and their heads, or by bribing tribal sheikhs to contain
their military hegemony in the desert.

STATUS GROUPS AND STRATIFICATION

One of the outstanding features of Jabal Shammar, with the
exception of Hail, was the ethnic and linguistic homogeneity of the
population. Status groups were not characterized on the basis of
ethnicity or language. Rather, the nomad versus sedentary
distinction (*badu vs hadar*) had always been the axis dividing the
population into two distinct, but not necessarily isolated groups. It
has been shown earlier in this book that the sedentary and
nomadic population of the region had always been engaged in
intense social, economic and political interaction.

Nevertheless, both the *badu* and the *hadar* developed their own
distinct identities and self-images. The study of local self-
perceptions in the nineteenth century and the way both groups
maintained their separateness requires a diversity of sources of
information. For this purpose, I use the literature of the European
travellers of the nineteenth century who had the opportunity to
come into contact with both groups and to document some of the

values, attributes, self-images, and local perceptions which they held of themselves and of others.[8] In addition, I rely on the still remembered and recited oral poetry of the Shammar and their amirs in which they described themselves and portrayed their values and attributes. These two sources combined should clarify the meaning of being *badu* or *hadar*, why people invoked such identities and how relevant it was to emphasize which group one belonged to during a period of political centralization carried out by a ruling group who were based in a sedentary environment, yet claimed *badu* origins. In other words, the distinction is regarded as a component of the historical setting in which it is invoked. This distinction was embedded in relations of inequalities relating to status, origin, attributes and power. Consequently, it was not merely a mechanism for categorization which the local population used to maintain their separateness and exclusiveness; it is also relevant to our anthropological understanding of the inter-connection between identity and self-image on the one hand, and history, power, and military hegemony on the other. When people stressed their *badu* identity and origin, they made political claims which placed them in a position superior to that of the *hadar*. Without these claims to superiority, the distinction would be void and irrelevant to the study of social and political relations.

The Badu

It is simplistic to translate the term '*badu*' as pastoral nomads because the word involved something more than animal-herding and nomadism. Although nomadism was an essential component of the notion of *badu*, it was not the determining factor which allowed a group to be so classified. It can be argued that within the context of Arabia, all animal-herders were *badu*, but not all *badu* were pastoral nomads. This was true of the nineteenth century and is still valid in the twentieth century (U. Fabietti 1984, R. Fernea 1985, and W. Lancaster 1981). Groups could still be classified as *badu* even if they were no longer animal-herders. In the nineteenth century, the Shammar tribal sections which took residence in Hail and the other villages of Jabal Shammar while leaving their animal herds with their relatives in the desert, regarded themselves and were regarded by others as *badu*. Wallin described those Shammar sections who inhabited Jubba, the oasis in the Great Nafud Desert: 'Their mode of living is quite the same as that of the nomadic

Bedawies, excepting that they dwell in fixed abodes and houses. Most of them possess great herds of camels, which they either give in charge to their bedawy brothers, or send out with their own herdsmen on the pasture grounds in the neighbourhood of their village.' (G. Wallin 1854: 163)

Being sedentarized does not necessarily mean the loss of *badu* identity and values. In fact some of the 'sedentarized *badu*' were renowned for their military superiority which exceeded that of their brothers in the desert: 'Contrary to the inhabitants of other desert villages, the townspeople of the Shammar are regarded as superior to their bedawy brothers in courage and in the art of using arms; and it is doubtlessly more to them, than to the nomads, that the sheikh family of Ibnu Alrashid owe the victories they have gained over all their neighbours.' (ibid: 178) Although these sedentarized sections were no longer practising camel-herding, they continued to own camels and endorse *badu* values and life styles. Wallin added that 'We find the villagers, to a certain degree, still clinging to the customs and manners of nomadic life, while the bedawies on the other hand, apply themselves to avocations, which are generally regarded as not becoming.' (ibid: 198)

The term *badu* referred to a cultural category which included both the pastoral and the sedentarized nomads. Both shared a set of images of themselves with regard to their tribal origin, values, attributes and qualities. The *badu* often had elaborate genealogies defining their ancestors and lines of descent which they located in a distant past. These genealogies were ideologies of descent invoked to justify their high status arising from their links with ancient Arab tribes. They emphasized their *asil* (nobility) and the purity of their origin uncontaminated by contacts and marriages with outsiders. In their oral poetry, they had images of themselves as pure Arabs of traceable and unmixed origins, an asset which guaranteed superiority *vis-à-vis* other groups, especially the *hadar* – who were considered to have lost the purity of descent, or to have had no noble descent at all. In addition, the *badu* held a set of values regarding the ideal life-style. They despised occupational specialization and regarded activities other than animal-herding and raids as humiliating and dishonourable. They regarded farmers and artisans as humble, subservient, and weak. These activities, claimed the *badu*, inflicted on those who engaged in them disgrace, humiliation, and vulnerability. The true *badu*, however, was someone who was able to enhance his ascribed status, i.e. his nobility, by achieving a set of valued attributes. To have *asil* without these achieved attributes would immediately place individuals and groups outside the *badu* category.

The *badu* valued their independence and despised submission to higher authority. Although they recognized the authority of their own sheikhs, they did not perceive it as oppressing, binding, or requiring total submission. These conditions were thought to describe the relationship between the *hadar* and their leadership, who were believed to have lost their autonomy as a result of centuries of domination.

Other aspects of *badu* values included those relating to hospitality, defending the weak, and eloquence. The *badu* thought of themselves as generous and capable of providing hospitality – to the extent of sacrificing their only animals to honour a guest. Also, they asserted that a generous *badu* could be identified by the smoke coming out of his tent as a result of continuous food preparations for his guests. He would always help the poor and provide for them and extend his protection to all those asking for it. He would not hesitate to go to war on behalf of his guests and protégés if the latter were attacked in his *hima* (territory within his sphere of influence). The *badu* believed themselves to be the speakers of pure language which was not contaminated by contact with foreigners and non-Arabs, a quality lost by the *hadar*. They believed that eloquence was reflected in their ability to compose *qasaid* (oral poetry) in which their memoirs, deeds, and battles were preserved.[9] These were the self-images held by the *badu*.

Within the category '*badu*', further internal distinctions can be observed. There were those *asil badu* (noble), a group consisting of the camel-herders such as the Shammar, the Anizah, the Dhafir, and the Harb tribesmen. Their nobility of origin, coupled with the military superiority which their camels guaranteed in raids and tribal battles, granted them the highest position in the status hierarchy. The sheep- and goat-herders were also *badu*, but from a group inferior to the *asil badu* as they lacked the means to demonstrate their military supremacy in the desert. The sheep- and goat-herders often placed themselves under the protection of the strong camel-herders, a gesture reflecting their lack of power and loss of independence. Consequently, they were incapable of displaying certain attributes such as chivalry, bravery and courage.

The distinction within the *badu* groups depended little on material wealth and much on non-material assets and attributes.

This was clear in the marriage patterns of the *asil badu*. It was always honourable to marry off one's daughter to a poor, but *asil badu* rather than to give a girl in marriage to a wealthy sheep-herder or a prosperous merchant or farmer from the towns and oases. It was also preferable for sons to marry a *badu* woman of the same group or compatible groups with whom equality of origin and status could be guaranteed. Montagne reported on the Shammar views with regard to the unacceptability of marriages with tribes such as the Shararat or Howeitat whom they considered to be unequal: 'Jamais une fille des Semmar n'épouserait un homme de ces tribus qui appartient à la masse des gens "à la fumée courbe" (awag ed dehhan), ainsi nommés parce qu'on ne verrait jamais s'élever de leur tente de fumée marquant des préparatifs importants pour la réception honourable d'un hôte de passage.' (R. Montagne 1932: 74)

At the bottom of the *badu* society were the Sulab – often hunters of gazelles and ostriches and believed to have no known tribal origin. They never participated in raids and tribal wars. Their property and belongings were not considered to be worth plundering by the strong camel-herding tribes as this would not constitute an activity which would honour those who engaged in it. In addition to their hunting, the Sulab used to manufacture baskets and utensils. They were also guides and travel companions (H.R.P. Dickson 1951). They were known for their gentle manners and their women were reputed to be the prettiest in the whole desert. Huber commented that the Arabs regarded them as an inferior race. 'There is no intermarriage between them and the other Arab tribes. They have no religion and their language lacks the range of holy formulas which Arabic uses so profusely . . . They suffer from the detestable reputation of eating the blood of animals with the dead flesh, and of eating dogs.' (C. Huber in P. Ward 1983: 434) These mythical or real views confirmed the inferior status of the Sulab.

The Shammar regarded other *asil badu* such as the Anizah, Dhafir, Qhatan and so on as their equals. These were either allies of the Shammar and enjoyed good relations with them, or enemies with whom the outbreak of violence and hostilities were frequent occurrences. The Shammar entered into alliance relations with other equal *badu* tribes who constituted the *hilf* (alliance) tribes – a group including at times the Harb, Muntafiq and Dhafir. However, the *hilf* tribes did not form a stable category as the fluctuating nature of intra-tribal political relations allowed tribes to enter into alliance relations with other tribes whenever this suited them, and opt out of these binding agreements when they contradicted their interests.

As descendants of the Shammar Jaafar lineage, the Rashidi amirs of Hail enjoyed a high status in the eyes of their own tribe and other non-Shammar groups recognized them as part of the *badu* nobility. This gave them intra-tribal credibility. Although the amirs settled in Hail, they represented a sedentarized *badu* élite which managed to maintain their cultural contacts with their desert cousins. Their sedentarization was preceded by conquest and the ability to show military hegemony and chivalry, which added to their credibility and increased their prestige. They continued to wear *badu* dress, marry into *badu* families, and endorse *badu* values of bravery, hospitality, courage, and eloquence. They occasionally left their Hail residence and encamped among their *badu* tribesmen in the desert where they prepared for raids, discussed future alliances and demonstrated their military supremacy. At the level of self-image, the Rashidi amirs regarded themselves as *badu* chiefs.

However, differences of wealth began to emerge between them and ordinary *badu* chiefs. Their income was not strictly dependent on local resources. Their revenues were derived from private landownership (date plantations and fruit gardens) in Hail and other oases such as Al Jauf, trade, tribute from the nomadic and sedentary population and subsidies from central governments (mainly the Ottoman Empire). In contrast, ordinary Shammar tribesmen rarely had individual rights to land and only a few Shammar sheikhs owned land and date plantations in the oases. The revenues of the Shammar were highly dependent on pastoral production which was supplemented by subsidies from the amirs and trading contacts with the towns and caravans.

The revenues of the amirs were under their total control through their financial *wazirs* (ministers). The wealth which was accumulated in Barzan palace was displayed in various ways. Euting commented on the amir's wealth:

> Ibn Rashid's treasure was kept in this castle and consists mainly of Turkish and English gold pieces, worth between 1½–2 million pounds sterling, a very large sum, especially in cash, in Arabia. Of course I am not certain if this is accurate, but it is quite possible since Ibn Rashid is very rich and one can estimate that

after deduction of his outgoings there is an annual surplus revenue of approximately 60,000 to 75,000 pounds sterling (J. Euting in P. Ward 1983: 617)

This wealth was spent on military expeditions, warriors, slaves, daily meals for over 300 persons, horses, and subsidies to tribal sheikhs. Doughty estimated the expenses of the amir:

The ordinary government expenses for castle service, for the maintenance of armed bands, the slave groom of his stud and herdsmen of his live wealth in the wilderness, stewards, mutasallims, his residents in outlying towns as Teyma and Jauf, the public hospitality at Hail, and for the changes of clothing may be nearly £1200. His extraordinary expenses are nearly £1000 yearly in gun powder and provision for the general ghrazzus and yearly gifts. (C. Doughty 1979: 35 vol II)

Their wealth and their highly valued *badu* origin, contributed to the transformation of this ruling group into a sedentary *badu* aristocracy which began to have interests not necessarily compatible with those of their fellow tribesmen. By the end of the nineteenth century, the rulers of Hail had been involved in the caravan economy for almost half a century. Their commercial interests coincided with those of the merchant communities. Trade was highly dependent on the establishment of peace and order and this could not have been done without the neutralization of the *badu* tribes and their pacification. The Hail amirs were also interested in maintaining the flow of tribute from the peripheral areas which fell under their control. These areas included sedentary and nomadic groups who resented the imposition of tribute and tried constantly to free themselves from this burden. As a result the amirs organized raids against those rebellious groups and those who challenged their authority by either refusing to pay tribute or by attacking the caravans under their protection.

Furthermore, the amirs had maintained relations with the Ottoman government and its representatives in Syria, Mesopotamia, and the Hijaz since the Egyptian invasion of central Arabia.[10] Ibn Rashid's co-operation with Khurshid Pasha enabled him to receive a monthly allowance from the Egyptian government and to keep one-third of the *zakat* (Islamic tax) of Jabal Shammar for himself. With the withdrawal of the Egyptian troops from Arabia in 1841, the Ottoman government tried to play a more active role in the region. Its representatives in the Hijaz, Iraq, and Syria became the channels which linked local tribal chiefs to the Ottoman Sultan. The second half of the nineteenth century was marked by the revival of Turkish interests and greater involvement in central Arabia. The Rashidi amirs, and in particular Abdullah Ibn Rashid, maintained the tradition of sending gifts (mainly horses) to the Ottoman governors in the region. Wallin reported on this tradition: 'A couple of these animals are sent yearly to Almedina with the pilgrim Karawan as a present for the Turkish Pasha: another couple to Mekka for the governor of the town: sometimes a third for the Pasha of Baghdad.' (G. Wallin 1854: 188)

Mohammad Ibn Rashid also negotiated with the Ottoman governor of Damascus the payment of 1500 majidie per year in return for his subjugation of Al Jauf. Moreover, he had an obligation towards the Sherif of Madina: 'He paid a small sum yearly in tribute to the Sherif of Medina, partly as a religious offering, partly to insure immunity for his outlying possessions, Kheybar, Kaf, and the rest from Turkish aggression.' (A. Blunt 1968: 267–8 vol I). The Hail amirs sent gifts to the Ottoman officials in an attempt to bribe them into accepting their position in central Arabia. These gifts symbolized their nominal submission to the Ottoman government.

However, by the end of the nineteenth century, the Ottoman government reversed its policies in central Arabia. Instead of receiving gifts, they subsidized the amirs in order to guarantee their loyalty at a time when Britain had already won to its side a number of tribal powers in the region. During the years which preceded the First World War, the Ottoman government tried to win the co-operation of tribal chiefs. The Rashidi amirs received a monthly allowance from Ottoman officials in addition to weaponry, four Turkish infantry regiments each 600 strong, 4,000 liras, and 800 Martini rounds of ammunition. These were sent to Hail from Baghdad in 1904 (IOR, R/15/5/25). These subsidies increased when the war became imminent: 'Ibn Rashid has the support of the government of all the neighbouring Ottoman Vilayet and is highly esteemed by the Ottoman Parliament and by the Committee of Union and Progress ... The allowance paid by the Turkish government to the young Amir of Jabal Shammar, Saud Ibn Abdulaziz has lately been raised from £150 to 200 a month.' (ibid)

Involvement in the caravan economy, coupled with their

relations with the Ottoman government, contributed to the creation of a gap between the amirs and their ordinary Shammar followers. Although the amirs were constantly emphasizing their *badu* origin and identity, by the end of the nineteenth century, the *hadar* community was beginning to assume hegemony over the *badu* of Jabal Shammar.

The Hadar

a. The farmers

The term '*hadar*' referred to those who inhabited the towns, oases, and villages. In Hail, the *hadar* were the farmers, artisans, and merchants, whom the *badu* regarded as inferior in status. They attributed this inferiority to the fact that the *hadar* often had mixed tribal origins or no origin at all. The *hadar* were considered to have lost the purity of their descent as a result of intermarriages with foreign groups. The occupations of the sedentary population added further to their inferiority in the eyes of the *badu*. These beliefs were grounded in the fact that the oases and towns used to attract a number of the *badu* who had been squeezed out of the desert as a result of their impoverishment and weakening. Some of the villages and oases of Jabal Shammar became a refuge:

> such places become then so many refuges for poor and reduced nomads, who having lost their herds and cattle in some manner or other, are unable to continue their pastoral life, or who with blood upon their head, have been obliged to leave their tribe and home, in order to escape the revenge of the murdered man's relations. (G. Wallin 1854: 199)

While immigration to the oases carried a stigma of inferiority, settlement there as a result of conquering it was regarded as a positive move revealing strength and military supremacy. The towns and oases also attracted those who were rejected by their group as a result of committing dishonourable deeds such as murder or theft, and these people would find it easier to live in the towns where they would be lost among the diverse population. Some of these dispossessed nomads took up agriculture only if they were forced by necessity as they expressed an aversion to farming.

In Hail, the majority of the oasis farmers belonged to an ancient sedentary Arab tribe, Bani Tamim, sections of which were settled in the oases of Jabal Shammar such as Raudhah, Mustajjidah, and Feid, and other oases in central Arabia. According to Wallin, Bani Tamim had retained some peculiarities in their language and manners, as well as a particular cast in their features, which easily distinguished them from the Shammar. 'Though their forefathers chiefly and originally were nomads, the present inhabitants are exclusively an agricultural people, who seldom engage in traffic or partake in war and plundering expeditions with the Shammar; nor is there ever, as I think, any of them found among the Bedawies leading here a nomadic life.' (G. Wallin 1854: 201–2) The sedentary Bani Tamim had retained their tribal origins in their genealogies. However, they were no longer an independent tribe as they acknowledged the authority of the Rashidi amirs over their oases and villages in Jabal Shammar (Admiralty 1920: 81).

The fact that the farming community did not participate in the military expeditions of the *badu* immediately placed them outside the *badu* value system. The *hadar* had no narratives in which they took pride in their courage during raids, their virtues, and military hegemony. However, they had memories of the outbreak of epidemic diseases such as cholera which used to wipe out considerable sections of the sedentary population, and demoralize them. They remembered abandoned settlements and burnt fields and date plantations, resulting from raids by the nomadic population. They documented their helplessness in the face of violence by the *badu* of the desert.

b. The artisans

In addition to the farmers, the oases of Jabal Shammar attracted a number of artisans (*senna*) and craftsmen. Huber listed the following *senna* families in Hail: al Amamah, al Jabara, al Abid, al Khazam, al Juray, and al Jazay. These families were regarded as inferior by the 'most ragged of the baduin' (C. Huber in P. Ward 1983: 430). The artisans occupied a lower position in the oasis status hierarchy because of their occupation. In Arabia in general, only individuals of humble origin would engage in the manufacture of artefacts such as weapons, knives, saddles, shoes, and cooking utensils. The craftsmen of Hail were either dispossessed nomads or people of foreign origin who had migrated to the oasis after failing to find work in their home towns (G. Wallin 1854: 199). Lorimer described the industry in Hail: 'Artisans are not many: they belong to the smiths' caste and their implements are few and clumsy; nevertheless copperware, spearheads, and horse shoes are manufactured, wooden bowls are turned, and camel saddles are built. There are a few house builders and gypsum plasters.' (J. Lorimer 1909: 602)

Although the *senna* were in general based in the oases, some lived and travelled with the *badu*. Montagne observed:

> Au milieu des Semmar bedouins habitent enfin des artisans, forgerons pour la plupart (sané: pl. senna), repartis habituellement au nombre de trois ou quatre par fraction. Bien qu'ils se déplacent avec leur patrons, les senna restent entièrement étrangers au monde bedouin; aucun mariage n'est possible avec eux. Ils sont originaires des oasis. (R. Montagne 1932: 74)

The low position of the *senna* both in the oases and among the *badu* in the desert was reflected in the fact that they were denied marriage rights among their hosts. The *senna* were also incapable of organizing themselves into associations or guilds because of their weakness and fragmentation as a group.

c. The merchants

As seen earlier, a considerable number of the Hail merchants were of foreign origin while others were from Hail families and the Qasim region in central Arabia. Their involvement in the caravan economy made them into an important status group which represented the link between the local population, including other oases dwellers, the nomads, and the outside regions which were beyond the reach of the local population. As some of the merchant families of Hail became very prosperous, they had a vested interest in the maintenance of peace and security along the trade routes. The disruption which often resulted from tribal raids threatened the flow of trade and slowed down, if not suspended the caravan traffic, thus affecting the prospects of the merchant community. The merchants had access to the amir's *majlis* (council) where they discussed their concerns (C. Doughty 1979: 604 vol I). They were able to win the approval, support, and trust of the amirs who had similar interests. We are told about personalities such as Abdullah Al Muslimani who was:

> an unrivalled merchant and experienced in business matters, he

was greatly honoured by al Ubaid, the warrior-father of
Hamud: he administered his estate and successfully increased it,
desired nothing for himself, and enjoyed the confidence of the
wolf . . . by the diligent conduct of his business, by his dealings
in loans and profits which affords the resident bedouins, he has
augmented his estate to such an extent that he can gradually
call his own large gardens and houses in Qafar and Aqda. (J.
Euting in P. Ward 1983: 458)

Such personalities were excused from participating in the amir's
military expeditions because of their involvement in business or
their lack of military skills. However, the wealthy merchants 'must
in compensation pay a certain sum of money or pay in kind, and
this compensation is settled in advance for each man and each
ghazu in turn'. For example, Abdullah, the wealthy merchant,
'must offer the loan of a gun and pay between 2 and 3 riyals. In
1883, before the raid on the Majmaa, Abdullah had to supply three
guns, all of them returned to him after the raid was over.' (C.
Huber in P. Ward 1983: 429) The merchants were also subject to
ad hoc taxes which they sometimes paid in goods. While attending
the amir's *majlis*, Euting observed that one of the Persian
merchants 'The Meshadi, Umran . . . paid a visit to the amir and
displayed before him goods which had recently been brought in by
the caravan from Mecca. He selected – naturally free of charge
(bila shay) – a few lamps. This is a convenient method for the
sovereign to collect tax from the Persian merchants, who are
becoming rich here.' (J. Euting in P. Ward 1983: 557)

The amirs and the merchants had common interests regarding
the flow of trade. The first benefited by sending their own caravans
and extracting tribute from all those involved in the caravan trade.
Their revenues from tribute were so important that they could not
alienate the merchants who would channel their trade through
other routes if they were not guaranteed protection. Towards the
end of the nineteenth century, the amirs increased their punitive
raids against those nomadic tribes who showed disrespect for their
authority by raiding and plundering the caravans and merchants
under their protection. These attempts at the pacification of the
badu reflected a change in the amirs' policies which in the past had
been in their favour. When Abdullah Ibn Rashid established
himself as amir of Hail he was ready to promote the interests of his
badu kinsmen who had been supporting him throughout the power

struggle between him and his cousin Ibn Ali. However, under the leadership of his son, Talal, concerns for the security of trade routes took precedence over those of the *badu*. The clash of interests between the amirs and the merchants on one hand, and the *badu* population on the other increased during the rule of Mohammad Ibn Rashid who almost every year organized military expeditions aimed at pacifying the *badu* in the vicinity of Hail (A. Blunt 1968: 267–8), enforcing order and security along trade routes, and reasserting his power and military hegemony among the *badu*. Contrary to the often repeated views which emphasized the *badu*'s domination over the *hadar*, the Rashidi dynasty towards the end of the last century represented the hegemony of the *hadar* over the *badu* – though this was achieved through a tribal aristocracy of *badu* origin.

Although the merchants represented an important financial community, it is difficult to assert that their material wealth was matched by a similar social status. As most of the merchants were of foreign origin, they were automatically regarded as outsiders who were external to the indigenous *badu* and oasis populations. Some merchants were regarded as *ahrar* (people of free birth) of a relatively respectable background, although no matter how much wealth a merchant possessed, he was still not fully integrated in *badu* society. Marriages between the *badu* and the merchants were impossible and most probably the latter chose wives from the sedentary families such as the farmers.

d. The slaves

The majority of the slave population in Jabal Shammar was found among the oasis dwellers. Only a small number was owned by Shammar bedouin sheikhs and other nomadic families who were able to purchase slaves in the major markets of the Arabian Peninsula, such as Mecca and Jidda, and the smaller slave markets in Hail, Unaizah, and Boreidah. Most of the slaves of Hail had African origins, although white slaves probably of Caucasian origin were also reported to have lived there. One such slave was Mubarak, the amir's chief slave. Blunt commented that though a slave, Mubarak had not in appearance the least trace of negro blood (A. Blunt 1968: 230). Doughty also reported that: 'Captain of the guard, the prince's chamberlain at home, and his standard bearer in battle, was Imbarak, a pleasant but fanatic strong man. He was a stranger from el-Aruth.' (C. Doughty 1979: 33)

Other white slaves included Caucasian women in the amir's castle. Bell was met by one of these slaves when she visited Hail in 1914. Hogarth described the encounter between them: 'of these a lively Circassian, once sent by the Sultan Abdul Hamid for a concubine to Mohammad Ibn Rashid and now married, took her fancy, this woman's mission no doubt included espionage; but her reports, in the end, did Miss Bell some service, she seems to have reciprocated the latter's liking.' (Hogarth in P. Ward 1983: 684)

The slaves' status was very much dependent on whether they performed domestic tasks or were part of the military apparatus of the dynasty. Domestic slaves were found in the amir's castle and in the houses of wealthy merchants and farmers. The amir's domestic slaves were cooks, cleaners, *gahwajis* (coffee makers and servers) and water carriers. They also looked after the amir's stables, date plantations and fruit gardens. Agricultural slaves were also employed by the farmers of Hail. Unlike the artisans who were believed to have no known origin, the slaves, claimed Montagne, were believed to be 'the descendants of Noah, their father is Ham' (R. Montagne 1932: 77). It is, nevertheless, unclear whether these claims had much relevance to their position as an inferior group. The only difference between the slaves and, for example, the artisans was that female slaves were more acceptable as wives for the amirs than their counterparts from artisan families. Mitab Ibn Abdul Aziz, the seventh amir of Hail, was said to have married a slave woman, Wasmiya, the mother of Abdullah, the eleventh amir. Other members of notable families in Hail such as the Sibhan were known to have had slave mothers, for example, Saud Ibn Sibhan, the amir's *wazir* (minister) in the 1920s.

A considerable number of the amirs' bodyguard consisted of slaves who carried arms and were often seen at the gates of the castle in Hail. Some trusted slaves were even sent by the amirs to represent them in the conquered oases. These slaves played an important role in the consolidation of Abdullah Ibn Rashid's power, helping him to overthrow his cousin Ibn Ali. Wallin reported that Abdullah's bodyguard at that time consisted of 200 persons, 'the greater part of whom were manumitted negroes and Egyptians who had been left behind the army of Ibrahim Pasha' (G. Wallin 1854: 180). With the expansion of the amirs' powers, the number of their slaves increased – Musil claimed that they numbered 400 who dwelt in groups of twenty (A. Musil 1928a: 303). These became the most loyal group in the dynasty, because 'having no relatives among the sedentary population, they were able to give effect to every order of their lord and to protect him against all enemies including his own kin.' (ibid) The amirs' bodyguard, though of slave origin, constituted a powerful group. Doughty referred to personalities such as Aneybar, who controlled access to the amir and was trusted by him:

> Aneybar was a habashy, a home-born Galla in Abdullah Ibn Rashid's household, and therefore to be counted slave-brother of Talal, Metab, and Mohammed; also his name is of the Lord's house, Ibn Rashid. This libertine was a principal personage in Hayel; in affairs of state-trust and under the Emirs since Telal's time. (C. Doughty 1979: 655 vol I)

Aneybar and many other slaves were brought up in the amir's household. It was common for a young amir to have a slave brother assigned to him who was often the same age as the amir. The task of the slave brother would start in childhood and would be expected to continue in adult life. He accompanied the amir, looked after him, took his side in disputes and defended his master in battle. Some slaves were so loyal to their masters that they were able to intervene in the internal power struggles of the Rashidi family – as when Saud Ibn Rashid was killed by his cousin Abdullah Ibn Talal, who was then murdered by one of Saud's slaves, most probably a slave brother. The pseudo-kinship arrangement created a strong bond between the slave and his master and fostered the creation of obligations and loyalties. The slave carried the amir's name next to his own and benefited from the amir's patronage and favours. In return, the slave was expected to show undisputed loyalty towards his master.

The cornerstone in this pseudo-kinship system was based on the practice of wet-nursing (*ridaa*) in which female slaves breast-fed the young amirs together with their own children. The milk bond is recognized by Islam as a legitimate basis for the creation of kinship relations which are equal to those established as a result of blood (*nasab*) and affinity (*musahara*) (S. Altorki 1980: 233). Milk kinship is established when a woman (slave or non-slave) breast-feeds a child together with her own children.

The milk-kinship allowed the amirs to refer to their slave wet-nurse as *umm* (mother), and those slaves with whom they shared milk as *akh* (brother). The internal power struggles between members of the Rashidi family in which uncles, cousins, and even brothers entered into fierce competition against each other weakened the natural bond between them. The pseudo-kinship system fostered the development of an alternative support system in which the slaves were outside the blood kinship relations, yet not completely outside it. When the slaves supported their master's claims to power, they knew that their destiny was tied to his and that his success or failure inevitably influenced their chances. Their master's rise to the office of amir accrued to them benefits and privileges. However, some slave brothers were actually murdered with the assassination of their master by a member of the ruling group. For example, when Mohammad Ibn Rashid carried out the massacre of his brother's sons in 1869, the young amirs were assassinated together with their slave brothers.

5

THE MILITARY APPARATUS

The establishment of the amirs in Hail and their involvement in the caravan trade economy were accompanied by the development of a military apparatus including a force of coercion which consisted initially of the Shammar human resources, but later became independent of them.[1] The amirs had conquered Hail with the military support of their *badu* kinsmen, members of the Jaafar lineage and their personal slaves, but towards the end of the century it was clear that their *badu* relatives were no longer the core of the military apparatus. The armed force of the amirs consisted mainly of townsmen and slaves. This shift in the composition of the military forces towards the *hadar* was a reflection of the growing pre-eminence of Hail and its sedentarized *badu* aristocracy and is crucial to our understanding of the political system which was in the process of being created. The recruitment of a stable and permanent military force independent of shifting tribal political relations and military alliances and loyal only to the amirs, was the crucial step towards the formation of dynastic rule.

This permanent armed force differed from that available to Shammar tribal section sheikhs, who relied on the human resources of their tribal section against an external threat or to launch a raid. After military encounters the tribesmen would resume their daily lives. In contrast, the amirs' armed force became a specialized body employed on a permanent basis for the purpose of expansion and defence. As it was under the command of the amirs, they could rule, suppress rebellions, punish criminals, enforce order and peace, and extract tribute through direct use of force or the threat of violence.

THE COMPOSITION OF THE FORCE OF COERCION

The change in the composition of the amirs' armed force and the shift towards an oasis-based military group can only be observed over time. When Abdullah Ibn Rashid became ruler of Hail in 1836 he had spent a period of exile mobilizing the Shammar *badu* and in particular his Abde tribal section. He relied on the support of the Abde whose camps were already in the vicinity of Hail. Abdullah had built a reputation for bravery and military competence during this period of exile and these achievements motivated the Shammar to gather around him and offer their support and allegiance. In other words, they became ready to put their human resources at his disposal. The lineage of Jaafar in particular constituted his kin military force and Palgrave claims that their support was essential for the conquest of Hail. It was in the Jaafar interest to see a member of their own descent group in control of the oasis (W. Palgrave 1865: 130 vol I). Montagne also shares these views as he argued that Abdullah's force consisted mainly of the Abde Shammar, the tribal section of the Jaafar (R. Montagne 1947: 154). Abdullah worked on gaining his lineage's support and trust by demonstrating his leadership abilities, especially in the field of armed conflict. His success meant that the Jaafar could guarantee their political and economic pre-eminence over both the sedentary population of the oasis and the nomadic groups of Jabal Shammar. Some lineages of the Abde were already resident in Hail where they owned date plantations. Consequently, they had a vested interest in controlling the leadership position in the oasis. Those partially sedentarized groups of the Abde Shammar provided a considerable number of Abdullah's armed men. According to Wallin, the sedentarized Abde were regarded as superior to their nomadic brothers in courage and in the art of using arms (G. Wallin 1854: 178). The conquest of Hail was not achieved by the collective assembly and participation of a tribal force consisting of various dispersed Shammar sections, but rather by the participation of one lineage, the Jaafar. Obviously, their success in pushing the claims of Ibn Rashid placed them in a hierarchical relationship *vis-à-vis* other Shammar sections, which had a strong military basis.

It is difficult, therefore, to assume that the various Shammar sections (Abde, Aslam, Sinjara, and Tuman) and lineages constituted equal parts or segments of a totality. First, according to the available estimates, the Abde outnumbered the other three sections as they were estimated to have had 1,500 tents.[2] Second, they established their military supremacy with the conquest of Hail by Ibn Rashid, a member of one of the lineages of the section. Third, this conquest produced a leadership which was able to rule in Hail for almost ninety years not only as leaders of the Abde, but also as representatives of the whole tribe. These three dimensions laid the foundation for unequal relations between the Abde and the other sections.

The emerging military inequality puts into question certain aspects of the segmentary lineage model which works on the assumption that first, equal tribal segments coexist in a balanced opposition, and second, that tribal leadership is limited as the system does not allow room for the consolidation of power in the hands of a sheikhly family drawn from one of the lineages. The predominance of the Abde within the Shammar tribe, and the leadership of the amirs enable us to re-evaluate these assumptions which have already been challenged by new material from other parts of the Middle East.[3] For example, Dresch examined the same processes in his study of north Yemeni tribes in which he reported the emergence of sheikhly families and the maintenance of their powers over long periods of time (P. Dresch 1989 and 1984). He argued that a 'particular shaykhly family is identified first with a particular section but then becomes identified also with a larger unit; often enough it then loses its grip, as it were, and reverts to being identified with the section it comes from. The tribal structure remains largely unchanged and shaykhly houses rise and fall within it.' (P. Dresch 1984: 38) The enlargement of the sheikh's sphere of influence is done in Yemen through signing a document in which the various minor tribal sheikhs recognize the authority of one man who becomes 'Shaykh al Mashaykh'. The sheikh's domain of influence and the tribal entity of which he is sheikh are not identical. The crucial factor, Dresch argues, is related to the fact that great sheikhly houses have powers of their own. These powers in turn are described and in practice circumscribed, by ideas which are as fundamental a part of tribalism as are those of brotherhood (ibid: 6).

Material from other parts of the Middle East shows that strong military leadership was often a prelude to the establishment of lineages and sheikhly families in positions of authority. The Qaids

of Morocco (R. Montagne 1930), the Shaalan amirs of the
Rwala bedouins (W. Lancaster 1981), the ilkhani of the
Bakhtiyari Iranian nomads (G. Garthwaite 1983), and the ilkhani
of the Qashqai (L. Beck 1986) all had strong military leadership alongside segmentary lineage structures and inequalities
between lineages based on military success. These examples raise
many questions: How is inequality maintained or enforced in a
milieu where there is a strong orientation towards segmentation?
How does a military leader who is identified with one section
become identified with a larger tribal unit? In the presence of
strong military fragmentation, how does such a leader assume
power and maintain his position? In the case of the Shammar, the
change in the composition of the amirs' military forces was
crucial.

Although Abdullah Ibn Rashid conquered Hail with the support
of his Jaafar lineage, it has been shown in the last chapter that he
also relied on slaves and foreign troops. Wallin refers to the
presence of 200 'negroes' and 'Turko-Egyptian' soldiers who were
'able-bodied men, skilled in the use of arms, experienced in war
and ready to obey blindly the commands of their master' (G.
Wallin 1854: 180). Musil confirms this account though there
appear to be some variations concerning the number of slaves and
Egyptians: 'The new Lord, Abdullah, was supported by some 250
Turko-Egyptian soldiers, who had deserted to him with their arms
and formed his bodyguard. With the help of his dauntless brother,
Obejd, he soon established peace in all the settlements about the
two ranges of Ega and Salma and endeavored to win over the
various heads of the Shammar by kindness and generosity.' (A.
Musil 1928a: 238)

The Egyptian soldiers were part of the army sent to Arabia
during the first Egyptian invasion. Some of them left their units
due to disease and lwo pay and about 200 soldiers joined Ibn
Rashid in return for shelter and protection from attack by hostile
local tribes. Their foreign origin won them Ibn Rashid's trust and
there is evidence that these Turko-Egyptian deserters remained
with him and constituted the core of his personal bodyguard.
During the rule of Mohammad Ibn Rashid, some 'foreign men'
were reported to have been serving in the amir's armed force:
'Among the strangers, in my time, in Hayil, that lived of Ibn
Rashid's wages, were certain Moghrebies ... The Moors, fifteen
persons, were transported to Hail: where they became of the

Prince's armed service. One of them (grown unwieldly to ride) has been made the porter of his castle gate, and no man may pass in threat but that Moor's allowance.' (C. Doughty 1979: 33)

Having no kin or tribal connection in the region, they became the amir's personal slaves, completely dependent on him for their survival. The slaves and the foreign men constituted a military force whose loyalty was not derived from traditional kinship allegiances. Musil argues that the loyalty of the slaves to the amir was stronger than that of his kin relatives because 'having no relatives among the sedentary population, they were able to give effect to every order of their Lord and to protect him against all enemies including his own kin' (A. Musil 1928a: 303). In addition, some slaves were tied to the amir through the pseudo-kinship system described in the previous chapter.

The slaves, together with the foreign troops, represented the core of the amirs' forces of coercion and were the permanent nucleus after the conquest of Hail. The Jaafar lineage and other Abde lineages were dispersed as they were not a 'specialized military group'. Their participation in enforcing Rashidi rule was situational. In other words, they temporarily put their human resources under the amir's disposal to achieve a particular end. Once they had fulfilled their duties, they saw no reason why they should continue their military services, a gesture typical of military alliances in such a tribal context. By the 1840s, they had already installed the Rashidi amir in a position of power and thus saw no merit in suspending their daily activities and remaining in the amirs' service.

Nevertheless, it is difficult to assume that they ceased to play any role in the consolidation of the amirs' powers – a view that Rosenfeld tends to hold: 'It was, I believe, non-kin elements, slaves (in part manumitted), and mercenaries that served as the initial nucleus and primary military strength used in establishing the superiority of the ruling house and protecting its continuity.' (H. Rosenfeld 1965: 177) I am inclined to agree with Rosenfeld's claim that slaves and the Turko-Egyptian deserters, which he calls mercenaries, constituted the nucleus of the amirs' armed forces, but it is difficult to accept his second assumption that the Jaafar lineage became marginalized. Although they might have suspended their military service, they nevertheless represented the source of legitimacy needed for the consolidation of the amirs' rule and remained a reservoir for potential alliances and strength. The support of the slaves and mercenaries would not have given the amirs the required legitimacy. It is, therefore, a mistake to assume that the Rashidi ruling house quickly separated itself from its 'equals of birth' as claimed by Rosenfeld (ibid 176). The amirs tended to develop separate commercial interests in the later decades of the nineteenth century, but they could not afford to alienate those who brought them into power in 1836. It is perhaps more appropriate to argue that towards the end of the last century, the amirs' force was not totally dependent on their *badu* kinsmen as they were able to create a permanent military force which consisted initially of slaves and mercenaries, but was later supplemented by townsmen.

In addition to the permanent force, there was a body of armed men who were known as '*rajajil es shuyukh*' (men of the sheikhs). These were seen in the castle at a later period and during the rule of Mohammad Ibn Rashid. Blunt estimated the number of these men to be '800 or 1000 men dressed in a kind of uniform, in brown cloaks and red or blue kefiyehs [head cover] and armed with silver-hilted swords' (A. Blunt 1968: 265 vol I). *Rajajil es shuyukh* were recruited by voluntary enlistment from the oases and villages of Jabal Shammar. Their duties included police work in the oases, the maintenance of peace in the markets, in addition to the protection of trading caravans: 'These were recruited from among the young men of the towns and villages by voluntary enlistment, those who wish to serve inscribing their names at the castle, and being called out as occasion requires.' (ibid 265–6)

Clearly, the *rajajil es shuyukh* were a sort of reserve army called upon when required. Being volunteers, they lived with their families and received no pay from the castle except when employed away from home. Their expense to the amir was, therefore, little more than that of their clothes, meals and arms. They were not a substitute for the amirs' military kin group but were recruited to perform a new and different function. The establishment of peace and order in the oases became important with the growth of Hail as a commercial centre. Any military involvement of the *badu* at that time had to be derived from the roles they perceived themselves as capable of performing. They could raid other groups, but not establish order in a settlement on a daily basis. It is worth noting here that the amirs continued to rely on the support of the Shammar *badu* during their raids, but they were aware that it was inconceivable for the *badu* to perform a policing role in Hail.

With the expansion of the amirs' realm, the recruitment of the sedentary population for military service became institutionalized, for voluntary enlistment was no longer sufficient. Huber gives a detailed account of the number of townsmen who were required by the amirs to join their forces: 'Tribute for war is given to the Amir of Jabal Shammar as follows: 30 to 40 men by Hail, 4 to 5 by Rawdah, 4 by Muwaqqaq, Qafar and Qasr, 3 each by Mustajiddah and Sabaan, and 2 or 3 by Gazalah. None of the other villages of the Jabal give money or men.' (C. Huber in P. Ward 1983: 435)

During the leadership of Mohammad Ibn Rashid, the imposition of military service was carried out on a larger scale. Doughty described the composition of the amir's sedentary armed group. In addition to the voluntary *rajajil es shuyukh*, there was a military force consisting of the Hail townsmen in particular: 'In the Prince's general ghrazzus there ride, his rajajil and Hail townsmen and men of the next villages, about four hundred men, and nearly as many of the tributary bedaw that are ready at the word of the Emir to mount with him in the hope of winning.' (C. Doughty 1979: 21)

The amir tried to diversify the sources of his armed force. *Badu* tribesmen were recruited and supplemented with a constant core consisting of the townsmen. Doughty reports that even the merchants of Hail were incorporated: 'About half of the men of Hayil were now in the field with Ibn Rashid; for besides his salaried rajajil, even the salesmen of the Suk are the Prince's servants, to side with him.' (ibid: 272) However, it would be difficult to imagine that all members of the merchant community actually participated in the military expeditions. Those who had no military skills or were too old were asked to make a contribution in cash or kind.

This gradual transformation of the amirs' forces of coercion reflected two tendencies: the creation of a permanent and specialized military force and the attempt to maintain a monopoly over the legitimate use of violence. These were the two important characteristics which accompanied the process of dynastic rule in the absence of a well-developed bureaucracy. The permanent military apparatus was meant to ensure the enforcement of the amir's command as it was loyal to him only. The assembly of this force and its dispersal were no longer dependent on negotiations and tribal alliances in which two or more sections used to join together for the purpose of defence or attack. Rather, it was a military apparatus under the amir's sole command which enabled him to exercise relative monopoly over the legitimate use of force. One of the functions of this force was to undermine the military hegemony of all those who possessed the ability and human resources to exercise their own military control over others or threaten the hegemony of the amirs.

Second, the military force was an indication of the increasing tendency towards the partial marginalization of the *badu*. In other words, this transformation reflected the growing military domination of Hail and its sedentarized ruling group over the *badu* and the countryside – although this domination was not completely successful. To use Radcliffe-Brown's words, military organization influences social structure, mainly by determining the distribution of naked power, or to use another word, the ability to use violence (forward in S. Andreski 1968: 1). Military organization also reflects the changes which take place at the political and economic levels. The major political changes taking place in Hail were related to the establishment of the Rashidi ruling group and the growth of its commercial interests, which were no longer in line with the *badu*. The marginalization of the *badu* as a military force was a consequence of their political and economic marginalization. As they no longer constituted the core of the amir's force, it was clear that their political predominance was being undermined. However, the complete breakdown of their military hegemony was not feasible. They retained their cohesion and control over their human resources which they could mobilize for military purposes. Furthermore, the amirs were concerned not to alienate their *badu* allies as this would inevitably undermine their legitimacy.

These remarks put into question the well-established view of Ibn Khaldun who stressed in *The Muqqadimah* the opposition between the *badu* and the *hadar*, the warlike character of the *badu*, their savage nature, and their opposition to *umran*, the civilized sedentary life (Ibn Khaldun 1987). These views were later repeated by European travellers in the nineteenth century. The frequency of armed conflict and raids among the *badu* themselves, and between the *badu* and the *hadar* in Arabia has always captured the imagination of European travellers. They were also fascinated by those accounts and narratives in which the *badu* celebrated their military encounters. Travellers' reports were often full of either romanticized comments about *badu* courage and chivalry, or degrading descriptions of the *badu*'s savagery and inherent instincts for plunder, i.e. comments of the Ibn Khaldun type. This literature has been recently scrutinized and critically evaluated by specialists in the field and will not be repeated here.[4] Anthropologists of the Middle East, especially those concerned with the problem of violence and armed conflict in the nineteenth century, were influenced by the travellers' descriptive accounts although their monographs were more analytical. Perhaps Rosenfeld's work was the most systematic attempt to investigate the alleged domination of the *badu* over the *hadar*. Rosenfeld wrote: 'This appears to be an ancient process. The military bedouin "protect" the settlement from raiders, thieves, and plunderers. Essentially they "protect" the settlers from the tribe that gives protection and from other raiders as well.' (H. Rosenfeld 1965: 78).

In spite of his understanding of the mechanisms and economic relations behind this process, Rosenfeld has been criticized for his failure to follow through the implications of his own data. Asad argues that Rosenfeld represents relations between pastoralists and cultivators as inherently antagonistic and lays great stress on the alleged military advantage that the nomads have over the sedentary population (T. Asad 1973: 61). On the contrary, argues Asad, a thriving agricultural–commercial centre has greater resources for dominating nomadic tribes than the other way round (ibid: 102). Using an historical perspective and drawing examples from the Hira and Mecca, Asad corrects these views in the light of evidence from the sixth century. He claims that pastoralists may help to conquer new territory, but they cannot constitute a regular state army and remain pastoralists (ibid: 66). In the past, he emphasizes, pastoralists have been more successful at resisting than imposing structures of domination.

It is true that Hail was able to produce its own military force which succeeded to a great extent in imposing peace and order in the markets, and to a lesser extent in pacifying the nomads in the vicinity of the oasis. Clearly, this challenges the assumption that the *badu* have a tendency to dominate the *hadar*. However, it is not easy to claim that because of Hail's predominance at the political, military, and economic levels, the *hadar* population was able to dominate the *badu*. The reversal of the relations of domination is not as straightforward and simple as it might appear. Although the leadership in Hail and its military force was able to pacify the nomads and curb their military supremacy in the desert from time to time through bribes, subsidies, and punitive expeditions, they failed to establish a situation whereby the *badu* were totally subjugated and encapsulated. This raises the question of why this was so when Hail possessed the means to do so.

Answers to this question lie in the nature of the amirs' leadership and sources of legitimacy. Their *badu* origin and tribal connection with the Shammar remained, throughout their rule in Hail, an important legitimating ideology. The amirs were caught in a dilemma. On the one hand, they tried to maintain their rule and their control over the countryside in order to secure their commercial interests and those of the Hail population. On the other hand, they did not want to alienate the *badu* population. As long as they were able to maintain a precarious balance between these two objectives, they guaranteed the loyalty of the *badu* without resorting to punitive measures. The crucial factor was their ability to keep the flow of subsidies to various tribal sheikhs which, in turn, guaranteed their loyalty. These subsidies represented an alternative to direct domination and open confrontation between Hail and its leadership on the one hand, and the autonomous tribal population on the other. It is worth noting that this pattern is not peculiar to the Shammar. Valensi, in her study of the Tunisian southern tribes, argues that the loyalty of the men of the tents is not based on their status as subjects, but on their voluntary accord with the dynasty. The relations between the central power and the hinterland can be described as relations of alliance or hostility rather than of subjugation (L. Valensi 1977: 34).

Even with their organized permanent armed force, the amirs were unable to break down the military integrity of the *badu* tribal sections which remained in control of their only surplus, i.e. their human resources. The tribal armed men constituted an independent auxiliary force which occasionally responded to the amirs' call for military support. Evidence of this can be found in those accounts and narratives in which both the amirs and the Shammar took pride in their support of each other during political and military crises.[5] However, this support was situational and very much dependent on the physical proximity of the Shammar camps to Hail, their interests at the time, and the purpose of the military action for which support was invoked. Lack of systematic military integration between the Hail leadership and its *badu* periphery was one of the reasons for the decline of the amirs' leadership during the first two decades of the twentieth century. The *badu* remained capable of switching allegiance and transferring their human resources to other rising power centres in central Arabia. This was exactly what happened when Ibn Saud undermined the Rashidis' power by attracting some sections of the Shammar to his side. His successful military expeditions and alliance with Britain offered the prospect of more subsidies which motivated some impoverished and marginalized subjects to join his military forces and turn against their Hail leadership.[6]

Instead of focusing on the general question of domination between the *badu* and the *hadar*, Burckhardt has concentrated on the actual context of violence, the *ghazu* (raids). He described the Shammar *ghazu* which, in his opinion, had the purpose of capturing *ghanima* (booty). The *ghazu*, however, was not an uncontrolled outbreak of violence and killings; it had specific strategies and rules:

> The Shammar Arabs had a peculiar custom of attacking by night the enemy's camp when it happens to be situated near their own. If they can reach it unobserved, they suddenly knock down the principal tent poles; and whilst the surprised people are striving to disengage themselves from the tent coverings which had fallen on them, the cattle were driven off by the assailants. (J. Burckhardt 1831: 141–2)

In other aspects of the raid, the Shammar were said to have observed the general rules. These can be summarized as follows: first, the objective of the exercise was not to exterminate the enemy, but to capture booty. Second, women, slaves and herdsmen were immune from attack. Third, the life of the defender who submits was spared and it was dishonourable to violate this rule. And fourth, raiding parties avoided killing the *dakhil*, i.e. those groups who had already placed themselves under the protection of the tribal section. Consequently, if their property was captured by mistake, they could claim it back from the raiding group. Of all these rules, the avoidance of killing the enemy was perhaps the most respected since the consequences were hard to control. The importance of the obligation of revenge acted as a deterrent prohibiting the growth of hostilities into perpetuated conflicts.[7]

Anthropologists working on the actual context of violence have used Burckhardt's monograph and others to reconstruct tribal raids of the nineteenth and early twentieth centuries. For example,

Sweet discusses camel-raiding among the north Arabian tribes, arguing that these mutually prosecuted raids are mechanisms for the circulation of camels among various tribal groups. Her cultural–ecological argument led her to claim that raiding was not a simple response to a particular crisis in the supply of camels, but rather a system-sustaining mechanism which functions throughout the bedouin niche: 'Reciprocal camel-raiding, as a continuous practice, operating at both long and short distances between tribal breeding areas, maintains a circulation of camels and of camel husbandry over a maximum physical range for camels and the societies which specialise in their breeding and depend on them.' (L. Sweet 1965: 1132)

Sweet's analysis of raids may be applicable to instances when not more than fifty individuals launch an attack on other groups, an attack which often results in the capture of camels. However, there were other large-scale military encounters between competitive and hostile groups, which cannot be described as a means for the circulation of camels. I shall argue later that some military expeditions of the Rashidi amirs were known as *ghazu*, but aimed at conquest, expansion and defence. Raiding between the Hail amirs and other groups, including tribes and other power centres in the region, became more than a military activity ensuring the circulation of surplus in camels. Raids were the means which made possible the establishment of political and economic hegemony. Some minor raids between small *badu* lineages were inevitably motivated by the possibility of capturing camels, but when these raids were carried out by established power groups, they became entangled with centralization of political leadership, dynastic ambitions, and territorial expansion.

The shortcomings of Sweet's argument have recently given rise to a new genre of anthropological literature. Meeker was one of the first to look at tribal raids from a new perspective. In his opinion, political violence and mounted camel-herding nomadism were closely connected among the north Arabian tribes: 'There was constant pressure among the pastoral nomads all over the arid zone to invest in personal instruments of aggression. With time, this investment embroiled men increasingly in political strategies and struggle.' (M. Meeker 1979: 9) The vulnerability of the camel as wealth predisposed the *badu* to invest in instruments of aggression to defend this wealth. The camel itself was, however, an instrument of aggression. Meeker argues that bedouin culture was highly political. 'The vulnerability of domestic possession (camels) precipitated by the aggressive potential of a political resource (camels) carried men away from a materially productive domestic life toward an uncertain, agonistic, political adventurism.' (ibid: 18) At the core of this political culture was the exercise of political violence, an exercise conceived sometimes as an absorbing and joyful play of life and sometimes as a serious struggle against death.

Meeker shifts the focus of analysis from the actual raids to the *badu* poetry and narratives which document their raids. He regards the raids as a genre of political adventurism. As camel-herding was not a labour-intensive activity, the bedouins had what Meeker calls 'Bedouin leisure': 'And there was, as well, nothing with which to fill this world of leisure other than talk. The words of these talks (poems and narratives) were the centre of an effort to work out the various possibilities and impossibilities of uncertain political relationships.' (ibid: 27) In other words, the literary voice crystallizes as a centre of formal life in the absence of certain relationships. In contrast, the oasis dwellers, according to Meeker, share the culture of political adventurism with the bedouins, but tend to deal with it by developing elaborate kinship rules and obligations. The settled population developed a set of distinct social norms centred around the integrity of family life. For example, the preference for parallel cousin marriage was an expression of the oasis dwellers' attempt to guarantee a secure domestic interior against an uncertain political exterior.

These arguments can be criticized on many grounds. First, Meeker ignores other mechanisms that both the nomads and oasis dwellers of the Arabian Peninsula have employed to deal with the problem of anarchy. For example, central Arabia has witnessed the rise of tribal dynasties (in the case of the Shammar) and religious reformist movements (Wahhabism) which aimed at the stabilization of political and military relations. These were reactions against the anarchic tendencies inherent in the region. Second, to assume that tribes reacted to the situation of political uncertainty by developing elaborate rules regulating family life is not peculiar to the bedouins. Almost all societies have some sort of kinship rules with varying degrees of complexity. Furthermore, the causal relationship between political uncertainty and the emergence of kinship rules needs, in my opinion, further justification and evidence from other cultural areas. Third, Meeker's argument that the oasis dwellers dealt with the problem of anarchy by enforcing kinship rules can be developed in the opposite direction. Settled communities can define themselves territorially and in terms of stable economic and political structures, whereas the nomads perhaps need such rules in the absence of a strong sense of territoriality.

Meeker's treatment of bedouin poems and narratives also raises questions. For example, he unquestioningly uses a quotation from Doughty which shows the influence of nineteenth-century travellers' ideas (ibid: 28). His preoccupation with the force of poetry led him to adopt Doughty's view that the *hess* (voice) appears in the desert as a striking human artefact commanding attention (ibid). Also, as Abu-Lughod has argued, Meeker's interest in the relationship between poetry and politics has led him to exclude other aspects of social life in which men play an important role. Abu-Lughod argues that a felicitous correspondence between the views of Arab tribesmen and European men has led each to reinforce the interest of the other and to slight other aspects of experience and concern. Women in bedouin society are concerned with political issues, the tribe, and conflict. On the other hand, bedouin men have other non-political interests which spring from the fact that they have families and experience love and desires, and suffer personal tragedies. She suggests that we broaden our vision of Middle Eastern tribal societies to encompass these dimensions of experiences in the analysis of social life (L. Abu-Lughod 1986: 30).

Any analysis of nineteenth and early twentieth century tribal *ghazu* has, by definition, to be given with an historical perspective. Our knowledge of tribal raids can be constructed from historical records (both primary and secondary) and from surviving *badu* poems and narratives which are still remembered and recited. These sources may lead to two different, but not necessarily, opposed results. An interpretation of raids based on historical data may focus attention on the consequences of these raids and their relevance to the formation of political structures. In contrast, an analysis based on the accumulated *badu* poetic tradition takes the researcher into the realm of literature, symbolism, and normative culture, that is it enables us to examine poetry, not only as an expression of social and political life, but also as an artisitic reflection of *badu* values, norms and concerns relating to *badu* life in general. In the following section, I look at the *ghazu* from the perspective of their objectives and consequences as constructed

from historical sources, and in the next chapter, the poetics of raids
will be dealt with.

CONQUEST, EXPANSION AND DEFENCE

As the composition of the amirs' military forces changed over time,
so did the objectives of their military expeditions. During the
amirs' rule in Hail, three phases can be discerned: an early phase
of conquest (pre-1836), a middle phase of territorial expansion
(1836–1900), and a final phase of defence (1900–1921). Although
specific dates are given here, they should be understood as a rough
estimation of the time when these changes took place. The shift
from conquest to expansion and defence was a gradual process
stimulated by a number of factors and circumstances, such as
political disputes, the extent of the amirs' military and political
hegemony, and the rise of new power centres in the region.

Conquest

In the pre-1836 era, the military efforts of Abdullah Ibn Rashid,
were concerned with resolving the power struggle between him and
his paternal cousin, Ibn Ali, the ruler of Hail at that time. Ibn
Rashid's political ambitions coincided with rising discontent
among the Shammar and in particular the Jaafar. In Chapter 2 I
have described how the area of Jabal Shammar and Hail fell into
the Saudi–Wahhabi sphere of influence, threatening Shammar
autonomy and successfully undermining their independence. The
Shammar resented Ibn Ali's friendly relations with the rulers of the
first Saudi–Wahhabi dynasty, and the attacks by the Egyptian
troops who came to central Arabia with the intention of
terminating Saudi domination.

These factors paved the way for Ibn Rashid's success in gaining
the military support of the Shammar and channelling it to
overthrow his cousin. During the period of his exile, Ibn Rashid
tried to mobilize the Shammar and win their allegiance. This was
achieved through his participation in their military expeditions
against other tribes in the region. Such expeditions were common
practice especially during the period of chaos which followed the

Egyptian invasions and the withdrawal of the troops from central
Arabia. Raids and counter-raids were intensified as a result of
the power vacuum created by the disintegration of the first
Saudi–Wahhabi realm and the fragile power of the second dynasty.
Competition between various local tribes over the distribution of
the natural resources of the region often led to the outbreak of
violence and aggression. The Shammar were at that time
struggling to create a safe niche for themselves amidst that
confusion and chaos. They had always competed with their
neighbouring tribe, the Anizah, over the exclusive use of pasture
and water – not only in central Arabia, but also in the Syrian
desert where some sections of the Shammar had migrated and
settled. The constant outbreak of violence between the two tribes
has led Burckhardt to believe that the Shammar were the mortal
enemies of the Anizah (Burckhardt 1831: 30). The armed conflict
between them is still remembered in the region where narratives
and poems are recited as reminders of the long period of hostility
between the two tribes.

One of the Shammar narratives describes in detail how the
Anizah under the leadership of Okab and Hijab, the sons of their
sheikh, Sadoun al Awaji, reached an area which was six hours' ride
from Hail with the intention of raiding the Shammar. As soon as
the Anizah arrived in the region, they imposed a siege on the
Shammar nomads who were encamping there. The Shammar
claim that the Anizah raided them and captured their camels. This
raid was known as *al manakh*, a term which indicated the
Shammar's failure to continue their pastoral and herding activity
as a result of the siege which paralysed their camels. The narrative
reveals that the besieged Shammar were rescued by Abdullah Ibn
Rashid who succeeded in killing the sons of Sadoun al Awaji. This
was a famous incident in the history of violence between the
Shammar and the Anizah. Both tribes had elaborate accounts of it
and continue until the present to recite those *qasaid* (oral poems)
which were composed at that time in response to the event (S.A.
Sowayan 1985).

One of the major occupations of the Shammar at that time was
the organization of military units to face external threat and raids.
The mobilization of large tribal units for the purpose of conquest
and the maintenance of autonomy favoured the crystallization of
centralized leadership. The successful organization of conquest,
raids and counter-raids by the dispersed Shammar was to a great

extent dependent on such leadership, whose role involved the co-ordination of various military expeditions. This coincided with Ibn Rashid's desire to conquer Hail and establish his power base there. Co-ordinated military activities were channelled by Ibn Rashid towards the achievement of this objective. The conquest of Hail was crucial for consolidation of the office of amir. However, it should be stressed here that it was not warfare or armed conflict *per se* which stimulated the centralization of leadership among the Shammar. Tribal raids and counter-raids had always been common among the nomadic tribes of the region and elsewhere, but did not necessarily lead to the formation of centralized political systems. Some of the most warlike tribes, such as the Nuer or the Masai of East Africa, have dealt with situations of armed conflict and aggression without stimulating the rise of centralized chiefly office.[8] In the case of the Shammar, the conquest of Hail and the establishment of the amirs seemed to have enforced the tendency towards political centralization.

Andreski was perhaps one of the first to draw our attention to the dangers involved in putting forward deterministic views with regard to the causal connection between armed conflict and the rise of centralized leadership. He argues that it is not warfare in itself but the conquest to which it may lead that constitutes the matrix of monocracy (S. Andreski 1968: 94). Therefore, it is important to identify the context of warfare, its consequences, and the actors involved before drawing generalizations regarding the existence of a causal connection between armed conflict and political structure and organization.

In the case of the Shammar, it is possible to say that their military encounters with the Anizah and other tribes would not necessarily have resulted in the establishment of amir's office. Had this conflict not been followed by the conquest of Hail and the economic benefits this ensured, the amirs' leadership would probably have disintegrated after the raids and threats of violence were terminated. It would be misleading, therefore, to hold deterministic assumptions such as those of Irons (1971 and 1979) and Carneiro (1978) who both stress that the need for the co-ordination and resolution of conflict inevitably leads to the rise of centralized leadership. Irons argues that these are the precondi-tions for the development of chiefly office with an authority to compel the peaceful resolution of conflict, whereas Carneiro emphasizes that warfare is the mechanism for political evolution and the formation of supra-community political units (R. Carneiro 1978: 210). These issues are also discussed by E. Marx who adopts a less deterministic tone as he correctly points out that in the case of the Arab bedouins, competition over economic resources such as water and pasture does not necessarily bring about strong tribal leadership and certainly not the formation of bedouin states. Only under the pressure of hostile neighbours, are the bedouins compelled to seek the patronage of a ruler or to create for themselves a political association that can match that of their enemies (E. Marx 1977: 343–63). However, it is essential to add that hostility between neighbouring tribes at least in the Arabian Peninsula did not always foster the development of patronage. Patronage relations were more likely to emerge when the bedouin leadership succeeded in conquering an oasis with important economic resources not necessarily generated in the oasis itself. In the case of the Hail amirs, their revenues from control over trade and tribute enabled them not only to subsidize the heads of the Shammar tribe, but also to launch military expeditions with the objective of territorial expansion.

Expansion

After the conquest of Hail, the amirs' military expeditions revolved around territorial expansion. The first attempt resulted in the subjugation of the oasis of Al Jauf, which early in the nineteenth century had fallen under Saudi–Wahhabi domination. However, as the Egyptian invasion put an end to this domination, Al Jauf seemed to have freed itself from Saudi control. According to some accounts, it suffered from internal power struggles:

> But when the power of the Wahhabies fell before the Egyptian Pasha, whose troops occupied every province of Negd and Northern Arabia, except Algawf alone, the town reverted to its former state of confusion and discord, which lasted until Abd Allahibnu-r-Rashid, after having strengthened his own power to Gebel Shammar, sent his brother Ubeid-Allah to Algawf, in order to put an end to the above mentioned hostility. (G. Wallin 1854: 146)

It seemed that the internal disputes among the various quarters of Al Jauf took place between the Dilhamiya and Shaara neighbourhoods on the one hand and the Khuthma and Qarawi on the other. Although the causes of the dispute remained unclear, it seemed that the outbreak of violence between the two sides led to the destruction of the Qarawi quarter which was partially inhabited by the Rumal section of the Shammar. The latter had migrated to Al Jauf from another oasis in the Great Nafud Desert, Jubba. Perhaps Abdullah's subjugation of Al Jauf was an attempt to guarantee the security of the Rumal Shammar.[9]

Ibn Rashid sent his brother Obeid with 3,000 camel riders against the disunited oasis which later became tributary to him. Both Wallin and Musil claim that Ibn Rashid did not immediately appoint a governor in the oasis as each quarter had its own sheikh. These dealt with the internal affairs of their quarters and brought matters of greater importance to the amir in Hail. Tribute from Al Jauf was collected by five men appointed by the amir from among the population of Al Jauf.

In 1853, Abdullah's successor, Talal, organized another expedition against the oasis whose population refused to pay tribute after the death of Abdullah Ibn Rashid. Talal's expedition not only aimed at restoring the tribute relations, but was also a strategy to increase his power and influence:

An opportunity offered itself in 1853, when the settlement of al Gowf, which had merely paid tribute to their overlord at Hajel, entered upon a fresh war with one another, and the more powerful party refused to pay the tribute. As soon as this news reached Hajel, Talal sent out a strong force under the leadership of his uncle Obejd and his brother Mitab, to whom the settlement of al Gowf soon capitulated. (A. Musil 1928a: 239).

This final encounter in Al Jauf brought the oasis within the Rashidi amirs' sphere of influence which became extended to the north of Jabal Shammar.

The amirs' expansion to the south led to the outbreak of violence in the Qasim region where the battle of Beqaa took place in 1842. Beqaa was a small village situated ninety-five miles away from Hail. In this battle, Ibn Rashid and his Shammar supporters on the one hand fought against the amir of Boreidah in the Qasim and his supporters among the Anizah tribe on the other. Hostilities between Jabal Shammar and the Qasim were stimulated by the competition between the two areas regarding their control over the caravan trade. The Shammar and the Rashidi amirs had already established their control over Jabal Shammar and its oases, whereas the Qasim was within the sphere of influence of the Anizah tribe.

The outbreak of hostilities was attributed to a raid by Ghazi Ibn Thubian, the sheikh of the Dahamshah section of the Anizah, on the Aslam section of the Shammar. This raid was encouraged by the amir of Boreidah. The Dahamshah defeated the Aslam and captured some of their camels. Ibn Rashid's reaction was to avenge the defeat by raiding the Dahamshah and gaining booty from them. The escalation of hostilities would have stopped at this stage had not the amir of Unaizah (Unaizah is an oasis in the Qasim and should not be confused with the Anizah tribe) mobilized the Suqur and Salatin sections of his tribe against the Shammar and their leadership.

Ibn Rashid summoned his Shammar followers to defend their territory and if possible attack the Qasim region (F. Al Marek 1386 AH: 130–2). The two parties met at Beqaa and the Shammar won the battle. The local Najdi historian, Ibn Bishr, mentions that eighty people from the Anizah tribe, seventy townsmen from Boreidah, and 300 people from the Qasim region were killed (Ibn Bishr 1930: 117–18 vol II). However, military skirmishes between the two regions continued even after the battle was over.

During the rule of Mohammad Ibn Rashid (1869–97), the objectives of the military expeditions continued to revolve around territorial expansion and the acquisition of new oases. Ibn Rashid's expansion at this stage included the subjugation of territories belonging to other power centres in central Arabia, including the Qasim and Riyadh. The population of the major towns of the Qasim, i.e. Unaizah and Boreidah, became tributary to the Hail amir. In addition, the amir's expeditions led to the disintegration of the rather fragile power of he Saudi imams. The collapse of the second Saudi–Wahhabi dynasty was brought about by the Rashidi amirs rather than by a foreign intervention as was the case with the first dynasty.

Ibn Rashid's ability to expand his sphere of influence over the Saudi–Wahhabi domain can only be considered with reference to the internal dissension which broke out among the four sons of Imam Faisal in 1865. After Faisal's death, his eldest son Abdullah became imam. His brother Saud resented his exclusion from power and started a series of contacts with the rulers of Asir, Al Aidh, in an attempt to gain their support. He also negotiated an alliance with the Al Murrah tribe of the Empty Quarter, the Ajman and the Dawasir. The latter were attempting to maintain their autonomy and political independence by allying themselves with Abdullah's rival. These alliances culminated in the battle of Jarba in 1870. According to Abu Aliya, the internal struggle between the Saudi brothers was fuelled by the desire of various nomadic groups to free themselves from Saudi domination. After his defeat at Jarba, Abdullah fled from Riyadh to Hail in an unsuccessful attempt to win the support of Mohammad Ibn Rashid (Abu Aliya 1969: 156–97). As seen in Chapter 3 Ibn Rashid took advantage of this internal dissension and planned for the subjugation of their capital Riyadh.

The military encounter between Mohammad Ibn Rashid and the Saudis resulted in the battle of Muleida, when tribal alliances began to crystallize. Ibn Rashid fought against an alliance of tribes which at that time had an interest in halting his territorial expansion to the south. The autonomy of the two major towns in the Qasim, Unaizah and Boreidah, had already been undermined by the expansion of the Rashidi amirs. The rulers of these towns had realized at an early stage that their interests coincided with that of the Saudis who had been put under mounting pressure by the Hail amir. Furthermore, the Anizah and Mutair tribes were hostile to the growing hegemony of the Shammar. A community of interest and opposition had grown among these various groups (R. Winder 1965: 275–6).

Towards the end of the 1890s, a loose anti-Rashidi confederation was formed. The people of Unaizah under the leadership of Zamil, those of Boreidah under the leadership of Hassan Ibn Muhanna, and the Saudi ruler were determined to stop Ibn Rashid's expansion. To face this alliance Ibn Rashid formed his own *hilf* tribes (alliance tribes). According to Musil, Ibn Rashid sent forty messengers on forty she camels covered with black tent cloth to the various Shammar sections who were at that time encamped between Karbala and Basra in Iraq. The black covers were meant to express clearly that their countenance and their honour would be covered in black shame if they did not immediately come to help their leadership (A. Musil 1928a: 279). Ibn Rashid also sought the support of the Harb, Muntafiq and Dhafir. The Rashidi and Saudi camps met in Muleida, twenty miles west of Boreidah in the

Qasim (D. Ibn Rashid 1966: 13, A. Musil 1928a: 279–80, J. Lorimer 1908: 1177 vol I and J. Philby 1955: 270–3).

Ibn Rashid defeated his enemies and was able to expand his sphere of influence over their territory. Zamil, the amir of Unaizah lost his life in the battle whereas the amir of Boreidah, Hassan Ibn Muhanna was taken to Hail as a hostage. The Qasimi army was defeated and suffered casualties of between 600 and 1200 men. The last Saudi imam, Abdul Rahman, fled together with his family to Kuwait.[10] To consolidate his power in the conquered areas, Ibn Rashid appointed Salim Ibn Sibhan as governor of Boreidah and a member of Zamil's family to the comparable post in Unaizah. The Saudi capital, Riyadh, was also incorporated in Ibn Rashid's realm and he appointed his representatives in the town (R. Winder 1965: 277, A. Abu Aliya 1969: 185, and A. Al Rihani 1973: 104).

In the battle of Muleida, Ibn Rashid relied on four groups. First, he summoned the sedentary and nomadic Shammar population, portraying his rivals as the common enemies of the Shammar. The skirmishes against Shammar territory acted in favour of Ibn Rashid who won approval for his military expeditions. Second, the *hilf* tribes allied themselves with Ibn Rashid as they were motivated by the possibility of capturing *ghanima* (booty) from the defeated party. Third, the amir's slaves and bodyguard fulfilled their duty towards their master and participated in his military expeditions. Fourth, conscripts from the towns and oases of Jabal Shammar provided a reliable military force which Ibn Rashid used regularly for his expansion. Their participation was thought to guarantee the predominance of Hail, both economically and politically.

At the end of the nineteenth century, the territorial expansion of Ibn Rashid, the realization of his dynastic ambitions, and the spread of his sphere of influence had been the major objectives of his military expeditions. When Mohammad Ibn Rashid died in 1897, Rashidi hegemony had already been extended from the borders of Aleppo and Damascus to Basra, Oman and Asir (A. Musil 1928a: 248). His successor, Abdul Aziz, was faced with the problem of defending these acquisitions, for although representatives and governors had been appointed in the conquered areas, firm control had not been established. The scanty resources of the region, coupled with the poverty of the transport infrastructure militated against the full integration of these areas in one unit. It is more accurate, therefore, to describe this expansion as a spread of influence rather than direct control over the conquered territories.

Defence

The move from expansion to defence was triggered by the re-establishment of Saudi power in Riyadh in 1902. Abdul Aziz Ibn Saud, known as Ibn Saud, the son of the last Saudi imam, Abdul Rahman, was determined to recapture his ancestors' capital from the Rashidi amirs and this paved the way for future confrontations.

During their exile in Kuwait, the Saudis tried to mobilize the support of the amir of Kuwait, Mubarak Ibn Sabah. Furthermore, they maintained contacts with the *badu* tribes of Muteir, Muntafiq and Ajman in an attempt to form an alliance which was mainly directed against Ibn Rashid. Kuwait became the seat from which Ibn Saud was to launch his negotiations with tribal sheikhs for the purpose of attacking the rulers of Hail. When faced with the revival of Saudi power, the Hail amir, Abdul Aziz Ibn Rashid, sought support from the Ottoman *wali* of Basra. He managed to win him to his side as the *wali* had a vested interest in attacking Kuwait which appeared at that time to have fallen increasingly within the sphere of influence of Britain (A. Vasiliev 1986: 250).[11] Ibn Rashid sent a telegraph to the Grand Vizir in Istanbul repeating his request for the authorization of the Imperial Government 'to attack sheikh Mubarak Ibn Sabah of Kuwait on the ground that the latter had attacked and plundered Shammar territory.' (IOR, R/15/5/24, O'Conor to the Marquess of Lansdowne, 15 Feb 1904). The first military expedition took place between the amir of Hail on the one hand, and the amir of Kuwait and Ibn Saud and the tribes which were allied to them on the other. Ibn Rashid defeated their camps in a place called Al Sarif in 1901.

Ibn Sabah had put Ibn Saud under his wing, and together they retreated to Kuwait. Ibn Rashid followed them with the intention of attacking them in their own land. He was eager to expand his sphere of influence to Kuwait to minimize the dangers it represented with the settlement of Ibn Saud there. Ibn Rashid was seeking also to break the geographical isolation of Hail from the sea and to establish his control over the port of Kuwait through which the flow of arms and ammunition to Hail could be guaranteed.

The attack on Kuwait was not successful due to the intervention of the British naval forces which opened fire on the Shammar and forced them to retreat to central Arabia. At the same time, the British consul in Istanbul complained to the Ottoman government about the military expeditions of Ibn Rashid against Kuwait. An agreement between the British and Ottoman governments concerning the maintenance of the *status quo* in the area was reached. This agreement encouraged the preservation of the balance of power between the local power centres in the region, i.e. between Ibn Sabah, Ibn Rashid and Ibn Saud (R. Bidwell, FO Confidential Print, Affairs of Arabia, 1905–6, vol I, p. XIII).

During this phase, Ibn Rashid's military expeditions were in defence of the possessions gained during the last two decades of the nineteenth century. The major challenge facing the Hail amirs was the rising power of Ibn Saud who was determined to re-establish his control over Riyadh – and did so in 1902. With the help of the amir of Kuwait, the Ajman, the Sbei, the Suhul, and the Murrah tribes, Ibn Saud recaptured Riyadh from Ibn Rashid after killing his representative in the town, Ajlan Ibn Mohammad (Ibn Hithlul 1961: 57–60, F. Hamza 1933: 132, A. Al Rihani 1973: 108–113, and J. Philby 1955: 231).

Once established at Riyadh, Ibn Saud started to expand his domination over Najd. Consequently clashes with Ibn Rashid over the Qasim region became inevitable. In 1904, Ibn Saud marched on the Qasim in an attempt to terminate Ibn Rashid's control over the province and was able to capture the town of Unaizah and establish Abdul Aziz Ibn Salim as governor of the town (Ibn Hithlul 1961: 245, and J. Philby 1955: 245). Boreidah, the second major town in the Qasim was later incorporated in Ibn Saud's realm and the Shammar forces (150 men) in the region were allowed to return to Hail. These events were watched by the Ottoman officials who eventually decided to back Ibn Rashid in an attempt to restore the balance of power in the region. The Ottoman government regarded the military expeditions of Ibn Saud in the Qasim region as a challenge to its authority in Najd especially when it was clear that the British government and her representatives in the Gulf had already given their sanctions to Ibn Saud's activities (A. Vassiliev 1986: 257). The clashes between Ibn Rashid and his Turkish allies on the one hand and Ibn Saud on the other reached their peak in the battle of Bukeiriya in 1906. The Ottomans lost 1,000–1,500 men whereas Ibn Rashid lost 300–500 men (ibid: 258). Ibn Saud's losses were estimated to have been over 1,000 men. However, the Turkish troops were defeated and

Abdul Aziz Ibn Rashid lost his life in the battle in 1906 at Rawdat Muhanna.

After the defeat of Ibn Rashid there followed a series of minor clashes between his successors and Ibn Saud. Perhaps the most famous battle was that of Jirab in 1915 when Captain W. Shakespear who was accompanying Ibn Saud lost his life. During this battle, the Shammar forces invoked their tribal war cry which was meant to arouse their courage and enforce their solidarity as a tribal unit, whereas the Saudi forces repeated their war cry which stressed the religious character of the encounter and their perception of it as a holy war (*jihad*).[12]

In addition to losses in the southern regions of Najd and the Qasim, Ibn Rashid lost his control over the northern town, Al Jauf, which switched allegiance to the Rwala amir, Ibn Shaalan. In general, the events of the first two decades of the twentieth century were not in favour of the Rashidi amirs. Their rule became restricted to the area of Jabal Shammar and Hail. Their capital was completely lost to Ibn Saud in 1921, thus ending their rule in their own homeland.[13]

To conclude, the outstanding feature of the military encounters of this last phase was the greater involvement of the foreign powers, the Ottomans and the British, in the area. This involvement materialized in sending greater subsidies and weapons to the local power-holders in the region, a practice which contributed to aggravating violence and conflict in central Arabia. At the beginning of the twentieth century, Ottoman intervention involved greater subsidies to Ibn Rashid who was expected to carry out Ottoman plans: 'The allowance paid by the Turkish government to the young amir of Jabal Shammar, Saud Ibn Abdulaziz, has lately been raised from £150 to £200 a month. He has also received the title of Amir al Umara in 1910.' (IOR R/15/5/25)

In addition to these cash subsidies, the Ottomans supplied Ibn Rashid with rifles and ammunition and even participated in the fighting, especially in the Qasim and Hasa regions. Lorimer estimated the number of Ottoman troops sent to Najd between 1904 and 1905 to have been 4,500 men (J. Lorimer 1908: 1155–6). Similarly, the British government maintained greater interest in central Arabia towards the beginning of the twentieth century. British officials in the Gulf region subsidized friendly amirs and sheikhs such as Ibn Saud and Ibn Sabah. Furthermore, they tried to increase the dependence of local groups on their resources through a series of protection agreements. For example, the Amir of Kuwait signed a secret treaty with Britain in 1899. In return for protection, Kuwait had to offer particular concessions to Britain such as freedom of movement and a privileged position with regard to other foreign powers (ibid: 1049–50). Ibn Saud also signed a similar treaty with Britain in 1915, which prevented him from maintaining any contacts with other foreign powers without prior consultation with the British government and its representatives in the region. In return, Britain sanctioned Ibn Saud's control over Najd, the Hasa, Qatif, Jubeil, and all the towns and ports within this territory. He was also entitled to receive a monthly subsidy of £5,000 in addition to weapons and ammunition (A. Vasiliev 1986: 282–284 and C.V. Aitchison 1933: 206).

Finally, the introduction of modern weaponry such as rifles and firearms aggravated the consequences of military conflict in the region. Raids and counter-raids were no longer military expeditions of short duration leading to the capture of camels. Although the participants may have regarded them as traditional raids, military conflict began to develop into actual warfare with the involvement of foreign agents and the use of modern weaponry. In the nineteenth century, the major weapons used in tribal raids consisted of lances, clubs, maces, swords, and matchlocks (J. Burckhardt 1931: 52). Traditionally raiding weapons and techniques involved face-to-face engagement with the enemy. The possibility of identifying the raiders and the dreadful consequences of blood revenge prohibited the development of these raids into bloodbaths. The objective of the military expedition was not to exterminate the enemy, but to gain booty from him. In contrast, modern weaponry, in particular firearms made killing anonymous as it was possible to kill the enemy from a distance. Consequently, the raiders could ignore the raiding rules and conventions which had been respected not because of the good intentions of the raiders, but because of fears that a minor raid might develop into perpetual hostility.[14]

6

MAKING HISTORY
The Power of Poetry

Today, whenever members of the Rashidi family discuss episodes of their past, their rise to power in the nineteenth century, their internal disputes, or the decline of their influence, these discussions always take the form of tales, narratives, and anecdotes. These are frequently interrupted by the recitation of long poems or verses of poems composed by one of their poet ancestors or by other Shammar poets. Narratives and poems constitute common topics of conversation among members of the Rashidi family. A considerable amount of time is spent in telling tales and reciting the oral poetry of the ancestors. This is done to enrich each other's knowledge of the past and exchange bits and pieces of information about the events of the nineteenth century. It is also done for entertainment purposes motivated by both a nostalgia for a glorified past and a bitterness about a wasted dynasty. This exercise is also part of a socialization process whereby young members of the family are introduced to a history which cannot be found in textbooks.

Although six generations separate the present members of the Rashidi family from the founders of the dynasty, the narratives and poems are still remembered. They belong to a reservoir of an oral tradition which is invoked whenever the appropriate occasion arises. While carrying out this research, I relied heavily on information provided by members of the Rashidi family whom I interviewed.[1] I asked questions relating to the causes of the original disputes between the descendants of Ibn Ali and Ibn Rashid, the exile of the Rashidi brothers from Hail in the 1830s, the expansion of their sphere of influence in central Arabia and their wars with other tribal groups and major power centres in the region. These questions and other similar ones gave members of the family the opportunity to indulge in an exercise of historical construction.

They told stories and referred to events which they themselves neither witnessed nor took part in. They were told these stories by members of the previous generation who in turn received this reservoir of knowledge from the generation before.

The authenticity of the stories, claimed the Rashidis, is highly dependent on the status of the narrator, his age, his reputation for possessing good memory and his relationship to what is being narrated. A key element in judging the authenticity of the narratives and oral poems is transmission. When narratives are told, the audience is always keen to know the line of transmission before listening to the speaker. Once this is established, the narrative is enhanced by the recitation of poems which have a wider circulation than the narrative. The clever narrator would be able to recite the right poem at the right moment. By doing so, he enhances the authenticity of his story.

In this genre of the oral tradition, actors are portrayed as wise grandfathers, brave fathers, eloquent uncles, dissident nephews, or treacherous cousins. In this oral history, one finds examples of actors who were 'real politicians', 'brave marshals', and 'traitors' betraying the lineage and surrendering to its enemies. Both 'good' and 'bad' characters are described. They belong to the ancestors whose deeds and words are not forgotten. There is always a story to be told about each one of the amirs who ruled in Hail and their relatives. The amirs of the nineteenth and early twentieth centuries become alive again as individuals experiencing glory over victory, and sorrow over defeat. Their life is told in the form of a narrative. As some of these amirs were famous poets, their poems are recited, thus making their words immortal. The narrator always allows the amirs to speak for themselves by reciting their *qasaid* (sing: *qasidah*: oral poem).

The narratives and oral poety which I collected for the purpose of this research seem to have a wide circulation among the Shammar; although they discuss the lives of members of a ruling lineage, they are part of the oral tradition of the whole tribe. It is not surprising, therefore, that some of these narratives (called *salfah* in Shammar dialect) had already been told to R. Montagne in the 1930s during his research among the northern Shammar of the Syrian Gezirah. The stories collected by Montagne referred to events which had taken place in central Arabia in the previous century (R. Montagne 1932). The northern Shammar took their memories with them when they migrated and these same stories are remembered today by the Rashidis. I give the following example to illustrate this point.

One of the narratives which Montagne documented was told by an Abde narrator who explained his section's rise to power in Jabal Shammar after the defeat of the ruler of that region, a man called Bahij. According to this story, the Abde Shammar arrived in Jabal Shammar and attacked Bahij who took refuge in the fortress of Agde. The Abde ordered him to come out, but Bahig refused unless he was granted protection. The Abde offered him the protection of the Mheisen, the Efrit, the Gedie which were various lineages of the Abde. Bahij remained inside the fortress and refused to accept these offers. He finally came out when the Abde mentioned that the Merdan, who were renowned for keeping their promises, had agreed to put him under their protection. Later Bahij was allowed to leave Jabal Shammar; he migrated to the north, thus leaving the Abde as the sole leaders in the region. Here is Montagne's translation of this *salfah*:

Histoire de Behig de Agdé:
Behig habitait Agdé. Ses gens étaient le Obeid. Les Semmar les chassèrent de Agdé. Behig s'y maintint, resta dans la forteresse et n'en sortit pas. On lui dit: 'Sors!'. Il dit 'je n'en sortirai pas!. Il me faut un protecteur. – Sors sous la caution des Mheisen – (Ceux-la ont des) petits yeux de formis qui se communiquent entre elles des malheurs comme une bonne nouvelle – Sors sous la protection de Efrit – Je ne sortirai pas sous la caution de Efrit – Pourquoi?. Sa colère (dure) jusqu'au midi et il s'appaise!. – Sors sous la caution de Gedi!'. Il ne sortit pas – 'Pour quelle raison ne veux – tu pas sortir?. – Cet âne, si je monte dessus, il ne se fatigue pas de moi, et s'il est sur mon dos, il n'en descend pas. Je ne sortirai pas sous sa protection – Sors sous la caution des Zegrut – Je ne sortirai pas – Pourquoi? – Ils forniquent avec la voisine et mettent en déroute la change de cavalerie. – Sors!. De qui aurai – je la caution?. – Sors sous la protection de Merdan!. – Oui – je sors!. – Pourquoi?. Il n'abandonne pas sa réclamation.' Behig sortit, emigra vers la Geziré – Après lui, Eben Ali commanda au Negd. (R. Montagne 1932: 76–7).

The same story was told to me by a member of the Rashidi family in 1987:

The Abde migrated to Jabal Shammar from the Yemen four centuries ago. When they arrived, Behij, one of the Sheikhs of Zbeid, was the local ruler. The Abde fought a war with him. He escaped to the fortress of Agde and stayed there for some time. The Abde defeated him. He left the fortress and escaped. The Abde were courageous men; they expelled Bahij and ruled in Jabal Shammar which became their *dira* (tribal territory). Obeid Ibn Rashid referred to these events in one of his *qasaid*. Obeid said:

> Before you, Bahig, defeated by the Sanais
> in Agde, the strong fortress

> gablak bahij haddaroh assanais
> min Agdah illi ma yahaddir ganaha

It is noticeable that some details about the various lineages which constituted the Abde were emphasized in Montagne's version whereas they are dropped in the more recent one. In spite of these variations, the theme of arrival to Jabal Shammar and the expulsion of the local ruler is retained as the central theme of the narrative. This theme is important as a justification for the group's presence in Jabal Shammar.

As parallels can be found between the narratives of the northern Shammar which were collected by Montagne almost fifty years ago and the recent accounts of the Rashidi amirs, it is clear that these narratives represent an oral tradition belonging to the whole tribe. The rise and fall of the amirs signify the rise and fall of the tribe as a whole. The narratives do not unfold an 'élitist' history. On the contrary, they are full of references to the Shammar, their relations with their amirs, their support for or disagreement with them, the joy of the supporters over the victory of the amirs or the discontent of the dissenters. The narratives tell us about both the amirs and their tribesmen and this seems to be an important feature of the oral tradition. Goody argues that one of the features of communication in pre-literate societies lies in its capacity to swallow up individual achievement and to incorporate it in a body of transmitted custom that can be considered as the approximate equivalent to what Tylor called 'culture' and Durkheim 'society' (or rather the 'social factor'), and which both writers regarded as *sui generis* (J. Goody 1977: 27).

THEMES IN RASHIDI NARRATIVES AND ORAL POETRY

What we call oral tradition refers to the bulk of the verbal messages that are reported statements from the past beyond the present generation (J. Vansina 1985: 27). These verbal messages can take various forms depending on the modes of transmission. Vansina gives a list of what can be classified as oral tradition: *memorized speech* (poems), *accounts* (historical gossip, personal tradition, group accounts of origin and genesis, and cumulative accounts), *epics*, and *tales, proverbs and sayings* (ibid: 14–27). Societies might have an oral tradition consisting of all these, or just one or two predominant forms.

The Shammar and Rashidi oral tradition seems to consist mainly of narratives (*salfah*) and oral poems (*qasidah*) which usually occur together in the process of accounting for the past. The theme of the *salfah* is often preserved during the different performances of the same narrative, while some versions are more detailed than others. The narrator often includes dialogues between two or more persons. The words of the dialogue are repeated with more precision than the narration of events, which has a cumulative character and often leads to a climax provided by the recitation of a *qasidah*.

The *qasidah* is memorized oral poetry of a known or anonymous poet who reacted to or participated in historical events and documented them in a poem with a special rhythm and metre. There is more accuracy in poetry recitation than in the narration of the *salfah*; the Rashidis claim that the musical sound of the *qasidah* makes it easier to memorize. Also any verbal deviation from the original version is easily detected by the audience – especially if this deviation upsets the rhythm. When a *qasidah* is recited, the person repeats the opening verses two or three times to remember the rhythm or the musical sound while waiting for the remaining verses to be recalled from the reservoir of his memory.

The *salfah* is not complete unless it is accompanied by a *qasidah*, which equally does not stand on its own. The narrative usually represents a commentary or explanatory prelude to the *qasidah*, placing it in its historical context and telling us who composed the *qasidah* if known.

Scholars of bedouin oral tradition have noticed the interconnectedness between the narrative and the *qasidah* and analysed them together (B. Ingham 1986 and S. Al Sowayan 1985) whereas others have treated the two components separately. For example, Meeker, in his study of Rwala oral literature, discussed narratives and poems in two separate parts of his book. It is worth noting that he did not collect this oral literature himself, but relied on the transcriptions in Musil's work (1928). Consequently, Meeker tends to treat them as literary texts which lend themselves to analysis. His analysis automatically shifts in the third chapter of his book towards literary criticism, stressing the musicality of the poems, their eloquence, and artistic features as manifested by the choice of words, the rhythm, metre, imagery, and metaphors. In addition, he comments on the shortcomings of Rwala poems of raid and war:

> We do not know if the war to which the poem refers involved a single battle on a particular day, an extended battle over several days, or several battles over a period of months. The Rwala of course do not share our ignorance since their narrative tradition fills out the details which are missing from the poem. However, this is just the point. The necessity of knowing the narrative tradition in order to place the scenes in context only emphasises how discontinuous, fragmentary and unstory-like the poem is. (M. Meeker 1979: 120)

Why then uproot the poetry from the historical context which the narrative provides and analyse it as a literary text? The Rwala do not recite poems for the sake of it. Their oral poetry is meaningless without the context which is so inseparable from the poem. This seems to be a characteristic of oral poetry in general. Finnegan argues that oral literature is dependent on its social context. She stresses that we cannot concentrate on the text alone, but must take account of the nature of the audience and the context (R. Finnegan 1977: 29). Other scholars of bedouin oral tradition, such as Caton, stress that the *qasidah* is not a narrative or a chronology of historical events (S. Caton 1984: 371). It has a *munasabah* (context or occasion) which is important for its composition. Caton, therefore, argues that the text of the poem bears on a real historical event, without knowledge of which the audience will fail to understand the poem (ibid: 423).

My aim here is not to analyse the literary and linguistic aspects of Shammar oral literature but to deduce from this tradition significant themes which were relevant to that society and which can only be gleaned from the oral tradition. For this purpose, I select two themes: exile, which is expressed in the first narrative (the narrative and poems of exile), and secondly herosim (the heroic narrative and poems). The selection of these particular themes from a rich oral tradition is guided by my aim to show how various experiences are reflected in that tradition. Although the following narratives and poems have a strong political preoccupation, in the sense that they refer to important political conflicts and events, each accounts for the experience of political struggle in a different way.

THE NARRATIVE AND POEMS OF EXILE

In Chapter 2, the rise of the Rashidi amirs to power in Hail was reconstructed by using information from primary and secondary sources. Here, we move to a different level of historical construction as we consider a more personalized account of the political struggle in Hail based on information gathered from members of the family. This information is derived from the narratives and poems in which the story of the exile from Hail of Abdullah Ibn Rashid, his brother, and their mother is told. As I asked why Abdullah and Obeid challenged the authority of their cousin Ibn Ali, the narrator responded by telling me this story:

> Abdullah and Obeid were brave young men. Their father Ali Ibn Rashid was a simple man who had a farm in Hail where he cultivated dates. Ali Ibn Rashid was *ibn amm* (paternal cousin) of the ruler of Hail, Saleh Ibn Ali. The young Abdullah and Obeid were ambitious; they could not accept their cousin's authority. In particular, Abdullah wanted power. He was a man of arms, a war leader. Abdullah wanted to raid with the Shammar to satisfy his ambition. The opportunity came when the Aslam Shammar were attacked by the Anizah who captured the camels of the Aslam. Abdullah rode his camel to the Aslam to defend them and stand by their side. He fought with them a war against the Anizah and succeeded in returning their captured camels. Abdullah's fame started to grow bigger and bigger among the *badu* and the *hadar*. Saleh Ibn Ali resented this. He thought that if Abdullah married his daughter, he would probably stop making trouble. This did not work for there was nothing which could discourage Abdullah. Saleh asked Abdullah and his brother Obeid to stay quietly in Hail or leave.

Abdullah preferred to leave. His father tried to persuade him to abandon his ambition and stop making trouble. Abdullah said to his father before leaving Hail: *lau tu' ayt shorak ma taadit dhanab thorak.* (If I accept your advice, I will never go beyond the tail of your bull). Abdullah left and took refuge in Jabal Aja. His wife came to visit him and to assure him that he had her support and trust. She came with Abdullah's friend, a man called Hossein. Abdullah was pleased to see his wife; he was also worried about her. Abdullah addressed his friend in a *qasidah* in which he asked this friend to look after his wife on the return journey to Hail. Abdullah said:

1 Oh! Hussein, she is wearing no shoes
  Oh! Hussein, it hurts me to know she is tired
2 Look after her and be lenient with her
  follow her steps and do not rush her
3 Take care of the beloved and if necessary
  make her slippers out of your clothes
4 Oh! Hussein, only those who are bad
  will mistrust the good
5 Even if you needed to carry her
  that is all right, for only a friend can be trusted

1 ya Hsen wallah malaha sabt rijlen
  ya Hsen, shayab baldhamir haka'anah
2 irfag baha ya Hsen witba' baha allin
  walli mishat ya Hsen famsh mashyanah
3 irfag bimadhmun sakan hajir al eyn
  wishlag laha min ras ridnak liyanah
4 ya Hsen ma yishtak kud arraddiyn
  wla tara attayib wasin ridanah
5 win shiltaha ya Hsen tara mabaha shin
  tara alkhawi ya Hsen mithl alamanah

News about Abdullah and Obeid's plot to assassinate Ibn Ali aggravated the latter's anger. He even sent their mother into exile. She was an old woman. Her exile depressed her. She addressed her children in a *qasidah* in which she said:

1 Oh! the light of my eyes, the love of my heart
  I look like one of those poor Indian pilgrims
2 I was expelled in the hot summer from my country

where the palms have become so dry
3 I hope justice will be restored
and we return to the country in peace

1 ya nur eyni ya mawaddat fwadi
ma kini illa min khimam addarawish
2 jalloni balgedh alhamar 'an biladi
u dirat hali fogi kima ghiyat alhish
3 assa yiji 'adil u mamshah gadi
u tikthar adhar illi ydawwir attahawish

When Abdullah heard his mother's poem, his determination to
return to Hail and overthrow his cousin increased. Abdullah left
his brother Obeid in Jabal Aja to look after his family. He went
to the Jaafar, his lineage who gave him all their support. A few
years later, Abdullah and Obeid killed their cousin. Abdullah
ruled in Hail bringing happiness and justice.

Not all the Shammar approved of Abdullah's action. Ibn
Twala, the sheikh of the Aslam, and Al Timyat, the sheikh of
the Tuman had a *hilf* (covenant) with Ibn Ali according to
which they swore allegiance to him. Obeid defended his
brother's action and addressed the Aslam and the Tuman in his
qasidah:

1 Oh! messenger, ride the camel, the free breed
like an army, fast
2 Visit Udwan, and stop at Nais[2]
say: the country belongs to those who defend it
3 Abu Talal, the sheikh, the fox who frightens the horses[3]
attacks his enemy and spreads fear
4 The country belongs to the Yitman, even if
Nais and the Tuman do not agree
5 Our country since the days of Tai and Qais[4]
the Dhayagim defended it with their swords
6 Why disapprove and question his right
which he achieved by the sword

1 ya sharikh irkab fog nab annasanis
hurr arib min hadhayib nadhaha
2 sayyir ala udwan u nawukh ala nais
u gil addar darali hathi ghathaha
3 abu Talal ashshekh dhib almalabis

kam hajmitin yagta' halla min rajaha
4 addar lilyitman lo yaza'al nais
lo taza'al attuman w' illi waraha
5 Darin lina min gabul tayy illya qais
bassef sibyan adhdhayaghim hamaha
6 lo azza'al min shan hagak flabes
bas tabi hugug alli bassef khadhaha

In this narrative, the narrator takes us from the general realm of political struggle to the personal level of emotions and tells a story about political conflict between kinsmen. This particular type of conflict makes the two levels of experience, the general and the personal, merge together. Abdullah is portrayed as a young dissident challenging an established authority, i.e. that of his cousin who could not tolerate any infringement of his sphere of influence. Abdullah not only questions the authority of his opponent, but also defies parental wisdom. His refusal to listen to his father's advice is an indicator of his unwillingness to suppress his ambition for political hegemony. In this struggle, Abdullah seeks the support of his brother who is now drawn into the arena of political conflict. At a later stage in the narrative, political struggle against Ibn Ali involves a group bigger than the Rashidi brothers. The Jaafar become involved in this conflict as they give refuge to Abdullah.

After focusing on the political conflict, the narrator moves to explaining how this conflict is lived by Abdullah, who in addition to being brave and ambitious, experiences emotions of sorrow, worry, and upheaval caused by separation from his wife and family. Pursuing a political career becomes entangled with an agonizing separation. The extent of worry is lessened by the presence of a loyal and trustworthy friend who brings Abdullah's wife to visit him in exile. In his poetry, Abdullah, worried and ill at ease, accepts this and reminds his friend of the bond of friendship. Abdullah chooses to do this in poetry so that his words remain as evidence for his approval of his wife travelling alone with this friend. As long as his words are remembered, shame could not fall on him or his wife.

Once again, the circle of this political conflict is widened as the curse of exile hits the old mother who is forced to leave her country under difficult circumstances. Her experience brings about a quest for justice with the hope that this will restore peace and harmony.

The mother reacts to these humiliating events by composing a poem. After hearing their mother's plea, how could the sons not defend their honour? How could they not do something about their mother's humiliation especially after she had left words which kept her suffering alive in everybody's memory?

The narrative and poems of exile represent a genre of the oral tradition in which one finds references to a public world characterized by political conflict, dissidence, and disputes. In this world, men fight for political hegemony. Consequently, they are portrayed as political actors with strong claims to power. Their struggle, however, affects those around them such as their relatives and their dependents. The impersonal nature of the field where political struggle takes place, is contrasted with the warmth, affection, and closeness characterizing relations between a man and his wife or friend. The aggressive 'political man' has another important dimension to his personality – like everybody, he experiences emotions. In this genre of the oral tradition, the hero is not a 'mythical' one, or in other words, an idealized person. He is brought down to earth by his own words in which he expresses sorrow and worry.

By focusing on this type of the oral tradition, I show that the so-called bedouin political adventurer, to use Meeker's terminology, is also a social man. Abu Lughod has rightly argued that our understanding of bedouin culture and oral tradition is limited if we concentrate solely on raids, war and political struggle (L. Abu-Lughod 1986: 31). The Shammar narrative and poems of exile show that the predominant values of society, especially those praising political supremacy, courage and bravery as desired virtues enabling men to assume leadership positions, allow room for the expression of emotions of a less manly nature with no shame. The fact that Abdullah, a potential leader, allows himself and is allowed in the narrative to express his worries, love, and care proves this point. His mother's plea for political justice, on the other hand, reflects a role that women were allowed to play. From her personal experience of exile, the mother ventures into the political realm of men. Her poem is a political statement, a plea or a request for action which she herself is unable to carry out. Nevertheless, her voice and words remain as important stimulants for this action.

After success is achieved, there comes the problem of justification. Abdullah and Obeid kill a cousin who has the support of two sections of the Shammar. How could the Rashidis rule in Hail without explanations which, above all, aim at persuading, convincing and winning the approval of all. Obeid's poem is a justification of a *fait accompli*. It is a claim to legitimacy in which the right to rule in Hail is portrayed as a historical and above all an inherited right. Obeid aims to convince his audience that his brother's actions are not an innovation, rather they are in line with an ancient tradition. Obeid is surprised that the Aslam and the Tuman disapprove of Abdullah's success, a success established through the use of the sword. The Rashidi hereditary right is restored through an act of bravery which cannot be classified as a crime of murder. In the context of political struggle against a usurper, killing is not a crime. It becomes a justified heroic act which itself establishes a claim to power.

THE HEROIC NARRATIVE AND POEMS

This genre of narrative and oral poetry has as its subject matter the celebration of intra-tribal wars. It derives its material from historical events which are related in most cases to raids and battle. These events give the narrator and the poet the opportunity to celebrate victory through the demonstration of heroic deeds and at the same time ridicule the enemy. The following is the translation of one of the narratives told by a member of the Rashidi family, which celebrates the Shammar victory over their Anizah enemies in the battle of Beqaa:[5]

After Abdullah Ibn Rashid had succeeded in establishing himself as ruler of Hail and Jabal Shammar, he was involved in a battle with the Anizah and the people of the Qasim. Hostilities started when Ghazi Ibn Dhubian, the sheikh of the Dahamshah (Anizah) raided the Aslam Shammar and their sheikh, Ibn Twala. The Dahamshah attacked the Shammar and captured their camels. Abdullah Ibn Rashid knew about this incident and wanted to organize a raid on the Dahamshah with the intention of recapturing the Shammar camels and returning them to the Aslam. Abdullah could not accept the defeat of his *ibn amm*, the Aslam. Abdullah defeated the Dahamshah and killed some of their men. This annoyed the amir of Boreidah who promised to take revenge and attack Abdullah Ibn Rashid. The amir of

Boreidah had the support of the people of the Qasim whom he
summoned to raid Ibn Rashid. He also convinced the Salatin
and the Suqur sections of the Anizah to join in the raid against
Ibn Rashid. He led this group and marched to Beqaa where he
attacked the Shammar who were encamped in that area.
Abdullah Ibn Rashid knew about this aggression. He immediately sent his brother Obeid with his army to Beqaa. Obeid
fought the Qasimis and the Anizah. He was later joined by
Abdullah who arrived in Beqaa with arms and men. The
Shammar captured many camels in this battle. The Anizah were
defeated by Ibn Rashid who killed many of their men. Obeid
Ibn Rashid celebrated the Shammar victory in his poem:

1 Oh! my heart, varied thoughts
  some are right others are unclear
2 Ninety thoughts turn in the chest
  some are small others are big
3 I left all but two
  Saadi and my sword capable of healing the heart[6]
4 And a big army and a gun
  with mares of noble breed
5 Our country! we defend you against attackers
  at night, evening and morning
6 Let the enemy come themselves
  there is no need to send messengers
7 We faced them with an army, more than two thousand
  like a water deluge fast and high
8 The *hadar* and the *badu* of the Jabal come
  followed by our women, with long black hair[7]
9 We attacked them in the morning while they were hiding
  the flames of the battle rose in the air
10 Victory won by a favour from God
  defeated the Qasimis and the sons of Wayil
11 A battle which brings joy, oh! Hussein
  a tribe like no other tribe
12 My people! swords covered with blood
  left the pebbles of Beqaa red
13 Ninety I killed with my sword
  no worry over expelling the rest
14 Events witnessed by admirers
  no lies can be told

15 They desired our land and fields
   they wanted Gofar and Hail
16 Today they want us but we defy them
   we defend ourselves with our swords from all comers

 1 ya min ligalbin hajs u hajus
   hajs u hajus u 'adil u mayil
 2 yidir fi dulab alafkar tisin
   bassadur yinshir daqahin u al jalayil
 3 asbaht minham khalin gheyr thinten
   Sa'adi u masgul ydawi l ghalayil
 4 u khmasi ghumg sawabah wa jouzen
   iliya karribaw shahs almhar alasayil
 5 ya darna min jak jinah ajlin
   ballel wa ssafar wal guwayil
 6 fain kan hum anna bilanshad muhfen
   min arras ma nihtaj dazz arrasayil
 7 nati min awwal bisurbah fog alalfen
   kunna ash har bih didahan al masayil
 8 hadhar al jabal wal badu nati salben
   yatlin'nana jamlat sud aljadayil
 9 jina sabah uhum lana mistikin' nin
   u thar addakhan min harr salo alfatayil
10 min fadhl wali al'arsh 'adl almawazin
   sarat 'ala' lgusman u awlad wayil
11 ajajah tijli' il galub ya Hsen
   dbelah mahi bkul eddebayil
12 rab' yi marwiyat essiuf al missanin
   khallu safa Baqaa min addam sayil
13 u illi dhibaht bshathrat essef tis'en
   minham wa lani a'n radduhum bsayil
14 u illi wateyna ma yushuf al muhibbin
   u alkithb tanfah ul'ulum assamayil
15 jona yabghun dy'yarna wal basatin
   yabghun manzilhum Qufar u Hayil
16 wal' yum yabghunna u hinna ma'ayin
   nisnid bhadd assayf min jah ayil

Both Abdullah and Obeid demonstrated their courage in the battle and their reputation spread all over Arabia. Abdullah described his courage in his own words:

1 My country where there is nothing but cold hunger
  I defended with Indian swords
2 Protected it from the greedy
  we salute one group and calm them down another
3 Brother of Obeid, as the cowards run away
  I stay alert while people sleep
4 I try my luck in life
  with money or with sharp swords
5 Oh! the poor, the hungry who come to us
  have seen days of misery
6 Even if we do not know them, they leave satisfied
  with money collected to be dispersed

1 li diritin mabaha hatha albard wal ju'
  lolay affeiytah btharb al hanadi
2 hamaytaha 'an kul dawar matmu'
  hay nsabbuhum u hay nhadi
3 akhu Obeid illa haba kul masbu'
  as' har alla namat 'ayoun assaradi
4 uhawyl addunya bdakhil wa madlu'
  bilmal walla murhfat alhadadi
5 kam khayyir anin lana shaki yal ju'
  hadih min lawat alayam hadi
6 lo ma na'arfuh rah minna bmatmou'
  min ras malin nijma ah linnifadi

Abdullah died after the battle. He left the *imarah* to his son, Talal. His death brought relief to his enemies who thought that the Shammar would be weakened. Obeid reminded all those who received the news of Abdullah's death with joy that nothing had changed; the Shammar supremacy was guarded by Abdullah's successors:

1 Tell the enemy who rejoice at the news
  joyed over a matter descending from the sky
2 No doubt, the flame has vanished
  but we are the fire which rises high

1 gul lila'du illi tibahaj bilakhbar
  u freh 'alla amrin nazilin min samaha
2 u qata' brayi in tefat shi'lat nar
  hinna shibat annar nughid sanaha.

This heroic narrative refers to a political and military conflict between the Shammar on the one hand and the Qasimis and the Anizah tribe on the other. Reference to this conflict can be found in written sources.[8] In the narrative, the narrator mentions events rooted in Shammar history, although there is no reference to time. Questions regarding when the Shammar were first raided by the Anizah, when Abdullah Ibn Rashid counter-attacked, when the Anizah and the Qasimis reached Beqaa, how long the battle lasted, when the Shammar achieved victory, and when Obeid composed his poems are not dealt with. The major characteristic of the narrative is the absence of chronological dating, which prevents it from being considered as an historical text.

However, the narrative describes structural social and political relations between the Shammar and other groups in the region and, in particular, it documents a perpetuated conflict between the Shammar and the Anizah. Both tribes have a rich narrative tradition whose themes revolve around the ancient conflict between them.[9] The emphasis is not put on 'historical time', rather, the structure of intra-tribal relations becomes the focus of the story. As a result, the narrative does not reveal 'historical truths'; its major contribution lies in the fact that it spells out the nature of these intra-tribal relations and the way they are structured around opposition and conflict.[10]

The narrator introduces the actors as two parties with latent and old hostilities. The Shammar and the Anizah represent two opposed groups who in the past had been engaged in minor clashes. This information clarifies the background and places the present events in context. The opposed groups are not entering a fresh war but simply perpetuating the *status quo*.

This long-lasting opposition is brought to the surface again as a result of a raid designed by the Anizah and directed against the Aslam Shammar. Tribal raids become the occasion where this opposition is manifested. Raids are motivated by previous hostilities; they in turn determine future opposition. As the Aslam are raided and their camels are captured, this requires a counter-raid to restore the Shammar camels to their owners, and above all to re-establish Shammar honour. Abdullah Ibn Rashid, a well-established amir, cannot but respond to these events for the Aslam are his tribal kinsmen with whom he shares a common ancestor. The Abde Shammar to whom Abdullah belongs are the classificatory *ibn amm* (paternal cousins) of the Aslam – the two have a common destiny. Abdullah, therefore, launches his counter-raid and restores to the Aslam their dignity.

The conflict between the Shammar and the Anizah grows bigger and bigger as the amir of Boreidah becomes involved and assembles to the battle other sections of the Anizah, the Salatin and the Suqur. Here we have a situation whereby a minor raid develops into a major war in which several tribal groups become involved. The military encounter lasts for several days. The battlefield becomes the arena where military skills, bravery and courage are demonstrated. Abdullah and Obeid participate in the actual fighting and compose poems to celebrate their victory and that of the Shammar and above all, to ridicule the defeated enemy. The narrative ends with the recitation of three poems composed by Abdullah and Obeid.

Obeid's first poem celebrates the Shammar victory in the battle of Beqaa and belongs to that genre of *qasidah* which is common among bedouins and other groups in the Middle East and whose composition is stimulated by military encounters and intra-tribal conflicts.[11] Obeid's *qasidah* does not describe an imaginary situation, rather it refers directly to an actual event, a battle, in which the poet himself had participated.

In this poem, Obeid launches a verbal war on his enemies after the fighting had stopped. He documents the defeat of the Shammar's enemies in words which are meant to last forever. Obeid's opening verses set the context for the events which follow. He begins by portraying himself as someone perturbed with all the thoughts turning in his head. In this state of turmoil, he takes refuge in two precious objects: his horse Saadi and his sword. Obeid immediately invokes the image of a huge army with thousands of noble mares. This is an image which can be translated into reality. The army is for the defence of his *dira*, his home and territory. Both the *hadar* and the *badu* assemble to defend this territory as they face a common enemy, an external enemy heading towards Jabal Shammar with the intention of attacking the land, the fields, the oases, Gofar and Hail. As the *badu* and the *hadar* assemble and head for the battlefield, they are followed by the Shammar women who praise the fighters and encourage them. This army attacks the enemy. The opportunity comes at last for Obeid to use his sword; he kills ninety people and expels the rest of the enemy group. Victory for the Shammar is achieved with the help of God. Obeid addresses his friend Hossein in the poem:

memories of this victory bring pleasure to the heart. A victory achieved by a tribe which is like no other tribe. This tribe is known for the bravery of its members who left Beqaa covered with the enemies' blood.

The victory of the Shammar is also celebrated in Abdullah's poem, which constitutes a genre of self-praise. By composing a poem, Abdullah asserts his first prestigious quality, his eloquence. Here we have a case whereby the amir is also a poet capable of surpassing the limited level of ordinary speech. He communicates his message in the form of brief artistic verses which have the advantage of being powerful instruments easily remembered, memorized and repeated among both his followers and enemies. The ability to communicate verbal messages in a poetic form is a valued quality especially if possessed by the amir. To be able to express oneself clearly and eloquently in short verses as a result of possessing poetic talents is a sign of prestige not only for the poet, but also for his tribe. It reflects mastery over a poetic form of speech which is preserved from the past. This ability also signifies that the poet has maintained mastery over a pure form of speech uncontaminated by contacts with foreign people. Poetic talents reveal an authentic origin, pure ancestry and nobility. Here poetic language is a status symbol accompanied by prestige. The poet-amir proves his authenticity and high status in addition to that of his group. His eloquence is not solely a personal quality but one which is enriched and enhanced through a process of socialization whereby the amir becomes familiar with the dialect and poetic tradition of his tribe and ancestors.

The poet-amir is a powerful propagandist who spreads his fame, announces his virtues and enhances his reputation. In his poem, Abdullah lists his personal qualities such as generosity and heroic skills (courage and bravery). These qualities characterize tribal leaders, both sheikhs and amirs. They are prestigous assets which constitute in this society the basis of leadership and are regularly stressed in oral poetry. It is important to discuss these qualities as they find expression in the *qasidah* in an attempt to decipher their meaning and their relevance to the realm of politics.

In his poem Abdullah, the poet-amir, stresses his generosity towards the poor and the hungry. He asserts that he never turns people away empty-handed. The description of the act of generosity is accompanied by the image of the country where poverty and scarcity are common. The poet aims to show that to give generously in an environment characterized by scarcity is an ultimate virtue. As generosity seems to be a recurrent theme in oral poetry, this raises the question of why it finds expression in this type of speech and why the poet-amir constantly reminds his audience of this particular asset. To answer these questions, one had to consider first, the importance of poetic messages in this society and second, assess the socio-political implications of generosity. Generosity as a virtue and a prestigous asset is communicated to the audience through oral poetry. When messages take a poetic form, they have a strong effect and a wide circulation. In oral poetry, messages become endowed with extra powers. Once composed, a poem is memorized and recited over generations.

The generosity of the amir stands as a disguised coercive force over the receivers. When the receivers of generosity happen to be of equal status to the generous man, generosity is a latent coercive instrument. This point can be illustrated in the following example. When the Rashidi amirs used to receive Shammar sheikhs and other non-Shammar notables in their *majlis*, meals were cooked for the guests, animals were slaughtered, coffee was served, and gifts of rice, weapons, and dates were distributed. These were generous acts celebrating the presence of important guests. After these feasts, political matters were usually discussed with the guests, tribal alliances were negotiated, and disputes were settled. Generosity in this context was a strategy with political implications, intended to impress equals who would no doubt propagate the news to those who had not been present in the *majlis* at that time. Generosity creates an aura around the amir which attracts supporters and potential political allies. Simply, when the amir is generous towards his equals, he enhances his political status and increases his prestige.

On the other hand, generosity towards weaker groups is a coercive force in a naked form. It creates economic dependence on the amir's resources which eventually leads to political submission. In this case, generosity acts as a bribe for loyalty and acceptance of political authority. Furthermore, generosity here is a mechanism for the circulation of wealth in which rich groups pass on a proportion of their wealth to the poor. In a society lacking formal or institutionalized means for such circulation, generosity, in addition to kin obligations, can play an important role in bridging the gap between those who have and those who have not.

The amir who proves his generosity through deeds (generous acts) and words (the communication of the quality in oral poetry) acts in accordance with the Shammar expectations which are best revealed to us through a proverb. The Shammar say that the amir is *saif wa mansaf* – literally sword and *mansaf* (meal consisting of rice and lamb). This means that there are two bases for his leadership: his ability to demonstrate heroic skills and his ability to provide meals for his followers.

Heroic skills consist of courage and bravery in battle. The ability to defend one's group and territory is an heroic act which is constantly invoked in oral poetry. Abdullah praises himself for being able to maintain an alertness which enables him to quickly discover trespassers and aggressors. He is also proud of his mastery over the use of arms, a valued quality in a society where aggression was a common feature of everyday life. To defend tribal territory against raiders provides the opportunity to experience *fakhr* (glory) and increase personal honour. Associated with this *fakhr* is a strong sense of belonging to a territory. In the poem, it becomes clear that the *dira* (territory) *per se* does not constitute the focus of pride, love or affection. What is stressed is sovereignty over a given territory. Abdullah mentions the poverty of his territory, the scarcity of its resources, and its harsh environment, features which do not make it attractive. This also implies that it has no inherent value to justify defending it; yet, Abdullah enjoys asserting the sovereignty of this territory under his leadership.

The amir-poet is a propagandist not only for his personal virtues and assets, but also for the tribe as a whole. In the poem, he projects his personal qualities on the tribe. The Rashidi poets are not unique in playing this role. In his study of Yemeni oral poetry, Caton stresses that poetic forms have a quasi-magical effect on the audience. Mastering poetic forms is necessary to defend the tribe's honour since it is equivalent in its potency to the fire-power of a gun or the cutting edge of the blade. Caton emphasizes that the poet sheikh is endowed with the power of persuasion, a quality which makes him a successful mediator in disputes as he persuades his clients to accept peaceful settlements of their conflict through the magical power of the poetic art (S. Caton 1984: 421). Oral poetry, according to Caton, becomes political rhetoric which he defines as communicative acts of persuasion made in response to conflict in the segmentary social order (ibid: 405).

Among the Shammar, a large number of poems are endowed

with the function of being integrated into political discourse. Obeid's second poem, for example, illustrates this point. Obeid uses poetic speech to communicate a political message of great importance to his enemies: that Shammar hegemony is not likely to disappear with the death of Abdullah Ibn Rashid. He addresses the enemies of the Shammar who had expressed their joy upon hearing the news of Abdullah's death. Obeid uses the strong image of a glowing fire to refer to the hegemony and leadership which his brother maintained over the years. He then claims that if one of the flames of this fire has vanished, there are other flames which keep the same fire glowing. The use of such images in oral poetry makes it a strong political discourse of a distinguished character. Images add to the message an emotional dimension, they add resonance. These occur, according to Vansina, spontaneously in the audience who hears the message (J. Vansina 1985: 137–8).

Obeid's poem not only communicates a message to the enemy, it has the advantage of doing so in a way which glorifies the group and demoralizes its enemies. This poem and other similar ones achieve a strong effect through a clever way of using words, symbols and images, and are easier to remember than prose. As this poem was composed after the death of Abdullah, it can be compared to the political statements one hears today on the radio after the death of kings or presidents – both are meant to restore faith, confidence, trust and assert continuity after the death of a leader. There is always a deliberate attempt at dissociating the political system from the personal influence of the deceased ruler while at the same time stressing his role in achieving hegemony.

In both the narrative of exile and the heroic narrative, oral poetry stands as a sacred evidence through which experience is communicated and documented. This leads us to consider the following questions. What role did oral poetry play in Shammar society at that time? What significance did this form of communication have in the context of the Rashidi dynasty?

THE POWER OF POETRY

A number of theories have been put forward by folklorists and literary critics to account for the significant role of oral poetry.[12] What concerns us here is the sociological explanations that regard oral poetry as a reflection of society and aim at identifying its role in that society. For example, the functionalist approach as represented by Malinowski and Radcliffe-Brown considers oral poetry as promoting solidarity and self-awareness among the group like any other form of the oral tradition.[13] The Marxist approach, on the other hand, sees poetry as a tool or an ideological charter of the ruling classes propagating and endorsing its ideas.[14]

These two approaches have been criticized for being monolithic and too generalized. Finnegan, for example, rejects any grand theory in which universal functions are allocated to oral poetry: 'Oral poetry can be used to reconcile, divide, maintain established authority or undermine it, propagandize, soothe. To judge which if any of these are in play it is essential not to begin from an abstract analysis of first principles, but from a consideration of the occasion and, above all, of the audience and of its reception and understanding of the performance.' (R. Finnegan 1977: 243). She also rejects the simplisitic view that oral literature reflects society, its norms, and circumstances. She asserts that what comes into poetry may reflect certain aspects of society and express ideas and reactions of concern to people at the time, but to take literary forms as a direct and full reflection or as a direct source of social history can only be misleading. She points out that: 'All literature in an indirect and subtle way must reflect the society in which it exists . . . A poet is a product of his own culture, rather than the free untrammelled genius of romantic theory.' (ibid: 263)

Finnegan puts forward an understanding of oral poetry which accommodates both the poet and his society. She argues that while the sociologist must insist on the significance of the social context of literature, he should also remember the role of literature as the medium for the creative imagination of men (ibid: 271).

Three recent studies have dealt with the question of the relationship between oral poetry and bedouin society in the Middle East. Meeker stresses that oral poetry is a reaction against the uncertainty of formal political relations among the north Arabian bedouins (Meeker 1979). In a society where men's relationships with one another are in question, the literary voice crystallizes as the centre of formal and public life. In contrast, Caton, adopts a more pragmatic view and identifies the functions that oral poetry plays in particular political situations such as dispute settlement, persuasion and mediation (S. Caton 1984). Abu-Lughod, on the other hand, criticizes these two studies for overemphasizing the centrality of politics and conflict in bedouin society. She tries to rectify these biased views which are in large a product of the concerns of anthropologists and bedouin males. She focuses on the bedouin *ghinnawa* (song) which can be considered as the poetry of personal life. Individuals recite this genre of poetry in specific social contexts, for most part private, articulating in it sentiments about their personal situations and closest relationships. It is worth noting that the *ghinnawa* seems to be common among women and young male members of Awlad Ali (L. Abu-Lughod 1986: 31).

In this chapter, I have selected two illustrative examples of Shammar narratives and poems. These showed that when political conflict is central to people's experience, it is natural that it finds expression in poetic forms, one of the media of expression in that society. However, the oral poetry recited earlier shows a considerable degree of flexibility. It can convey personal, sentimental and emotional messages in addition to heroic, public and glorified messages. While I agree with Meeker and Caton that political conflict is central in bedouin society, I stress that bedouin oral poetry is flexible enough to incorporate human experiences other than those of political struggle.

Shammar oral poetry is associated with particular socio-political and historical events. When poets, including those of the Rwala, the Shammar and the Yemeni tribes, compose or recite a *qasidah*, they make history. The poems are the medium of historical construction. They are local 'oral archives' but they do not tell us a history whereby events are structured chronologically and there is a causal connection between events. The history embedded in oral poetry is a structural history. It unfolds social and political relations which stand above and outside chronology. The only reference to time is found in general statements like 'today', 'long time ago', or 'in the past'. This seems to be a general characteristic of tribal history among many groups in the Middle East. For example, Davis observed the way tribesmen make history in Libya. The Zuwaya have two types of 'historians'. The first are old men who tell stories about past events which they witnessed themselves or heard about from their ancestors. The poet among the Zuwaya is also an 'historian'. History in this case is a product of a specialized group and the arguments about the quality of the product were about its beauty, metre, wit, rather than about its truth, typicality and meaning (J. Davis 1987: 207).

With the emergence of centralized authority such as that of the Rashidi amirs, the preservation of past historical events in a collective memory becomes essential. Historical construction involves accounts of defeat and victory. When such history is preserved in an oral tradition, one learns lessons from defeat and derives joy from victory.

Making history in the context of a centralized polity is just another aspect of the exercise of power. Poetry becomes the medium of history and the amir-poet is his own historian, not of peace, order, stability and prosperity, but rather of political and military conflict, opposition and competition. The history which he constructs reveals episodes in which his survival and that of his tribe come under threat. Facing that threat by action is not enough. The amir-poet documents challenges through poetry. He makes history for future generations.

At this stage, the following questions have to be asked. Is this tribal history, which in most cases takes the form of narratives and poems, relevant to our 'historical-anthropological' research? What sorts of 'historical truths' can we derive from this poetic history?[15]

THE VALUE OF ORAL TRADITION IN HISTORICAL RESEARCH

Both the narratives and poems of the Rashidis communicate messages of a culturally-specific 'historical truth' which may or may not correspond to what anthropologists and historians call 'historical truth'.[16] To the Shammar, their oral tradition encompasses a true history about individuals and incidents and is not concerned with unfolding a chronological history.[17]

It is also a selective tradition because of the failure of human memory, personal prejudices and changes in what is considered important over time. Consequently, a large body of information can be lost and selected knowledge may contribute to the creation of a history derived from present concerns which are projected on the past. This limitation need not undermine its value for the use of other sources may reveal events which have been intentionally or unintentionally omitted. This would inevitably lead one to investigate why the oral tradition remains silent about some events and is rich when it comes to others.

Oral tradition can also be very élite-oriented. Shammar oral tradition tells us more about predominant lineages, their achievements, heroism, and oral literature than about the lives of ordinary tribesmen. This is significant because it reflects Shammars' perceptions of their past. It is not about general laws, historical forces or successive stages and progression. Their history is a history of lineages, amirs and sheikhs.

As long as the oral tradition gives accounts of how people in the past have interpreted their experiences, it should be considered as a legitimate and indispensable source in our construction of people's history.[18] Vansina argued that 'oral tradition should be treated as hypotheses and as the first hypothesis the modern scholar must test before he or she considers others. To consider them first means not to accept them literally and uncritically. It means to give them the attention they deserve, to take pains to prove or disprove them systematically for each case on its own merits.' (J. Vansina 1985: 196).

By considering oral tradition, the scholar gives the people he studies the opportunity to speak for themselves.[19] He allows them to construct their own history and no matter how imprecise, biased, and distorted this history may be, we learn by incorporating it in our research. When people construct their history, they produce hypotheses about their past, a task which the professional historian shares. Both the professional historian and the people he studies constantly subject their historical data to reinterpretation. People do this depending on new social circumstances and the historian does the same thing in the light of new historical evidence and theoretical developments in his field. Therefore, there is no reason to portray our historical knowledge as sacred, unchanging and scientific but that of the people as mythical, changing and unreliable. Our task is to analyse people's historical versions of their past and look for the reasons behind the predominance of one version of history over others.

7

THE POLITICS OF MARRIAGE

Among the Rashidi amirs, marriage was an institution which stemmed from the necessities both of human reproduction and of political life. The complexity of their political relations was reflected in the diversity of their matrimonial strategies which combined endogamy and exogamy. When these strategies are put in their historical and political context, one can determine why some marriages were politically meaningful acts whereas others were not. What is important, however, is that marriage practices are part of an overall strategy whereby social and political relations are maintained, recreated, and reproduced. Every marriage tends to reproduce the conditions which have made it possible. Bourdieu correctly points out that matrimonial strategies belong to the system of reproduction strategies, defined as the sum total of the strategies through which individuals or groups objectively tend to reproduce the relations of production associated with a determinate mode of production by striving to reproduce or improve their position in the social structure (P. Bourdieu 1977: 39 and 70).

In Hail, the patrilineal kinship system based on blood was flexible enough to allow for other kinship relations parallel in importance, for example the milk bond between the amirs and their slave brothers. Here I focus on those relations created by marriage.

The blood kinship was based on the ideology of patrilineal descent with a distinct set of terminology and key indigeneous notions. Among the Shammar, the term *beit* (household) referred to ego, his wife or wives, and his children. The Rashidi amirs were known as members of *beit* Rashid although they represented a group larger than the household. The following terms are used to refer to members of the *beit*: *jid*: grandfather, *jida*: grandmother, *ab*: father, *umm*: mother, *ibn*: son, *bint*: daughter, *amm*: father's brother,

184

amma: father's sister, *ibn amm*: father's brother's son, *bint amm*: father's brother's daughter, *akh*: brother, *ukht*: sister.

These terms are used to refer to the male and female descendants of the same paternal *jid*. The *jid* does not have to be a grandfather; sometimes it is used to refer to a distant ancestor. Equally, the term *ibn amm* can be used in a classificatory sense which allows a person to include a large number of distant paternal relatives into a close kinship relationship with him when an actual kinship or genealogical relationship does not exist. For example, the male members of the same *fakhd* (maximal lineage) may refer to each other as *ibn amm* given that the different *biut* (extended families) of the *fakhd* meet genealogically at a higher level of segmentation, i.e. at the level of *ashira* (tribal section) and *gabila* (tribe).

Another set of kinship terms is used to refer to the members of the mother's *beit* (extended family): *jid*: mother's father, *jida*: mother's mother, *khal*: mother's brother, *khala*: mother's sister, *ibn khal*: mother's brother's son, *bint khal*: mother's brother's daughter, *ibn khala*: mother's sister's son, *bint khala*: mother's sister's daughter.

The maternal relatives are usually referred to as *khawal* and this is extended to all maternal relatives who are not actual mother's brothers. In this respect, the term *khawal* is similar to *ibn amm* in the sense that both can be used in a classificatory sense to refer to a group of relatives on the side of either the mother or the father without the existence of a clearly recognized kinship relationship. The fact that two different sets of kinship terminology are used to refer to the maternal and paternal kin is typical of lineage systems. The terminological distinction implies that the relationship between ego and his consanguine relatives is different from his relationship with his affines.

The first distinctive feature of ego's relationship with his paternal relatives concerns descent. Ego derives his name from his agnatic ancestors and in particular from his paternal *jid* (grandfather or distant ancestor). This is manifested in the use of the term 'Ibn Rashid' to refer to all the amirs of Hail, regardless of their first names. For example, the founder of the dynasty, Abdullah Ibn Ali Ibn Rashid was always referred to as simply Ibn Rashid. The individual's identity which is expressed in the use of his first name is sacrificed to the advantage of that of his *beit*.

The same rule of patrilineal descent applies to the female

members of the *beit*. For example, a female member of *beit* Rashid is referred to as *bint* Rashid and will retain her name and jural rights within the *beit* even if she marries outside it.

The relationship between ego and his agnates is best described in the use of the indigenous notion of *asab* (literally: backbone). When people refer to their agnates as one *asab*, they are using the image of the bone, i.e. the hard matter or the core from which the lineage is derived. This imagery invokes the centrality of the agnates in the kinship system. The notion of *asab* reflects the official kinship ideology whereby emphasis is put on paternal descent.

With respect to the maternal relatives or *khawal*, the notion of *luhma* (flesh) describes a different relationship between ego and his maternal kin – linking ego secondarily to a kin group of which he is not a member. In contrast with the image of the bone, the flesh is a cover of an auxiliary nature. However, the predominance of patrilineal descent does not undermine the importance and intensity of the relationship that exists between ego and his *khawal*. Although the *khawal* do not share their *asab* with ego, they are believed to influence his character. It is common to describe someone who shows signs of bravery, chivalry, and courage as *juthuboh khawaloh*, a phrase which emphasizes that ego's characteristics are inherited from his maternal kin through a process whereby he is metaphorically pulled in their direction.

The maternal kin can unite and divide agnates. Their role varies depending on the situation and the degree of their involvement in the internal affairs of the agnates. Among the Cyrenaican bedouins, when a man permits his maternal kinsmen to use the land and water facilities of his lineage, his agnates may give ready consent or bicker about it. However, when it comes to cleaning a well, disputes are almost certain to break out between those who argue that their maternal relatives should not be expected to assist in its cleaning and those who insist they should (E. Peters 1960: 46). In this case, the maternal kin act as a dividing force among the agnates. On the other hand, when the maternal kinsmen allow someone to use their grazing land and wells, his agnates would be pleased as this decreases the pressure on their own resources. In this situation, the maternal link strengthens the agnatic group (ibid).

The amirs' *khawal* played a crucial political role at certain moments. As shown in Chapter 3 they were involved in succession disputes; but they also participated in dynastic murders, and conspiracy. Some maternal relatives encouraged rebellion and dissent among their sister's brothers who were members of the Rashidi family. They acted as an informal support group which interfered and divided agnates. The following two examples illustrate this point.

Abdullah Ibn Rashid's father was married to Alya bint Abdul Aziz Ibn Himiyan who was from a prominent *beit* of the Jaafar Shammar. During Abdullah's dispute with his paternal cousin, he was unable to seek support from his close paternal relatives who were not very influential in Hail at that time. One of the options available to him was to resort to his maternal kin who had a vested interest in Abdullah's success. In the event, their overt support and involvement in the dispute between Abdullah and Ibn Ali widened the gap which was already emerging between the two agnates.

The Sibhan, another *beit* of the Jaafar Shammar, provided wives for the amirs for generations. Consequently, various members of this family were influential maternal uncles who became closely involved in the political affairs of the dynasty, often occupying the post of *wazir* (minister) and treasurer. Some Sibhan members became regents during the leadership of Saud Ibn Abdul Aziz (1910–20), whose maternal uncles played an active role in installing him as amir of Hail (see Chapter 3). Bell mentions how their intervention led to placing a sister's son in the post of amir: 'Saud Ibn Hamud was assassinated by one of the Sibhan family, hereditary viziers to the Rashids who placed his nephew, son of Abdul Aziz and Mudhi bint Sibhan upon the throne.' (G. Bell 1914: 76–7) The British consul in Jeddah also reported this: 'The Subhan, the viziers of the amirate, wished the boy to govern under the tutelage of the Subhan who had from old times always been viziers of Ibn Rashid and are of the best blood of the Shammar, closely allied by marriage with Ibn Rashid, men of weight and wealth.'[1]

The Sibhan case illustrates how the maternal kin were directly involved in political disputes between the Rashidi agnates. As it is difficult to find examples whereby the *khawal*'s intervention did actually unite the agnatic group, one is more likely to consider the maternal kin as a potentially dividing force which could be employed during times of political crises. Their direct intervention especially in massacres and disputes over succession, widened the gap between rival agnates and upset the balance of power between the various branches of the Rashidi family.

TABLE 6: *The Amirs' Marriages*

Amir	Name of Wife	Male Offsprings	Origin of Wife
1 Abdullah Ibn Rashid (1835–48)	a Muneira bint Abdul Rahman Al Jabr	Talal & Mitab	CBA
	b Salma bint Ibn Ali	Mohammad	CBA
2 Talal Ibn Abdullah (1848–68)	a Al Jawhara bint Faisal Ibn Turki		Saudi
	b Namsha bint Sahan Ibn Ali	Naif*	CBA
3 Mitab Ibn Abdullah (1868–9)	a Sita bint Jaza Ibn Ajil	Abdul Aziz	Abde (Sh)
	b Fatima bint Sibhan		Jaafar (Sh)
4 Bandar Ibn Talal (1869)	a Sita bint Jaza Ibn Ajil		Abde (Sh)
5 Mohammed Ibn Abdullah (1869–97)	a Mudhi bint Sibhan		Jaafar (Sh)
	b Amusha bint Obeid		ABA
	c Turkiya bint Jadaan Ibn Muheid		Sh Boreidah
	d Loulowa bint Muhanna		Boreidah
6 Abdul Aziz Ibn Mitab (1897–1906)	a Mudhi bint Sibhan	Saud	Jaafar (Sh)
	b Mudhi bint Hamud Ibn Obeid	Mohammad-Mitab & Mishal	ABA
	c Hisa bint Saleh Al-Dakhil		Dawasir
7 Mitab Ibn Abdul Aziz (1906–7)	a Sakina		unknown
	b Wasmiya	Abdullah	slave
8 Sultan Ibn Hamud (1907–8)	a Tureifa bint Muheisin Al Jabr		CBA
	b Mudhi bint Hamud Ibn Sibhan	Ali	Jaafar (Sh)

TABLE 6: *continued*

Amir	Name of Wife	Male Offsprings	Origin of Wife
	c Loulowa bint Muhanna		Boreidah
9 Saud Ibn Hamud (1908–10)	unidentified		
10 Saud Ibn Abdul Aziz (1910–20)	a Fahda al Shureim	Mishal	Abde (Sh)
	b Loulowa bint Saleh Al Sibhan	Abdul Aziz	Jaafar (Sh)
	c Shaha bint Al Wajaan	Mohammad	Aslam (Sh)
	d Anud bint Salem Ibn Hamud Ibn Obeid	Saud	ABA
11 Abdullah Ibn Mitab (1920–21)	a Anud bint salem Ibn Hamud Ibn Obeid	Mitab & Mishal	ABA
12 Mohammad Ibn Talal (1921)	a Loulowa bint Faisal Ibn Hamud Ibn Obeid		ABA
	b Nura bint Hamud Al Sibhan	Bandar	Jaafar (Sh)
	c Abta bint Sultan Ibn Hamud Ibn Obeid	Talal & Mitab	ABA

NB. CBA = classificatory *bint amm*; ABA = actual *bint amm*; Sh = Shammar tribe.
* = Other sons include Bandar, Badr, Nahar, Muslat, Zaid, Sultan and Abdullah.

MARRIAGE STRATEGIES

I was able to collect information on twenty-eight marriages which took place over a period of almost ninety years.[2] Ten unions out of twenty-eight were conducted with actual or classificatory *bint amm* (see Table 6: amir 1, 2, 5, 6, 8, 10, 11, 12). To look at this from another angle, one can say that eight amirs out of twelve had among their wives an actual and/or classificatory *bint amm*. An actual *bint amm* is a father's brother's daughter with whom a kinship relation can be identified and spelled out within the degree of the first, second, third, fourth and fifth *jid*. An actual *bint amm* belongs to the same *beit* as ego.

For example, the fifth amir, Mohammad Ibn Abdullah married Amusha bint Obeid who was his father's brother's daughter, i.e. a first generation *bint amm*. The sixth amir Abdul Aziz Ibn Mitab married Mudhi bint Hamud Ibn Obeid, the daughter of his grandfather's brother, i.e. a second generation *bint amm*. Abdul Aziz and Mudhi meet genealogically at the level of their first grandfathers.

An actual *bint amm* can also be more distanced from ego than in the two above-mentioned cases. The eleventh amir Abdullah Ibn Mitab married Anud bint Salem Ibn Hamud Ibn Obeid who was his third generation *bint amm*. The last amir, Mohammad Ibn Talal, married Abta bint Sultan Ibn Hamud Ibn Obeid who was a third generation *bint amm*, but was also married to Loulowa bint Faisal Ibn Hamud Ibn Obeid who was a fourth generation *bint amm*.

On the other hand, a classificatory *bint amm* belongs to another *beit* of the same lineage. Usually, the kinship relationship is established at the level beyond the fifth *jid*. For example, the second amir of Hail, Talal Ibn Abdullah married Namsha bint Sahan Ibn Ali who was a classificatory *bint amm* belonging to the Alis, who together with the Rashidis constitute two *beits* of the Jaafar lineage.

Furthermore, in eleven cases the wives were recruited from the Shammar tribe and in the majority of those marriages the wives were members of the Abde Shammar (see Table 6: amir 3, 5, 6, 8, 10, 12). In these marriages the husband and wife belonged to the same *ashira* (tribal section).

Four marriages out of a total of twenty-eight took place between the amirs and women from outside the Shammar tribe (see Table 6: amir 2, 5, 6, 8). One of the women was a daughter of the Saudi ruler of Riyadh, another one was a member of the ruling family of Boreidah. This woman married twice into the family of Ibn Rashid. The last outside marriage was with a woman from the Dawasir tribe of central Najd.

Out of twenty-eight marriages, the name of three wives was

TABLE 7: *Types of Marriages*

No. of Amirs	Endo. marr. ABA CBA	Shammar marr.	Out-marr.	Unidentified
	6 4			
12	10	11	4	3
%	35.7	39.2	14.2	10.7

NB. Endo. marr. = endogamous marriages, ABA = actual *bint amm*, CBA = classificatory *bint amm*

either forgotten or unidentified. Table 7 is a summary of the types of marriages and their statistical importance. The figures in Table 7 show that polygamy was widely practised among the amirs. It is worth mentioning here that the recorded marriages did not include infertile or short-term marriages.

The second feature of the amirs' marriage practices was endogamy. Endogamous marriages (35.7 per cent) included those unions with actual *bint amm* (6) and classificatory *bint amm* (4). Marriages with Shammar women (39.2 per cent) can also be considered as endogamous. In-marriages therefore constituted 74.9 per cent of the recorded marriages.

With respect to the amirs' endogamous marriages, it is worth emphasizing the distinction between *beit* endogamy and lineage endogamy. The category '*beit* endogamy' or actual *bint amm* marriage refers to those marriages in which the wife is an actual patrilateral parallel cousin. However, lineage endogamy refers to those marriages in which the wife is a classificatory *bint amm*. In this case, husband and wife are related genealogically at the level of their lineage in spite of the fact that each one is a member of a different *beit*.

On the other hand, marriages with Shammar women (see Table 7) can be classified under the category 'tribal endogamy', where the wife belongs to the same tribe as that of the husband. In the case of the marriages of the amirs, the category 'tribal endogamy' included the marriages in which the wife was from one of the various Shammar tribal sections. These marriages can be considered as endogamous given the fact that both husband and wife meet genealogically at a higher level of segmentation – for example *fakhd* (maximal lineage), *ashira* (tribal section) and *gabila* (tribe).

INTERPRETATIONS OF *BINT AMM* MARRIAGE

The occurrence of *bint amm* marriage has been reported from many areas in the Middle East and different explanations given for it. It is believed that the practice of endogamy in general dates back to ancient times before Islam (G. Tillion 1966: 27–30). *Bint amm* marriage is regarded as a special phenomenon in the sense that it occurs in societies where the kinship structure is based on patrilineal/unilineal descent. Unlike their African counterparts, Middle Eastern unilineal descent groups are endogamous.[3] The preference for patrilineal parallel cousin marriage marks them as distinct from those unilineal descent groups in Africa and Oceania.

This 'anomaly' or deviation from the rule of exogamy has attracted the attention of many anthropologists.[4] So far, most explanations have been given in terms of the political, economic, structural and psychological functions that this practice performs in society. It is believed that the *bint amm* marriage contributes to reinforcing unity and integration within the lineage. Lineage endogamy is regarded as a type of delayed exchange in which the father receives political allegiance in his lifetime from his brother's son in return for the daughter which he gives in marriage. The girl's father creates an obligation on the part of his brother's son to give him political support by exempting him from paying the brideprice. As a result, *bint amm* marriage plays a role in solidifying the minimal lineage as a corporate group in factional struggle (F. Barth 1954: 168). This view stresses the immediate and long-term political functions of the marriage strategy, an emphasis which is sometimes combined with showing that the strategy aims at retaining matrimonial wealth within the same lineage. A second approach focuses on the psychological benefits to be gained from indulging in this practice. It is believed that *bint amm* marriage does not contribute to the creation of conflicting roles nor does it create tense affinal relationships like those associated with out-marriage. By marrying a paternal parallel cousin, a man does not create significant affinal ties nor does he alter the consanguine relationships which he learns from childhood (F. Khouri 1970: 607).

The functionalist approach has been criticized by those who oppose an explanation given in terms of the immediate functions. Thus, Murphy and Kasdan focus on the less visible structural function of the practice. They argue that the consolidation of wealth or of power may constitute a motivation for those who wish to marry their father's brother's daughter; however, one structural function of the institution is to promote the segmentation process. The preference for the father's brother's daughter deepens the gulf between collateral branches by turning affinal bonds inward. As a result, each minimal-sized unit becomes virtually self contained and encysted (R. Murphy and L. Kasdan 1959: 18).

Anthropologists' interest in *bint amm* marriage is still sustained even after Bourdieu declared that the way out of the difficulties encountered in formulating cross-culturally valid generalizations about this practice is to dissolve it as a meaningful category to be explained (P. Bourdieu 1977: 48). In spite of the assertion that this phenomenon is sociologically inexplicable, in a recent study, Holy shifts the focus of analysis from the actual practice of *bint amm* marriage and its pragmatic functions to its meaning, context, and symbolic significance. According to Holy, marriage is above all a culturally-meaningful act: 'It is possible to show how actors use the existing preference to solve practical problems; however, it is not possible to argue conversely that it is these practical problems which generate the preference; i.e. that people have certain preferences because they serve useful practical functions.' (L. Holy 1989: 68)

As a cultural notion, the preference for *bint amm* marriage exists independently of the practical functions it might fulfil in the course of strategic behaviour. Its meaning is inseparable from the context in which it occurs. Holy analyses this preference in the context of gender relations in the Middle East. The preference relates to the system of gender relations in which men are charged with controlling the unharnessed female power, combined with under-evaluation of affinal relationships at the expense of kinship ones, and with the conceptualization of agnatic links as those of the closest – and in extreme cases the only – kinship (ibid: 126). The preference is an outcome of gender notions relating to honour while at the same time it contributes to their production.

Of more relevance to the present study is Garthwaite's work on the Bakhtiyari of Iran, for the discussion concerning the marriage practices of the ilkhani is strictly limited to the marriages of the ruling group (G. Garthwaite 1983: 76). He argues that the predominant marriage pattern for the khans' daughters was parallel cousin marriage which was utilized as a means of obtaining continued family-*tayafah* (tribe) support, of retaining some control over the wealth that accompanied these brides, and of keeping their sons in the family. Furthermore, it was a means of lessening uncle–nephew tension over inequalities in inheritance (ibid: 78). According to Garthwaite, one can generalize that daughters' marriages were arranged to reaffirm family ties and to lessen family tension. The sons often included a parallel cousin among their wives but then chose brides from a range of *tayafah* as a means of broadening their base of outside alliances and support. However, the khans were not bound by the same rules as other tribesmen. They took brides outside their *tayafah* but did not usually reciprocate with their own sisters and daughters, a very common strategy among political élites (ibid). The frequency of the khans' outside marriages demonstrates their willingness to broaden their political influence and alliance with other lineages and groups. Nevertheless, during the nineteenth century when family rivalry over political leadership between uncles and nephews was strong, parallel cousin marriage was practised in an attempt to lessen tensions and heal political divisions in the family.

In the next section my aim is to explain the occurrence of various marriage strategies or practices among the Rashidi amirs including *bint amm* marriage rather than focusing on the preferences which are assumed to be reflected in practice.

THE ENDOGAMOUS MARRIAGES OF THE AMIRS

The high frequency of endogamous marriages can be explained by placing these marriage strategies in their relevant political and historical context.

Beit *Endogamy*

The strategy of actual *bint amm* marriage aimed at neutralizing the conflict-laden relationship between paternal uncles and nephews (brothers' sons). Furthermore, such unions tended to lessen inequalities over political rather than economic inheritance. Political inequalities were inherent in the system of succession to the office of amir, for which there was no fixed rule.

When the amir marries his paternal parallel cousin, he is in fact marrying the daughter of a political rival and a potential enemy, namely, his paternal uncle who has equal claims over the office which he occupies. This was evident among the ruling *beit* where male members were competing for the chieftaincy. This type of marriage brings the daughter of a political rival into the amir's household and contributes to the transformation of the relationship between the amir and his paternal uncle (or the amir and his nephew when the uncle is amir). The paternal uncle becomes father-in-law and maternal grandfather for the amir's sons who are potential amirs. Marriage with a parallel cousin results in merging the paternal and maternal kin.

I argued in Chapter 3 that the office of amir was occupied by the descendants of Abdullah who extracted an *ahd* (covenant) from his brother to guarantee that his successors maintained a monopoly over the office of amir. The two lines of descent remained equal in status and jural rights although there were obvious political inequalities. In genealogical terms, Abdullah and Obeid were equal brothers. However, Abdullah was the senior son of the Rashidi family; consequently, his descendants became senior in status *vis-à-vis* the descendants of Obeid. Furthermore, Abdullah was the amir and as he managed to guarantee the supremacy of his descendants through the *ahd*, the inequality was sustained. We have a situation here whereby fraternal equality was upset by two factors: age (the seniority of Abdullah) and politics (the fact that he became amir of Hail). As a result, the descendants of Abdullah became the core of *beit* Rashid.

In an attempt to compensate for political inequalities, the amirs who were descendants of the Abdullah line took wives who were their Obeidi *bint amm*. These female cousins were members of a junior branch of the family. They circulated upward when they married members of the Abdullah line and the sons who were born as a result of these marriages became members of the senior branch. In addition, these hypergamous marriages in which women moved upward towards the senior branch of the family lessened political inequalities and conflict emerging from the unequal access to political office. They also blurred the division between the maternal and paternal kin who were members of the same group.

Lineage Endogamy

With respect to the second sub-category of the amirs' endogamous marriages, i.e. lineage endogamy or classificatory *bint amm* marriage, these unions fostered the development of affinal ties with

other extended families which were proliferations of the same
lineage of *beit* Ibn Rashid. These marriages were conducted in an
attempt to neutralize hostilities and rivalries emerging between two
or more *beit* rather than within the same *beit*.

Two marriages of the founder of the dynasty Abdullah were
contracted with classificatory *bint amm* (see Table 6 no. 1a and 1b).
His second wife, Salma, was a member of *beit* Ibn Ali, the rival
ruling group of Hail before the establishment of Rashidi rule. Once
in power, the Rashidis took wives from *beit* Ibn Ali. Hypergamy
was practised. Wives moved from the ranks of the politically junior
branch to the more dominant one. The junior branch became the
group of wife-givers. The tradition of marrying into *beit* Ibn Ali was
maintained by Abdullah's successor, Talal (Table 6, no. 2b). Even
after a lapse of ten years, it was felt that a marriage with a member
of the previous ruling group in Hail was crucial. These marriages
aimed at blurring the severe political divisions between the two
groups by merging them through a sequence of marriages but at
the same time maintaining the hierarchy between them.

Tribal Endogamy

I mentioned earlier that the category 'tribal endogamy' includes
those marriages in which the wife was a member of one of the four
Shammar tribal sections. Statistical analysis showed that 39.2 per
cent of the amirs' marriages were conducted with Shammar
women. This high frequency can be explained by reference to the
political relations which existed between the amirs and the various
Shammar tribal sections.

Neither *beit* endogamy nor lineage endogamy allows for the
creation of a wide network of kinship, social and political relations.
In fact, both restrict political contacts to a limited number of
individuals with whom there is already a kinship relation. On the
other hand, tribal endogamy offered the amirs the opportunity to
expand their sphere of influence and political contacts given the
fact that most of their tribal endogamous marriages were
conducted with daughters of Shammar chiefs. The marriages
fostered the development of political alliances between the oasis-
based leadership of the amirs and the tribal leadership of the
Shammar sheikhs. These alliances were essential since the sheikhs
had direct contact with the Shammar tribesmen whose support and

participation in military expeditions against outsiders was frequently sought by the amirs in Hail. Furthermore, the support of the Shammar sheikhs and their tribal sections would provide a wider geographical and political legitimation for the oasis-based leadership. Alliances between the tribal sheikhs and the amirs were further cemented by tribal endogamy which generated a set of affinal ties with dispersed nomadic Shammar groups.

The tribal endogamous marriages of the amirs led to the emergence of some Shammar sections as wife-givers. In general, tribal endogamy was in favour of sub-groups of the Shammar tribe such as the Abde and the Aslam. Most of these marriages were with daughters of tribal sheikhs, i.e. members of the chiefly lineages of the sub-groups. On the one hand, these unions strengthened the contacts and cemented the political alliances with the Shammar sections and their tribal sheikhs. On the other hand, the internal rivalries and dynastic murders among the ruling group threatened constantly to split up the Shammar tribe, members of which were the maternal kinsmen of one amir or the other. Consequently, conflict within the ruling group was easily transmitted to a grass-root level, i.e. to the level of the Shammar tribe.

One can equally argue that because the various Shammar tribal sections were entangled with the ruling group through marriage, they were able to push their claims through supporting one amir against his paternal uncle, nephew, or even half brother. The Shammar sections and their rivalries reached the top level of political leadership in the dynasty, i.e. the level of amirs, who responded by indulging in dynastic murders against each other.

THE EXOGAMOUS MARRIAGES OF THE AMIRS

Statistics in Table 7 showed that only four marriages out of twenty-eight were conducted with women who were outsiders, i.e. 14.2 per cent of the unions were exogamous marraiges. Although these marriages were statistically insignificant, they had great political importance.

One such marriage was conducted by Talal Ibn Abdullah (1848–68) who married into the Saudi family. This marriage took place at an early period when the amir was still engaged in consolidating his power. At that period, an out-marriage was preferred because it promised the creation of affinal ties with the

Saudi–Wahhabi dynasty.[5] Consequently, hostilities between Hail and Riyadh were not recorded at that time. It was only at a later stage that enmity between the two power centres in Najd did emerge. The transformation of the relationship between the two groups took place during the leadership of the fifth amir, Mohammad Ibn Rashid (1869–97).

Two of the exogamous marriages were with a descendant of the ruling family of Boreidah, a town in the Qasim region. These two marriages took place after the defeat of the ruler of Boreidah in the battle of Muleida (1891). It seems that, being defeated and imprisoned, the ruler had no say over the proceedings of these two marriages, which were conducted according to the rule of marrying into the rival group.

The last exogamous marriage was with a woman from the Dawasir, one of the tribes of central Najd. Alliance with the Dawasir tribe was regarded as important by the amir, Abdul Aziz Ibn Mitab (1897–1906) who wanted to solidify this political relationship by marriage.

The political context of the amirs' exogamous marriages was relevant to the explanation of these unions. In the four cases discussed above, the affinal ties created by marriage tended to encourage political alliances, cement old political relations, and create new ones. However, although the amirs of Hail took brides from outside their *beit*, lineage and even tribe, they did not reciprocate with their own daughters and sisters.

The practice of polygamy allowed the amirs to diversify their wives as they were capable of marrying a parallel cousin, a Shammar woman and an outsider at the same time. However, the Rashidi family did not become a group of wife-givers. In the case of their females, the tendency was towards circulating them within the group. This was in line with a tradition whereby the most aristocratic groups kept their females to be married by close cousins. The only exception to this rule was to marry off an aristocratic female to another aristocratic family which was considered to be equal in status to those giving the wife. These marriages operated according to a strict equal exchange system whereby one female was given out by the group who immediately received from the wife-takers another female. This equal exchange system seemed to have been practised among the Rashidis. I mentioned earlier that the second amir of Hail, Talal Ibn Rashid married the daughter of the Saudi ruler, Al Jawhara bint Faisal

Ibn Turki. To complete the exchange, Talal's sister, Nura, was given to Abdullah Ibn Faisal Ibn Turki, the ruler in the second Saudi–Wahhabi dynasty. The Saudis gave the Rashidis a woman and received from them another one. In an oral account of the events of these marriages, I was told that Nura, Ibn Rashid's sister, left her Saudi husband and returned to her family in Hail after a clash with him. The reasons behind this separation were not remembered. However, what is interesting about this story is the fact that the Saudi ruler Abdullah Ibn Faisal immediately proposed to another Rashidi woman, Tureifa bint Obeid to replace his first Rashidi wife and re-establish the balance.

After the capture of Hail by Ibn Saud in 1921, this situation was changed. A number of marriages took place with the Saudi family. However, these marriages were no longer in line with the rules of the equal exchange system. More Rashidi women married into the Saudi family then Rashidi men. The daughter of the last Rashidi amir, Juwahir bint Mohammad Ibn Talal, was taken as wife by King Abdul Aziz Ibn Saud whereas her sister, Watfa, was taken by his son, Musaid. This started a trend. Many Rashidi women married into the various branches of the Saudi family, although it was not counter-balanced by Rashidi men doing so.[6]

These observations give an insight into the change in power relations. In the nineteenth century, the equal exchange system was a symbolic representation of the equal power relations between the Rashidis and the Saudis. In contrast, in the twentieth century, when power shifted with the collapse of Rashidi hegemony to the advantage of the Saudis, so did the symbolic marriage practices; the Rashidis became wife-givers *vis-à-vis* the Saudi family.

The practice of exogamous marriages among the Rashidi amirs in the nineteenth century can be contrasted with the marriage practices of the Shammar. The latter chose brides who were either actual *bint amm*, classificatory *bint amm*, or distant Shammar women. Only on rare occasions did Shammar marry complete outsiders. Furthermore, marrying into the sedentary population was considered degrading. This was not the case among the amirs who married into the ruling family of a sedentary population, namely the Al Muhanna ruling group of Boreidah, believing that the political relations that would be created through this marriage outweighed the stigma attached to marrying into a sedentary group. The marriage strategies of the Shammar reflected their immediate concerns. It was believed that marrying an actual *bint amm* fosters the unity of the *beit* whereas lineage endogamy contributes to solidifying the whole lineage by fusing the various *biut* which compose it.[7] On the other hand, it was believed that tribal endogamy contributes to maintaining the cohesion and solidarity of the Shammar. The rule of endogamy was even stricter when the marriages of Shammar women were concerned. These were rarely allowed to marry outside the group. In this case, both the Shammar women and the Rashidi ones married inside the group.

8

THE EMPIRE AND
THE DYNASTY

During the second half of the nineteenth century, the area of Jabal
Shammar and Hail was within the claimed territorial boundaries of
the Ottoman Empire, and the Porte tried to maintain a nominal
suzerainty over the amirs of Hail. This situation was sustained
until the defeat of the Ottoman government in the First World War
as a result of which Britain replaced the Ottomans in dealing with
the local power centres in the region.

The relationship between the Ottoman government and local
tribal leaders was complex as it did not follow a fixed pattern. The
general tribal policy of the Ottomans oscillated over time.
However, like most power centres which tried to govern a
heterogeneous population with a strong tradition of autonomy and
independence, their policy aimed at exercising direct control
whenever it was possible to do so and indirect rule when it was
advantageous and less risky. The guiding principle behind this
policy was to maintain maximum control over the local population
and its leaders at a minimum cost. This was achieved through
direct use of force and diplomacy. In both cases, their policies
influenced local political processes.

Khazanov has stressed that relations with the outside world are
important factors behind the emergence of political centralization
and economic differentiation among the nomads. He observed that
only when bedouin society came into contact with sedentary
society, when some nomads became sedentary and the nomadic
aristocracy became the ruling class over the sedentary population,
did class differentiation begin to develop (A. Khazanov 1984: 277).
The entry of the nomads into relations with a central state even in
those cases where they retained a considerable degree of autonomy,
frequently enabled social differentiation to increase. In fact, the
particular relations which the amirs of Hail maintained with the

201

Ottoman government and the flow of subsidies from outside the local economic resources were the crucial factors which influenced this process. As far as the category 'the outside world', to use Khazanov's terminology, includes external central states, his argument is relevant to the interpretation of political centralization and differentiation not only in Hail, but also in other parts of the world where local nomadic groups established contacts with outside states (L. Beck 1986, G. Garthwaite 1983, M. van Bruinessen 1978, and R. Tapper 1983).

To the north of Jabal Shammar, in Syria and Jordan, similar processes were generated as a result of the increasing involvement of local tribal sheikhs with the Ottoman government and its governors and representatives. For example, Bani Sakhr, one of the tribes of Jordan, maintained contacts with Ottoman officials who were implementing a policy of playing off tribal sheikhs against each other. This was believed to ensure that the various tribes of the region respected Ottoman authority. Those local sheikhs who participated in the game received farming land from the Ottomans, which was usually close to water resources, towns and villages. Tribal sheikhs used this land as their summer headquarters when it was important to be situated near permanent wells and water resources. Lewis argues that this set in motion an irreversible process whereby the Bani Sakhr sheikhs became land-owners. The heads of the tribal sections regarded these summer headquarters as theirs in a more proprietorial way than they regarded the steppe and the desert in which they wandered widely in winter (N. Lewis 1987: 127). The sheikhs were also given titles by the Ottomans such as *sheikh al mashaikh* (chief of the whole tribe). This policy led to the emergence of rivalries among the tribal heads, and speeded up the process of political centralization among an otherwise politically decentralized tribal group.

Ottoman tribal policy in Syria and Jordan was observed in Jabal Shammar with some variations. The Porte was geographically distant from central Arabia, yet it maintained contacts with local tribal chiefs. The latter were not given farming land in return for their co-operation with the government. However, they received various subsidies and monthly allowances which allowed them to distance themselves from their tribal groups. As a result of these subsidies, many local sheikhs and amirs became part of a sedentarized tribal ruling group. Moreover, throughout the nineteenth century, the Porte's policies revolved around preventing the emergence of one single power in central Arabia which could challenge their position in the more vital regions of the empire such as the Hijaz, Syria, and Mesopotamia. Ottoman fears resulted from their helplessness during the eighteenth century when Saudi–Wahhabi expansion threatened the integrity of the empire. To eliminate the possibility of similar threats, Ottoman policy was based on the old principle of divide and rule. In the following section, I discuss how this general principle operated in central Arabia and what consequences this policy had for the development of political centralization among the Hail amirs.

OTTOMAN TRIBAL POLICY

After the success of the first Egyptian invasion of central Arabia in 1818, contact between the local sheikhs and the Ottoman government was made through Egypt (see Chapter 2). Mohammad Ali's army officers maintained a military presence in the major towns of Najd and the Hijaz. The major feature of the submission of Najd to Egypt was the payment of the *zakat* (Islamic tax) to the Egyptian officials in the area. This situation lasted until 1841 when Mohammad Ali's forces had to withdraw from the whole of the Arabian Peninsula under international pressure. The presence of the Egyptian forces was regarded as a threat to the integrity of the Ottoman Empire and the British interests in the Persian Gulf. Mohammad Ali was actually intending to replace the Ottoman Empire in Arabia, Syria and Palestine. The dangers that Mohammad Ali represented were perceived by Britain as early as 1816 and reported by the French Consul in Alexandria: 'Les anglais seraient assurément fachés de voir Mehemet Ali avoir des succès qui lui donneraient de la prépondérance sur le golfe Persique et sur la mer Rouge; il faut donc qu'ils croyent que l'expedition ne réussira pas.'[1]

With the withdrawal of the Egyptian forces, the administration of central Arabia became the responsibility of the *wali* (governor) of Basra. Najd became a *mutassarifiyah* (sub-administrative unit) of this *wilayat*. Hail and Jabal Shammar were part of this administrative unit. This arrangement was not supplemented by any practical measures to incorporae Najd in the Ottoman Empire nor to guarantee its submission to Ottoman rule. During the 1850s and 1860s, Ottoman suzerainty over Najd remained nominal, and Ottoman officials and military officers were entirely absent in central Arabia: 'Cette domination – en grande partie purement nominale – ne s'excerce guère plus loin que Medine et s'arrête aux vagues frontières du Nejd.'[2] With respect to Hail, during the rule of Talal Ibn Rashid (1848–68) the vague recognition of nominal Ottoman suzerainty was manifested in mentioning the Sultan's name during the Friday prayers: 'Talal had to preserve appearance with the sultan whose name looms large in the Friday prayers at Hail but who derives no other benefit from the province.'[3]

However, no measures were taken by the Ottoman government to enforce its domination over Hail. Philby describes the situation in Jabal Shammar with regard to Ottoman rule: 'Jabal Shammar accepted the vague and profitable suzerainty of the Ottoman Empire as one of the axioms of existence and the Ottoman Empire regarded Jabal Shammar as a neutral part of its clumsy far-flung heritage.' (St. J. Philby 1930: 129) As long as the Rashidi amirs and the Shammar did not impose any threat to the security of the 'Imperial Pilgrimage Route' from Damascus to the holy cities of Arabia, the Ottoman government refrained from interfering in their internal affairs. This situation was preserved until the 1870s. The last three decades of the nineteenth century were characterized by the Ottoman government's desire to enforce its control over central Arabia in general. Consequently, this resulted in clashes of interest between the central government and local power centres in the area.

The change towards greater political involvement in the Arabian provinces of the Ottoman Empire can be attributed to the desire of the Ottoman government to compensate for its territorial losses in Europe.[4] Furthermore, the involvement of Britain in the Persian Gulf at that time was regarded as a threat to Ottoman interests in the region. By the end of the nineteenth century, the Ottoman government was extremely eager to behave like a modern state and to acquire real control of its territories. The Porte wanted to enforce its authority over those Arabian provinces which so far had been outside its direct and effective control. The Ottoman government's involvement in Arabia materialized in a series of military campaigns whose aim was to guarantee firm domination over the peripheral Arabian provinces of the empire. Although the Ottoman military campaigns of this period took place on the periphery of Najd, their aim was to undermine the political autonomy of the local rulers and to prevent the expansion of their sphere of influence to the adjacent territories.

The military campaign against the oasis of Al Jauf to the north-west of Jabal Shammar was an indicator of Ottoman intentions. The oasis was ocupied by Talal Ibn Rashid in 1853 and thereafter the population of the oasis paid tribute to the amirs of Hail. However, in 1870, the Ottoman government took advantage of the disturbances in Hail over succession to the office of amir and encouraged the sheikh of the Rwala tribe, Satam Ibn Shaalan to invade the oasis with the help of the *wali* of Damascus and some Turkish troops. (A. Musil 1927: 242 and J. Lorimer 1908: 1111, vol Ib)

The Ottoman expedition failed to disentangle the oasis from the domination of Ibn Rashid and an agreement was reached with him to allow a Turkish official with eighty soldiers to remain there. Ibn Rashid continued to receive tribute from the population of the oasis while agreeing to pay 1500 Turkish majidis to the Ottoman government in return for his subjugation of the oasis.[5] This payment was a symbolic gesture of his nominal submission.

This incident revealed the policy of the Ottoman government of playing off one tribal leader against the other (in this case, Ibn Shaalan against Ibn Rashid), in an attempt to enforce its own control over the political affairs of the region. The ability to manipulate tribal political relations between rival groups was considered to be a prerequisite for the enforcement of Ottoman domination. The Ottoman government sometimes refrained from taking any direct action against dissident tribal units, but preferred this policy of setting off one tribal leader against the other.

The military campaign of 1871 against the Hasa, a province on the eastern periphery of Najd, was another Ottoman attempt at greater involvement in the affairs of central Arabia. The Ottoman government sought to establish a permanent military and political presence on the Arab littoral of the Persian Gulf. The appropriate moment for the attack came in 1871 when Abdullah Ibn Faisal, the Saudi ruler, disputed with his brother Saud over the leadership of the second Saudi–Wahhabi dynasty (see Chapter 3). Abdullah sought help from the Ottoman authorities against his disloyal brother, with the result that an Ottoman force under the leadership of Midhat Pasha, the *wali* of Baghdad, occupied the province of Al Hasa.[6] It was alleged that the people of the Hasa had addressed a petition to the sultan praying His Majesty to take Najd under his direct rule and appoint a Turkish governor instead of a member of the Al Saud family. When pressed for explanations by the British officials in the Persian Gulf, the Ottoman government, and in particular Midhat Pasha, stressed that the true and sole objective of the present enterprise was to pacify the two Saudi brothers, to prevent the protraction of disorder and to restore tranquillity.[7]

However, by 1872, the true objectives became apparent. Abdullah Ibn Faisal was said to have addressed a letter to the Ottoman authorities complaining that though they had entered his country with the avowed intention of restoring him to power, in reality they had put him under restraint and intended to undermine his dynasty by substituting their own authority.[8] The Ottoman plans for the province of Al Hasa soon materialized in a series of administrative measures which aimed at further direct control. The administration of the region including the town of Katif was conducted by a *mutassarif* appointed by the *wali* of Basra, and a *kaimmakam* (deputy governor), appointed by the *mutassarif*. Furthermore, a local commandant was appointed for military purposes.[9] Later, the Ottoman government changed its administrative policy; the governorship of the Hasa was conferred upon Ibn Urayer, the chief of Bani Khaled, a local tribe subjugated by the Saudi–Wahhabi forces towards the end of the eighteenth century. In addition, it was decided to withdraw the Ottoman regular troops and entrust the defence of the frontiers between Najd and the Hasa province to a body of gendarmerie to be raised in the country for that purpose.[10]

Once the Ottomans had succeeded in establishing a permanent presence in the Hasa province, they started a series of contacts with Mohammad Ibn Rashid, encouraging him to get involved in joint military expeditions under their auspices. For this purpose, frequent correspondence was maintained between the *mutassarif* of the Hasa province and Ibn Rashid.[11] In 1888, reports indicated that the government was trying to encourage Ibn Rashid to invade Oman in conjunction with Sheikh Jassim of Qatar.[12] This was confirmed in a report by the British political resident in Bahrain: 'The Turkish Government is friendly to Ibn Rashid, and shortly in the cool weather, Ibn Rashid will, without fail or doubt, arrive at El Hasa and thence proceed to Oman, and this is well known and the common topic of conversation among people of El Hasa, and privately among the Turks.'[13]

These plans were abandoned because they met the opposition of Britain, but the friendly relationship between Ibn Rashid and the Ottoman government continued. In 1886, an Ottoman mission went to Hail to induce Ibn Rashid to allow the construction of a mosque and a government school, but was unsuccessful.[14]

Friendly relations between Ibn Rashid and the Ottoman authorities did not last for long, for they had different plans and interests. Towards the end of the nineteenth century, Mohammad Ibn Rashid's influence was continuously being extended. By that time, he had completed the subjugation of the Qasim province and Riyadh, the Saudi capital. He wanted to incorporate the Hasa region into his territories and wished the Ottoman sultan to place the province legally under his jurisdiction.[15] However, the Ottomans aimed at extending their own jurisdiction over the Arab littoral of the Persian Gulf. The ambition of Ibn Rashid to be an independent ruler only nominally acknowledging the suzerainty of the sultan met the opposition of the Porte which was planning on turning Najd into an Ottoman province.[16] The concentration of power in the hands of Ibn Rashid and the expansion of his sphere of influence over the whole of central Arabia were good reasons for the Ottomans to re-evaluate their poliices towards him. Although Porte officials openly supported him, they privately maintained contacts with his rivals in an attempt to use these against him if he tried to detach himself from Ottoman suzerainty and claim his independence.

When Mohammad Ibn Rashid captured the Saudi capital, and expelled its ruler, Abdul Rahman, in 1891, the latter took refuge in the Hasa province which was still under Ottoman occupation. The Saudi ruler went there at the invitation of the *wali* of Basra who assigned him a monthly allowance of 33 liras.[17] This shows how the Ottomans relied heavily upon using one tribal force against another for they could afford to allow neither Ibn Rashid nor the Saudi ruler to rule supreme in central Arabia. This was revealed in the joy of Ottoman officials on the borders of Ibn Rashid's territories upon the death of the ruler of Hail in 1897:

Le vali et le grand cherif de la Mecque qui étaient attendues ces jours-ci à Djeddah ont retardis leur voyage à cause de cet événement qui a une importance au point de vue de la domination turque dans l'arabie centrale ... La mort d'un adversaire redoutable, jaloux de son independance et les divisions intestines servirons mieux les intérêts turc dans ce pays.[18]

During the last decade of the nineteenth century, the Ottoman government had watched carefully the emergence of Mohammad Ibn Rashid as the sole undisputed ruler in central Arabia. However, his death removed from the scene a strong ruler who would only openly confess nominal loyalty to the Ottoman government without actually compromising his independence or offering total submission. Later, Mohammad's successors had less bargaining power *vis-à-vis* the government as they were faced by the re-establishment of Abdul Aziz Ibn Saud (known as Ibn Saud) in Riyadh. This coincided with the plans of the Ottoman government to initiate an active policy in central Arabia and their decision to support Ibn Rashid in any future clash between him and Ibn Saud. At the same time the Ottoman government began to prepare in 1904 for a military campaign which was to take place in the Qasim region between the territories of Ibn Rashid and that of Ibn Saud: 'The Sultan has finally decided upon an active policy in the Nejd direction and has ordered that a new and more powerful expedition shall be prepared without loss of time, for the ostensible purpose of assisting Ibn Rashid to crush Ibn Saud and his Wahhabi followers.'[19]

Despite the stated purpose of the expedition, Ottoman officials kept the channels of communication open with Ibn Saud. The *wali* of Basra invited Ibn Saud's father, Abdul Rahman, for a meeting which took place in Basra. In this meeting, Abdul Rahman professed his loyalty and devotion to the sultan and promised to obey his commands. He also stated that he was prepared to do all he could to assist the Ottoman expedition to the Qasim.[20] Eventually, the expedition proceeded from Basra under the command of Faiz Pasha and occupied the major towns of the Qasim. However, the Turkish troops had to withdraw due to difficulties in maintaining the security of the supply routes, disease and the hostility of the local tribes. Consequently, an alternative policy was developed to deal with the situation.

This policy aimed at maintaining a balance of power between Ibn Rashid and Ibn Saud. If the political situation proved to be favourable to one, the Ottoman government would immediately intervene through military aid and subsidies to the other, so as to restore the balance and the *status quo* in the region. Although the government acknowledged both as legimate rulers in Najd, it undermined the authority of one ruler by supporting his rival. The Porte tried to prevent the emergence of a single unchallenged ruler with strong political ambitions who would inevitably challenge Ottoman authority in the more vital regions of the empire such as Iraq and Syria. Such fears were not without historical precedent since the rulers of the first Saudi–Wahhabi dynasty had reached Karbala in Iraq and made encroachments on the Syrian borders. Furthermore, towards the end of the nineteenth century, Mohammad Ibn Rashid forced Palmyra in the Syrian desert to pay him tribute.[21] The only way to prevent such incidents was to keep two rulers in Najd whose hostilities towards each other would prevent them from expanding to the north.

In addition, the government sought the construction of a transportation system to link the peripheral parts of the empire with the major cities such as Damascus and Baghdad. In 1900, under the auspices of Sultan Abdulhamid II, a commission began investigating the possibility of constructing a railway to join Damascus to the holy cities of Arabia, Mecca and Madina. This railway was later known as the Hijaz railway. Sultan Abdulhamid II attributed a special importance to Islam as the basis of loyalty to the state; consequently, he was willing to pay due attention to winning the hearts of the Arabs.[22] This materialized in his attempts to guarantee the safety of the pilgrims who annually visited Mecca and Madina. However, religious factors were not the only motivating force. M. Arif, an Arab apologist for Turkish rule, advised the sultan on the benefits of this railway.[23] He stated that 'the railway would assist in repopulating southeastern Syria, pacifying the nomadic tribes and halting their raids, developing agriculture, exploiting natural resources, reaffirming the Sultan's authority and enabling Muslims from all over the world to make the pilgrimage.' Therefore, it was clear that the political and military advantages to the Ottoman government were as important, if not more important, than the religious ones.

The constructions of the Hijaz railway was bound to meet with the opposition of the local bedouin tribes who had for years benefited from the transport of the pilgrims and extracted a tax from them in return for protection. It was clear that the manipulation of the pilgrims' caravans would no longer rest in the hands of these nomadic tribes after the construction of the railway. The Ottoman government dealt with these problems by force and diplomacy. Troops were sent to pacify these tribes and military clashes accompanied the construction of the railway.[24] However, sometimes the Ottoman government tried to win the approval of the powerful nomadic sheikhs through subsidies and gifts:

> La tâche sera difficile et on ne voit pas quelle compensation le gouvernement pourra offrir aux bedouins, pour les décider à assister avec sérénité à l'achèvement d'une entreprise qui doit leur enlever l'unique source de profit, qu'il faut employer la force, pour exécuter les travaux du chemin de fer dans le désert, de nombreux troupes et beaucoup d'argent seront nécessaires.[25]

As a result, Ottoman officials paid tribal chiefs in return for a promise to restrain their followers. In spite of these difficulties, the railway reached Madina in 1908 though the extension to Mecca was never finished.

In Mesopotamia the Ottoman government carried out a similar project. Towards the end of the nineteenth century, a concession was given by the sultan to a German company to build a railway to join Anatolia to the Persian Gulf and pass through Baghdad. This project, known as the Baghdad railway, did not meet any opposition from local groups. Rather, it was perceived by Britain as a threat to its interests in the Persian Gulf where it had already established its unchallenged supremacy almost a century before. Consequently, in 1899, Britain encouraged the Sheikh of Kuwait, Mubarak Ibn Sabah, to sign a secret treaty which would guarantee his independence *vis-à-vis* the Ottoman government in return for some concessions to be granted to Britain.[26]

The secret treaty with Kuwait aimed at preventing the establishment of a terminus for the railway in Kuwait and promised greater intervention by Britain in the local affairs of the town. It marked the growth of British interests in central Arabia and a permanent British presence in Kuwait by 1904. This provided the ground for local groups to manipulate the rivalry between Britain and the Ottoman government to their own advantage. For example, at the beginning of the twentieth century, Ibn Rashid tried to open lines of communication with British officials in the region. His emissaries told the British consul in Iraq that he wanted to enter into treaty relations with the British government. He would also accept the British position in Kuwait and grant a concession for a trans-Arabian railway if the British government so desired. In return, he expected Britain to permit a free flow of arms through the Gulf to Hail.[27] Similarly, Ibn Saud in Riyadh tried through his ally, Mubarak Ibn Sabah of Kuwait, to win the sympathy of Britain to his cause. The strategy of Ibn Saud was to involve Britain more in the affairs of Arabia as a counterpoise to Turkey.[28]

The Ottoman government watched these attempts suspiciously. Ottoman officials objected to the British ambassador in Constantinople and accused Britain of having the intention of proceeding to Najd to persuade Ibn Saud to rise in rebellion against the Imperial government, and accept British protection. The British ambassador assured the Ottoman authorities that there was no evidence for these accusations: 'I said that I had not heard of the alleged movement of British ships, but that the report that His Majesty's Government contemplated the establishment of a British protectorate in the interior of Arabia was ridiculous and I could not suppose that anyone would suspect us of such designs.'[29]

At the same time Britain did not respond to the overtures made by Ibn Rashid and Ibn Saud although a deliberate policy of not alienating them was adopted. Britain's main interest was to guarantee that Kuwait remain within its sphere of influence, and in this respect Ibn Saud represented no threat. The main concern therefore was to prevent any attack by Ibn Rashid on Kuwait. It was believed that 'though the British government did not have direct relations with the Hail amir, there was no need to pointlessly antagonise him. Besides, a struggle for power between Hail and Kuwait would weaken both the participants and thereby increase Turkish influence over Arabia. British interests demanded that there be no conflict between Mubarak and Ibn Rashid.[30]

Faced with Britain's unwillingness to actively support him, Ibn Rashid responded to the encouragement of the Ottoman authorities to attack Kuwait. The Ottoman government feared the consequences of a direct confrontation with Britain and thought that if Ibn Rashid would attack Kuwait on their behalf, the chances of an outbreak of hostilities with Britain would be diminished. Ibn Rashid prepared an attack and defeated Mubarak in 1901. He then encamped for some time on the confines of Kuwait where he kept up communication with the Turkish authorities at Basra, demanding their assistance for the purpose of extracting redress from the amir of Kuwait for his aggression on Najd territories.[31]

The victory of the amir of Hail caused concern for British officials in Kuwait and when he continued his attacks on Kuwait, the British naval forces opened fire and forced him to withdraw to Najd. In the light of these events, it became clear that the Ottoman government was willing to support Ibn Rashid against the amir of Kuwait and his British and Saudi allies. On the other hand, British political agents in Kuwait drew the attention of their government to the importance of sending a mission to central Arabia to gather information which would enable the government to redefine its position and formulate active policies concerning the situation in Najd.[32]

When these suggestions reached the Foreign Office in London, they encountered some opposition. While the British government desired more information on the interior of Arabia, the Foreign Office thought that the mission would probably lead to further proposals for establishing closer relations with Ibn Rashid's rival, i.e. Ibn Saud. Consequently, it was decided that no mission should be sent to Najd. Instead, an agreement between Britain and the Ottoman government was reached to the effect that both governments would preserve the *status quo* in central Arabia. This meant that the Ottoman authorities would restrain Ibn Rashid from attacking Kuwait while the British government would restrain Sheikh Mubarak of Kuwait from attacking central Arabia. Furthermore, it was agreed that Britain should not enter into negotiations with Ibn Saud. By 1906, Ibn Saud had already accepted the Ottoman sultan as a nominal suzerain and agreed to the cessation of hostilities with Hail.

During the first decade of the twentieth century, Britain was still maintaining a policy of not openly antagonizing the Ottoman government. As long as the Ottomans and their allies in central Arabia respected British interests in the Persian Gulf, Britain saw no benefit in entering into negotiations or secret treaties with local groups who might use British support to challenge Ottoman authority in the area. This was reflected in an unwillingness to negotiate a protectionist treaty with Ibn Saud in spite of his attempts to establish a rapport with British officials in the Persian Gulf and Kuwait. Rather, Britain preferred to enter into negotiations with the Ottoman government regarding the protection of its interests in the Persian Gulf. This resulted in the Anglo-Turkish Convention of 1913 in which Britain recognized Al Hasa, the province on the Arab side of the Persian Gulf that had been under Ottoman occupation since 1871, as Ottoman territory. This recognition implied that Britain had accepted Ottoman sovereignty over the Hasa and Najd itself.[33]

However, in the same year, the province of the Hasa was recovered by Ibn Saud who wrote to the Ottoman authorities in Basra saying that the action was 'forced upon him by the complaints of the inhabitants that they were being oppressed by the Turkish subordinate officials'. He added that he would willingly represent the Turks as *wali* and that he would underake responsibility for the tranquillity of the district.[34] The Ottoman authorities had no alternative but to recognize Ibn Saud as *de facto* ruler in the Hasa. In May 1914, a treaty was signed with Ibn Saud in which the Ottomans recognized him as the ruler of Najd. Also, Ibn Saud was appointed as *wali* and commander-in-chief of Najd. It was agreed that all taxes and rates were to remain in his hands; he was to pay from these revenues the expenses of the country and what was left over would be sent to the palace. However, there is no evidence that Ibn Saud sent any taxes or rates to the Ottoman government – on the contrary, he received a monthly allowance of 250 Turkish majidis as ruler of the Hasa.[35] This allowance was regarded as a salary from the Ottoman government to imply that he was acting in accordance with its will.

At the same time, the Ottoman government communicated with Ibn Rashid and encouraged him to recover the Hasa from Ibn Saud:

> During a recent meeting which took place between the Vali of Basra and Bin Rashid, the Vali asked the Amir whether, if necessary, he was in a position to reconquer Hasa and restore it to the Turks. Bin Rashid is said to have professed his willingness to do so, and to have stated that he merely required the cooperation of 200 Turkish soldiers for the purpose.[36]

Consequently, a high Ottoman officer was sent to Hail to discuss the details of the war which Ibn Rashid was expected to launch against Ibn Saud. Furthermore, arms and ammunition including three mounted guns, breech loaders with 500 rounds of shell, and 30,000 rifles were sent from Damascus to Ibn Rashid through the Hijaz railway.[37] Although the railway did not fall within his territory, it was possible to send him weapons and ammunition that way.

In 1913, the British government was still adopting a policy of non-intervention in the affairs of central Arabia. British officials in the Persian Gulf were under strict orders that:

> His Majesty's Government cannot intervene in any way in the dispute and must maintain the strictest neutrality between the two parties. As long as Bin Saud confined himself to El Hasa, he could be ignored with impunity. The British Government should abstain from any communication whatsoever, other than that of a purely formal nature where inevitable with Bin Saud or any other Arabian chief with whom His Majesty's Government have not treaty relations. Moreover, British Officials stressed that it should be clearly understood that the influence and interests of His Majesty's Government are to be strictly confined to the coast line of Eastern Arabia, and that no measures are to be taken or language used, which might appear to connect them even indirectly with the tribal warfare, now in the progress in the interior.[35]

This policy was respected throughout the first decade of the twentieth century. Britain recognized Ottoman authority over Najd and refrained from any intervention in the clashes between Ibn Rashid and his Ottoman allies on the one hand and Ibn Saud on the other. However, the outbreak of the First World War in 1914 freed both Britain and Turkey from their previous policies.

OTTOMAN AND BRITISH POLICIES DURING THE WAR

As the shadow of the war approached, the Porte officials endeavoured to reconcile the two rulers in Najd and obtain a promise of their military co-operation.[39] They apparently felt that the old method of setting off one Arab sheikh against another would no longer be as successful even in maintaining that semblance of Ottoman sovereignty over them.[40] The involvement of the Ottoman government in the war required a more positive policy towards the rulers of Najd. However, Ottoman attempts at reconciliation failed and hostilities were resumed between Ibn Rashid and Ibn Saud.

Equally, the outbreak of the war freed Britain from its previous policy of non-intervention in central Arabia. Britain was searching for some local allies in Najd whose support and co-operation were essential to end Ottoman authority in the region. As Ibn Saud was willing to co-operate with the British government in this matter, he received Captain Shakespear, a British envoy whose role was to advise on matters related to the war and the necessary military actions. This was followed by signing a treaty with Ibn Saud in 1915.[41]

When Ibn Saud's allegiance to Britain was guaranteed, the British government tried to win over Ibn Rashid and deprive the Ottomans from their local ally. Consequently, British officials suggested that the Sherif of Mecca open communications with Ibn Rashid on their behalf.[42] In a letter to the sherif, British officials declared that if Ibn Rashid agreed to side with Britain, 'the Turks will lose their chief source of camel supply, and will have a troublesome enemy on their flank east of the railway, (the Hijaz railway).'[43] Moreover, Britain encouraged Ibn Saud to reconcile with Ibn Rashid, in the belief that it would help British interests – especially if the two rulers acted together against Turkey.[44] These attempts were doomed to failure because Ibn Rashid declared through his envoys that he would certainly join the Ottomans if they sent troops to support him.

By that time, Ibn Rashid had already been appointed by the Ottoman authorities as 'commander of the whole of Najd' and he was sent 25 German and Turkish officers with 300 soldiers.[45] The Ottoman government was convinced that Hail was an important centre and if it was lost, the whole of the Arabian Peninsula as far as Damascus would unite against them. Therefore, their alliance with Ibn Rashid was essential since he was the only influential local ruler who did not join their enemies in Arabia.

Once it became clear that Ibn Rashid's alliance with the Ottomans was well-established, Britain abandoned its policy of reconciliation and encouraged Ibn Saud to attack Ibn Rashid from the south. This, it was believed, would keep Ibn Rashid busy and prevent him from providing military aid to the Ottomans in the north. By December 1917, the initiative with regard to the proposal for attacking Hail had already come from the British authorities (the Arab Bureau) in Cairo.[46] A messenger, Colonel Hamilton, was sent to Ibn Saud to discuss the possibility. In a report he explained that:

Bin Saud said it was an impossible task because Ibn Rashid was a sheikh of a single, powerful tribe, which would unite at once for self-defence in case of Hail being attacked. Ibn Saud also explained that the composition of his forces would not render the campaign against Hail successful. His forces consisted of an amalgamation of different tribes such as the Mutair, the Dawasir, the Subai, Ataiba, Hajar, and Dhafir, all of them would gather and would be a large mob difficult to control or to keep concentrated for more than a few days in one locality. Consequently, anything like prolonged operations against Hail with such levies was not to be thought of.[47]

Ibn Saud claimed that the terrain between the region which he controlled in the Qasim and Hail was barren ground and this would inevitably make it difficult for troops and camels to survive for long and, in addition, Hail was a well-fortified oasis difficult to conquer with the weapons in his possession. British officials recognized that:

Ibn Saud may not find it possible to undertake operations on such a large scale as to enable him to capture Hail and there is no necessity to press him unduly in this connection, but at any rate, it is still important that he should maintain more effective control, and put real pressure on the Shammar. It was agreed that Britain should assist him with 1000 rifles and 100,000 rounds to achieve this end.[48]

Furthermore, Britain employed another strategy to put pressure on Ibn Rashid. It was agreed that the Shammar and Ibn Rashid's subjects should not be granted access to the markets of Baghdad, Basra and Kuwait which had already been put under the control of Britain. It was thought that a pass should be given to friendly tribes whereas those loyal to the Ottoman government should be deprived of *Mussabalah* (access to the market).[49] This economic pressure would induce the Shammar and Ibn Rashid's subjects to abandon him and declare their allegiance to Britain or Ibn Saud – whose subjects were granted access to the markets.

As the settled population of Hail and the Shammar depended heavily on supplies from Iraq and the port of Kuwait, this economic blockade was effective in partially isolating the oasis and causing trouble among Ibn Rashid's subjects. It was believed that the economic conditions of the Shammar would force them to give in. To prevent this, Ibn Rashid immediately sent his messenger, Ibn Leiyla, to Damascus in an attempt to bring food supplies and ammunition from the Ottoman authorities there. The messenger proceeded to Constantinople where he aimed to discuss further plans concerning Ibn Rashid's role as an ally of the Ottomans in Arabia. While Ibn Rashid was waiting in Hail for the return of his envoy, the British political agent in Kuwait received information that Ibn Rashid was at the same time contemplating opening negotiations with Britain: 'Ibn Leiyla (Ibn Rashid's messenger) has returned to Damascus from Constantinople with money and presents. Ibn Rashid awaits Ibn Leiyla's return with money to Hail and then intends opening negotiations with us.'[50]

However, Ibn Rashid was hesitant to abandon his traditional role as an ally of the Ottomans and news concerning his unwillingness to start immediate negotiations came from Ibn Saud: 'Ibn Rashid cannot be bought, of that Ibn Saud was certain, nor can he be brought over to our side because it is the fundamental policy of Hail and the Shammar to lean on the Turks so as to remain independent in Najd.'[51]

Ibn Rashid realized that his independence and that of the Shammar would be better sustained if he maintained his alliance with the Ottoman government which for centuries had been unable to directly control Najd. This was made clear through observing Britain's policies towards her allies such as Ibn Saud in Najd and Sherif Hussein in the Hijaz. Britain was determined to encourage its local allies to take positive measures against the Ottoman authorities. The Arab revolt of 1916 by Sherif Hussein and the tribes of the Hijaz was the outcome of this policy. In contrast, the Porte continued during the war to provide Ibn Rashid with supplies and subsidies without being able to force him to actively participate in the war on their side. The poor communication network with local Arab sheikhs prevented the development of real control over them. Furthermore, communication lines such as the Hijaz railway were soon attacked by hostile local tribes and this increased the inability of the Ottoman government to sustain an effective command over Ibn Rashid. From the point of view of the latter, an alliance with a weak central government was regarded as beneficial to the maintenance of local autonomy. However, the defeat of the Ottomans in the war in 1918 had put an end to Ottoman suzerainty in Arabia. Britain replaced the Ottoman

Empire in dealing with the local power centres in the Arabian Peninsula as a whole.

BRITISH POST-WAR POLICIES IN NAJD

Towards the end of the war in Arabia, Britain defined its policy as the pursuit of three objectives: the security of the annual pilgrimage routes, the immunity of the Arabian Peninsula from any foreign occupation, and the preservation of peace and the promotion of trading facilities on the borders of an autonomous Arabia.[52]

The events of the war resulted in the emergence of an autonomous ruler in the Hijaz. Sherif Hussein of the Hijaz had already declared himself 'King of the Arabs' and was waiting for Britain to fulfil the promises which she had made during the war in return for his co-operation against the Ottoman Empire. King Hussein expected Britain to support his claims in the peace conferences which followed the war and prevent any local group from challenging these claims on the ground. On the other hand, in central Arabia, British subsidies and support resulted in the growth of Ibn Saud's sphere of influence. By the end of the war, Ibn Saud was already in control of central Najd including the region of the Qasim between his capital, Riyadh and the domain of Ibn Rashid. This was achieved by his warriors, the *ikhwan*.[53] Ibn Saud and his warriors were interested in the expansion of their control over areas beyond the borders of central Arabia such as the Hijaz. Clashes with the King of the Hijaz were therefore inevitable. However, any confrontation between Ibn Saud and King Hussein was embarrassing for the British, as both were close allies of Britain and received considerable subsidies during the war. To support one ruler against the other would put Britain in a difficult position given the fact that both rulers had strong claims and a substantial number of followers.

The defeat of the Ottomans contributed to the marginalization of Ibn Rashid, whose sphere of influence became restricted to Hail and Jabal Shammar although he was still able to extend his control over the pilgrimage route from Iraq to the holy cities. Furthermore, Ibn Rashid had lost some of his tribal subjects who joined King Hussein or Ibn Saud. His authority was limited to the oasis of Jabal Shammar and some Shammar tribal sections.

Taking these developments into consideration, British officials thought it would be in their interest for Ibn Rashid to remain as an independent ruler in Hail: 'As regards after war conditions, it would seem that the balance of power in Arabia would be better preserved if Ibn Rashid continued to rule independently there.'[54]

Furthermore, when Britain succeeded in capturing Jerusalem from the Ottomans in April 1918, British officials in the Persian Gulf advised their government that Ibn Rashid was in no position to do any harm or to provide any support to the Ottomans through the territory now controlled by Britain. As a result, it was argued that his retention would assist in the maintenance of the balance of power between Ibn Saud and the King of the Hijaz. The Viceroy of India advised the Foreign Office concerning the necessary measures: 'We, therefore, recommend that Cox should keep Ibn Saud in play by presents of money, but that assistance in arms and instructors should not be given except very sparingly. Otherwise, we seem to risk the establishment of two powers in Arabia mutually hostile, but to both of whom we have given pledges of support.'[55]

In the light of this advice, the British government decided against the complete elimination of Ibn Rashid by Ibn Saud. It was believed that the possession of Hail by Ibn Saud would only increase British difficulties in central Arabia since it would inevitably be regarded unfavourably by King Hussein and would increase the friction between himself and Ibn Saud.[56]

In spite of the change in British policy towards Hail, Ibn Saud continued to organize minor attacks on the Shammar and Ibn Rashid's territory. In August 1918, accompanied by his British adviser, Philby, and his *ikhwan* warriors, Ibn Saud launched an attack on Jabal Shammar and Hail. However, when it became clear that he was almost winning the battle, the British government, through her envoy in Riyadh, ordered him to retreat. This reflected the British policy of diverting Ibn Saud's attention from the Hijaz by keeping him occupied in minor attacks against Hail.

The King of the Hijaz realized that Ibn Saud entertained ambitions regarding his territories, especially when Ibn Saud's forces began a series of attacks on the borders of the Hijaz which culminated in the battle of Khurma in 1918. Consequently, in an attempt to isolate Ibn Saud, King Hussein of the Hijaz started negotiations with Ibn Rashid through his son, Abdullah. British officials in the area received news to the effect that peace was made between Ibn Rashid and King Hussein and negotiations were proceeding regarding the affairs of the northern areas of central Arabia: 'If attacked by Ibn Saud, Ibn Rashid will probably make terms without delay either with the King of the Hidjaz or with us and in either case will be placed in a difficult position. If he joins the King of the Hidjaz, we shall doubtless be asked to call off Ibn Saud.'[57]

The peace negotiations between Ibn Rashid and the King of the Hijaz were regarded by Ibn Saud as leading to an alliance directed mainly against him. If this alliance was to be taken to its logical end, Ibn Saud would find himself isolated and could be put under pressure from the west by King Hussein and from the north by Ibn Rashid. Moreover, he could no longer take for granted the security of his eastern territories since Sheikh Salem of Kuwait was already in communication with Ibn Rashid: 'There are indications that the Shareef of Mecca, Bin Rashid and Shaikh Salem of Kuwait are in communication with one another. The general intention being to check Bin Saud's increasing power, the immediate object being to prevent him from going to Mecca by threats of war and invasion.'[58]

At the same time, Sheikh Salem was offering refuge to the Ajman tribes who were constantly challenging Ibn Saud's authority and revolting against him. It seemed that Kuwait redefined its previous policy *vis-à-vis* Ibn Saud once it became clear that his power was growing faster than the Kuwaiti sheikhs had anticipated.

As a result, Ibn Rashid's sphere of influence was being extended to the limits of Iraq. As the pilgrimage route from Iraq to the holy places was still under his control, British officials tailored the principles of their policy to take this into account. It was believed that in order to make Ibn Rashid respect their borders in Iraq and keep open the route for the pilgrims, it was desirable to enter into relations with him to the extent of subsidizing him.[59] At the same time, Ibn Rashid sent an agent to the British civil commissioner in Baghdad to settle the amount of subsidy to be given in return for his co-operation. The civil commissioner believed that the amount should be fixed at Rs 3,500 per month of which the Mesopotamia administration would contribute half.

All these events were carefully being watched by Ibn Saud whose ambition to unite all Najd under his leadership was growing. Furthermore, he looked at the Hijaz territories and in particular the holy cities of Mecca and Madina as possible targets.

His *ikhwan* followers were eager to extend their influence to these places but Ibn Saud realized that it was essential to unify Najd first by removing Ibn Rashid from the scene. After achieving this objective, the incorporation of the Hijaz territories in his domain would inevitably become easier. The opportunity offered itself during the period of internal disturbances in Hail over the issue of succession.

In 1920, the ruler of Hail, Saud Ibn Rashid, was assassinated by his paternal cousin, Abdullah Ibn Talal, who was immediately killed by Saud's slaves. Succession reverted to the young amir Abdullah Ibn Mitab who imprisoned the assassin's brother, Mohammad Ibn Talal, because he feared the possibility of revenge.[60] These events created a favourable milieu for Ibn Saud who immediately wrote to the British political agent informing him that he would not make peace nor conclude a treaty with the new amir of Hail, for he did not trust the leadership's attitude towards alliances and friendship in general.[61] Ibn Saud immediately started to organize his forces, determined to end Ibn Rashid's rule in Hail and Jabal Shammar. The campaign began in 1920 and the oasis was conquered in the following year.[62]

The major concern of Britain at that time was to establish her control over Iraq and Trans-Jordan through creating friendly monarchies there. It was thought that this would help solve the problem of the King of the Hijaz who was still waiting for Britain to fulfil her promises by recognizing his leadership as the 'King of the Arabs'. As a result, the incorporation of Hail by Ibn Saud was not perceived as a threat to British interests in the north since he was still maintaining friendly relations with Britain at that time.

In conclusion, it must be pointed out that external governments, whether Ottoman or British, were not themselves immune from manipulation by local groups. These external power centres represented a source of power outside the local system which local leaders were eager to manipulate to their own advantage. Moreover, the availability of more than one external source provided the opportunity for local groups to manoeuvre and play risky political games. Consequently, the bargaining power of these local leaders *vis-à-vis* the Ottomans was enhanced by the mere appearance of Britain on the scene.

The relationship maintained by the amirs of Hail with external governments generated some economic and political changes in the dynasty especially at the level of leadership.[63] As allies of the

Ottoman government, these amirs became recipients of various kinds of subsidies, allowances, weapons and presents in spite of the fact that sometimes they were asked to pay *ad hoc* tribute which symbolically indicated their submission to the government. Since, no serious effort was made to guarantee that payment was made, the flow of subsidies was to the advantage of the amirs and was in most cases a one-way process.

External relations therefore contributed to the creation of a surplus in the hands of the ruling group and although part was poured back into the political community as gifts and subsidies to tribal sections, a substantial amount remained under the control of the amirs, resulting in an increase in economic differentiation. This differentiation was a characteristic feature of the oasis-based leadership of the Rashidi amirs which differed from the leadership of the Shammar tribal section sheikhs. The latter had minimal contacts with outside governments.[64] They remained politically and economically undifferentiated from the rest of their tribal section. Furthermore, they were leaders only of their tribal section and had no authority outside that section. On the other hand, the amirs of Hail were expected by the external government not only to restrain their followers from challenging the government's authority, but also to act as rulers with a military force ready to obey commands from above.

In his work on the development of Ibn Rashid's 'state', Rosenfeld tends to ignore the significance of relations with external power centres. Rosenfeld attributes the development of beit Ibn Rashid as a differentiated stratum in Shammar bedouin society to purely economic factors emerging from nomadic sedentary interaction within that society. He sees the hegemony of the Hail amirs as a function of trade, commerce and tribute relations (H. Rosenfeld 1965: 80). Although these were important factors maintaining Rashidi hegemony, one has to remember the significance of interaction with outside governments in the process of economic differentation beween rulers and subjects.

9

THE DECLINE

EXTERNAL PRESSURES

Both the Ottoman Empire and the British government played a crucial role in upsetting the balance between the local power centres in central Arabia. The association of the Hail amirs with the Ottoman Empire and the defeat of the latter in the First World War deprived the ruling group in Hail of an imporant ally. The Rashidi amirs lost their only source of subsidies and weapons. In contrast, their rival, Ibn Saud, had already succeeded in establishing strong ties with Britain, the victorious party after the war.

Between 1918 and 1920, the amirs of Hail constantly tried to compensate for their losses and break their isolation in central Arabia. They entered into negotiations with the Hashemites in the Hijaz and Al Sabah, the amirs of Kuweit who began to realize the threat that Ibn Saud represented – especially after it became clear that Britain's support for him during the war had strengthened his position in central Arabia. By that time, it seemed that Ibn Saud was planning to extend his sphere of influence beyond his ancestors' traditional territory in southern Najd. These two rulers regarded this as a threat to their interests and aimed at establishing an alliance with the Rashidi amirs against Ibn Saud. The British political agent in Bahrain reported to the civil commissioner in Baghdad: 'There are indications that the Sherif of Mecca, Bin Rashid, and shaikh Salem of Kuweit are in communication with one another. The general intention being to check Bin Saud's increasing power, the immediate object to prevent him going to Mecca by threats of war and invasion.'[1]

Although these negotiations succeeded in breaking the isolation of the Rashidis after the war, they did not materialize in any joint military activity against Ibn Saud. The Hail amirs were not able to prevent Ibn Saud's attack on their territories in the 1920s.

As early as 1918, Ibn Saud realized that in spite of successive internal power struggles and assassinations, the Hail ruling group still enjoyed the support of the Shammar tribe. Ibn Saud revealed his doubts about the success of any major attack on Hail to the British officials in the Persian gulf.[2] He expressed his inability to guarantee the expansion of his power over Ibn Rashid's territory as long as he had grass-root support among the Shammar. In an attempt to undermine this support and contribute to his further isolation, Ibn Saud tried to win over to his side some Shammar sections. This was reported by Philby to the British commissioner in Baghdad. 'Today Ibn Saud sent out fifteen letters to chiefly Shammar Shaikh communicating to them and offering them alternatives of friendship on condition of taking up residence within his effective borders or war if found elsewhere.'[3]

Furthermore, Ibn Saud realized that if his attack was to have any success, it was important to cut all lines of communication between Hail and the Shammar and force the latter to settle down in areas like the Hasa or southern Hajd. It was believed that this would prevent the Shammar from providing any support or military help in the north should the Rashidi amirs be attacked by Ibn Saud. In fulfilling this policy, Ibn Saud tried to put economic pressure on the Shammar by denying them access to the markets of the towns which had already fallen within his sphere of influence (such as Riyadh, Unaizah, Qatif, and Boreidah) and reached an agreement with the British political agent in Kuwait that only friendly tribesmen would be given *mussabalah* (market transactions) in places within British control. Ibn Saud was convinced that under no circumstances would the Shammar fight with him against their Rashidi traditional leadership.[4] However, in the years following the war, he constantly tried to guarantee at least the neutrality of some Shammar sections should he launch an attack on Hail. To implement his objectives, he promised the Shammar food rations from the British officials in Kuwait if they showed signs of willingness to remain neutral or switch allegiance to him.

One Shammar section, the Aslam, had already been in contact with British officials in Kuwait. Their sheikh, Dari Ibn Twala, convinced the British authorities to allow his section to enter Kuwait and purchase food, rice, and other important goods. The Aslam were given the right to *mussabalah* on condition that they remain near Kuwait and sever contacts with the Rashidi amirs. It took British officials in Kuwait a long time to discover that Dari Ibn Twala and his Aslam section were involved in the leakage of goods to Ibn Rashid.[5] Consequently, Philby, the British envoy to Ibn Saud, recommended that British officials in Kuwait maintain strict control over the issue of passes which were to be immediately withdrawn in case of any hostilities against Ibn Saud: 'The proved participation of any such person in raids and hostilities against Ibn Saud should be followed by withdrawal of privileges from whole sections and paramount chiefs.'[6]

These economic pressures were not very successful in undermining Shammar support for the Rashidi amirs. However, during the first two decades of the century, Ibn Saud had offered an alternative ideology defined in terms of religion. He reinvoked Wahhabism in an attempt to provide an overarching ideology under the banner of which the various antagonistic tribes of the region could be unified.[7]

Ibn Saud portrayed his military expansion and political ambitions as a holy war against his enemies and rivals, appealing to the various tribes of central Arabia in the name of God. Those who adopted Wahhabism became his *ikhwan* (Muslim brothers) followers. They were organized to settle in the *hujar* (village settlement created for this purpose) where they were given religious education and were prepared to accept fighting Ibn Saud's wars. In return for abandoning their nomadic existence, settling down, and offering their alliance to Ibn Saud, the *ikhwan* received subsidies from *beit al mal* (public treasury). For example, the *al qaidah* was a cash sum distributed among the *ikhwan* whose name appeared in Ibn Saud's register of fighters. In addition, there were other subsidies distributed in kind, such as handouts of rice, butter, sugar, and clothes.

At the beginning of the *ikhwan* settlement in the *hujar* in 1913, the Shammar were reluctant to join Ibn Saud whose Wahhabi teachings and accompanying life-style did not appeal to them. However, by 1918, under the above-mentioned economic pressures, almost one-fourth of the Shammar had become *ikhwan* and allied themselves with Ibn Saud. Towards the end of the war, the Shammar became more susceptible to accepting the Wahhabi movement as this promised obvious economic rewards.

Traditionally the Shammar migrated to the north towards Syria and Iraq in search of water and pasture. War operations between the Ottomans and the British government in that region forced the Shammar to maintain their subsistence within the confines of central Arabia. These pressures, coupled with drought and bad climatic conditions undermined the viability of their pastoral economy and made them vulnerable to accepting settlement in Ibn Saud's *hujar*.

The Shammar economy was further weakened by the Hijaz railway which joined Damascus to Madina. It was believed that the railway would gradually replace the camel caravans which carried both the pilgrims and the various goods imported into the Arabian Peninsula. In addition, cheap steamship transport to the major ports of the peninsula, especially Djeddah, contributed to the decline of the number of pilgrims using the camel caravans to make the journey. As a result, there was a decreasing demand for camels, guides and escorts; camel prices fell as camels began to be replaced by other means of transport.

The pastoral economy of the nomadic tribes not only in the Arabian Peninsula, but also in the Middle East in general, was undergoing a process of marginalization. It is worth mentioning here that the introduction of modern means of transport acted in favour of Ibn Saud's plans to settle the nomads. A weakened pastoral economy predisposed the impoverished nomads to abandon their pastoralism and join the *ikhwan* movement. Settlement in small *ikhwan* villages became a viable and attractive alternative which was inevitably more acceptable to the nomads during times of economic scarcity than during economic prosperity.

Arrangements for the Shammar who turned into *ikhwan* included their settlement in southern Najd where it would be difficult for them to join Ibn Rashid and other Shammar sections in the north who were still hostile to Ibn Saud.[8] This contributed to both the fragmentation of the tribe and the weakening of tribal unity. It also generated hostilities and antagonisms between those Shammar who still swore allegiance to the Rashidi amirs and those who joined Ibn Saud.

Wahhabism was not only adopted by some sections of the Shammar. The movement found supporters among the sedentary population of Hail as well. In spring 1920, the British political agent in Bahrain received news that a group of merchants and *qadis* (judges) from Hail had written to Ibn Saud expressing their views about the unsatisfactory way in which they had been ruled in the past and asking Ibn Saud to take advantage of the present situation and take charge of their interests.[9]

In contrast with Ibn Rashid's inability to take serious punitive measures against the Shammar who switched allegiance to Ibn Saud, he was able to exercise some control over the population of the oasis. As soon as the *qadi* of Hail and his followers were discovered, they were summoned in the market square where they were executed as traitors.[10] However, this attempt to establish contact with Ibn Saud reflected the growing dissatisfaction of the oasis population with their leadership, for a number of reasons. First, the instability resulting from successive assassinations undermined the amirs' legitimacy. While this instability had been tolerated in the nineteenth century when there was no obvious challenge to Rashidi domination, the emergence of Ibn Saud provided an alternative to the population of Hail. His wealth from British subsidies and the prosperity and security of his territories encouraged other groups in central Arabia to establish contacts with him, which undermined the legitimacy of local leaders and rulers. Second, the population of Hail, and especially its merchant community began to feel the pressure of the economic blockade and the marginalization of Hail as a caravan transit station.

In the nineteenth century, the prosperity of Hail was highly dependent on the caravan economy and it became the third most important caravan city after Mecca and Madina. While the strength of its amirs at that time enabled them to divert the caravan traffic to their oasis, the weakened amirs of the first two decades of the twentieth century were unable to prevent the caravan trade being diverted to other growing commercial centres in central Arabia. The political instability in Hail pushed the merchants away from its market. The decline was further aggravated by the fact that the Rashidi amirs failed to spread their sphere of influence over a port. Hail had always been dependent on the Ottoman centres in Syria and Iraq (the ports of Basra and Kuwait) for its supplies of goods. The amirs encouraged trade especially with Kuwait which received a variety of goods from India, Europe and Persia. However, access to the port of Kuwait was highly affected by the political relations between the Hail amirs and those of Kuwait. During times of conflict, it was common for the Kuwait amirs to restrict both the flow of goods to Hail and the access of the Shammar to the market. In an attempt to reduce this dependence, Abdul Aziz Ibn Rashid tried in 1901 to incorporate Kuwait in his realm by launching a series of attacks on the outskirts of Kuwait. British officials in Kuwait resented Ibn Rashid's activities which they believed were backed by Ottoman approval. However, the British naval forces compelled him to retreat to central Arabia, leaving Hail without an outlet on the coast of the Persian Gulf.

According to Rosenfeld, the Hail merchants were in many respects similar to the Shammar nomads. As a result of economic pressures, both groups showed their willingness to switch their allegiance to Ibn Saud. As they both had mobile wealth and no important landed property, they were able to do so with ease. Their wealth consisted of items which could easily be transported: 'Because they are landless, or practically so, because they have no deep interest in fixed production, no real investment in agriculture, but in trade, the loyalty of the merchant class, who were in part strangers, shifts with the focus of power.' (H. Rosenfeld 1965: 185–6) Therefore, as the focus of power shifted from Hail to Riyadh, the merchants were able, according to Rosenfeld, to follow their fortunes where strong leadership and more security were available. Since most of the Hail merchants came from the Qasim, Hasa, Syria and Iraq, they had no deep roots or long-lasting ties in the region. They had been attracted by the security of Hail in the second half of the nineteenth century, but when the Hail leadership could no longer provide this security the merchants moved out in search of better localities.

The similarities between the nomads and the merchants which Rosenfeld invokes is not very convincing. Although it is true that the nomads were able to move off easily, it is less evident that the merchants could. The nomads were genuinely mobile and could not be restrained from the centre if they wanted to move. In contrast, the geographical proximity of the merchants to the centre of power in Hail restricted their ability to move away freely. It is probably more accurate to say that the political instability in Hail discouraged the settlement of new merchants there.

The Hail amirs lost some revenues as a result of the decline of their power and military strength. With diminished revenues, the ruling group were unable to maintain the system of subsidies to tribal section sheikhs, in return for which the tribal sheikhs had offered their loyalty and that of their section. As these subsidies diminished or stopped, the sheikhs shifted their loyalty and were ready to offer their allegiance to a rival group who would provide such benefits. Even the Shammar sections who were constantly bribed into keeping their loyalty transferred their fidelity to the strongest enemies of Ibn Rashid when they saw that Rashidi hegemony was no longer a viable power (ibid).

All these conditions constituted a favourable background to Ibn Saud's invasion of Jabal Shammar. He managed to secure at least the neutrality of one-fourth of the Shammar and maintained contacts with local Hail personalities. This coincided with the outbreak of a fierce power struggle in Hail. When the amir Saud Ibn Rashid was assassinated in 1920 the new amir, Abdullah Ibn Mitab, was a young boy with no political experience. Ibn Saud was determined to take advantage of the situation and terminate the rule of his traditional rivals in central Arabia. He immediately approached Hail from the south and imposed a siege on the oasis.

The new amir sent his representative to Ibn Saud in an attempt to negotiate a treaty which would lead to the cessation of hostilities between Hail and Riyadh. Ibn Saud declared that he was ready to make peace with Ibn Rashid if the latter agreed to the following conditions. First, Ibn Saud required that Hail had no foreign relations except with him. Second, all relations with the Shammar were to be dealt with by Ibn Saud. Third, Ibn Saud agreed that Hail would remain independent in the management of its internal affairs on condition that final control stayed in his hands. Fourth, final appeals in all disputes were to be submitted to Ibn Saud for settlement.[11]

Ibn Rashid's representative returned to Hail to discuss the conditions of the treaty. According to a report by the British political agent in Bahrain, two-thirds of the population of Hail were in favour of the conditions and the remaining third were opposed.[12] The amir himself found the conditions unacceptable and denounced the treaty. Instead, an agreement among the ruling group was reached to the effect that they were willing to continue resisting Ibn Saud's attacks on Hail and Jabal Shammar.[13] Once news of the rejection reached Ibn Saud, he continued to put more military pressure on Hail. He also wrote to the British political agent in Bahrain in an attempt to justify his military campaign and point out that the sherif of the Hijaz was involved in the dispute between him and Ibn Rashid: 'Regarding Bin Rashid, for long I have been trying to win his good will, but he avoids my advances because of the false hopes held out to him by the Sherif. The Sherif has now promised his support in money and arms. Munition and supplies have already reached Hail and more are about to leave from Madina.'[14]

Ibn Saud immediately launched three consecutive attacks on Jabal Shammar. The first was led by his son, Saud, and succeeded in reaching Beqaa to the north-east of Hail. The second was under the leadership of the two famous *ikhwan* leaders, Ibn Rabian of the Ataiba tribe and Faisal Al Duwish of the Mutair tribe. The final attack was organized by Ibn Hameid of the Ataiba tribe who was also a sheikh of an *ikhwan* settlement called Ghatghat.[15]

These attacks generated some confusion in the oasis. Although the young amir, Abdullah Ibn Mitab, favoured peace with Ibn Saud under the mounting pressure, he was not able to express this view because of the strong objections made by the factions of his cousin, Mohammad Ibn Talal who was in prison. These factions were strong enough to influence Abdullah's decisions even when Mohammad was still in prison, and indeed forced the amir to free him.[16] Abdullah Ibn Mitab immediately took refuge with Ibn Saud whose forces were camped on the outskirts of Hail unable to enter the oasis. The freed amir, Mohammad, was expected to lead the resistance against Ibn Saud and defend the oasis.

Although Ibn Saud's military campaign succeeded in putting enormous pressure on Hail, he failed to go beyond the surrounding wall. He had underestimated the fact that some Shammar sheikhs were still willing to support the Rashidi amirs. When Mohammad Ibn Talal sent letters to the Shammar warning them of the imminence of Ibn Saud's attacks on Hail, informing them of the mounting pressure on its population, and asking them for support, three sheikhs responded to his call. Ibn Ali of the Abde Shammar, Ibn Zumeil of the Sinjara and Ibn Twala of the Aslam gathered their sections and headed towards Hail in an attempt to save what they regarded as their traditional legitimate leadership. These Shammar sections were again united with the exception of those who became *ikhwan* and were forced to settle in southern Najd.[17]

As the military pressure on Hail increased, Mohammad Ibn Rashid wrote to King Faisal of Iraq and the British officials in Baghdad asking them to mediate in the dispute and to intervene to lift the siege of Hail.[18] Ibn Saud refused the appeal for mediation, insisting on the personal surrender of Mohammad Ibn Rashid as a prerequisite for peace.

As a result of the siege, Hail was cut off from all lines of supplies as caravans carrying food were not allowed by Ibn Saud's forces to enter the oasis. Under these economic pressures, Mohammad Ibn Rashid agreed to allow Ibn Saud to enter Hail after receiving from him a guarantee of personal safety. Consequently, the gates of Hail were opened on 3 November, when Ibn Saud and fifty of his men were received by Ibn Rashid as his guests.[19] Ibn Saud immediately asked Ibn Rashid and four members of the Rashidi family to accompany him to Riyadh where they were expected to live under strict supervision.[20] Ibrahim Ibn Sibhan, whose family was allied to the Rashidi amirs through marriage, was appointed as governor of the oasis. Ibn Saud justified these measures by claiming that he did not want to completely alienate the Shammar and their leadership by appointing a representative of foreign origin. However, this was a temporary arrangement because Ibn Saud later replaced this governor by his own cousin whose loyalty was not questioned.[21]

After the departure of the ruling group from Hail, some Shammar sections who did not adopt Wahhabism and continued to support the Rashidi amirs, migrated to Iraq where they joined the Jarba, one of the sections of the Shammar who had been in Mesopotamia for two centuries. As Iraq was under British mandate, the British authorities there decided that: 'The Iraq government is being placed in great difficulty by the influx of the Shammar into Iraq. It is exceedingly difficult to keep them out and we are using all our endeavour to send them to join the Shammar Jarba in northern Jazirah.'[22]

This statement was meant to reassure Ibn Saud who feared that the Shammar might use Iraq as a base for future raids on his territories. The British high commissioner promised Ibn Saud that everything possible was being done to prevent this although it would be difficult to prevent it effectively until the Shammar were driven off to the north of the Euphrates. However, the majority of the Shammar remained in their traditional Jabal Shammar territory which Ibn Saud added to the provinces under his control. This territory became part of the present Saudi state.

We have seen how external factors constituted a favourable background for the decline of the Rashidi rule. In the following section, I analyse how the intervention of these historical events in the overall political and economic structure only accelerated the decline of Rashidi rule which was characterized by inherent structural contradictions.

INTERNAL STRUCTURAL WEAKNESSES

Throughout the nineteenth and twentieth centuries, the Rashidi dynasty was characterized by internal structural weaknesses at the political and economic levels which did not predispose it towards the formation of stable and permanent political entity.

Political Structural Weaknesses

The political system created by the Rashidi amirs can be described as having the following characteristics. First, instability at the level of leadership generated by an indeterminate pattern of succession to office. Second, fluidity of dynastic boundaries resulting from fluctuation in power. Third, lack of formal and institutionalized channels for contact and communication with the grass-root level of the tribe brought about by the amirs' settlement in Hail. Fourth, inability to maintain a monopoly over the legitimate use of violence. I shall argue that the first and second characteristics were not sufficient to bring the disintegration of the amirs' power whereas the last two characteristics heavily impinged on the viability of the political structure.

I have described in Chapter 3 how leadership in the dynasty was invested in *beit* Rashid with no fixed pattern for succession. Succession by assassination became the rule – out of twelve amirs, only three died of natural causes, one died in battle with Ibn Saud, and the remaining amirs were assassinated by members of their own family.[23] What consequences did this have for the political structure? The absence of a defined pattern of succession, coupled with the high turnover of the amirs, contributed to the instability of political leadership. A substantial number of amirs were overthrown after a year or two in office. Furthermore, the successive assassination of the amirs and their close relatives reduced the demographic base from which future amirs could be drawn. This resulted in the appointment of inexperienced young amirs in the absence of eligible senior ones.

The instability at the level of leadership does not constitute a handicap in itself. Internal power struggles over succession occur in almost all political systems and forms of government regardless of whether they have defined rules for succession. The case of the

Rashidis is not unique; history provides many examples of internal power struggles and assassinations. In particular in the Arabian Peninsula, among both the sedentary and nomadic populations, succession by assassination seems to have been prevalent. The Kuweiti amirs, the Omani sultans, the Rwala sheikhs, and the Saudi rulers of the nineteenth century, all had periods when assassination was a legitimate means for succession. In fact what might appear a negative characteristic can be considered as a positive attribute. Conflict is not inherently negative. Internal power struggles among ruling groups are mechanisms whereby the political structure ascertains its dynamic nature. Succession struggles are historical events which contribute to weakening the rigidity of the political structure by inserting checks on the exercise of power.

Successive assassinations among the Rashidi ruling group were events impinging on the political structure at definite historical moments without actually constituting causal factors for its disintegration. It is only when internal power struggles and frequent assassinations coincided with external threats and challenges to leadership that these struggles constituted favourable conditions for the decline of their dynasty. However, even then, these struggles cannot be considered as causing the decline.

Equally, the fluidity of dynastic boundaries over which the amirs' authority was extended cannot be said to have speeded up the process whereby Rashidi rule came to an end. The dynastic boundaries of Rashidi rule were dynamic. The delimitation of the boundaries was highly dependent on the amirs' military strength and the weaknesses of their neighbours. The presence of a militarily strong leadership, coupled with fragile neighbours allowed the amirs to expand beyond their traditional tribal territory. In contrast, the weakened amirs of the first two decades of the twentieth century and the emergence of Ibn Saud as a rival power in the region resulted in the shrinking of the Rashidi territory to the traditional tribal frontiers.

The fluidity of the amirs' dynastic boundaries does not necessarily imply lack of legitimate rule over those territories which came under their control and were outside their traditional tribal *dira* (tribal territory). The legitimacy of their leadership was not dependent on exercising power within their defined traditional territory. Expansion beyond Jabal Shammar established the right to rule over the newly acquired territories. Equally, the concept of territory was closely linked to sovereignty. In other words, if an amir was capable of extending his control over territories beyond the traditional Shammar *dira* and extracting tribute from the population, this constituted by itself a legitimate claim to rule. This was recognized by the amirs and by other groups in central Arabia.

These two characteristics of the Rashidi dynasty did not undermine the viability of the political structure. Nevertheless, the question to be asked is why the dynasty disintegrated at a time when other power centres such as that of Ibn Saud succeeded in turning the traditional power structure on which the leadership was based into a 'state'.

To answer this question, I consider the major drawback resulting from the lack of formal channels for contact and communiction with the tribal base, a characteristic which weakened the Rashidi amirs. As the majority of the Shammar remained nomadic, their mobility in search of water and pasture meant travelling over long distances away from the centre of leadership in Hail. Although their tribal territory included a large area in the Great Nafud Desert and Jabal Shammar, their search for pasture required them to travel further to the north in the direction of Syria and Iraq. During their seasonal migration, it was difficult to maintain contacts with them and the Hail amirs tried to overcome this problem by employing three strategies. First, they maintained a tradition of camping among the Shammar nomads for at least a few months every year. Second, they contracted marriages with daughters of the Shammar sheikhs in an attempt to cement political alliances. Third, during times of external threats and raids, the amirs used to send messengers to the scattered sections of the Shammar to inform them about any imminent military campaigns against the Rashidis and encourage them to actively participate in defending their leadership.

These informal strategies were successful as long as the leadership in Hail was strong and prosperous. However, the same strategies failed when they were used by the amirs of the twentieth century whose power and wealth were declining. These amirs had no institutionalized means to guarantee first their contacts with the Shammar and most importantly, their control over their tribal followers.

This was aggravated as the amirs' settlement in Hail became permanent and they moved towards greater political centralization. The case of the Rashidi amirs can be contrasted with that of the

Shaalan amirs of the Rwala bedouins of the Syrian Desert. The Shaalans took advantage of the general decline of Hail at the beginning of this century and conquered the oasis of Al Jauf whose population had been paying tribute to Hail. The people of Al Jauf switched allegiance to the Shaalans and paid tribute to them. The Shaalan preferred not to settle permanently in the oasis which they only used as their summer headquarters. They remained as traditional sheikhs of a camel-herding nomadic tribe, which allowed them to maintain close contacts with their own tribe, move with them and live like the rest of their group. It was only after the division of Rwala territory among three states, Saudi Arabia, Jordan and Syria that the Shaalans settled down (A. Musil 1928 and W. Lancaster 1981). In contrast, the Hail amirs became urbanites, living in a palace in Hail where they enjoyed the luxuries of sedentary life. They were no longer traditional bedouin sheikhs. This further detached them from the Shammar and weakened their ties with them.

This was combined with the amirs' inability to maintain a monopoly over the legitimate use of violence. The tribal sections continued to have control over their own means of coercion, above all their human resources. The Shammar sections were cohesive military units. All those who accepted Rashidi authority remained in charge of their manpower, the major pillar of violence. Furthermore, the cohesion of these groups was intact as they retained their traditional leadership which was represented by their sheikhs. These sheikhs together with their section enjoyed the freedom to dispose of their military strength which was not broken down by a higher political authority. The inability of the Hail amirs to diminish or neutralize the military strength of the tribal sections stemmed from the following factor.

Although the amirs possessed their own means of coercion which was independent of tribal alliances, they were only capable of occasionally pacifying the nomads without actually succeeding in eliminating their strength completely. Their regular punitive raids against rebellious tribal sections illustrate this point. Even at the height of his military and political domination, Mohammad Ibn Rashid had to organize raids every year to punish rebels and enforce loyalty to his leadership. These raids, however, succeeded only in demonstrating his might and functioned as deterrents against future rebellions and potential dissension. In general, the raids failed to create a situation whereby the military strength of the tribes and their control over their own means of coercion were formally incorporated in the dynasty's military apparatus.

In contrast, Ibn Saud's first step towards creating a stable political system was to undermine local tribal politico-military autonomy. His aim was to integrate the tribes' military strength in the state apparatus, thus maintaining a monopoly over the legitimate use of violence. This was done through the *ikhwan* movement and the *hujar* system in which tribal sections were forced to settle in specially created villages. The various tribes which accepted the Wahhabi call were expected to abandon their wandering habits which in the past had been conducive to raids and defection (J. Kostiner 1991). By adopting agriculture and religious revivalist facets, Kostiner argues, these tribes were also supposed to develop a new sense of loyalty to the state that would replace tribal bonds. Finally, Ibn Saud sought to benefit from these tribes' military skills by turning them into a standing army in the state's service. However, this system was not initially as successful as hoped due to the predominance of tribal autonomy. Until the 1920s, Ibn Saud's attempt at state-building in Najd was counter-productive, Kostiner argues: 'Manifested in a combination of territorial expansion and the Ikhwan phenomena, this process tended to regenerate characteristics typical of tribal confederacies which Ibn Saud found hard to control.' (ibid)

In spite of Ibn Saud's attempt to contain tribal autonomy through centralization, the *ikhwan* rebellion of 1927–9 illustrates the difficulties which he encountered in the process of consolidating his leadership. The *ikwan* movement grew as a separate entity ready to challenge him.[24] It was only with the help of external sources such as modern weaponry and British advisers that the strength of the *ikhwan* was broken down and efficiently guaranteed.

The Rashidi dynasty did not have this advantage. The political structure continued to be based on traditional informal arrangements between the Hail leadership and the tribal groups. The amirs failed to create a bureaucratic infrastructure ensuring contacts and communication with the tribes. Furthermore, there was no military apparatus helping to integrate the dynasty's military sources with those of the tribes. Lack of integration meant that the various tribal sections which declared loyalty to the amirs possessed at the same time the means to challenge their authority. This was coupled with contradictions manifested at the level of the economy.

Economic Contradictions

I demonstrated in Chapter 4 that the Hail dynasty was dependent on caravan trade for its survival and the maintenance of the political structure. The oasis itself did not have the means to ensure its subsistence but depended on supplies from Mesopotamia, Syria and the Persian Gulf.

The viability of the caravan trade economy was linked to the military power of the amirs. The more power they had, the more they attracted trade and merchants to their capital. This in turn allowed them to impose tribute which made possible their investment in the means of coercion. The delicate balance between military strength, trade, and tribute affected the amirs' ability to gain loyalty and enforce their rule. Any alteration in one of these three pillars automatically affected their political status in central Arabia.

The prosperity of Hail suffered as a result of the diversion of trade routes. This was brought about by the rise of Ibn Saud to power and the expansion of his sphere of influence. Hail was cut off from all lines of supplies as it had no developed internal agricultural infrastructure, its population experienced food shortages during the siege of 1920–21. With the decline of the Hail trade, its ruling group also lost a substantial revenue of tribute collected from the trading caravans.

In addition to its vulnerability to external influences, the caravan trade economy embodied an internal contradiction resulting from the inconsistency between the requirements of caravan trade, such as security of routes, and local tribal conditions. The continuity of trade was guaranteed at the expense of the nomadic population which represented the majority of the groups living within the amirs' sphere of influence.

The prohibition of tribal raids was the first prerequisite for ensuring the flow of trade to Hail which received the token of protection (*khuwa*) from the trading caravans. Although the *khuwa* was partially redistributed in the form of subsidies to tribal sheikhs, the redistribution was not complete. In other words, the benefits from the trade economy failed to reach all tribal groups in whose territory the caravans travelled. Consequently, there were tribal groups that did not benefit from the subsidy system and continued to raid the caravans. A cleavage of interest between the Hail amirs and some nomadic tribal sections began to emerge. As mentioned earlier, the nomadic sections possessed the means to raid caravans as their military strength was not encapsulated. When the Hail amirs bribed these sections through subsidies, they provided an extra revenue which replaced the benefits resulting from raiding caravans or from imposing their own *khuwa* on the caravans.

However, this was not enough to deter the tribal sections from launching raids and counter-raids against caravans. This was so because raids were not military strategies with the sole objective of gaining extra economic resources.[25] Tribal raids were entangled with the bedouins' life style and value system, and took place during times of prosperity and of scarcity. Furthermore, the tribes with a strong tradition of raids were not the poorest in Arabia. On the contrary, those who frequently raided others were the richest in camels and the most powerful. There is also no substantial evidence to believe that raids increased as a result of, for example, drought which increased the vulnerability of the pastoral economy.

Prohibiting raids for the sake of maintaining the caravan economy was not only a practical problem. It was a social and cultural problem. For the prohibition to be successful, it required altering the values in bedouin society which were attached to this activity and changing the very foundation of this society. Neither task was possible in the nineteenth or even the early twentieth century. As long as the Hail amirs were incapable of controlling tribal raids, the prosperity of the caravan economy and their own political domination remained at the mercy of external pressures. They therefore constantly organized punitive raids against those who attacked the caravans, but could not succeed in establishing total security for trade. The decline of the amirs' military strength towards the beginning of this century meant that they were not in a position to punish raiders and restore faith in the security of their territory and their power. Traders, consequently, followed trade routes that were more secure as a result of the protection of stronger local chiefs and rulers.

The inability of the Rashidi amirs to inhibit tribal raids can be compared with Ibn Saud's attempts to resolve the contradiction between the trade economy and raids. Ibn Saud's fortune depended on revenues from trade and tribute on trading and pilgrims caravans in addition to substantial subsidies from the British government. However, instead of curbing tribal raids, a task difficult to achieve, he channelled them to his advantage by turning what used to be called tribal raids into a holy war, i.e. a *jihad* against those who did not follow his Wahhabi call. The tribes which became *ikhwan* continued to practise raids under a different umbrella. Raids became a valued pursuit entangled with chivalry, courage and honour, but also the means to spread a message of a religious and political nature as well as Ibn Saud's sphere of influence. After his expansion reached the point of threatening British interests in Trans-Jordan and Iraq, Ibn Saud was under pressure from Britain to stop these raids. That was precisely the moment which brought to the surface the latent conflict between his objectives and perception of these raids and those of the *ikhwan*. The *ikhwan* rebelled when they were forced to stop their raids on the territories that were internationally recognized as outside Ibn Saud's sphere of influence.

Thus, the internal economic structural weaknesses of the Rashidi dynasty were to a great extent responsible for its decline. The inherent shortcomings of the economic structure impeded the development of a stable political entity in Hail. Also these shortcomings were not particularly favourable grounds to predispose the Rashidi dynasty to move in the direction of state-formation at the beginning of this century.

Competing Ideologies

In *La civilisation du desert*, R. Montagne argued that the Rashidi dynasty lacked the stabilizing effect of a religious ideology as a result of which the dynasty was fragile and unstable:

> Il faut la puissance de la religion pour fonder, avec les matériaux sociaux, des empires théocratiques qui meritent vraiment de retenir l'attention des historiens . . . La tradition de son gouvernement est trop incertaine. Les institutions, sur lesquelles il pourrait se reposer, sont trop rudimentaires pour que l'oeuvre subsiste au delà de deux ou trois générations. (R. Montagne 1947: 159)

It is not difficult to notice the influence of Ibn Khaldun in Montagne's statement. The fourteenth century north African scholar was the first to emphasize that tribal solidarity (*assabiya*), coupled with the strong effect of religion, constitutes the basis for stable political structures at least in his part of the world. In the

Muqqadimah, Ibn Khaldun declared that the dynasties of wide powers and large royal authority have their origin in religion based either on prophethood or truthful propaganda. The rise of the Muslim empire with the beginning of the prophet's call in the seventh century and the successive caliphates, in addition to the north African dynasties of the later period were the examples which allowed Ibn Khaldun to draw this conclusion. However, he equally argued that religious propaganda cannot materialize without group feeling or what he calls *assabiya* (Ibn Khaldun 1987: 125–7).

According to Ibn Khaldun, the conditions of pastoralism in his part of the world, coupled with the insecurity of desert life, endows people with cohesion. Those who have no cohesion cannot survive in the desert. To have group feeling and internal cohesion becomes a matter of survival arising from the harsh environmental conditions and the resulting insecurity. Common descent and blood ties lie at the heart of this group feeling or cohesion. However, although Ibn Khaldun argues that the natural blood ties which exist between people constitute the basis for cohesion, he does not ignore the importance of alliance and clientship in establishing equally strong ties between groups which are not related by descent. He claims that a client-master relationship leads to close contacts in exactly, or approximately the same way, as does common descent (ibid: 98).

By definition, group feeling is exclusive and introverted. It encompasses all members of the group who are related genealogically according to the rules of descent. It is by its nature a superior ideology. Ibn Khaldun argues that group feeling is geared towards supremacy: 'Once one group feeling has established superiority over the people who share in it, it will, by its very nature, seek superiority over people who have other group feeling unrelated to the first.' (ibid: 108) The solidarity of the descent group and the clients provides the leader with the support needed to establish his superiority and that of his own group. It is only when this solidarity is combined with a homogenizing religion that dynasties maintain longer lives and become more stable. According to Ibn Khaldun, tribal cohesion and religion seem to be two important elements in the establishment of dynasties.

In the light of Ibn Khaldun's model, the Rashidi dynasty can be described as a tribal dynasty which at the beginning of its establishment enjoyed the solidarity of the Shammar tribe, but failed to invoke a religious ideology. When they came to power in 1836 the amirs were totally dependent politically and militarily on the support of their own tribal group. They appealed in their requests for support to their own descent group which enjoyed a strong internal cohesion. This endowed their leadership with both strength and legitimacy. Furthermore, their leadership became distinct from other leaderships in central Arabia such as that of the three Saudi dynasties. Hogarth commented on the difference between the Rashidi leadership and that of the Saudis:

> To take the ruling family for example, the chiefs of the house of Rashid are not as the chiefs of the house of Saud in Riad, rulers of settled communities with which they are at one and surrounding tribes of bedouins, distinct from themselves, but they are chiefs, in the first instance of a great dominant bedouin tribe, and in the second of the settlements which serve that tribe for markets and rallying points. (D.G. Hogarth 1905: 166)

As the Rashidi amirs expanded their sphere of influence in central Arabia, they were in fact asserting the dominance of the Shammar tribe. The non-Shammar conquered groups regarded the predominance of the Hail leadership as an imposition of an alien rule of one group over others. These groups could not free themselves due to their weaknesses *vis-à-vis* the Shammar and their leadership. They remained as clients or tributary groups of an inferior status.

The foundation of the Rashidi rule, tribal cohesion, remained unchallenged in the nineteenth century in spite of the presence in central Arabia of a rival religious ideology for government and leadership. The second Saudi–Wahhabi dynasty remained faithful to its religious fundamentalist call and failed to constitute a challenge to Rashidi rule. Towards the end of the last century, the Rashidi tribal rule triumphed over the religiously orientated dynasty of the Saudis.

At the beginning of the present century, the situation was reversed. Rashidi rule stumbled when it was faced with the Saudi return to central Arabia with strong religious claims for the establishment of their rule in the region. Saudi leadership was armed with Wahhabism which provided the basis for unifying various tribal groups under its banner. It was an overarching ideology which appealed during the first two decades of the twentieth century to a wider range of tribes who had been disunited as a result of tribal divisions. With its emphasis on equality between Muslims and its rejection of hierarchies based on tribal nobility, Wahhabism was attractive to many tribes in Arabia which had enjoyed in the past an inferior status. Wahhabism, as a result, appealed to groups such as the Sulab who were regarded as the most inferior and despised communities in the region. They became the most dedicated and ferocious warriors among the *ikhwan*, receiving a new status as Muslim fighters and the promise of being freed from their servitude.

If we apply Ibn Khaldun's model, we have in the twentieth century two rival dynasties in central Arabia, the Rashidi dynasty with its tribal government based on an appeal to Shammar tribal solidarity and the Saudi dynasty which claimed legitimacy by invoking the strong Muslim alternative geared towards the establishment of a Muslim state. The Islamic alternative triumphed, proving the validity of Ibn Khaldun's conclusion that government benefits from religious propaganda which renders it more powerful and stable.

However, this would be a simplistic way of explaining the decline of the Rashidi dynasty and the success of the Saudi one in establishing a permanent state, at least until the present day. It is true that Wahhabism was a strong unifying ideology which succeeded in providing the basis to contain tribal autonomy, a condition important to the consolidation of the centralizing government of Ibn Saud. Since its rise in the eighteenth century, Wahhabism represented the basis for Saudi rule and expansion, although both the movement and Saudi rule were challenged twice in the nineteenth century. Their first dynasty disintegrated as a result of the Egyptian invasion in 1818 and their second attempt at establishing their hegemony in central Arabia collapsed in the face of Rashidi expansion in 1891. Their third attempt at establishing their rule in Najd at the beginning of this century succeeded with the help of Wahhabism. However, this cannot be considered as the sole factor behind the permanence and stability of the third dynasty which became a state in 1932. Rashidi decline and Saudi success were two parallel processes which took place not in isolation, but in conjunction with a whole series of historical events such as the disintegration of the Ottoman Empire and the subsequent intervention of the British government. The competition between the two rival ideologies in central Arabia was resolved to the advantage of the Muslim alternative only as a result of the interference of these historical events.

The disintegration of the Ottoman Empire set in motion the process of state formation, not only in Arabia, but also in what became known as the Middle East. Although the majority of the Middle Eastern territories entered into mandatory relations with Britain and France, the victorious powers after the First World War, the trend in these territories was heading in the direction of state formation. The history of central Arabia until the formation of the present Saudi state followed a repetitive cycle whereby tribal dynasties rose to power, expanded over adjacent territories, and indulged in political centralization. These polities later disintegrated as a result of the inherent centrifugal tendencies which stemmed from a combination of the deep-rooted tradition of tribal autonomy and pastoralism which enforced this autonomy. The polities were themselves unstable whereas the general cyclical pattern of their rise and fall was not. The cycle was broken only with the intervention of the modern conditions of the twentieth century and the external pressures of foreign governments.

10

AMIRS IN EXILE

> Hail seemed like a city marooned among the sand, all the
> inhabitants of which had died . . . The population of Hail was
> plainly on the decline. Numbers of houses in the northern
> quarter of the town were in ruins . . . many of the people of Hail
> had fled to the comfortable realms of King Faisal of Iraq . . . ten
> years of Wahhabi rule had turned the people of Hail into
> fanatics. The old forts of Hail have been thrown down and a
> new stone fort has been erected on a small hill commanding the
> town. (E. Rutter 1931: 78–9)

After dominating the political scene in central Arabia for almost
ninety years, Hail entered a phase of decline with the elimination
of the Rashidi amirs as important political figures in Najd. The
oasis itself and the area of Jabal Shammar became provincial
districts in the realm which Abdul Aziz Ibn Saud endeavoured to
create. With the collapse of Rashidi power, Hail lost the pillar on
which its prosperity had rested over the years. After the conquest
of Hail, Ibn Saud declared himself the Sultan of Najd, the
undisputed ruler of central Arabia.

Although Hail did not suffer the massacres and atrocities which
became the fate of some towns in the Hijaz (for example Taif)
which fell under the sway of Ibn Saud's *ikhwan*, it nevertheless
failed to recover its former economic and political role. In 1930,
Rutter visited the oasis which he described in the above passage as
an oasis where the traveller could not fail to notice the urban decay
and sense of demoralization among its population. Ten years after
the collapse of the amirs' power, the population of the oasis
dropped sharply. Rutter estimated the number of inhabitants at
2,000, which was much lower than the population towards the end
of the nineteenth century. This was because most of the oasis

merchants migrated to Iraq, Madina, and the Qasim and a considerable number of the Shammar residents in the oasis decided to migrate to Iraq to join their tribal brothers who had been in Mesopotamia for generations. The exodus left most of the houses in ruin and this was combined with the demolition of the quarter of Hail where the amirs' palace had stood. In an attempt to wipe out traces of the Rashidi amirs in the oasis, Ibn Saud gave orders to destroy Barzan palace. A new palace was constructed to accommodate the governors of the new realm. Rutter also noticed that the once prosperous market seemed to be abandoned.

Wahhabi rule was enforced in Hail as most of the officials and local governors were brought from the Qasim and Riyadh. These officials not only established the tenets of Wahhabism in the oasis and ensured that religious laws were respected, but also were meant to keep an alert eye on both the sedentary and nomadic population which had lost its traditional leadership. The governors sent from Riyadh to rule in Hail were carefully selected; they were close relatives and cousins of Ibn Saud. Their loyalty was undisputed, an important condition for leadership in such a troublesome area. Ibn Saud's major concern at that time was to enforce his rule in Hail. He adopted a strategy whereby he maintained maximum control over the Shammar and prevented any contacts between them and the Rashidi amirs. To achieve this objective, Ibn Saud refused to leave Hail in 1921 without being accompanied by Mohammad Ibn Talal and the rest of his family.

When the gates of Hail were opened on the first days of November 1921, Mohammad Ibn Talal, together with his family, friends and supporters had taken refuge in the palace. The encounter between Mohammad Ibn Talal and Ibn Saud is still remembered by members of the Rashidi family. I was able to record a Rashidi narrative in which this encounter was described. Although my informant did not witness the events in 1921, he claimed that he heard the narrative from a person who was present.

Mohammad Ibn Talal retreated with his family and friends behind the wooden gates of Barzan, his palace. The doors were closed and remained guarded by his most loyal slaves. Ibn Saud's messengers started to arrive at the gate with assurances and promises of protection. One messenger was allowed to enter Barzan and meet Mohammad. 'Get ready to meet the *shuyukh* (the sheikhs by which he met Ibn Saud)', said the messenger. 'What *shuyukh*? isn't Ibn Saud called the imam?!', replied Mohammad.

Mohammad Ibn Talal started getting ready; he bathed and put on his best robes. He did not fear death which he expected to happen the moment he stepped out of his palace. He was ready to meet his fate. The Barzan gate was opened and Mohammad emerged with dignity. He thought that the moment had come.

As Mohammad entered Ibn Saud's *majlis* which was set up temporarily in Hail, Ibn Saud rose to greet and embrace him. 'Sit beside me,' Ibn Saud said, 'now the fighting is over between us. We are to become brothers. You and your family shall accompany me to Riyadh where you shall live like my sons *muazzazin wa mukaramin* (with dignity and generosity).' Ibn Saud added. They sipped coffee and Ibn Saud sprinkled perfume on Ibn Rashid. Later they rose together and headed towards Riyadh. Ibn Rashid was never to see Hail again.

This narrative does not only account for the meeting which took place between Mohammad Ibn Talal and Ibn Saud. It is the Rashidi version of that encounter and has its own poetry. The narrative begins by showing that Mohammad Ibn Talal realized that he could no longer defend his capital. As a result, he retreats in his castle with his supporters, reflecting his withdrawal from public life. This is interrupted by the arrival of Ibn Saud's messengers who bring reassurances to the defeated amir. Mohammad Ibn Talal receives an invitation to attend Ibn Saud's *majlis*.

The narrator stresses an important point when he repeats Mohammad Ibn Talal's response to the invitation. When the messenger says: 'Get ready to meet the *shuyukh*', Mohammad Ibn Talal is puzzled as he asks: 'What *shuyukh*? isn't Ibn Saud called the imam?!' This question brings to the surface two central themes. First, Mohammad Ibn Talal's response involves an implicit assumption on his behalf that Ibn Saud was an imam, a religious leader, rather than a tribal sheikh. Second, the question also reveals that there is a deliberate attempt to rule out the possibility that Ibn Saud could be regarded as a tribal sheikh. Here, the narrator makes a statement of great political importance. The defeat of the Rashidis remains at the background of the narrative, but Mohammad's question represents an attempt to impose order and meaning on the events. His question affirms an underlying assumption that in spite of his defeat, there is no room at least in his mind for ambiguity. The question seems to define Ibn Saud's role and clarify how this role was perceived at that time.

As Mohammad accepts the invitation, he 'bathes' and 'put on his best robes'. These are significant symbolic acts. Mohammad is portrayed as going through a purification ritual which is meant to prepare him for the encounter with Ibn Saud. At this moment, the future is not clear and there is a possibility that Mohammad will be executed as soon as he leaves the castle gates. Therefore, the purification ritual becomes meaningful as it prepares him for death.

Mohammad enters Ibn Saud's *majlis*. The narrator tells us that Mohammad is embraced by Ibn Saud who rises to greet him as a guest, offering him coffee and perfume, both symbols intended to establish security, generosity, reassurance and friendship. Moreover, kinship is invoked here as Ibn Saud tells his guest that he will live in Riyadh as a son or a brother. The narrator repeats Ibn Saud's words (*muazzazin wa mukaramin*) which are meant to guarantee the guest's dignity and preserve his honour. This narrative not only describes an encounter between a loser and a winner, but also invokes expectations relating to the future. In many respects, the narrative is a statement about how the Rashidis saw their future in Riyadh.

In the following section, I describe Mohammad's experience of exile based on information provided by his son, Talal. I also had access to a diary written in prose and poetry which Mohammad left with his son. This diary includes poems which Mohammad had memorized and composed.

THE FATE OF MEN AND WOMEN

Mohammad Ibn Talal arrived in Riyadh with his family and, despite Ibn Saud's promises and assurances in Hail, was immediately put in prison where he stayed in a small, dark cell for two years. His only contact with the outside world was through a tiny window with iron bars, which overlooked one of the streets of Riyadh where the prison guards used to assemble. The guards regularly talked in a loud voice so that he could overhear their conversation without being able to see them. The guards always discussed Mohammad's fate and exchanged rumours that he was going to be executed after the Friday prayers of the week. For two years Mohammad waited for the day when his execution was to be carried out in the public square of Riyadh. That Friday never came and he was released from prison to live under house arrest.

Ibn Saud organized a policing force of fifty men to monitor Mohammad's activities. These men resided with Mohammad in the house allocated to him; they ate with him and were always present in his *majlis*, where he was not allowed to receive any important Shammar guests and sheikhs nor was he allowed to meet up with his most intimate friends and companions.

Ibn Saud forbade Mohammad to meet his most loyal poet, a Qasimi man called Al Oni who had allied himself to Mohammad before the conquest of Hail. Al Oni was amongst the men who were forced to move to Riyadh where their control was easier to organize. He had the skill of composing oral poetry and Ibn Saud feared that any encounters between the two men might result in the composition of some *qasaid* in praise of Mohammad which had the power of spreading all over Arabia. On one occasion, Mohammad met secretly with Al Oni in the latter's house. They were found out by Ibn Saud's loyal slaves. Al Oni was immediately sent to prison in Al Hafuf where he became blind. Later he developed tuberculosis, was released from prison and died immediately afterwards (S.A. Sowayan 1985: 86–7). This was the price that this famous oral poet paid for his loyalty to the Rashidi amir and his unwillingness to abide by the rules which Ibn Saud imposed. Al Oni's last years in prison and his unfortunate death set up an example to be avoided by those who contemplated future contacts with the Rashidi amir.

Ibn Saud loosened the restrictions on Mohammad who was allowed to leave his house and visit people if he was accompanied by the fifty men whose main task was to watch his movements. Mohammad was even allowed to attend Ibn Saud's *majlis* together with other sheikhs and amirs. Nevertheless, restrictions on whom he was allowed to see and socialize with continued to be enforced.

Mohammad lived in a house which Ibn Saud had set up for him. As all his property in Hail was confiscated by Ibn Saud, he was deprived in Riyadh of any income. His household depended on provisions from Ibn Saud who regularly sent out sacks of rice, coffee, sugar and dates. These provisions were closely controlled by Ibn Saud's financial *wazir* (minister). It was decided that the provisions should allow Mohammad and his family to live comfortably while keeping them at a level which would not allow him to give generously, invite guests or entertain people. This policy was meant to guarantee Mohammad's isolation and maintain his inability to rebuild a reputation for himself in Riyadh or attract followers and supporters.

The restrictions on Mohammad's movements were loosened once again in the early 1950s when he was allowed to travel with his two sons outside Saudi Arabia. The trip, however, was to be organized and supervised by the Saudi embassies abroad. Mohammad travelled to Egypt and Lebanon and later went on a tour which took him to France, Belgium and Germany. Ibn Saud objected to Mohammad visiting England at that time, fearing even then that he might start up contacts with British officials in London with the objective of shaking the foundation of his power.

Mohammad Ibn Talal remained politically marginalized until his death in 1952. He was assassinated by his own slave Faris who was found dead immediately after killing him. Ibn Saud ordered an investigation which came to the conclusion that the slave was mentally deranged and that he planned the murder alone. It was also claimed that the slave committed suicide as a result of feeling guilty over the assassination of his master. According to Mohammad's descendants, it is still unclear whether there was enough evidence to support the conclusion that the slave committed suicide or whether he was himself assassinated to remove the only clue which would reveal the identity of the murderer.

Other members of the Rashidi family escaped Mohammad's fate in Riyadh. For example, the previous ruler of Hail, Abdullah Ibn Mitab, who had made peace and left Hail before its conquest in 1921 to join Ibn Saud, was also brought to live in Riyadh. Abdullah led a less restricted life, able to travel to other cities in Arabia. He spent the rest of his time travelling between Riyadh and Mecca (D. Al Rashid 1966: 168). Ibn Saud did not inflict on Abdullah the same punitive measures which he inflicted on his cousin. Mohammad's determination to continue the struggle against Ibn Saud and defend Hail to the last minute was obviously the reason for the restrictions imposed on him. Mohammad was often described even by his enemies as a young determined man with strong political ambitions who would not have missed the opportunity to regain his ancestor's power in Hail had Ibn Saud allowed him to live under less restricting conditions. Whether he would have succeeded is a matter which cannot possibly be determined.

History and politics equally changed the lives of Rashidi women. As their fathers lost their power, they too paid the price. After the capture of Hail, they were brought to live in Riyadh with their men.

As marriage with tribal groups was part of Ibn Saud's state policy, a series of marriages with Rashidi women was planned and carried out in Riyadh. Immediately after imprisoning Mohammad Ibn Talal, Ibn Saud married Nura bint Sibhan, one of Mohammad's wives whom he had to divorce under pressure. Members of the Rashidi family claim that on the wedding night Ibn Saud was struck by an eye disease as a result of which he lost the sight in one of his eyes. Ibn Saud thought that this marriage was bound to bring him bad luck so he immediately divorced Nura and sent her back to Hail. Although it is difficult to find evidence to support the Rashidi version the story is nevertheless significant. First, it shows that this marriage was a violation of the honour code as Ibn Saud put pressure on Mohammad to divorce the woman whom he wanted to marry. Ibn Saud, claim the Rashidis, used his power to humiliate Mohammad. Second, the story stresses that Ibn Saud's eye disease was a penalty or punishment inflicted on him as a result of violating Rashidi honour.

Ibn Saud married another Rashidi woman. This time he chose Saud Ibn Rashid's widow, Fahda bint Asi Al Shuraim. Fahda became the mother of Ibn Saud's eighth son, Abdullah, the present crown prince who was born two years after the capture of Hail. A third marriage was arranged with the daughter of Mohammad Ibn Talal, Jawaher. As Jawaher lived until 1982, I became familiar with her life history. She married Ibn Saud when she was fourteen years old and lived in his palace amongst his other wives. As she was young, the marriage was not consummated until two years later. Jawaher was attractive and able to win Ibn Saud's admiration. This caused the jealousy of his senior wives who managed to make her life in the palace very uncomfortable. Jawaher did not bear children. She remembered being seen regularly by Ibn Saud's doctor who prescribed weekly injections to strengthen her and treat her infertility. She became a widow at the age of twenty-six without seeing the child that she always wanted. After Ibn Saud's death in 1953, Jawaher did not remarry. In the 1960s, she began to develop health problems and sought treatment in Paris and Lebanon where she was told by various doctors that the injections she had as a young woman affected her health badly and were in fact responsible for the fact that she never was able to bear children. The doctors claimed that these injections were meant to make her barren rather than treat her problem. At that moment, her bitterness over her fate in Ibn Saud's household was aggravated. Later as she observed what happened to her sister who married Ibn Saud's son and did bear four children, two of whom were killed by their paternal relatives, she began to realize that she was in a way lucky not to have had a child from Ibn Saud.

Jawaher's younger sister Watfa married Ibn Saud's son Musaid and became the mother of Princes Khalid, Faisal, Bandar and Princess Al Jawhara. Watfa was later divorced by Musaid. She had a miserable life as she lost two sons whose tragic death left her with no hope or energy. In 1965, Watfa's eldest son Khalid was involved in a demonstration which he organized to protest against the introduction of television in Saudi Arabia. Khalid adhered to a strict interpretation of Wahhabism and was also against the marginalization of the Wahhabi *ulama*, a process for which King Faisal was preparing the country. As a result of his involvement in the protest, Khalid was shot dead by the Saudi police in his own home. This event left a sense of bitterness among the remaining brothers of Khalid who became closer to their maternal uncles and aunts, the Rashidis. Khalid's brothers regarded the assassination of their brother as an unjustified act, a crime committed by their own paternal relatives and carried out by their paternal uncle King Faisal himself. This event would have been forgotten had it not been brought to the surface in 1975 with the assassination of King Faisal by Khalid's brother, Prince Faisal Ibn Musaid.

On 1 April 1975, the Saudi radio announced that the king had been assassinated in his own *majlis* by his nephew, Faisal Ibn Musaid, who had entered like most Saudi princes with the objective of greeting the king. As these princes were not searched at the gates of the royal palace, Prince Faisal managed to enter with a small gun. As soon as he met the king, he fired three shots which led to his immediate death. Prince Faisal was at once arrested by the Palace Royal Guard. Saudi official statements at that time did not even mention that the assassin's brother had been shot dead in 1965 by the Saudi police. Instead, a biography of Prince Musaid was assembled by the media portraying him as an irresponsible young man who had led a hedonistic life in the United States when he was a student at the University of Colorado. Official Saudi announcements also claimed that the possibility that the assassin was mentally disturbed should not be ruled out.

Prince Faisal was put in prison where he was interrogated in an attempt to find out his motives and whether he was acting in collaboration with others. The Saudi government announced one month later that the murder was a calculated act of one man and that Prince Faisal was rational and responsible for his actions. He faced trial before an Islamic court which ordered his execution in a public square in Riyadh (*Time Magazine* 7 and 14 April 1975). Prince Faisal was Watfa's second son to be killed by his own paternal relatives. Her remaining son, Prince Bandar was put in prison for a year and was later released. He now lives in Saudi Arabia.

In spite of the findings of the Saudi enquiries which established that Prince Faisal was acting on his own, his Rashidi maternal uncles were interrogated by the Saudi secret police (*mukhabarat*). One of his maternal uncles, Mitab, was imprisoned for a year without trial. This angered other members of the Rashidi family who succeeded in putting pressure on the government to release him. After his innocence was proved, Mitab was released. He immediately left the country with his family and sought political asylum in Iraq where he now lives as an Iraqi citizen. Prince Faisal's other maternal uncle, Talal, was also interrogated by the police at that time and although he was not imprisoned, his movements in Riyadh were carefully watched. He also left Saudi Arabia in the summer of 1975. In recent years, Talal received many invitations for a reconciliation with the Saudi government. This was finally achieved in 1988 and Talal returned for a short visit to Saudi Arabia. It is uncertain whether he will move permanently to live in the country.

In this account, I have dealt with the experiences of the last ruler of Hail and his descendants in Riyadh. Other members of the Rashidi family who were also forced to settle in Ibn Saud's capital did not experience the same restrictions. Today there are four branches of the Rashidi family living in Riyadh, the Al Talal, Al Mitab, Al Obeid and Al Jabre.

The first branch consists of the descendants of Abdullah Ibn Rashid, the founder of the dynasty. The Al Talal are the sons and grandsons of the last ruler of Hail, Mohammad Ibn Talal. Mohammad's sons, Talal and Mitab are not now living in Saudi

Arabia as mentioned earlier. However, some of their sons, i.e. Mohammad's grandsons, have returned to seek employment. Although some have been educated abroad and hold university degrees, none managed to find a permanent job in the country. One of Mohammad's grandsons applied for a teaching post at the University of Riyadh where his application was rejected. Saudi suspicions and mistrust were perhaps the reasons behind his failure to get the job. Other grandsons tried their luck in business without being able to establish themselves even in a field remote from politics or education. The Al Talal receive small monthly salaries (an average of 5,000 Saudi riyals for males and 1,000 Saudi riyals for females) from the government, like most of the families in Saudi Arabia who had been connected through marriage to the Saudi ruling group.

The second branch, the Al Mitab, are also descendants of the founder of the dynasty. A number of their ancestors did hold power in Hail early in the twentieth century such as Saud Ibn Rashid (1910–20) and Abdullah Ibn Mitab (1920–21). One of Saud Ibn Rashid's sons, also called Saud migrated to Iraq in the 1940s and returned to live in Saudi Arabia eight years ago. The Al Mitab now receive monthly salaries from the government. However, none of them holds a government post. Like their cousins the Al Talal, the Al Mitab have been deprived from the many opportunities existing in Saudi Arabia.

The Al Obeid are the descendants of Obeid Ibn Rashid, the brother of the founder of the dynasty. The Al Obeid did not hold the office of amir in Hail except for a short period (1907–10). All of them live in Saudi Arabia. Like the Al Obeid, the fourth branch of the Rashidi family the Al Jabre were politically marginal in Hail. Consequently, when they settled in Riyadh, they were not subjected to restrictions or imprisonment.

In general, the Rashidi family seem to have retained some influence in Saudi Arabia although they were excluded from occupying any official government posts. They are part of the marriage network which the Al Saud maintained with various tribal groups in the country. One has to remember that the present crown prince has a Shammar mother. Furhermore, the various marriages which Ibn Saud and his sons conducted with Rashidi women fostered the development of kinship relations which drew the two groups together. Although the Rashidis were affected in a negative way by some of these links, especially in the case of

Watfa's marriage and her sons' assassination, these marriages allowed them to have access to a wide network of Saudi princes. They were able to exercise some influence through the use of these networks. If their influence was not strong enough to prevent the imprisonment of one of their members in 1975, they did succeed in putting pressure on the government to release him. Also, the government's contacts with the Rashidis abroad and its conciliatory approach proves that they are not completely deprived of power. Like most tribal groups in Saudi Arabia, the Rashidis were drawn into the patronage system which the state fostered.

THE PATRONAGE SYSTEM

Saudi Arabia has been described as a tribal state whereby the state is owned by a royal house organized as a tribe (F. Khouri 1980). The Saudi royal family resembles a clan with multiple factions and branches. Today the family consists of the sons and grandsons of Abdul Aziz Ibn Saud. Ibn Saud probably married 400 wives as a result of which he came to have forty-three sons (Dickson 1951: 162 and R. Lacey 1981). The demographic explosion within the Saudi family made it difficult for everybody to be involved in politics or government. The major political and economic decisions are made by a limited circle of brothers, the senior sons of Ibn Saud, assisted by appointed ministers.

The modern centralized Saudi state with its partially developed bureaucracy, economic infrastructure, and technological modernization evolved over a period of fifty years. In 1932 when Abdul Aziz Ibn Saud declared himself king and the country came to be known as the Kingdom of Saudi Arabia, the state which he endeavoured to create might have appeared to be a break from the traditional system of government which had existed for centuries in the Arabian Peninsula and was exemplified in the Rashidi dynasty. However, at that time political relations between Ibn Saud and the conquered tribes and former power-holders remained to a great extent based on the premises of tribal politics. This was true of the Saudi state until the discovery of oil in the 1940s. Wealth from oil allowed Ibn Saud and later his successors to centralize their powers and develop government bureaucracy (J. Kostiner 1991).

Today the Saudi government, that is the royal house consisting of the king and the princes, rules through patronage. Massive oil revenues and the unequal distribution of wealth in the country allow the rulers to play the role of patrons. In this society, instead of taxing the productive activities of its citizens, the government and the ruling group become the providers in a welfare state. This is believed to be one of the major characteristics of what Davis calls the 'hydrocarbon society' (J. Davis 1987). Where the prince (a sovereign or male members of royal houses) gets more than 90 per cent of his income from taxes on petroleum production, the basis of politics changes (ibid: 16). In Saudi Arabia as in other hydrocarbon societies (such as Libya and Kuwait), at the level of politics, the most important break from the past is the fact that today the prince does not need any consensus among his citizens. Davis argues that the hydrocarbon prince may conceal the extent of his revenues; may fail to distinguish treasury from pocket, may reward a restricted and exclusive coterie, a family, a descent group, without any public accounting (ibid: 18). The reward system in this society operates according to the rules of patronage. In the following section, I shall describe how patronage relations develop between members of the Saudi ruling group and their clients who constitute a considerable section of present day Saudi society. This description is based on observing how some members of the Rashidi family were drawn into the patronage network in the past fifteen years.

In Saudi Arabia, patronage involves the establishment of an unequal relationship between a patron, usually a Saudi prince, and a client, often a notable, a former power-holder or a tribal sheikh. The inequality in the relationship has an economic and political rather than a social basis. The patron has more resources than his clients. In most cases, his *maash* (monthly salary or pension) from the government is much higher than what the clients get. The patron's *maash* is not usually paid as a result of working in government departments. All Saudi princes receive salaries regardless of whether they work for the government. Furthermore, the prince is often capable of increasing his fortune through acting as a mediator between the government and foreign companies. Some princes organize contracts between the government and these companies as a result of which they receive a considerable commission. At the political level, the prince has more power than his client. Although some Saudi princes are more powerful than others and are involved in decision making, most of them have some varying degrees of influence.

Clients are usually attached to various princes as *khawi* (companions). They attend the prince's *majlis*, dine with him, and some *khawi* accompany princes on travel abroad. The clients become part of the prince's entourage; although the economic and political discrepancies between the client and the prince are obvious, socially the boundaries are ambiguous and difficult to draw. In terms of prestige, some clients do in fact enjoy a high status as members of noble tribes or ex-amirs and sheikhs. They are regarded by the prince himself and society in general as members of a distinguished status group. The client's high status allows him to have access to the prince in the first place. Without this status, a client would find it difficult to associate with the prince, socialize and develop an initimate relationship with him. In many aspects, the client can be said to enjoy a status similar to the prince.

As the prince is usually wealthy and politically influential, it is perhaps obvious how he becomes a patron. However, how someone becomes a client is a process which involves important factors. First, patron–client relations can develop as a result of affinal links with the prince. Polygamy results in the development of factions among half brothers and sisters, who often fail to have the unity which would exist among full brothers and sisters. Princes find themselves distanced from their paternal relatives and half brothers while at the same time they are drawn closer to their maternal kin. It is not unusual to find among the prince's clients a *khal* (maternal uncle), a maternal relative, or even a distant member of the mother's tribe. Patron–client networks can also be created through marriage. Members of the prince's wife's family usually stand a good chance of entering the patronage network of the prince.

Second, early childhood friendship can be the basis of patronage. Before the urban modernization of Riyadh, a process which started only three decades ago, young Saudi princes intermingled with other children in the streets and alleys of the city. One often hears comments like so-and-so used to play with the governor of Riyadh when they were young. These comments are interesting as they reveal how so-and-so became a client of the same governor. Today, friendships tend to develop in schools in the country or abroad where princes are sent to receive higher education and university degrees. Childhood friends tend to become grown-up clients.

Third, to enter a patronage network, one has to possess certain communication skills and social assets. A client has to be eloquent, conversant and entertaining as well as flexible and patient. Loyalty and secrecy are usually admired in a client as he stands a good chance of becoming familiar with the intimate details of the prince's life.

Patronage in Saudi society is a multi-functional mechanism. Above all, it fosters the development of economic relations between two unequal parties. The prince acts as the provider. He may distribute cash handouts whereas at other times he may help in the allocation of property and land. He can also give his sanctions for a contract or a deal to be won by a client. Patronage becomes the tool for sharing the enormous wealth to which the princes have access.

This particular form of patronage also has the advantage of giving the illusion of political participation. As clients find themselves in the *majlis* of influential princes who occupy high positions in the government, they enjoy the opportunity to have access to the government itself as they sometimes express opinions and political views on current issues.

Thirdly, this type of patronage has the capacity of diffusing political opposition. As a result of the growth of wide patronage networks, the various princes in the country become familiar with a broad section of society which tends to come from important families, tribes and notables. These princes develop with the larger society personalized relations which in many respects create bondages and ties. These ties make it difficult for any organized political opposition to find expression, especially among the wide circle of clients, their relatives and families.

Fourth, prestige is another important aspect of patronage for both the prince and his client. The prince gains prestige if a number of his clients are respectable sheikhs or amirs of noble tribes. Saudi society still adheres to the tribal ethos which stresses the importance of nobility and tribal origin. If the entourage of the prince are members of the once influential and powerful tribes, this tends to enhance his position in government. He will be treated with respect by his own group as he can be regarded as the link between the government and his clientele. The client too derives prestige from being seen in the prince's *majlis* where he is treated with courtesy. His prestige and power among his family and tribe is increased as he becomes the mediator between his group and the government. He is expected to bring thier cases to the prince's attention. His links with the government are seen as speeding up requests for passports, court hearings, demands for accommodation, allowances and various benefits from the government. In general, as a result of his involvement in the patronage network, the client is endowed with a new basis for prestige springing from the power of mediation with a depersonalized government bureaucracy which is open for manipulation.

In general, the patronage system has become the means through which the government and society function and operate. This system allows maximum control over the population which is tied through personalized relations with an otherwise distant political élite. It allows the partial distribution of wealth in the absence of formal and institutionalized channels. Those who succeed in entering the patronage network benefit from various favours, subsidies and preferential treatment. They develop a vested interest in the continuation and perpetuation of the system. However, to be left without a patron in the country is a handicap which impinges on every aspect of people's lives. As the system is informal and dependent on several factors, it is bound to leave some people out of the network. Those who choose not to be part of the network find themselves helpless in a society where it is difficult to function without a patron.

11

CONCLUSIONS

The exploration of a single example of nineteenth century central Arabia's regional politics allows us to draw two conclusions. The first addresses the complexity of the Arabian political structures prior to the formation of the modern Saudi state. The second tackles the interconnectedness between this regional politics and the general historical framework of the nineteenth century.

REGIONAL COMPLEXITY

It is true that central Arabia (Najd) was characterized by the absence of a unifying central state. It is true also that the population of this area of the Arabian Peninsula was living as wandering tribes in the desert. Although it is difficult to give accurate estimates of the nomadic population which led such an existence, there is general agreement that some tribes were nomadic and continued to nomadize until recently. It is also established that central Arabia had its sedentarized tribes, who did not wander in the desert yet retained a degree of tribal organization. The sedentarized groups inhabited the oases and towns of Najd where politics was made, as the case of the Hail dynasty and studies of other towns in Arabia demonstrate (Altorki and Cole 1989). It is a mistake, therefore, to assume that the local history of central Arabia was dominated until the present century by wandering groups who knew only war and plunder.

Perhaps the stereotype which describes the history of Najd as a perpetual battle between aggressive nomadic tribes and passive oasis dwellers stems from the unjustified rigid dichotomy made between the nomads and the sedentary population, i.e. the *badu* and the *hadar*. As I have argued, this dichotomy divided the population into two distinct, but not necessarily isolated groups. The *badu–hadar* distinction is above all a cultural distinction pertaining to people's identity and self-image. The intense social, political, and economic interaction between the sedentary and nomadic groups fostered the development of relatively stable political structures in the region.

Once we establish that politics in central Arabia was made in the oases, we have to acknowledge that this politics sometimes had depth in the desert. As centralized leadership grew up and flourished in the many oases, some oasis amirs derived their legitimacy and strength from the desert, i.e. from the nomadic tribes. This was not true of every dynasty or emirate in central Arabia. The first and second Saudi–Wahhabi dynasties (Chapter 2), the Unaizah emirate (Altorki and Cole 1989), and the Hashemite Sherifian dynasty in the Hijaz (Al Amr 1974) lacked the support of a single powerful bedouin tribe. In contrast, the Rashidi dynasty was a unique case in central Arabia in which an oasis-based leadership was from the very beginning combined with the support of one tribe. This important characteristic made politics in Hail different from that in other oases, for it impinged on every aspect of the political structure and determined the dynasty's prospects for stability and expansion.

The Rashidi dynasty combined political centralization with tribal autonomy. The amirs in Hail endeavoured to create a centralized state with the objective of establishing monopoly over the protection of trade routes. This was done through territorial expansion. Dynastic rule had to be reconciled with tribal autonomy. This reconciliation found expression in the coexistence of amirs and sheikhs. There was an underlying mutual recognition that one leadership could not intrude into the other's sphere of influence. The amirs could not coerce the sheikhs who together with their tribal section had complete control over their human resources. To achieve consensus and support from the tribal sections, the amirs could only buy their loyalty.

Wealth in Hail was derived from control over the caravan network which joined Mesopotamia, Persia, India and the Persian Gulf to the major towns in central Arabia and the Hijaz. Its strategic position coupled with the emergence of a centralized leadership in the oasis, enabled this leadership to exercise monopoly over the protection of trade routes. Control over trade allowed the amirs to impose tribute on the trading and pilgrim caravans which in most cases travelled together along the same routes. At a later stage, the amirs sent their own commercial caravans. Revenue from trade was invested in subsidizing tribal sheikhs, a mechanism which guaranteed their loyalty and support. Also, trade revenues allowed the amirs to invest in new means of coercion.

A military apparatus was established which was initially drawn from the Shammar, but later became independent of them. The amirs began to invest in the creation of a stable and permanent military force independent of shifting tribal alliances. This was an important step in the history of the dynasty as it involved a structural and organizational break from the traditional system. With this military force, the amirs moved beyond conquering Hail. They expanded their realm and later defended it. They also established a police force consisting of sedentarized bedouins and slaves to guard the interests of the dynasty, mainly to protect the market in Hail, enforce orders and commands and punish criminals.

In addition to economic and military might, the Rashidi amirs used the power of oral poetry to make history. Oral poetry had always existed in the Arabian Peninsula as an effective means of communication in political and social life. In the context of a centralizing dynasty, oral poetry became endowed with the power of spreading fame and hegemony. The amirs were their own poets; they documented their own experiences and those of their tribe. The poetry of the period refers to important historical events, tribal conflicts, personal experiences, victory and defeat. Hence, it is an essential source of information which unveils many aspects relating to tradition, values and people's concerns at that time. Above all, the Rashidi poetry was one of the means which they employed to enforce their power.

Equally, marriage was used as a political strategy. The analysis of the amirs' marriages revealed that a combination of a number of matrimonial strategies reflected the diversity and complexity of political relations in the dynasty. The well-established practice of endogamy (including *beit*, lineage, and tribal endogamy) was combined with a number of outside marriages which, although statistically insignificant, were in fact of great political and strategical importance. Once the amirs' marriages were analysed and put in their relevant political context, they became comprehensible.

The examination of a single case study does not allow us to make great generalizations regarding the nature and origin of tribal dynasties in the world, their characteristics, and development. However, throughout this book I draw attention to the existence in central Arabia of complex and varied political structures. The Rashidi dynasty was one political development. Other forms of political centralization crystallized with the rise of the Wahhabi movement and the Saudi's adoption of it. A detailed account of the various political entities would lead us to question the dichotomy between state and stateless society. In the nineteenth century, Central Arabia did not have a continuous state authority, but nevertheless, it had various forms of government, some centralized and others less so. Different types of leadership, amirs, imams and sheikhs, coexisted and competed with each other. There were periods of stability, competition, and conflict. Centralization and decentralization were two processes which went hand in hand. Fluctuation in political power was a deep-rooted characteristic of all political entities in the region.

The instability in the past of dynasties and political leadership in central Arabia cannot be regarded as a negative attribute, a characteristic enforcing the stereotype of the so-called 'rebellious and ungovernable tribes'. Fluctuations in the power of the amirs and the rise and decline of dynasties were positive attributes, following a repetitive cycle whereby rulers were overthrown, dynasties rose and fell, and political boundaries were redrawn in the pursuit of political change mainly at the level of leadership. The instability of political structures was a check on the exercise of power. Dictators and ruthless rulers could be overthrown and replaced. The system worked until it was stabilized with the creation of the present Saudi state. Now, the stabilization of the political system as a result of the intervention of external forces and modernization has left Saudi Arabia without a system ensuring political and leadership changes. The country has lost its previous dynamism and above all its indigeneous capability for political change.

The analysis of the Rashidi dynasty allows us to revise some of the well-established assumptions that state formation in Arabia began with Ibn Saud's attempt to unify Arabia early in the twentieth century. Central Arabia was not an area of chaos and tribal warfare. It produced economic, military and political structures which reflected the specificity of the region as a cultural area. However, the specificity of this area does not stem from geographical isolation. Although central Arabia was never an integrated part of the Ottoman Empire, it was nevertheless drawn into the realm of international politics. Its regional politics was entangled with development taking place elsewhere. Consequently, the emergence of the Rashidi dynasty has been discussed in the context of nineteenth-century Ottoman politics.

REGIONAL AND INTERNATIONAL POLITICS

Regional political development in central Arabia cannot be studied in isolation. Although Najd was geographically and economically peripheral to the major centres of Ottoman domination, it was close enough to one of the most important provinces of the empire, the Hijaz. Central Arabia had no significant economic wealth to attract the Ottoman Porte. However, it produced a rival ideology which caused the Ottomans great concern. The Wahhabi call and the expansion of the first Saudi dynasty towards the end of the eighteenth century into the more vital provinces of the empire threatened the stability of the area. This generated a series of interventions to curb the threat which Wahhabism represented. Early in the nineteenth century, local political leaders came into contact with the Porte's officials and governors. Although the latter never established a permanent base in central Arabia, they continued to communicate with the population and its leadership from the adjacent territories. These channels of communication opened new doors for further intervention, subsidies, and manipulation. As the Ottomans began to realize the futility and perhaps the difficulty in exercising direct control over central Arabia, their policies shifted towards maintaining only nominal suzerainty over the region. Throughout the nineteenth century, however, their policies towards the various tribes and powers oscillated between direct military intervention and indirect rule.

Whether a central government exercises direct or indirect rule in areas over which it claims jurisdiction, its interaction with regional political figures is responsible for many economic and political changes at the local level. In the case of the Rashidi dynasty, relations with the Ottoman government did in fact set in motion some processes which cannot be understood without reference to the influence of external factors. To win their loyalty, the Ottomans subsidized the amirs with cash, weapons, ammunition and various other items. These subsidies and benefits were meant to enable the amirs to exercise greater control over their tribal followers. As a result, Ottoman intervention created the means for the emergence of greater differentiation between the amirs and their subjects. The amirs were no longer tribal sheikhs with limited resources as a considerable proportion of their revenues now came from outside the local economy.

In the twentieth century, central Arabia began to be caught up in the rivalry between the Ottoman Empire and the British government. With the approaching First World War, foreign interests in the region intensified. In a desperate search for local supporters, Britain began to look in the region for allies who could shake the foundation of the Ottoman Empire from within. They found a few supporters such as Ibn Saud and the Sherif of the Hijaz who in return for their loyalty were granted various favours and subsidies. These new interventions upset the balance in central Arabia between its local rival groups.

The international power struggle and its resolution which resulted in Britain emerging as the victorious party after the war, affected the political affairs of central Arabia. Victory in Najd was the lot of those who allied themselves with Britain. The Rashidi dynasty did not survive the rapid changes taking place at that time. It stumbled as a result of the intervention of new actors on the international scene. As external factors moulded the political structure of the dynasty, its decline, in addition to being a product of its particular internal characteristics, was to a great extent a result of external factors. Equally, the creation of the present Saudi state was influenced by external intervention in the region.

When it was created in 1932, the Saudi state resembled to a great extent the tribal chieftaincies or dynasties which had been common in Arabia for centuries. The state at that time lacked the economic, bureaucratic, and technological infrastructures which would have enabled it to be transformed into an efficient centralized political system. It is only with oil revenues that the present Saudi state was capable of undermining tribal autonomy and fully encapsulating the various former power-holders in Arabia. The state began to operate through a personalized patronage system and succeeded in establishing political central-ization to the detriment of political participation. As a result, former power-holders such as the Rashidi amirs became increasingly marginalized. Whether the present Saudi state will survive as it is, or adapt to the new conditions that it created itself is a question which future events and research will perhaps answer.

GLOSSARY

Ahd: covenant
Ahl al Bidaa: innovators
Ahl al Tawhid: unitarians
Amir: ruler, commander, or prince
Amghar: chief (Berber)
Asab: backbone
Assabiya: tribal solidarity
Ashira: tribal section, (pl. *ashair*)
Asil: noble tribal origin
Baraka: grace
Bedouin: the nomads of Arabia
Badu: bedouin
Badawa: nomadism
Beit: house, household, and extended family, (pl. *biut*)
Beit al Mal: public or state treasury
Bled el Makhzen: the central government (Moroccan Arabic)
Bled el Siba: the region of anarchy or dissidence (Moroccan Arabic)
Dakhil: someone under the protection of an individual or a powerful tribe
Dawa: religious call
Dira: tribal territory and homeland
Diyya: blood money
Fakhd: segment or maximal lineage, (pl. *fukhud*)
Gabila: tribe, (pl. *gabayil*)
Gahwaji: coffee maker and server
Ghanima: booty
Ghazu: raid
Gibla: the direction to Mecca in prayers
Hadar: the settled population

Hajj: pilgrimage to Mecca
Hamula: lineage
Harb: warfare
Hayy: quarter in an oasis or town
Hess: voice
Hilf: alliance
Hujar: the village settlement of the *ikhwan*
Ijtihad: independent judgement
Ikhwan: brothers; in this context, the Muslim brothers who
    adopted Wahhabism early in the twentieth century
Imarah: emirate
Imam: religious leader of prayer
Jahiliya: the age of ignorance
Jabal: mountain
Khan: leader (Persian)
Khatib: orator or preacher
Khawi: companion
Khuwa: brotherly tax
Khutba: the speech before the Friday noon prayer
Kufr: blasphemy
Luhma: flesh
Majlis: council
Maash: pension or monthly salary
Maslakha: slaughterhouse
Mithaq: covenant
Musabala: market transactions
Musahara: affinity
Nasab: blood kinship
Qadi: Islamic judge
Rajajil: men
Ridaa: wet nursing
Sadaqa: Islamic charity
Senna: artisans
Shafaa: absolution
Sheikh: religious personnel or tribal chief
Shirk: polytheism
Sunna: the sayings and deeds of the Prophet
Shura: negotiations and consultation
Suq al Abid: slave market
Tayafah: tribe (Persian)
Ulama: religious scholars

Umma: the Muslim community
Umran: civilization
Urf: tribal custom
Wadi: valley
Wali: governor
Wasm: tribal brand on camels or wells
Wazir: minister

NOTES

1 THE COUNTRY AND THE PEOPLE

1. The word 'Shammar' appears in some legendary accounts as the name of a south Arabian king among the tribes of the Yemen. M. Rodinson mentions the legend in his book on the life of the Prophet, Mohammad:

   'Un cycle de légendes se forma sur la gloire des anciens rois, transmettant des faits historiques, en les déformant et en les exagérant. C'est ainsi qu'un roi, Shammar, qui effectivement fut un conquérant à l'échelle de l'Arabie se voyait attribuer des incursions jusqu'en Chine dont temoignerait le nom de la ville de Smarkand, qu'il aurait fondée.' (M. Rodinson 1961: 45).

2. Reference to Bahij is made in a poem by Obeid Ibn Rashid, the brother of the founder of the Rashidi dynasty in 1836. The relevance of this genre of oral poetry will be discussed later.
3. In her study of south Tunisian tribes, Valensi tends to support the view that oral tradition contains bits and pieces of true history, but cannot be viewed as a chronicle of events. She comments on the presence of gaps in tribal history which is constructed from oral narratives. She argues that as one moves back in time, the history becomes thinner, beyond a century chronological dating is no longer operative and time ceases to be measurable. But contrary to dated time, this portion of the past is richer the further back it goes; the closer to the founder, the more precise the account. In her study of the Hamama, Valensi noticed that the purpose of the sequence was not to establish 'historic truths', but to determine the position of the Hamama in relation to other tribes. For further details on this study, see L. Valensi 1985: 23–5.
4. These are rough estimates and cannot be taken for granted. Unfortunately, there are no accurate statistics with regard to the size of the population of Jabal Shammar in the nineteenth century. This applies also to the whole of the Arabian Peninsula.
5. The various status groups in Hail will be discussed in Chapter 4 which deals with the economy of Jabal Shammar.

6. See A. Musil 1927 and 1928a, G. Wallin 1854 and U. Fabietti 1984.
7. This includes the local historians of Najd such as Ibn Bishr and Ibn Ghanam. European travellers such as Wallin, Doughty, Palgrave, Blunt, Huber, and Euting who visited the region in the nineteenth century also regarded the Shammar as belonging to one tribe. This view is shared by foreign political agents especially the British officers in the Persian Gulf. Other groups in Arabia considered the Shammar as a single *gabila* among the various tribes of the Arabian Peninsula.
8. See D. Eickelman 1981, E. Marx 1977 & 1979, P. Salzman 1979, R. Tapper 1983, and E. Gellner 1983.
9. The rise of the first Saudi–Wahhabi dynasty in 1744 was linked to the emergence of the religious movement of Mohammad Ibn Abdul Wahhab. The Saudis adopted the mission and started a holy war to spread his teachings. Their expansion to the north brought them into conflict with the Shammar who resisted the incorporation of their territory in the Saudi realm. The Shammar were defeated by the Saudi forces in the 1790s and some sections of the tribe migrated to Mesopotamia. Details of the confrontation betweent the Shammar and the Saudi forces are given in Chapter 2.
10. The northern Shammar will not be dealt with here in great detail. For further information on their situation in Iraq, see J. Williamson 1975.
11. If the Shammar of Mesopotamia were to be included, the size of this tribal unit and its dispersion over a huge area would make collective action almost impossible.
12. These terms are used by other groups in the Middle East, but mean different things among different groups.
13. Early in the twentieth century, some sections of the Shammar abandoned the Hail leadership and joined the camps of their enemies. This was against their segmentary ideology which stressed the unity of the various groups especially during periods of external threat. Further historical evidence will be given in the following chapters.
14. When the Shammar were put under military and economic pressure by Ibn Saud at the beginning of the twentieth century, they were unable to remain faithful to their notions of cohesion, mutual support and co-operation. The Wahhabi movement divided them and weakened their tribal solidarity. These issues will be discussed later in the book.

2 CENTRAL ARABIA IN TURMOIL (1744–1841)

1. This brief introduction to Wahhabism is intended only to give the reader a general idea about its major concerns and emphasis.
2. Ibn Taymiyya's thoughts are elaborated in his book, *al siyasa al shariyya*, Cairo 1951.
3. The political situation in central Arabia prior to the rise of the Saudi–Wahhabi domination was characterized by the existence in the towns and oases of local amirs and sheikhs who were either

independent or under the protection of one of the major camel-herding tribes. The major oases and towns of central Arabia such as Hail, Boreidah and Unaizah had their own town rulers who maintained relations with the surrounding desert tribes. The latter frequently visited the towns to purchase agricultural and manufactured goods and to sell their animals, wool, and butter.

4. In the eighteenth century, the Hijaz had already been incorporated in the Ottoman Empire. The Ottomans ruled the area indirectly through the local Sherifian family.

5. The expansion of Mohammad Ali in Palestine, Syria, and Lebanon and his political ambitions were one of the major concerns of the Ottoman sultans in the 1830s and 1840s. This necessitated further action on behalf of the Ottoman Empire to curb the growing influence and powers of their representative in Egypt who had become independent and paid only lip service to the sultan.

6. As Mohammad Ali was increasingly being supported by the French government, Britain regarded his expansion in Arabia as a threat to her interests in the Red Sea and the Persian Gulf. This expansion meant greater involvement on behalf of the French in the affairs of the region. Consequently, more than the Ottoman sultan, Britain was eager to see the day when the Egyptian troops withdrew from the Arabian Peninsula.

7. The decline of the second Saudi–Wahhabi dynasty and the expulsion of the Saudi family from Riyadh will be discussed in detail in Chapter 5.

8. Some historians argue that the second Saudi–Wahhabi dynasty did not succeed in establishing a real power base until 1865 in spite of the return of Imam Turki Ibn Abdullah to Southern Najd in 1824 (see Vassiliev 1986).

9. The conflict between Mohammad Ali and the Ottoman sultan was stimulated by the former's expansion which was regarded as a threat to the integrity of the Ottoman Empire.

10. After the withdrawal of the Egyptian forces in 1841, the Ottoman sultan restored his sovereignty over the Arabian Peninsula. However, this sovereignty was nominal as the Ottoman Empire lacked the will to enforce its direct rule in the region. It was only towards the end of the nineteenth century that the Ottoman government showed signs of the exercise of direct rule in Arabia. These issues will be discussed in detail in Chapter 8.

3 PATTERNS OF LEADERSHIP: AMIR, SHEIKH AND IMAM

1. Most of the major towns of central Arabia had castles or fortified houses which were inhabited by the local ruler. Town or oasis rulers were recruited from the local population or from the surrounding nomadic tribes. When towns were conquered or put under the protection of an external ruler, the representatives of this external

power would usually reside in the castle. This is not a phenomenon peculiar to central Arabia; Montagne has observed the pattern in North Africa among the berber tribes of Morocco (R. Montagne 1930).

2. In most towns in central Arabia, prisons were part of the amir's residence. They kept rival members of the family in these prisons, in addition to dissident tribal sheikhs and town rulers. The emergence of the prison institution was often an indication of the changing nature of leadership. This change accompanied the settlement of the ruler in the town. The same phenomenon was observed by Montagne among the Berber *amghar* (chiefs) of Morocco: 'Deux innovations marquent à cet instant la victoire remportée sur les traditions Berbères: la construction d'une Kasba et l'aménagement d'une prison . . . Quant à la prison, elle est plus encore que la forteresse l'indice de changement importants dans la vie du pays; sa présence au-dessus des lois de la tribu à laquelle il n'a plus a rendre comptes de ses actes; on entre dans sa geôle quand il lui plait; on en sort quand Dieu le veut.' (ibid: 319)

3. The ahd (covenant) between Abdullah and Obeid constitutes a theme around which many anecdotes are told. The oral poetry of Obeid's son, Hamud is always recited as a proof of the existence of an agreement between the two Rashidi brothers regarding succession to office.

4. See G.A. Wallin 1854, W. Palgrave 1865, C. Doughty 1979, and A. Blunt 1968. The local historians of central Arabia are Ibn Bishr 1930 and Ibn Ghanam 1971.

5. IOR, R/15/5/24, p. 260, from O'Conor to Sir E. Grey, Kuweit 25 September 1907.

6. The construction of the Hijaz and Baghdad railways and the use of steamships contributed to the decline of pilgrim caravans at the beginning of the twentieth century.

7. The siege of Hail and the defeat of the last Rashidi amir will be discussed in Chapter 9.

8. Almost all members of the Rashidi family possessed some sort of poetic talents. Wallin described the importance of the art of oral poetry in his commentary on the amirs of Hail: 'That art is at home in Gebel Shammar, and every one young or old, knows a quantity of songs by heart; the princes of the family of Alrashid are poets, as was of old the celebrated prince and poet, Imroo Alkeis, who formerly reigned over them.' (G. Wallin 1854: 185). The political significance of oral poetry will be discussed in Chapter 6.

9. On the Ottoman Empire, see B. Lewis 1961 and H. Inalcik 1978.

10. The amirs' marriage strategies were significant at the political level as they tied the ruling group with various Shammar and non-Shammar families. For further details see Chapter 7.

11. When Abdullah Ibn Rashid established himself as amir of Hail in 1836, he had neither the intentions nor the means to depart from the traditional pattern of sheikhly leadership. It was only during the 1860s and 1870s that the crystallization of the role of amir began to take place.

12. Political leadership among the nomadic population of the Middle East is a popular reseach topic among anthropologists. For comparative research, see G. Garthwaite 1983, L. Beck 1986, J. Black 1972, F. Barth 1956, and P. Salzman 1974.

13. Early accounts of the Rwala political organization can be found in the study of A. Musil 1928.

14. The nomadic tribes of Syria were geographically closer to Ottoman supervision than the tribes of central Arabia, who for centuries had escaped direct encapsulation by the Ottoman Empire. N. Lewis argued that Ottoman policy towards these groups was uncertain and hesitant: 'One year they [the tribes] are attacked and another subsidized. Promises are made and broken. Bribes are given to them by the governors to keep them quiet, and received from them by the members of the council to obtain the pardon for their misdeeds.' (N. Lewis 1987: 27). The geographical proximity of these tribes to the centres of Ottoman bureaucracy, officials, *walis* and governors, had an impact on their political development. Their sphere of influence remained in the desert where they had total political and military monopoly over the area and its resources. However, the nomadic tribes were unable to extend their domination over the urban centres which remained in the hands of the Ottoman government and its representatives in the region.

15. Accounts of the second Saudi–Wahhabi dynasty can be found in R. Winder 1965, L. Pelly 1866, Abu-Aliya 1969, Ibn Bishr 1930, and Ibn Ghanam 1971.

16. Palgrave's account that the amirs were hostile to Islamic law was perhaps an overstatement. Religious attitudes and practices in Hail at that time would simply not allow the explicit manifestation of hostility towards religion. It is safe to argue, however, that if compared with the strictness and orthodoxy of the southern Saudi–Wahhabi provinces, the Rashidi amirs and the Hail population were more lenient when it came to the application of Islamic laws. Perhaps the romanticism of the European travellers of the nineteenth century concerning Arabian customary law influenced their opinions and the observations they made in Hail. This romanticism was responsible for their interpretation of the moderate religious attitudes which went as far as to claim that they were hostile to Islamic law.

4 THE CARAVAN ECONOMY: TRADE, PILGRIMS AND TRIBUTE

1. The composition of the amir's armed forces will be discussed in Chapter 5.

2. The *khuwa* system was also known in north Africa. However, it does not seem to be considered by those anthropologists working in that region as a mechanism regulating peaceful interaction between the weak and strong tribes. This is perhaps related to the fact that in north Africa the *zawiyas* where saint tombs are found functioned as a neutral territory where violence was under control. Consequently,

peace was established by invoking the *baraka* of the saint. The *khuwa* system will be discussed later in this chapter.

3. During the nineteenth century, the Saudi imams were not very successful in polishing their image and the reputation of their followers although they tried to adopt a less expansionist policy in the region. The massacres of the Shiite villages in southern Iraq were still remembered and the stories about Wahhabi fanaticism were constantly repeated by those European travellers who visited the area in the nineteenth century.

4. The *khuwa* system has been discussed by many anthropologists. For comparative material, see W. Lancaster 1981 and U. Fabietti 1983.

5. Traditionally, the collection of the *khuwa* was ad hoc and no fixed amount was imposed on the givers. The Hail amirs tried to institutionalize the payment through quantification.

6. The expansion of the amir's realm beyond Hail and Jabal Shammar and the increase in the number of the tributary groups was bound to undermine the face-to-face interaction which had been an important aspect of the relationship. The *khuwa* givers and receivers traditionally encamped in the same territory and in close proximity to each other. In contrast, the amirs had no close involvement with those paying them the *khuwa*. This led to the bureaucratization of the *khuwa* relations to the detriment of the brotherly relations involved in the system.

7. Lack of military integration between Hail and its nomadic periphery was one of the most important factors which weakened the amirs' power later in the twentieth century and contributed to their decline. As the nomads (both the Shammar and non-Shammar) remained in possession of their arms and human resources, they constituted a potential threat to the amirs. They were a potential reservoir for other rising power centres in the region to use against the Rashidi amirs. This was exactly what happened when Ibn Saud succeeded in winning the loyalty of the nomadic population through subsidies and the adoption of Wahhabism early in the twentieth century. Once he established his grip over the nomadic population outside Hail, he was able to proceed and conquer the oasis.

8. The literature of the European travellers of the nineteenth century has to be read with care as in many respects it reproduces stereotypes of the *badu* which are sometimes romanticized or pejorative. Also, it is important to supplement this literature with other sources, preferably those of the *badu* themselves.

9. For the purpose of this research, some *qasaid* (oral poetry) were collected from members of the Rashidi family. These poems have been passed from generation to generation and represent an important source for our understanding of their values, self-perception and above all history. They will be discussed in detail in Chapter 6.

10. Ottoman tribal policy in the region was not always consistent. Officials were prone to adopt various policies towards local chiefs and sheikhs depending on the situation and the pressures of the period. These policies and the amirs' relations with the Ottoman government will be discussed in Chapter 8.

5 THE MILITARY APPARATUS

1. 'The force of coercion' is used in this context to refer to the sum total of the human resources employed by the amirs for the direct exercise of violence or the threat of violence.
2. These are rough estimates drawn from British sources such as *Handbook of Arabia*, Admiralty, Naval Intelligence Division, GB, HMSO, 1916, 1917, 1920, and 1949.
3. For comparative material drawn from other parts of the Middle East, see E. Peters 1960 and 1967, J. Black 1972, and T. Asad 1970.
4. For a critique of European travellers' literature, see K. Tidrick 1981, R. Brent 1977, Z. Freeth & H. Winstone 1978, R. Bidwell 1976. E. Said 1978 and M. Rodinson 1988.
5. For example, in the battle of Muleida, which will be discussed later in this chapter, the Shammar played a major role in supporting their Hail leadership.
6. During the first two decades of the twentieth century, the Wahhabi movement was revived by Ibn Saud in an attempt to re-establish his family's hegemony in Arabia. This movement appealed to a small number of the Shammar who abandoned the Hail amirs and joined the camps of Ibn Saud. This will be discussed in detail in Chapter 9.
7. The rules of raids are repeated in the literature of the European travellers. See Burckhardt 1831, C. Doughty 1979, W. Palgrave 1865, A. Blunt 1968, and H.R.P. Dickson 1951.
8. Pastoral nomads in other parts of the world have dealt with the problem of armed conflict in different ways. For example, the Nuer of the Sudan lived amidst recurrent tribal wars and aggression, yet they did not develop highly centralized political office. For further details, see E. Evans-Pritchard 1940. Other groups such as the Berber of Morocco dealt with conditions of insecurity and anarchy by creating an elaborate Saint-oriented religious culture to cope with the problems involved as a result of the constant occurrence of raids and couner-raids. See E. Gellner 1969.
9. For further details on the Rumal section of the Shammar, see U. Fabietti 1984.
10. After 1891, the last Saudi imam, Abdul Rahman, fled to the Empty Quarter where he took refuge with the Al Murrah tribe. Later, he decided to accept the invitation of Mubarak Ibn Sabah, the Kuwaiti amir, to reside in his town. Abdul Rahman thought that this would give him the opportunity to plan his return to Riyadh.
11. By the end of the nineteenth century, Britain already had a well-established position in the Persian Gulf where its political agents had been residing. Kuwait became the seat for the Gulf political agent after the signing of the protection agreement with Britain in 1899.
12. The Shammar war cry was always chanted before the departure of the amirs' troops from Hail and along the way to the battle. It was meant to increase the courage and bravery of those participating in the raid.
13. The siege of Hail and the departure of the Rashidi family from their capital will be discussed in detail in Chapter 9.

14. The Shammar were not the only tribe in the area affected by the introduction of modern weaponry. The northern Rwala tribe also witnessed similar problems, all emanating from the widespread use of firearms. For further details on the Rwala, see W. Lancaster 1981.

6 MAKING HISTORY: THE POWER OF POETRY

1. The interviews carried out for the purpose of this research took place in December 1986 and between June and December 1987. Five members of the Rashidi family were interviewed. They prefer to remain anonymous. It is worth noting here that the narratives and poems are translated in such a way as to convey the meaning intended.
2. The Udwan are one of the sections of the Shammar whose sheikh, Ibn Timyat, resented the success of Abdullah Ibn Rashid in overthrowing his cousin Ibn Ali. Nais refers to another Shammar sheikh whereas Ibn Twala was the leader of the Aslam.
3. 'Abu Talal' is a common appellation for Abdullah Ibn Rashid. It consists of the word 'abu' (father) followed by the name of his eldest son.
4. Tai and Qais are the names of two ancient Arab tribes who are believed to have lived in the area now called Jabal Shammar.
5. The battle of Beqaa was very important as it led to the expansion of the Rashidi power in the Qasim region to the south of Jabal Shammar.
6. Saadi is the name of Obeid's horse.
7. In this verse, Obeid refers to a tradition among the Shammar and other tribes in Arabia going back to pre-Islamic times whereby the riders were often followed by the most beautiful women of the tribe. The latter sing songs and praise the raiders with the objective of encouraging them in battle.
8. See Ibn Bishr 1930, Ibn Ghanam 1971, and D. Ibn Rashid 1966.
9. The Shammar and the Anizah were engaged in continuous raids and counter raids. Hostilities between them were reflected in their oral poetry and narratives.
10. The fact that oral tradition reveals a structural rather than a chronological history is stressed in Valensi's work on the tribesmen of Tunisia. See L. Valensi 1985.
11. Arabian oral poetry before the rise of Islam is full of examples of this genre of *qasaid*. The heroic poems were composed by poets who documented various battles and raids between the various tribes of Arabia. For further details, see S. Al Sowayan 1985.
12. The study of oral poetry falls in the domain of the sociology of art. See K. Burke 1969 and A. Hauser 1982.
13. The functionalist approach is best represented in the work of Malinowski. See B. Malinowski 1922. See also the work of I. Lewis and B. Andrzejewski on Somali poetry (1964).
14. The Marxist approach is best represented in the work of M. Bloch 1975.

15. Historians have been concerned with assessing the value of oral tradition in historical research. The debate between historians can be followed in the writings of J. Vansina 1985, P. Thompson 1978, D. Henige 1982.

16. The problem concerning historical truths is discussed in J. Vansina 1985.

17. Lack of chronology is a characteristic common to most tribal histories which are constructed from oral tradition. This problem is discussed in Valensi's work 1985.

18. P. Skalnik has expressed the possibility of writing anthropological history by using the oral tradition. See P. Skalnik 1979: 197.

19. Thompson argued that oral history is as old as history itself. It was the first kind of history. (P. Thompson 1978: 19).

7 THE POLITICS OF MARRIAGE

1. IOR, file R/15/5/25 from Monahan to Political Agent, Kuweit.

2. It is unfortunate that no written record of the marriages under consideration is available. The data presented here are entirely gathered by interviewing members of the Rashidi family. It is worth noting that some of the marriages which did not lead to the birth of children were not remembered and, as a result, the wives involved were forgotten and their names dropped out of people's memory. On the other hand, the names of the wives who were outsiders or belonged to non-Shammar tribal groups were remembered even though some of these wives did not bear children. The omission of females' names who did not have children is significant because it reflects the attitudes at that time towards wives. Unless they bore children, they remained marginal and their names were immediately forgotten, unless they were outsiders. This is an indication of the importance of the political links created and maintained by these marriages.

3. See M. Fortes 1953 for his classical study of African unilineal descent groups. Parallel cousin marriage, however, is not strictly a Middle Eastern practice. It is reported that the Tswana of south Africa have a high frequency of such marriages. For further details, see I. Schapera 1963.

4. This topic has been dealt with by many anthropologists. See F. Barth 1954, M. Ayoub 1959, R. Patai 1965, G. Tillion 1966, R. Murphy and L. Kasdan 1959 and 1967, F. Khouri 1970, M. Meeker 1976, L. Holy 1989, P. Bourdieu 1977, E. Peters 1960, and S. Caratini 1989.

5. The rise of the second Saudi–Wahhabi dynasty in southern Najd was discussed in Chapter 2.

6. The defeat of the Rashidis in 1921 and their arrival in Riyadh will be discussed in Chapter 10.

7. See U. Fabietti 1984 for a discussion of the marriage practices of the Rumal sections of the Shammar tribe. For comparative data, see D.

Cole on the Al Murrah tribe of the Empty Quarter and W. Lancaster 1981 on the Rwala tribe of north Arabia.

8 THE EMPIRE AND THE DYNASTY

1. From Roussel to Richelieu, Alexandria 1 December 1816, in E. Driault p. 37.
2. Archive du Ministère des Affaires Etrangères, Paris, Correspondence Politique et Commerciale, Turquie: Arabie, Dossier Generale, vol. 139.
3. IOR, file L/P&S/20C 240, p. 48. Précis of Nejd Affairs 1804–1904, letter from Vice-Consul at Damascus, 22 July 1880.
4. On the history of the Ottoman Empire and its territorial losses in the Balkan, see S.J. Shaw and E.K. Shaw 1977 vol. II, B. Lewis 1961, and M.S. Anderson 1966.
5. IOR, file L/P&S/20C 240, p. 48, Précis of Nejd Affairs 1804–1904, letter from Vice-Consul at Damascus 22 July 1880.
6. IOR, file L/P&S/20C 238, p. 17, Précis of Nejd Affairs 1804–1904.
7. Ibid, file L/P&S/20C 238, p. 17, Précis of Turkish Expansion on the Arab Littoral of the Persian Gulf and Hasa and Katif Affairs 1871.
8. Ibid, file L/P&S/20C 240, p. 36, Précis of Nejd Affairs 1804–1904.
9. Ibid, file L/P&S/20C 238, p. 238, Précis of Turkish Expansion on the Arab Littoral of the Persian Gulf and Hasa and Katif Affairs 1871.
10. Ibid, file L/P&S/20C 240, p. 42, Précis of Nejd Affairs 1804–1904.
11. Ibid, file R/15/6/19, p. 14, from Political Resident Bahrein, to Political Resident Persian Gulf, Bushira, 21 October 1888.
12. Ibid, file L/P&S/20C 238, p. 135, Précis of Turkish Expansion in the Arab Littoral of the Persian Gulf and Hasa and Katif Affairs 1871.
13. Ibid, file R/15/6/19, p. 14, from Political Resident Bahrain to Political Resident Persian Gulf, Bushire, 12 October 1888.
14. Ibid, file L/P&S/20C 240, p. 51, Précis of Nejd Affairs 1804–1904.
15. Ibid, file R/15/6/19, p. 56, from Political Resident Bahrain to the Marquis of Salisbury, 9 May 1889.
16. Ibid, p. 52.
17. Ibid, Report on the Administration of the Persian Gulf Political Residency and Muscat Political Agency, 1891–92 and 1892–93, from Talbot to the Governor of India.
18. Archive du Ministère des Affaires Etrangères, Paris, Correspondence Politique et Commerciale, Turquie: Arabie, Dossier Générale, vol. 139, no. 50.
19. R. Bidwell (ed), Foreign Office Confidential Prints, Affairs of Arabia, 1905–6, vol. I, Part I, p. 6, 1971.
20. Ibid, p. 142.
21. It is worth mentioning here that because of Ibn Rashid's activities to the north of Jabal Shammar, the Ottoman authorities started thinking about incorporating the area of Maan and Karak (now in Jordan) in a *mutassarifya* so that the government could exercise more control over Ibn Rashid. The Ottoman authority's decision to extend its control

over this area was deemed necessary in order to check the 'adverse' activities of Ibn Rashid. See E. Akarli 1986: 29 in *Dirasat*.

22. E. Akarli in D. Kushner (ed) 1986: 74.
23. Manuscript by M. Arif translated by J. Landau 1971.
24. Archive du Ministère des Affaires Etrangères, Correspondence Politique et Commerciale, Turquie: Arabie, vol. 141, Part III, p. 24.
25. Ibid.
26. IOR, file L/P&S/20C 239 (1896–1904), Précis of Kuweit.
27. R. Kumar 1965: 196.
28. Ibid, p. 200.
29. R. Bidwell (ed), Foreign Office Confidential Prints, Affairs of Arabia (1905–1906), Part I, p. 4, 1971.
30. Ibid.
31. IOR, Report on the Administration of the Persian Gulf Political Residency and Muscat Political Agency 1900–1901.
32. J.B. Kelly 1968: 226.
33. IOR, file L/P&S/20/C 247A, Historial Summary of Events in Territories of the Ottoman Empire, Persia, and Arabia Affecting the British Position in the Persian Gulf 1907–1928.
34. Ibid, L/P&S/10/384, file 2184/1913, from Cox to the Governor of India, 30 May 1913.
35. Ibid, L/P&S/10/385, Treaty between Ibn Saud and the Turks, 15 May 1914.
36. Ibid, from Sir L. Mallet to Sir E. Grey, 23 June 1914.
37. Ibid, Report by Captain Shakespear: Notes on Ibn Rashid's Affairs, January 1914.
38. Ibid, L/P&S/10/384, file 2182/1913, Memorandum by Mr Parkes on British Policy of Non-Interference in the Affairs of Nejd.
39. Ibid, L/P&S/20/C 247A, p. 25, Historical Summary of Events in Territories of the Ottoman Empire, Persia, and Arabia affecting the British Position in the Persian Gulf 1907–1928.
40. Ibid, L/P&S/10/385, Report by Captain Shakespear: Notes on Ibn Rashid's Affairs, January 1914.
41. See C.V. Aitchison 1933.
42. In 1916, the Sherif of Mecca had already been won over by Britain. He started the Arab revolt against the Ottoman government in the Hijaz. This was pursued with the support and encouragement of Britain.
43. IOR, file L/P&S/10/387, p. 254, from Wilson to Sherif of Mecca, 3 October 1916.
44. Ibid.
45. Ibid, pp. 177 and 271.
46. Ibid, L/P&S/10/388, p. 13.
47. Ibid, R/15/5/104, p. 19, Report of Hamilton on Recent Journey to Nejd 1917.
48. Ibid, R/5.101, p. 34, from Cox Muscat to Foreign Office, 9 March 1918.
49. Ibid, R/15/5/104, p. 20, Report of Hamilton on Recent Journey to Nejd 1917.

50. Ibid.
51. Ibid, R/15/5/104, p. 20, Report of Hamilton on Recent Journey to Nejd 1917.
52. Ibid, L/P&S/11/131, p. 457, 1918, from Foreign Office to the Secretary to the State of India 1918.
53. For further details on the Ikhwan movement, see J. Habib 1978.
54. IOR, L/P&S/135, p. 2142, 1918.
55. Ibid, L/P&S/10/389, p. 179, from Viceroy of India, 5 January 1918.
56. Ibid, p. 485.
57. Ibid, p. 484.
58. Ibid, file R/15/5/99, p. 104, from Political Agent Bahrein to Civil Commissioner, 25 July 1920.
59. Ibid, p. 8.
60. Ibid, p. 12, from Civil Commissioner Baghdad to Political Agent Bahrein, 17 April 1920.
61. Ibid, p. 17, from Ibn Saud to Major H.R.P. Dickson, Political Agent Bahrein, 14 April 1920.
62. Details of the siege of Hail and the decline of Ibn Rashid's power will be discussed in Chapter 9.
63. The consequences of the relationship between central governments and local chiefs have been studied by many anthropologists in the Middle East and elsewhere. For further details, see G. Garthwaite 1983, P. Salzman 1967, 1974, and 1980, D. Bates 1971, E. Marx 1967 and 1978, P. Lienhardt 1975, L. Beck 1986, R. Tapper 1983, and B. Spooner 1969 and 1975.
64. Dari Ibn Twala, the sheikh of the Aslam section of the Shammar, was an exception. He maintained contacts with the British officials in Kuwait during the First World War. He was able to get a pass for his section to enter the market in Kuwait. In return, Ibn Twala was expected to give his loyalty and fight on the side of the British government. However, later, the British officials in Kuwait discovered that Ibn Twala was involved in smuggling goods to Hail.

9 THE DECLINE

1. IOR, file R/15/5/99, p. 104, from Political Agent Bahrain to Civil Commissioner, Baghdad, 25 July 1920.
2. Ibid, R/15/5/104, p. 19, Report of Hamilton on Recent Journey to Nejd 1917.
3. Ibid, file R/15/5/101, p. 41, from Philby to Political Agent Baghdad, 28 April 1918.
4. Ibid, file R/15/5/101, p. 163, from Political Agent Baghdad to Political Agent Basra, 23 July 1918.
5. Ibid, file R/15/5/103, p. 8, from Philby to Commissioner, Baghdad 18 July 1918.
6. Ibid, p. 55.
7. Ibn Saud realized early in the twentieth century the incompatibility of nomadism and kin affiliation on the one hand and statehood on the

other. The settlement of those who adopted the Wahhabi call in agricultural villages was given priority on the basis that true Muslims can practice their religion much better in the *hujar*. New settlement villages were created for this purpose. They were a combination of military camps, agricultural colonies, and missionary centres. Those who settled in the *hujar* became known as the *ikhwan*. Habib defines them as 'those bedouins who accepted the fundamentals of orthodox Islam of the Hanbali school as preached by Abdul Wahhab which their fathers and forefathers had forgotten or had perverted and who through the persuasion of the religious missionaries and with the material assistance of Abdul Aziz abandoned their nomadic life to live in the Hijrah which were built by him for them.' (J. Habib 1978: 16). The *ikhwan* remained the most ferocious warriors of Ibn Saud's armed forces which were to carry out the unification of the tribes under a cover of Islamic revivalism. For further details on the rise of Ibn Saud to power and the consolidation of his rule in the Arabian Peninsula, see J. Philby 1928, 1930, & 1948, J. Kostiner 1982, 1985 & 1991, T. Niblock 1982, D. Hopwood 1972, H. Lackner 1978, C. Helms 1981, H.R.P. Dickson 1951, and J. Habib 1978.

8. IOR, file R/15/5/25.
9. Ibid, file R/15/1/557 61/6 III D(33), p. 15, from Political Agent Bahrain to Civil Commissioner Baghdad, 12 May 1920.
10. Ibid, file R/15/5/25.
11. IOR, file R/15/2/40, p. 20, from Ibn Saud to Political Agent Bahrain, 8 May 1920.
12. Ibid, p. 30.
13. Ibid, file R/15/5/99, from Political Agent Bahrain to Civil Commissioner, Baghdad, 14 July 1920.
14. Ibid, file R/15/1/557 61/6 III D(33), p. 247, from Ibn Saud to Political Agent, Bahrain, June 1920.
15. Ibid, file R/15/5/25.
16. G. Bell argued that Mohammad Ibn Talal and his brother Abdullah were popular among the Shammar who made a point of attending the coffee *majlis* of the two amirs and of inviting them to their gatherings as early as 1917. See G. Bell 1940: 51.
17. IOR, file R/15/5/25.
18. Ibid, file R/15/5/28, from Political Agent to Ibn Saud, 17 September 1921.
19. Ibid, file R/15/5/25.
20. Ibid, file R/5/2/25, p. 65, from Political Agent Kuwait to High Commissioner Baghdad, 22 November 1921.
21. Ibid, file R/15/5/28.
22. Ibid, R/15/5/28, p. 18, from High Commissioner Baghdad to Political Agent Kuwait, 16 September 1921.
23. Mohammad Ibn Talal, the last amir of Hail died in Riyadh after being assassinated by his own slave. The events leading to his assassination and the parties involved in plotting it will be discussed in Chapter 10.
24. The *ikhwan* was the cheapest military force ever mobilized to conquer

large stretches of territory. However, once created, the movement had a momentum of its own. The fanaticism of the newly converted led them to despise the more relaxed approach taken by the townsmen. Also, they held strong views against communicating with the infidels or tolerating religious diversity. Their holy war which Ibn Saud initiated was not to be stopped. In 1927, the *ikhwan* started a series of attacks on Iraqi territories. Consequently, when Ibn Saud put pressures on them to respect the northern frontiers with Iraq and Trans-Jordan and restrain themselves from raiding other tribes beyond these borders, they rebelled against his authority. The famous *ikhwan* leaders, Faisal Al Duweish, Ibn Hithlain, Ibn Mashur and Ibn Bijad rebelled against Ibn Saud by continuing to launch attacks inside Iraqi territory. This provoked the British authorities in the country which reacted by ordering its air force to bomb the *ikhwan* fighters. Ibn Saud managed to curb the influence of the *ikhwan* in 1930. Some leaders were killed and others were imprisoned by Ibn Saud. For further details on the *ikhwan* rebellion, see J. Habib 1978.

25. I argued in Chapter 5 that L. Sweet's approach which regards raids as mechanisms for the circulation of camels does not take into account other cultural, political, and social factors which were of great importance to understanding tribal raids.

BIBLIOGRAPHY

ORIGINAL SOURCES

Archives in India Office Library and Records, (IOR) London

A. Residency Records: Persian Gulf Residency and Agencies:
Bushire Political Residency: R/15/1/135, 154 (vol. 197), 166 (vol. 251),
167 (vol. 253), 557 (vol. 61/6 III D33).
Bahrain Political Residency: R/15/2/40 E/12
Kuwait Political Residency: R/15/5/24, 25, 27, 29, 66, 99, 100, 101, 103,
104, 38, 59, 94, 45.
Muscat Political Agency: R/15/6/19, 34.

B. Departmental Papers: Political and Secret Annual Files (1912–30):
L/P&S/11/2, 55, 64, 71, 89, 106, 110, 119, 131, 135, 139, 140.

C. Departmental Papers: Political and Secret Annual Files (1902–31):
L/P&S/10/12, 135, 188, 259, 348, 384, 385, 387, 388, 389, 462, 560, 576,
586, 635.

D. Political and Secret Library (1800–1947):
L/P&S/20/C 227 *Selection from State Papers*
L/P&S/20/C 236 *Turkish Arabia 1801–1905*
L/P&S/20/C 240 *Précis of Nejd Affairs 1870–72*
L/P&S/20/C 239 *Précis of Koweit Affairs 1896–1904*
L/P&S/20/C 238 *Précis of Turkish Expansion on the Arab Littoral of the Persian
Gulf and Hasa and Katif Affairs*
L/P&S/20/C 247A *Historical Summary of Events in Territories of the Ottoman
Empire, Persia, and Arabia Affecting the British Position in the Persian Gulf
1907–28.*
*Report on the Administration of the Persian Gulf Political Residency and Muscat
Political Agency 1883–1905, Calcutta.*

Archives in 'Archive du Ministère des Affaires Etrangères', Paris

A. Correspondance Politique et Commerciale (1897–1918):
Turquie (Arabie) – Dossier Général: vol. 139, 140, 141, 142, 143, 144, 145.
Mésopotamie (Golfe Persique): vol. 149, 150, 151, 152.

B. Correspondance Consulaire et Commerciale (1793–1901):
Djeddah: vol. 1, 2, 3, 4, 5.
C. Memoires et Documents (Turquie): vol. 16, 20, 31, 104.
D. Serie E
Levant 1918–40.
Arabie (Hidjaz) 1918–29.

Published Egyptian Archival Material

Selection from the National Archives of Cairo (*Dar al Wathaiq al Qawmiyah*)
published by A. Abdul Rahim 1976 Cairo.
Selection from the same archives published by S. Al Jamal 1974 Cairo.

BOOKS AND ARTICLES

Abir, M. (1987) 'The consolidation of the ruling class and the new elite in
Saudi Arabia', *Middle Eastern Studies*, vol. 23: 149–71.
Abu-Lughod, L. (1986) *Veiled Sentiments: Honor and Poetry in a Bedouin Society*
(University of California Press).
Admiralty (1916, 1917, 1920, & 1946) *Handbook of Arabia* (Naval
Intelligence Division, Great Britain H.M.S.O.).
Ahmad, A. & Hart, D. (eds) (1984) *Islam in Tribal Society: from the Atlas to
the Indus* (London: Routledge and Kegan Paul).
Aitchison, C.U. (1933) *A Collection of Treaties, Engagements & Sanads Relating
to India & the Neighbouring Countries* (Delhi).
Akarli, E.D. (1986) 'Establishment of the Ma'an-Karak Mutasarrifiyya,
1891–1894', *Dirasat* vol. XIII: 27–42.
—— (1986) 'Abdulhamid II's attempt to integrate Arabs into the
Ottoman system', in *Palestine in the Late Ottoman Period*, edited by D.
Kushner.
Al Amr, S.M. (1974) *The Hijaz Under Ottoman Rule 1869–1914* (Saudi
Arabia).
Al Rasheed, M. (1987) 'The process of chiefdom formation as a function of
nomadic-sedentary interaction', *Cambridge Anthropology*: 32–40.
—— (1989) 'The Political System of a North Arabian Chiefdom: the
Rashidi Amirs of Hail 1836–1921', PhD. thesis, Cambridge University.
—— (1991) 'Le pouvoir et l'économie caravinière dans un oasis de
l'arabie du nord', in J. Bisson (ed.), *Le nomade, l'oasis et la ville*.
Al Rasheed, S. (1981) *Darb Zubeidah: the Pilgrim Road from Kufa to Mecca*
(Riyadh).
Altorki, S. (1980) 'Milk kinship in Arab society: an unexplored problem in
the ethnography of marriage', *Ethnography* (2): 233–44.
Altorki, S. and Cole, D. (1989) *Arabian Oasis City: the Transformation of
Unayzah* (University of Texas Press).
Altorki, S. and El Solh, C. (1988) *Arab Women in the Field: Studying your Own
Society* (Syracuse University Press).
Anderson, M.S. (1966) *The Eastern Question 1774–1923: a Study in International
Relations* (London & New York: Macmillan).

Andreski, S. (1968) *Military Organisation and Society* (London: Routledge & Kegan Paul).

Asad, T. (1970) *The Kababish Arabs: Power, Authority, and Consent in a Nomadic Tribe* (London: C. Hurst).

—— (1973) 'The Bedouin as a military force: notes on some aspects of power relations', in *The Desert and the Sown*, edited by C. Nelson.

—— (1979) 'Equality in nomadic social systems? Notes towards the dissolution of an anthropological category', in *Pastoral Production and Society*. Proceedings of the international meeting on nomadic pastoralism, edited by l'equipe écologie et anthropologie des sociétés pastorales (Cambridge University Press).

Ashkenazi, T. 'La Tribu Arabe: ses elements', *Anthropos*, Bd XLT–XLIV, HF 4–6: 657–72.

Awad, M. (1962) 'Nomadism in the Arab lands of the Middle East' in *The Problems of the Arid Zone*. Proceedings of the Paris symposium, UNESCO 18. Paris.

Ayoub, M. (1959) 'Parallel cousin marriage and endogamy: a study in sociometry', *Southwestern Journal of Anthropology*, vol. 15: 266–75.

Bacon, E. (1954) 'Types of pastoral nomadism in central and southwest Asia', *Southwestern Journal of Anthropology*, vol. 10: 44–57.

Bailey, F.G. (1969) *Stratagems and Spoils: a Social Anthropology of Politics* (Oxford: Basil Blackwell).

—— (ed). (1971) *Gifts and Poison: the Politics of Reputation* (Oxford: Basil Blackwell).

Balandier, G. (1970) *Political Anthropology* (New York: Random House).

Barth, F. (1953) *Principles of Social Organisation in Southern Kurdistan* (Oslo).

—— (1954) 'Father's brother's daughter marriage in Kurdistan', *Southwestern Journal of Anthropology*, vol. 10: 164–71.

—— (1959) *Political Leadership among Swat Pathan* (London: Athlone Press).

—— (1961) *Nomads of South Persia: the Basseri Tribe of the Khamseh Confederacy* (Oslo University Press).

Bates, D.G. (1971) 'The role of the state in peasant-nomad mutualism', *Anthropological Quarterly*, vol. VLIV: 109–13.

Beck, L. (1986) *The Qashqa'i of Iran* (Yale University Press).

Bell, G. (1907) *The Desert and the Sown* (London: William Heinemann).

—— (1914) 'A Journey in North Arabia', *Geographical Journal*, vol. 44: 76–77.

—— (1940). *The Arab War: Confidential Information for General Headquarters from Gertrude Bell* (London: Golden Cockerel Press).

Benet, F. (1970) 'Explosive markets: the Berber high-lands', in L. Sweet (ed.), *Peoples and Cultures of the Middle East* (New York: The Natural History Press).

Benoit-Mechin, J. (1957) *Arabian Destiny* (London: Elek Books).

Bidwell, R. (1971) *The Affairs of Arabia*, Foreign Office Confidential Print, vol. I & II. (London: Frank Cass).

—— (1976) *Travellers in Arabia* (London: Hamlyn).

—— (1985) *Arabian Gulf Intelligence: Selection from the Records of the Bombay Government*. New Series no. XXIV. (Cambridge: Oleander Press).

—— (1986) *Arabian Personalities of the Early Twentieth Century* (Cambridge: Oleander Press).

Birks, J.S. (1978) 'Development or decline of pastoralists: the Bani Qitab of the Sultanate of Oman', in *Arabian Studies*, edited by R. Serjeant & R. Bidwell, vol. IV: 7–19.

Bisson, J. (ed.), *Le nomade, l'oasis et 'la ville* (Urbama: Tours).

Black, J. (1972) 'Tyranny and strategy for survival in an egalitarian society: Luri facts versus an anthropological mystique', *MAN*, vol. 7: 614–34.

Bligh, A. (1984) *From Prince to King: Royal Succession to the House of Saud in the Twentieth Century* (New York University Press).

Bloch, M. (1975) *Marxist Analysis and Social Anthropology* (London: ASA).

—— (1975) Political Language and Oratory in Traditional Society (London: Academic Press).

Blunt, A. (1968) *A Pilgrimage to Nejd, The Cradle of the Arab Race: a Visit to the Court of the Arab Emir and 'our Persian Campaign'*, 2 vols. (London: John Murray, 1881, reprinted in 1968).

Bocco, R. (1987) 'La notion de dirah chez les tribus bedouines en Jourdanie: le cas de Beni Sakhr', in *Terroirs et sociétés au Maghreb et au Moyen Orient*, edited by B. Cannon.

Bombay Government (1985) *Selection from the Records* vol. XXIV. H. Thomas & R. Bidwell (eds) Bombay 1856. (New Edition Cambridge: Oleander Press).

Bonnenfant, P. (1982) *La Peninsule Arabique d'aujourd'hui*, 2 vols. (Paris).

Boucheman, A. De. (1939) *Une petite cité caravanière: Sukhné* (Damascus).

Bourdieu, P. (1977) *Outline of a Theory of Practice* (Cambridge University Press).

Brent, R.W. (1977) *Far Arabia: Explorers of the Myth* (London: Weidenfeld & Nicolson).

Briant, P. (1977) *Etat et pasteur au Moyen-Orient ancien* (Cambridge University Press).

Brown, L.C. (1984) *International Politics and the Middle East: Old Rules, Dangerous Games* (Princeton University Press).

Bujra, A. (1971) *The Politics of Stratification: a Study of Political Change in a South Arabian Town* (Oxford: Clarendon Press).

Bulliet, R.W. (1975) *The Camel and the Wheel* (Harvard University Press).

—— (1980) 'Sedenterisation of Nomads in the Seventh Century: the Arabs in Basra and Kufa', in *When Nomads Settle*, edited by P. Salzman.

Burckhardt, J.L. (1831) *Notes on the Bedouins and the Wahabys*, 2 vols. (London: Colburn & Benthey).

Burke, K. (1969) *A Rhetoric of Motives* (University of California Press).

Burling, R. (1974) *The Passage to Power: Studies in Political Succession* (New York: Academic Press).

Busch, B.C. (1967) *Britain and the Persian Gulf 1894–1914* (University of California Press).

—— (1971) *Britain, India and the Arabs 1914–1921* (University of California Press).

Bush, A. (1987) *Al Sabah: History and Genealogy of Kuwait's Ruling Family 1752–1987* (London: Ithaca Press).

Callocott, T. & Throne, J. (eds) (1961) *Chamber Gazetteer and Geographical Dictionary* (London).

Cannon, B. (1987) *Terroirs et sociétés au Maghreb et au Moyen Orient* (Lyon: Maison de l'Orient).

Caratini, S. (1989) 'A propos du mariage arabe: discours endogame et pratiques exogames: l'exemple des Rgaybat du nord-ouest saharien', *l'Homme*: 30–48.

Carneiro, R. (1978) 'Political expansion as an expression of the principles of competitive exclusion', in *Origins of the State: the Anthropology of Political Evolution*, edited by R. Cohen & E. Service.

Caskel, W. (1954) 'The Bedouinisation of Arabia', in *Islamic Cultural History*, edited by G.E. Von Grunebaum. The American Anthropological Association, vol. 56, no. 2, pt. 2, memoir no. 76, Wisconsin.

Caton, S. (1984) 'Tribal Poetry as Political Rhetoric: from Khawlan At-Tiyal, Yemen Arab Republic', Unpublished PhD. thesis, University of Chicago.

Chatty, D. (1977) 'Leaders, land, and limousines: emir versus sheikh', *Ethnology* (16): 385–97.

—— (1986) *From Camel to Truck: Bedouin in the Modern World* (Vantage Press).

Chelhod, J. (1965) 'Le Mariage avec la cousine parallele dans le systeme arabe', *l'Homme*: 113–73.

Claessen, H. & Skalnik, P. (eds) (1978) *The Early State* (The Hague: Mouton).

—— (1981) *The Study of the State* (The Hague: Mouton).

Cohen, A. (1974) *Two-Dimensional Man: an Essay on the Anthropology of Power and Symbolism in Complex Societies* (London: Routledge & Kegan Paul).

Cohen, B. (1980) 'History and anthropology: the state of play', *Comparative Studies in Society and History*, vol. 22: 188.

—— (1981) 'Anthropology and history in the 1980s', *Journal of Interdisciplinary History*, vol. 12: 227–52.

Cohen, R. & Service, E.R. (1978) *Origins of the State: the Anthropology of Political Evolution* (Philadelphia Institute for the Study of Human Issues).

Cole, D. (1975) *Nomads of the Nomads: The Al Murrah Bedouin of the Empty Quarter* (USA: AHM Publishing Corporation).

Coon, C. (1961) *Caravan: the Story of the Middle East*, revised edition, (New York: Rinehart & Winston Inc).

Corancez, L. (1810) *Histoire des Wahabis depuis leur origine jusqu'a la fin de 1809* (Paris).

Cuisenier, J. (1962) 'Endogamie et exogamie dans le mariage arabe', *l'Homme*: 80–105.

Cunnison, I. (1957) 'History and genealogy in a conquest state', *American Anthropologist*, vol. 59: 20–31.

—— (1966) *Baggara Arabs: Power and Lineage in a Sudanese Nomad Tribe* (Oxford: Clarendon Press).

Davis, J. (1987) *Libyan Politics, Tribe and Revolution* (London: I.B. Tauris).

Destre, A. (1969) 'Le Developpement des etats du Moyen-Orient et la crise du Nomadism', *Revue de L'Institut de Sociologie*: 236–81.

Dickson, H.R.P. (1951) *The Arab of the Desert: a Glimpse into Badawin Life in Kuweit and Saudi Arabia* (London: George Allen and Unwin).
Digard, J. (1978) 'The segmental system: native model or anthropological construction? Discussion of an Iranian example', in *The Nomadic Alternative*, edited by W. Weissleder.
Doughty, C. (1979) *Travels in Arabia Deserta*, 2 vols, first published 1888. (Cambridge University Press).
Dresh, P. (1984) 'The position of shaykhs among the northern tribes of Yemen', *Man*: 31–49.
—— (1986) 'The significance of the course events take in segmentary systems', *American Ethnologist*: 309–24.
—— (1989) *Tribes, Government and History in Yemen* (Oxford: Clarendon Press).
Driault, E. *La Formation de l'empire de Mohamed Aly: de l'Arabie au Soudan 1814–1823. Correspondance des Consuls de France en Égypte* (Cairo MPGGCC XXVII).
Dunn, R. (1977) *Resistance in the Desert* (University of Wisconsin Press).
Dyson-Hudson, R. (1980) 'Nomadic pastoralism', *Annual Review of Anthropology*, vol. 9: 15–61.
Earle, T. (1987) 'Chiefdoms in archaeological and ethnohistorical perspective', *Annual Review of Anthropology*: 279–308.
Easton, D. (1953) *The Political System* (New York: Knopf).
—— (1965) *A Framework for Political Analysis* (London: Prentice Hall).
Eickelman, D. (1976) *Moroccan Islam: Tradition and Society in a Pilgrimage Centre* (University of Texas Press).
—— (1981) *The Middle East: an Anthropological Approach* (New Jersey: Prentice Hall).
Eisenstadt, S.N. (1959) 'Primitive political systems: a preliminary comparative analysis', *American Anthropologist*, vol. 61: 200–20.
Elam, Y. (1973) *The Social and Sexual Roles of Himla Women: a Study of Nomadic Cattle Breeders in Nyabushozi Country, Ankole, Uganda* (Manchester University Press).
Elphinstone, W. (1945) 'The future of the Bedouin of Arabia', *International Affairs*, vol. 21: 370–75.
Euting, J. *Tagbuch einer Reise in Inner Arabien* 2 vols. (Leiden: Brill 1896–1914).
Evans-Pritchard, E.E. (1940) *The Nuer: a Description of Modes of Livelihood and Political Institutions of a Nilotic Tribe* (Oxford University Press).
—— (1949) *The Sanusi of Cyrenaica* (Oxford University Press).
Fabietti, U. (1983) 'Una citta dell'Arabia settentrionale: Hail', in *La Salvaguardia delle citta storiche in Europa e nell' area Mediterranea*, 147–60.
—— (1984) 'Centri carovanieri differenziazione sociale e potere tra: nomadi d'Arabia', in *Ethnicita e Potere*, edited by P. Chiozzi.
—— (1984) *Il Popolo del Deserto. I Bedouini Shammar del Gran Nefud Arabia Saudita* (Rome).
—— (1986) 'Control and alienation of territory among the Bedouin of Saudi Arabia', *Nomadic Peoples*: 33–9.
Farra, O.T.E. (1973) 'The Effects of Detribalizing the Bedouins on the Internal Cohesion of an Emerging State: Saudi Arabia', Unpublished PhD. thesis, University of Pittsburgh.

Fernea, R. (1987) 'Technological innovation and class development among the Bedouin of Hail', in B. Cannon (ed.), *Terroirs et sociétés au Maghreb et Moyen Orient*.

Field, H. (1950) 'Among the Bedouins of North Arabia', *ADIM*, no. 294: 1–20.

Finnegan, R. (1977) *Oral Poetry, its Nature, Significance, and Social Context* (Cambridge University Press).

Forder, A. (1902) *With the Arabs in Tent and Town* (London: Marshall Brothers).

Fortes, M. (1953) 'The structure of unilineal descent groups', *American Anthropologist*, vol. 53: 17–41.

Fortes, M. & Evans-Pritchard, E.E. (eds) (1940) *African Political Systems* (Oxford University Press).

Fortes, M. & Patterson (eds), (1975) *Studies in African Social Anthropology* (London: Academic Press).

Freeth, Z. & Winstone, H. (1978) *Explorers of Arabia: from the Renaissance to the end of the Victorian Era* (London: Allen and Unwin).

Fried, M. (1967) *The Evolution of Political Society: an Essay in Political Anthropology* (New York: Random House).

—— (1975) *The Notion of Tribe* (USA: Cummings Publications).

Fried, M., Harris, M. & Murphy, R. (1967) *War: the Anthropology of Armed Conflict and Aggression* (USA: Garden City).

Galaty, J. & Salzman, P. (eds) (1981) *Change and Development in Nomadic Societies* (Leiden).

Garthwaite, G. (1983) *Khans and Shahs: a Documentary Analysis of the Bakhtiyari in Iran* (Cambridge University Press).

Geertz, C., Geertz, H. & Rosen, L. (1979) *Meaning and Order in Moroccan Society* (Cambridge University Press).

Geertz, H. (1971) 'Review of Saints of the Atlas', *American Journal of Sociology* vol. 76: 763–6.

Gellner, E. (1969) *Saints of the Atlas* (London: Weidenfeld & Nicolson).

—— (1973) *Introduction* in *The Desert and the Sown* edited by C. Nelson: 1–9.

—— & Micaud, C. (eds) (1973) *Arabs and Berbers: From Tribe to Nation in North Africa* (London: Duckworth).

—— & Waterbury, J. (eds) (1977) *Patrons and Clients in Mediterranean Societies* (London: Duckworth).

—— (1981) *Muslim Society* (Cambridge University Press).

—— (1983) 'The tribal society and its enemies', in *The Conflict of Tribe and State in Iran and Afghanistan*, edited by R. Tapper.

—— (1991) 'Tribalism and the state in the Middle East', in *Tribes and State Formation in the Middle East*, edited by P. Khoury and J. Kostiner.

Glubb, Sir J.B. (1961) *War in the Desert* (New York: Norton).

Godelier, M. (1977) *Perspectives in Marxist Anthropology* (Cambridge University Press).

Goldberg, J. (1985) 'Philby as a source for early twentieth-century Saudi history: a critical examination', *Middle Eastern Studies*, vol. 21: 223–44.

Goody, J. (1966) *Sucession to High Office* (Cambridge University Press).

—— (1971) *Technology, Tradition and the State* (Oxford University Press).

—— (1973) *The Character of Kinship* (Cambridge University Press).

——— (1977) *The Domestication of the Savage Mind* (Cambridge University Press).

Guarmani, C. (1938) *Northern Najd: a Journey from Jerusalem to Anaiza in Qasim* (London: Argonaut Press).

Habib, J. (1978) *Ibn Saud's Warriors of Islam* (Leiden: Brill).

Halliday, Fred (1974) *Arabia without Sultans* (Penguin).

Hallpike, C.R. (1973) 'Functional interpretations of primitive warfare', *MAN*, vol. 8: 451–70.

Hamoudi, A. (1980) 'Segmentarity, social stratification, political power and sainthood: reflections on Gellner's theses', *Economy and Society*, vol. 9: 279–303.

Harrison, R. (1973) *Warfare* (USA: Burgess Press).

Hauser, A. (1982) *The Sociology of Art* (London: Kegan Paul).

Helm, J. (ed.) (1968) *Essays on the Problem of Tribe*, Proceedings of the 1967 Annual Spring Meeting of the American Ethnological Society (University of Washington Press).

Helms, C. (1981) *The Cohesion of Saudi Arabia* (Baltimore: Johns Hopkins University Press).

Henige, D. (1982) *Oral Historiography* (London).

Hilal, J. (1972) 'Father's brother's daughter marriage in Arab communities: a problem for sociological explanation', *Middle East Forum*, vol. 46: 73–84.

Hitti, P. (1937) *History of the Arabs* (London: Macmillan).

Hobday, P. (1978) *Saudi Arabia Today* (London: Macmillan).

Hogarth, D. (1905) *The Penetration of Arabia: a Record of Western Knowledge Concerning the Arabian Peninsula* (London: J.G. Bartholomew).

Holden, D. & Johns, R. (1982) *The House of Saud* (London: Sidgwick and Jackson).

Holy, L. (1989) *Kinship, Honour, and Solidarity. Cousin Marriage in the Middle East* (Manchester University Press).

Hopwood, D. (1972) *The Arabian Peninsula, Society and Politics* (London: Allen and Unwin).

Hourani, A. (1970) *Arabic Thought in the Liberal Age 1798–1939* (Oxford University Press).

Huber, C. (1888) *Journal d'un voyage en Arabie (1883–1884)* (Paris).

Hudson, M. (1977) *Arab Politics, the Search for Legitimacy* (Yale University Press).

Hurgronje, C.S. (1931) *Mekka in the Latter Part of the Nineteenth Century* (Leiden).

Ibn Khaldun (1987) *The Muqqadimah. An Introduction to History*, translated by F. Rosenthal 1967 (London, reprint).

Igbal, S.M. (1977) *The Emergence of Saudi Arabia: a Political Study of King Abd al Aziz ibn Saud 1901–1953* (Kashmir: Saudiya Publications).

Inalcik, H. (1978) *The Ottoman Empire, Conquest, Organisation and Economy* (London: Variorum Reprints).

Ingham, B. (1986) *Bedouin of North Arabia* (London: KPI).

Irons, W. (1971) 'Variation in political stratification among the Yomut Turkmen', *Anthropological Quarterly*, vol. 44: 143–56.

——— (1979) 'Political stratification among pastoral nomads', in *Pastoral*

Production and Society. Proceedings of the international meeting on nomadic pastoralism. Edited by l'equipe écologie et anthropologie des sociétés pastorales (Cambridge University Press).

Irons, W. & Dyson-Hudson, N. (1972) *Perspectives on Nomadism* (Leiden).

Issawi, C. (ed.) (1966) *The Economic History of the Middle East 1800–1914* (Chicago University Press).

Jaussen, A. (1908) *Coutumes des arabes au pays de Moab* (Paris).

Johnson, D. (1969) *The Nature of Nomadism* (University of Chicago Press).

Katakura, M. (1977) *Bedouin Village: a Study of Saudi Arabian People in Transition* (Japan).

Kelly, J.B. (1968) *Britain and the Persian Gulf 1795–1880* (Oxford: Clarendon Press).

Kennet, A. (1925) *Bedouin Justice* (Cambridge University Press).

Khazanov, A.M. (1978) 'The early state among the Scythians', in *The Early State*, edited by H. Claessen & P. Skalnik.

—— (1978) 'Some theoretical problems of the study of the early state', in *The Early State*, edited by H. Claessen & P. Skalnik.

—— (1984) *Nomads and the Outside World* (Cambridge University Press).

Khoury, P. & Kostiner, J. (1991) *Tribes and State Formation in the Middle East* (London: I.B. Tauris).

Khuri, F. (1970) 'Parallel cousin marriage reconsidered: a Middle Eastern practice that nullifies the effects of marriage on the intensity of family relationship', *MAN*, vol. 4: 597–610.

Kister, M. (1965) 'Mecca and Tamim', *Journal of the Economy and History of the Orient*, vol. 8: 113–61.

Kostiner, J. (1982) 'The Making of Saudi Arabia 1917–1936', PhD thesis, London School of Economics and Political Science, 1982.

—— (1985) 'On instruments and their designers: the Ikhwan of Najd and the emergence of the Saudi State', *Middle Eastern Studies*, vol. 21: 298–323.

—— (1991) 'Transforming dualities: tribe and state formation in Saudi Arabia', in *Tribes and State Formation in the Middle East*, edited by P. Khoury and J. Kostiner.

Krader, L. (1968) *Formation of the State* (Englewood Cliffs: Prentice-Hall).

—— (1978) 'The origins of the state among the nomads of Asia', in *The Early State*, edited by H. Claessen & P. Skalnik.

Krasner, S.D. (1984) 'Approaches to the state: alternative conception and historical dynamics', *World Politics*, December.

Kumar, R. (1965) *India and the Persian Gulf Region (1858–1907): a Study in British Imperial Policy* (London: Asian Publishing House).

Kushner, D. (1986) *Palestine in the Late Ottoman Period* (Leiden: Brill).

Lacey, R. (1981) *The Kingdom* (London: Fontana/Collins).

Lackner, H. (1978) *A House Built on Sand: a Political Economy of Saudi Arabia* (London: Ithaca Press).

Lacoste, Y. (1966) *Ibn Khaldun: naissance de l'histoire passé du tiers monde* (Paris: Maspero).

Lancaster, W. (1981) *The Rwala Bedouin Today* (Cambridge University Press).

——— (1982) 'The development and function of the shaykh in nomad/settler symbiosis', in *Arabian Studies*, edited by R. Serjeant and R. Bidwell. vol. VI.

——— (1986) 'The concept of territory among the Rwala Bedouin', *Nomadic Peoples*: 41–8.

Landau, J. (1971) *The Hijaz Railway and the Muslim Pilgrimage: a Case of Ottoman Propaganda* (Detroit).

Lattimore, O. (1940) *Inner Asian Frontiers of China* (Oxford University Press).

Leach, E. (1954) *Political System of Highland Burma: a Study of Kachin Social Structure* (London: G. Bell & Sons).

Leachman, G.E. (1910) 'A journey in North Eastern Arabia', *Geographical Journal*, vol. 37: 265–74.

Lewellen, T.C. (1983) *Political Anthropology: An Introduction* (Massachusetts).

Lewis, B. (1951) 'The Ottoman archives as a source for the history of the Arab lands', *Journal of the Royal Asiatic Society*: 139–55.

——— (1961) *The Emergence of Modern Turkey* (Oxford University Press).

Lewis, I.M. (1961) *A Pastoral Democracy: a Study of Pastoralism and Politics among the North Somali of the Horn of Africa* (Oxford University Press).

——— (ed.) (1968) *History and Anthropology* (London: Tavistock Publications).

——— & Andrzejewski, B. (1964) *Somali Poetry. An Introduction* (Oxford: Clarendon Press).

Lewis, N. (1987) *Nomads and Settlers in Syria and Jordan 1800–1980* (Cambridge University Press).

Lienhardt, P. (1975) 'The authority of shaykhs in the Gulf: an essay in nineteenth century history', in *Arabian Studies*, edited by R. Serjeant & R. Bidwell, vol. II: 61–75.

Linder, R.P. (1983) *Nomads and Ottomans in Medieval Anatolia* (Bloomington).

Lorimer, J.G. (1908) *Gazetteer of the Persian Gulf, Oman and Central Arabia*, vols I & II (Calcutta, 1908–1915).

Macro, E. (1968) *Bibliography of the Arabian Peninsula* (University of Miami Press).

Mahdi, M. (1957) *Ibn Khaldun's Philosophy of History* (London).

Mair, L. (1962) *Primitive Government* (London: Pelican Original).

Malinowski, B. (1922) *Argonauts of the Western Pacific; an Account of Native Enterprise and Adventure in the Archipelagoes of Melaesian New Guinea* (London: Routledge & Kegan Paul).

Marx, E. (1967) *The Bedouin of the Negev* (Manchester University Press).

——— (1977) 'The tribe as a unit of subsistence: nomadic pastoralism in the Middle East', *American Anthropologist*, vol. 79: 343–63.

——— (1978) 'The ecology and politics of nomadic pastoralists', in *The Nomadic Alternative: Modes and Models of Interaction in the African and Asian Desert and Steppes*, edited by W. Weissleder.

——— (1979) 'Back to the problem of tribe', *American Anthropologist*, vol. 1: 124–5.

Meeker, M. (1976) 'Meaning and society in the Near East: examples from the Black Sea Turks and the Levantine Arabs', *Journal of Middle Eastern Studies*, vol. 7: 243–70.

—— (1979) *Literature and Violence in North Arabia* (Cambridge University Press).

Meillassoux, C. and Forde, D. (eds), *The Development of Indigenous Trade: Trade and Markets in West Africa* (Oxford University Press).

Messerschmidt, D. (ed.) (1981) *Anthropologists at Home in North America: Methods and Issues in the Study of One's Own Society* (Cambridge University Press).

Middleton, J. & Tait, D. (1958) *Tribes Without Rulers. Studies in African Segmentary Systems* (London: Routledge and Kegan Paul).

Midhat Bey, A.H. (1903) *The Life of Midhat Pasha* (London).

Montagne, R. (1930) *Les Berbéres et le Makhzen dans le sud Du Maroc* (Paris).

—— (1932) 'Notes sur la vie sociale et politique de l'Arabie du Nord: les Semer du Negd', *Revue des Etudes Islamiques*, vol. 6: 61–79.

—— (1935) 'Contes poetiques bedouins', *Bulletin des Etudes Orientales*: 33–119.

—— (1947) *La Civilisation du Desert* (Paris).

—— (1973) *The Berbers, Their Social and Political Organisation* (London).

Murphy, R. & Kasdan, L. (1959) 'The structure of parallel cousin marriage', in *American Anthropologist*, vol. 61: 17–29.

—— (1967) 'Agnation and endogamy: some further considerations', *Southwestern Journal of Anthropology*, vol. 23: 1–14.

Musil, A. (1927) *Arabia Deserta. A Topographical Itinerary* (New York: American Geographical Society).

—— (1928) *The Manners and Customs of the Rwala Bedouins* (New York: American Geographical Society).

—— (1928a) *Northen Negd* (New York: American Geographical Society).

Nelson, C. (1973) *The Desert and the Sown. Nomads in the Wider Society* (University of California Press).

Nettleship, M. (ed.) (1975) *War, Its Causes and Correlates* (The Hague).

Niblock, T. (1982) *State, Society and Economy in Saudi Arabia* (London: Croom Helm).

Nolde, E. (1895) *Reise nach Inner Arabien, Kurdistan, und Armenien* (Brunswick).

Ochsenwald, W. (1984) *Religion, Society and the State in Arabia. The Hijaz under Ottoman Control 1840–1908* (Ohio State University Press).

Palgrave, W.G. (1865) *Personal Narrative of a Year's Journey through Central and Eastern Arabia (1862–1863)*, 2 vols (London: Macmillan & Co).

Parry, V. & Yapp, M. (1975) *War, Technology and Society in the Middle East* (Oxford University Press).

Patai, R. (1965) 'The structure of endogamous unilineal descent groups', *Southwestern Journal of Anthropology*, vol. 21: 325–50.

—— (1978) 'The cultural areas of the Middle East', in *The Nomadic Alternative*, edited by W. Weissleder.

Pelly, L. (1978) *Report on a Journey to the Wahabee Capital of Riyadh in Central Arabia 1865*. 1866 (Reprint Cambridge: Oleander Press).

Pershits, A. (1979) 'Tribute relations', in *Political Anthropology: the State of Art*, edited by S.L. Seaton & H. Claessen (The Hague).

Peters, E. (1960) 'The proliferation of segments in the lineage of the Bedouin of Cyrenaica', *Journal of Royal Anthropological Institute*, vol. 90: 29–53.

—— (1967) 'Some structural aspects of feuds among the camel-herding Bedouin of Cyrenaica', *Africa*, vol. 37: 261–82.

—— (1968) 'The tied and the free: an account of a type of patron-client relationship among the Bedouin pastoralists of Cyrenaica', in J. Peristiany (ed.) *Contributions to Mediterranean Sociology* (The Hague).

Philby, H.St-J.B. (1928) *Arabia of the Wahhabis* (London: Constable & Co).

—— (1930) *Arabia* (London: Ernest Benn).

—— (1933) *The Empty Quarter* (London: Constable and Company Limited).

—— (1948) *Arabian Days: an Autobiography* (London: Robert Hale).

—— (1952) *Arabian Jubilee* (London: Robert Hale).

—— (1955) *Saudi Arabia* (London: Ernest Benn).

Rabinow, P. (1977) *Reflections on Fieldwork in Morocco* (University of California Press).

Raswan, C. (1930) 'Migration lines of North Arabia tribes', *Geographical Review*: 494–502.

Richards, J. (1949) 'Desert city: an account of Hail in Central Arabia', *The Architectural Review*, vol. 105: 35–41.

Rodinson, M. (1961) *Mahomet* (Paris: Editions du Seuil).

—— (1988) *Europe and the Mystique of Islam*, (London: I.B. Tauris).

Rosenfeld, H. (1965) 'The social composition of the military in the process of state formation in the Arabian Desert', Parts I & II, *Journal of the Royal Anthropological Institute*, vol. 95: 75–86 & 174–194.

Rutter, E. (1931) 'Damascus to Hail', *Journal of Royal Central Asian Studies*, vol. 18: 61–73.

Safran, N. (1985) *Saudi Arabia: the Ceaseless Quest for Security* (Harvard University Press).

Sahlins, M. (1961) 'The segmentary lineage: an organisation of predatory expansion', *American Anthropologist*, vol. 63: 322–43.

—— (1968) *Tribesmen* (Prentice-Hall).

—— (1981) *Historical Metaphors and Mythical Realities: Structure in the Early History of the Sandwich Islands Kingdoms* (University of Michigan Press).

Said, E. (1978) *Orientalism* (London: Routledge & Kegan Paul).

Salzman, P.C. (1967) 'Political organisation among nomadic people', *Proceedings of the American Philosophical Society*, vol. 111: 115–31.

—— (1971) 'Adaptation and political organisation in Iranian Baluchistan', *Ethnology*, vol. 10: 433–44.

—— (1974) 'Tribal chiefs as middlemen: the politics of encapsulation in the Middle East', *Anthropological Quarterly*, vol. 47: 203–10.

—— (1979) 'Tribal organisation and subsistence: a response to Emmanuel Marx', *American Anthropologist*, vol. 81: 121–4.

—— (1980) *When Nomads Settle: Processes of Sedentarisation as Adaptation and Response* (New York: Praeger).

Salzman, P. & Galaty, J. (eds) (1981) *Change and Development in Nomadic and Pastoral Societies* (Leiden).

Sanger, R. (1954) *The Arabian Peninsula* (Cornell University Press).

Scoville, S.A. (ed.) (1979) *Gazetteer of Arabia: a Geographical and Tribal History of the Arabian Peninsula*, vols I & II (Austria).

Seaton, S. & Claessen, H. (1979) *Political Anthropology: the State of the Art* (The Hague: Mouton).

Service, E. (1975) *The Origins of State and Civilisation* (New York: Norton).

Schapera, I. (1962) 'Should Anthropologists be Historians?', *Journal of the Royal Anthropological Institute*, vol. 92: 143–56.

—— (ed.) (1963) *Studies in Kinship and Marriage* (London: Royal Anthropological Institute Occasional Paper no. 16).

Shaw, S.J. & Shaw, E.R. (1977) *History of the Ottoman Empire and Modern Turkey*, 2 vols (Cambridge University Press).

Smith, M.G. (1956) 'On segmentary lineage systems', *Journal of the Royal Anthropological Institute*, vol. 86: 39–80.

—— (1962) 'History and Social Anthropology', *Journal of the Royal Anthropological Institute*, vol. 92: 73–85.

Spooner, B. (1972) 'The status of nomadism as a cultural phenomenon in the Middle East', *Journal of Asian and African Studies*, vol. 7: 122–31.

Sowayan, S. (1985) *Nabati Poetry: the Oral Poetry of Arabia* (University of California Press).

Stacy International (1977) *The Kingdom of Saudi Arabia* (London).

Stein, L. (1967) *Die Sammar-Gerba. Beduinen im Ubergang Vom Nomadismus Zur Sesshaftigkeit* (Berlin: Akademie Verlag).

Sweet, L. (1965) 'Camel raiding of North Arabian bedouin: a mechanism of ecological adaptation', *American Anthropologist*, vol. 67: 1131–50.

—— (1968) *The Central Middle East: a Handbook of Anthropology*, 2 vols (New Haven).

—— (1969) 'Camel pastoralism in North Arabia and the minimal camping unit', in *Environment and Cultural Behaviour*, edited by P. Vayda.

Tapper, R. (1979) 'The organisation of nomadic communities in pastoral societies of the Middle East', in *Pastoral Production and Society*. Proceedings of the international meeting on nomadic pastoralism. Edited by l'equipe ecologie et anthropologie des societés pastorales (Cambridge University Press).

—— (1979) *Pasture and Politics: Economics, Conflict and Ritual among Shahsevan Nomads of Northwestern Iran* (London: Academic Press).

—— (ed.) (1983) *The Conflict of Tribe and State in Iran and Afghanistan*, (London: Croom Helm).

Thesiger, W.P. (1950) 'The Badu of Southern Arabia', *Journal of Royal Central Asian Society*, vol. XXXIV: 53–61.

Thompson, P. (1978) *The Voice of the Past* (London).

Tidrick, K. (1981) *Heart-Beguiling Araby* (Cambridge University Press).

Tillion, G. (1966) *Le Harem et les cousins* (Paris: Le Seuil).

Turney-High, H.H. (1949) *Primitive War. Its Practice and Concepts* (USA).

Valensi, L. (1977) *Fellah Tunisiens: l'economie rurale et la vie des compagnes aux 18ème et 19ème siecles* (Paris: La Haye).

—— (1985) *Tunisian Peasants in the Eighteenth and Nineteenth Centuries* (Cambridge University Press).

Van Bruinessen, M. (1978) 'Agha, Shaikh and State: on the Social and

Political Organisation of Kurdistan', Doctoral thesis submitted to the State University of Utrecht.
Van Nieuwenhuijze, C.A.O. (1971) *Sociology of the Middle East* (Leiden).
Vansina, J. (1985) *Oral Tradition as History* (London: James Curry).
Von Grunebaum, G.E. (ed.) (1954) *Studies in Islamic Cultural History* (The American Anthropological Association, Memoir No. 76, vol. 56, Wisconsin).
Wahba, H. (1964) *Arabian Days* (London: Arthur Barker).
Wallin, G.A. (1850) *Notes Taken During a Journey through Part of Northern Arabia in 1850* (London).
—— (1854) 'Narrative of a journey from Cairo to Medina and Mecca, by Suez, Araba, Tawila, al-Jauf, Jublae, Hail and Negd in 1845', *Journal of the Royal Geographical Society*, vol. 24: 115–201.
Ward, P. (ed.) (1983) *Hail: an Oasis City of Saudi Arabia* (Cambridge: Oleander Press).
Weber, M. (1964) *The Theory of Social and Economic Organisation* (New York: Free Press).
Weissleder, W. (ed.) (1978) *The Nomadic Alternative: Modes and Models of Interaction in the African and Asian Desert Steppes* (Leiden: Mouton).
Williamson, J. (1975) 'The Political History of the Shammar Jarba Tribe of al Jazirat 1800–1958', Unpublished PhD thesis, Indiana University.
Winder, R. (1965) *Saudi Arabia in the Nineteenth Century* (London: Macmillan).
Winstone, H.V.F. (1980) *Gertrude Bell* (London: Quartet Books).
Wolf, E. (1951) 'The social organisation of Mecca and the origins of Islam', *Southwestern Journal of Anthropology*, vol. 7: 329–56.
Wright, H. (1977) 'Recent research on the origin of the state', *Annual Review of Anthropology*: 379–97.

WORKS IN ARABIC

Abdul Rahim, A.A. (1976) *al Dawla al Saoudiya al oula 1745–1818* (Cairo).
Abu Aliya, A. (1969) *Tarikh al Dawla al Saoudiya al Thaniya 1840–1891* (Riyadh).
Abu Hakima, A.M. (1967) *Lama' al Shihab Fi Sirat al Shaikh Mohammad Ibn Abdulwahab* (Beirut).
Al Batriq, A. (1964) 'al Wahabiyya Din Wa Dawla', in *Hawliyat Kuliyat al Banat* (Cairo).
Al Jamal, S.A. (1974) *al Wathaiq al Tarikhiya li Siyasat Masr Fi al Bahr al Ahmar* (Cairo).
Al Hindi (1380 AH) *zahr al khamayil fi tarajim ulama hayel* (Djeddah).
Al Husari, S. (1960) *al Bilad al Arabiya Wa al Dawla al Uthmaniya* (Beirut).
Al Marek, F. (1386 AH) *min shiyam al arab* (Beirut).
Al Mawardi (1880) *al Ahkam al Sultaniyya* (Cairo). (French translation by P. Sagnan 1915).
Al Qasim, A. (1936) *al Thawra al Wahabiyya* (Cairo).
Al Rihani, A. (1973) *Tarikh Najd Wa Mulhaqatiha* (Beirut).
Al Tahir, A.N. & Hnaydi, M. (1954) *al Badu Wa il Ashair Fi Bilad al Arabiya* (Cairo).

Al Utheimin, A. (1981) *Nashat Imarat al Rashid* (Riyadh).
Al Yasini, A. (1987) *al Din Wa al Dawla Fi al Mamlaka al Arabiya al Saoudiya* (London).
Al Zakarli, K. (1970) *Shibh al Jazirat Fi Ahd al Malik Abdulaziz* (Beirut).
Chamieh, J. (1986) *Al Saud Madhihum Wa Hadhirhum* (London).
Hamza, F. (1933) *Qalb Jazirat al Arab* (Cairo).
Haraz, R. (1970) *al Dawla al Uthmaniya Wa Shibh Jazirat al Arab 1840–1909* (Cairo).
Ibn Bishr, O.A. (1930) *Unwan al Majd Fi Tarikh Najd*, 2 vols (Mecca).
Ibn Ghanam (1971) *Tarikh Najd* 2 vols (Cairo).
Ibn Hithlul, S. (1961) *Tarikh Muluk al Saud* (Riyadh).
Ibn Issa, I. (1966) *Tarikh Baadh al Hawadith al Waqia Fi Najd 700–1340 AH* (Riyadh).
Ibn Rashid, D. (1966) *Nabtha Tarikhiya An Najd* (Riyadh).
Ibn Taymiyya, T.D. (1951) *al Siyasa al Shariyya* (Cairo).
Ibrahim, A.A. (1981) *Hukumat al Hind al Birithaniya Wa al Idara Fi al Khalij al Arabie. Dirasah Wathaiqiya* (Riyadh).
Mahjoub, M. (1974) *Muqqadimah Li Dirasat al Mujtamaat al Badawiya* (Kuweit).
Rafiq, A. (1974) *al Arab Wa al Uthmaniuun 1516–1916* (Damascus).
Shararah, W. (1981) *al Ahl Wa al Ghanima* (Beirut).
Sharit, A. (1984) *Nusus Mukhtara min Falsafat Ibn Khaldun* (Algiers).
Vassiliev, A. (1986) *Tarikh al Arabiya al Saoudiya* (Moscow).

INDEX